OFF THE BEATEN PATH® SERIES

NINTH EDITION

OFF THE BEATEN PATH®
TEXAS

A GUIDE TO UNIQUE PLACES

JUNE NAYLOR

gpp®
travel

Guilford, Connecticut

For my parents—
I am grateful for your love and your
abundant Texan legacies.

All the information in this guidebook is subject to change. We recommend that you call ahead to obtain current information before traveling.

To buy books in quantity for corporate use
or incentives, call **(800) 962-0973**
or e-mail **premiums@GlobePequot.com**.

Copyright © 2012 by June Naylor

Editor: Kevin Sirois
Project Editor: Heather M. Santiago
Layout: Joanna Beyer
Text Design: Linda R. Loiewski
Maps: Equator Graphics © Morris Book Publishing, LLC

ISSN 1537-0526
ISBN 978-0-7627-7328-2

Printed in the United States of America
10 9 8 7 6 5 4 3 2 1

Contents

About the Author

A sixth-generation Texan and Fort Worth native, **June Naylor** has written for the *Fort Worth Star-Telegram* newspaper since 1984, starting in sports and writing for the state and metro desks before moving to the travel section in 1985 to write stories about Texas, the Southwest, the US, and the world. She added dining and food to the mix in 1987 and currently writes about dining, food, and travel for the *Star-Telegram*'s features sections. A contributor to numerous magazines and travel and dining websites, June is the coauthor of a cookbook, *The Texas Cowboy Kitchen*.

The author of GPP's *Quick Escapes from Dallas/Fort Worth, Romantic Days and Nights in Dallas/Fort Worth,* and *Recommended Bed & Breakfasts Southwest,* June has received several writing and photography awards from the Society of American Travel Writers. She is currently serving on the organization's board of directors and is a founding member of the Association of Women in Journalism.

Acknowledgments

Working on the ninth edition of this book was a pleasure, mostly because it allowed me to rediscover the backroads and oft-overlooked corners that make Texas live up to its vast legend. I owe a great debt to the kindly folks who work in tiny museums, cafes, shops, and inns in such towns as Leakey in the Hill Country, Uncertain in the Piney Woods, Marathon in the Big Bend, and Canyon in the Panhandle; it's people like this, in places like those, who make writing about Texas a joyful privilege. A great deal of thanks goes to my friend, Corinne DeFord, whose research and generous enthusiasm helped this newest edition immeasurably. I'm also deeply appreciative to my editors at GPP, who make the process of working on books as painless as possible. As for the support at home, I have endless gratitude for family and friends who make me keep my sense of humor—and still love me even during those moments when I seem to have misplaced it.

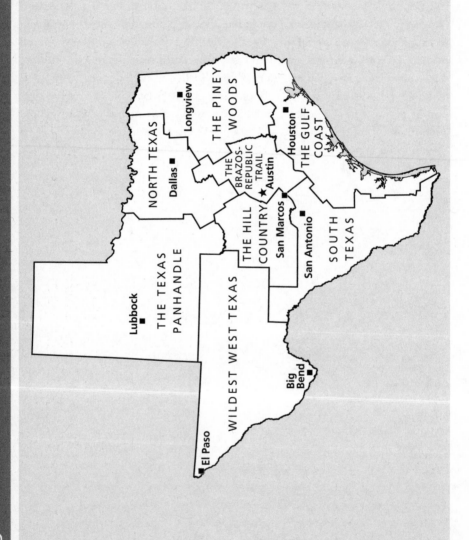

THE PINEY WOODS

Longview ■

NORTH TEXAS

Dallas ■

THE GULF COAST

Houston ■

THE BRAZOS-REPUBLIC TRAIL

★ Austin

THE HILL COUNTRY

San Marcos ■

San Antonio ■

SOUTH TEXAS

THE TEXAS PANHANDLE

Lubbock ■

WILDEST WEST TEXAS

Big Bend ■

El Paso ■

Introduction

John Steinbeck wrote in *Travels with Charley,* "Texas is a state of mind. Texas is an obsession. Above all, Texas is a nation in every sense of the word."

Sam Houston—first president of the Republic of Texas and hero in the defeat of Santa Anna—would have loved Steinbeck.

But for all its staunch independence, Texas is one big welcome mat. Folks coming to call from elsewhere are often taken aback when greeted on the street by total strangers with a "Howdy" or "Hey." There's no catch—Texans are just greeters by nature.

Let's go ahead and dispel some myths: Texas is flat if you don't count those 91 mountains that reach over a mile into the sky; Texas is dry if you ignore 3.07 million acres of inland water made up of streams, rivers, lakes, springs, creeks, and 624 miles of Gulf of Mexico shoreline; and Texas has no trees if you overlook those 23 million acres of woodlands.

Texas's farm-to-market roads serve not only today's farmers but also those wanderers who just want to absorb the gentle, uncluttered environs. The first such road opened in 1937 (redesignated in 1939 as a portion of TX 315), and now there are more than 3,000, making up 41,000 highway miles of the state's total of 79,000. The shortest, FM 742, in Molennan County, is 0.175 mile. Two of the prettiest farm-to-market vistas are in the Piney Woods of east Texas and the Trans-Pecos wilds of west Texas.

When eating in Texas, be aware that Mexican meets southern, Cajun greets soul, and, somehow, dissimilarities welcome one another. From such mingling, southwestern cuisine rides a crest of fame, and country cooking soars higher than ever on all palates.

You can trust places with signs that say If You Leave Here Hungry It's Your Own Fault, and put your faith in waitresses who are concerned you haven't been eating right and insist you need that piece of pie to keep up your strength. Also, if it sounds absurd, it's probably good; if it sounds French, it probably isn't Texan.

For fried alligator tail, a tender delicacy, look around east Texas lake joints, which also serve up lightly fried catfish with green tomato relish and jalapeño hush puppies. Barbecue, a critical Texas staple, is best from the old places in central Texas's Taylor, Lockhart, and Luling. If you can find barbecued pork or beef ribs, brisket, goat, shrimp, or sausage, eat it up.

How about buffalo? It's a tasty treat, lower in fat and cholesterol than beef, and a wonderful way to eat Wellington, burgers, and steaks. No bull. The best *wurst* turns up in thickly German towns such as New Braunfels and Fredericksburg, while *kolache* heaven is spread out over the Czech communities of West and Caldwell.

A word about chicken-fried steak: Sounds weird, but this could be the state food of Texas; go for it only if it's fork-cutting tender and its breading is homemade and light. And whence came chili? San Antonio or Fort Worth? Both claim it. Beef or venison, spicy or mild, beans or no, there's plenty of it for the sampling at cook-offs all year long. Just don't confuse it with chile, which can be a fire-hot stew if eaten on one of Texas's two Native American reservations, or a velvety green or creamy red pepper sauce if found in one of south Texas's Hispanic-infused towns. Now, you'll get plenty of argument from fajita lovers, but the best Mexican eats are breakfast goods—*migas, empanadas* (sweet and savory pastries)—found in cafes and bakeries.

For fruits of the Texas earth, look to Weatherford and Stonewall for peaches, Pecos for cantaloupes, and the Rio Grande valley for citrus. For the nectar of Texas gods, we have dozens of vineyards and wineries, among them international award winners **McPherson Cellars** in Lubbock, **La Buena Vida** in Grapevine, and **Fall Creek Vineyards** in Tow.

As any Texan will tell you, this is one recreation-crazed state. In water action alone, there's rafting, canoeing, and kayaking on Hill Country rivers and the Rio Grande, while sailing and sailboarding are Corpus Christi favorites, surfers flock to Galveston, catamaran rentals are booming business on South Padre Island, and fishing charters and tournaments subsidize the Port Aransas economy.

Texans are always looking for an excuse to have fun. There are festivals celebrating mosquitoes, flowers, berries, hush puppies, rattlesnakes, bluegrass music, fall foliage, and fire ants. Cowboys have a Christmas ball, Native Americans have a championship powwow, and Scottish clans gather in kilts.

When exploring the sprawling state, it's usually helpful to do so by region. Eight easily defined areas—each with its own personality and shape—will keep you busy, to say nothing of intrigued.

In **North Texas,** all Dallas and Fort Worth have in common are a shared river, 30 miles of connecting interstate highway, and one of the largest, busiest airports in the world. Which is just the beauty of the area—in about a half hour you can be someplace drastically different. Dallas is larger, more dashing, and aggressive. It glitters and bustles and has a lifestyle ridden with haute cuisine and couture. Fort Worth defines Texas succinctly: Businesspeople wear boots and make deals over barbecue, and cowboy-hatted police officers ride horses on their downtown beats. Dallas's Uptown neighborhood, Mavericks basketball, internationally flavored dining, and incomparable shopping bring Fort Worth folks over for visits. Conversely, Fort Worth's restored Stockyards and world-renowned art museums, the Bass Performing Arts Center, and the family-style Mexican food at Joe T. Garcia's bring Dallasites over in hordes.

East Texas's **Piney Woods** is something of an extension of the Old South, with several of the Republic of Texas's birthmarks. San Augustine and Nacogdoches are vintage towns packed with earliest history, while Jefferson appeals with its old riverboat town and antiques-shop charm. Marshall, a stop on stagecoach and Victorian train lines, has restored mansions and bed-and-breakfasts in lovingly refurbished homes. Train buffs delight in traveling between Rusk and Palestine on the Texas State Railroad's steam locomotives. Approximately one-fifth of all commercial rosebushes in the US are grown in Smith County, and more than half of the nation's rosebushes are packed and shipped from here. Canton brings several thousand people each month to its century-old First Monday Trade Days. Four national forests jam the region, and the Big Thicket National Preserve is home to a precious virgin forest where 20 kinds of wild orchids and carnivorous plants and 300 varieties of birds coexist in an impenetrable natural fortress.

Some of Texas's deepest heritage is found in the humid, lush environs of the **Texas Gulf Coast.** Sam Houston's ravaged army rid the Republic of Santa Anna's Mexican troops on a field named San Jacinto, where now stands a breathtaking, 570-foot commemorative monument against the backdrop of Texas's largest city. Houston is an oil city, home to the NASA-Johnson Space Center, a vibrant, resurrected downtown, and a sizable selection of theaters, museums, and shops.

A short drive east, Galveston has rebounded from the devastation of Hurricane Ike in 2008 to become one of Texas's more significant beach communities again. Once known as the Wall Street of the Southwest, the island-city boasts one of the nation's largest collections of restored Victorian buildings. The Strand, the 1894 Grand Opera House, Ashton Villa, and the *Elissa,* a square-rigged tall ship, highlight a long list of attractions. Padre Island is a long, thin finger of sand protecting the Texas coast from Corpus Christi to the Rio Grande. Most of the island's 113-mile stretch is national seashore, populated by more than 400 species of birds, sand dunes, and sea oats. The King Ranch—the largest privately owned ranch in the world—sits inland from the sailboarding, sailing city of Corpus Christi. South Padre Island is a resort town glistening with new high-rise hotels and sleek condos, boutiques, and sunbleached houses. Teens jam the beaches in spring, families ride the waves in summer, and anglers work the bay and beach year-round.

In **South Texas**'s Rio Grande valley, the communities of McAllen, Weslaco, and Mission are the heart of Texas's huge citrus industry and the home of Winter Texans, snowbirds from the Midwest. San Antonio, the most common gateway to south Texas, fairly reverberates with the passion of Texas's European origins and the hearty Hispanic culture still enjoying growth.

Some explorers make their way down to Langtry, home of revered Judge Roy Bean, whose justice was once the only law west of the Pecos. In this southwestern corner find the world's Spinach Capital, the state's oldest winery, the dramatic set of the epic film *The Alamo,* and an opalescent lake shared by two friendly countries.

If the spiritual heart of Texas is to be embraced, it will happen in the ***Hill Country.*** Spring-fed rivers course beneath limestone cliffs, through rolling hills dotted with live oak and wildflowers. It is a region for escape, for reflection, for rejuvenation. Small towns in the Hill Country embrace a serenity not quite duplicated elsewhere. Fredericksburg and New Braunfels gleam with their German heritage, displayed in the shops, historic lodgings, and plentiful wurst and beer. Kerrville is home to the Y.O. Ranch, and Burnet claims the Vanishing Texas River Cruise.

At the heart of Texas, figuratively and literally, is Austin; the state capital and an integral part of the ***Brazos-Republic Trail.*** This is an easy city to enjoy, one favored for its music and nightlife, where pleasures unfold from lakes and wooded hills, cultural centers at the University of Texas, and the Lady Bird Johnson Wildflower Center. To the east are more small towns forming the core of the old republic.

John Wayne should have been required by law to make all his westerns in the ***Texas Panhandle.*** The genuine, traditional Texan style is so thick here you could cut it with a knife. In the High Plains a great treasure is the shockingly beautiful and huge Palo Duro Canyon. An exciting musical drama plays under the stars there in summer, and real working cowboys take folks out to the canyon's edge for a Cowboy Morning Breakfast.

Texas's western heritage is defined and illustrated with great care at the Panhandle Plains Museum in Canyon and at the Ranching Heritage Center in Lubbock. Another Lubbock asset—wines produced from its sandy but rich land—is offered for sampling at three award-winning vineyards.

West Texas is a vast area distinguished by attractions as diverse as ancient Native American ruins and pioneer forts, mountains, and unexplained moving lights—this is a region that could take years to truly explore. El Paso is a reservoir of Native American, Hispanic, and Anglo influences characterizing the city's architecture, art, food, shopping, and pastimes.

Due east from El Paso, Guadalupe Mountains National Park contains a wealth of scenery, from McKittrick Canyon and its blazing fall foliage to Guadalupe Peak, Texas's highest point at 8,749 feet above sea level. Fort Davis lies between the Guadalupe Mountains and the Big Bend's Chihuahuan Desert. Home to Fort Davis National Historic Site with its restored cavalry fort, Fort Davis sits beside the Davis Mountains State Park and its romantic Indian

Lodge, and it claims Prude Ranch, a place with restorative qualities; McDonald Observatory, with fascinating "Star Parties"; and miles of cool, clean mountain air and vistas gained by a 74-mile mountain loop road.

The Big Bend is the site of a rugged, 800,000-acre national park, encompassing a wild stretch of the Rio Grande beloved by geologists, naturalists, and outdoorsy types who want to spend a day, week, or month camping and rafting in jagged canyons.

After driving around a spell, you'll notice bumper stickers with the image of the Texas flag emblazoned by the word *Native* or *Naturalized*. Texans, whether born or transplanted here, like to advertise their Lone Star State status.

Such boasts shouldn't detract from the amiable intent—it's simply a friendly state, as the official motto proclaims. It won't take you long to find that out for yourself.

Texas Fast Facts

- Texas is the largest of the contiguous states, with 266,807 square miles.
- Only Alaska has more fresh water than Texas.
- There are four national forests in Texas.
- The King Ranch in Kingsville is the largest ranch in Texas and is slightly larger than the state of Rhode Island.
- Texas has 23.4 million acres of woodland.
- Houston, San Antonio, and Dallas are among the nation's 10 largest cities; and Austin, Fort Worth, and El Paso are in the nation's top 20 most populated cities.
- Texas has more than 200,000 alligators.
- More than 20 million people call Texas home, making this the second-most populous state.
- State capital: Austin
- State motto: Friendship
- State nickname: Lone Star State
- State mammal: armadillo (small); longhorn (large)
- State bird: mockingbird
- State tree: pecan
- State flower: bluebonnet
- State dish: chili
- State gem: blue topaz
- State fruit: red grapefruit

- State dance: square dance
- State song: "Texas, Our Texas"
- State plant: prickly pear
- State pepper: jalapeño
- State reptile: horned lizard
- State fish: Guadalupe bass
- State flying mammal: Mexican free-tailed bat
- State grass: sideoats grama
- State insect: monarch butterfly
- State seashell: lightning whelk
- State ship: battleship *Texas*
- State sport: rodeo

Important Dates in Texas's History

1519   Spain is the first of six nations to claim Texas.

1685   France claims the Rio Grande as the western boundary of its Louisiana Territory, based on the exploration of La Salle.

1821   Upon winning independence from Spain, Mexico acquires Texas.

1836   After holding off a Mexican army of thousands for 13 days in the Battle of the Alamo, 188 "Texans" die. A month later General Sam Houston leads the Texas army in the successful Battle of San Jacinto to win independence from Mexico.

1845   Texas joins the US as the 28th state.

1861   Texas secedes from the US, joining the Confederates in the Civil War.

1865   Texas rejoins the US.

1901   Oil is discovered at Spindletop.

1917   Miriam A. Ferguson becomes the first woman governor of Texas when she finishes her husband's (James E. Ferguson) term after his impeachment.

1953   Dwight D. Eisenhower becomes the first Texas-born president of the US.

1963   John F. Kennedy is assassinated in Dallas; Lyndon B. Johnson, born in Stonewall, becomes the 36th president.

1965   National Aeronautics and Space Administration (NASA) opens the Lyndon B. Johnson Space Center in Houston.

1966   Barbara Jordan is the first African American elected to the Texas Senate.

1989   George H. W. Bush becomes the 41st US president.

2001   George W. Bush becomes the 43rd US president.

2005   The University of Texas's football team wins its fourth national championship.

2009   The Dallas Cowboys leave Dallas County and begin playing at the team's new billion-dollar stadium in Arlington, in Tarrant County.

2010   The Texas Rangers Baseball Club represents the American League in the World Series.

2011   The Super Bowl is hosted by North Texas at the Cowboys Stadium in Arlington.

2011   The Dallas Mavericks win their first NBA title.

Websites Worth Visiting

- **Abilene:** www.abilenevisitors.com/
- **Amarillo:** www.visitamarillotx.com
- **Arlington:** www.arlington.org
- **Austin:** www.austintexas.org
- **Big Bend:** www.visitbigbend.com
- **Corpus Christi:** www.visitcorpuschristitx.org/
- **Dallas:** www.visitdallas.com/
- **El Paso:** www.visitelpaso.com
- **Fort Worth:** www.fortworth.com
- **Fredericksburg:** www.fredericksburg-texas.com
- **Galveston:** www.galveston.com
- **Houston:** www.visithoustontexas.com
- **Irving:** www.irvingtexas.com/
- **Jefferson:** www.jefferson-texas.com
- **Lubbock:** www.visitlubbock.org
- **San Angelo:** www.visitsanangelo.org
- **San Antonio:** www.visitsanantonio.com
- **South Padre Island:** www.sopadre.com
- **State parks:** www.tpwd.state.tx.us
- **Statewide tourism:** www.traveltex.com
- **Waco:** www.wacocvb.com

Speed Limits

The maximum speed limit is 70 miles per hour during the day and 65 at night on all numbered highways in rural areas. Some counties in west Texas have

75- or 80-mile-per-hour speed limits. Lower limits are posted on many highways; limits on urban freeways are from 55 to 70 miles per hour. School zones are strictly monitored at 20 miles per hour, and many cities impose hefty fines for drivers using cell phones while driving through school zones.

Texas State Parks

The *Texas Parks and Wildlife Department* offers more than 100 parks, state natural areas, wildlife management areas, and historic sites. *The State Parks Pass* and the *Texas State Parklands Passport* afford visitors discounted or waived entry fees. Check www.tpwd.state.tx.us for details. The parks department has a centralized reservations office for camping. Call the office at (512) 389-8900 Mon through Fri from 9 a.m. until 8 p.m. and Sat from 9 a.m. until noon.

Texas Travel Information Centers

The Texas Department of Transportation operates travel information centers in 12 locations across Texas. Each center is staffed by professional travel counselors and offers thousands of pieces of free literature, including the excellent *Texas State Travel Guide,* road maps, and lodging guides. All services are free, and the centers are open daily from 8 a.m. until 5 p.m., except New Year's Day, Thanksgiving Day, Christmas Eve, Christmas Day, and Easter Sunday.

Find the travel centers located in Amarillo on I-40; Anthony on I-10 (near the New Mexico state line); Austin at the Capitol Complex; Denison on US 75/69 (near the Oklahoma state line); Gainesville on US 77/I-35 (near the Oklahoma state line); Langtry on US 90 at Loop 25; Laredo on I-35 (near the Mexican border); Orange on I-10 (near the Louisiana state line); Texarkana on I-30 (near the Arkansas state line); Harlingen on US 77 at US 83; Waskom on I-20 (near the Louisiana state line); and Wichita Falls on I-44 (near the Oklahoma state line).

For free road maps and information on travel destinations and road conditions, call the travel consultants at (800) 452-9292, or visit www.traveltex.com.

Texas state roads are designated in this book as Highways, as in Highway 261 and Highway 41. Farm Roads are FR; Park Roads, PR; and Ranch Roads are RR.

Admission Fees

Note that in many cases, attractions are noted with a phrase such as "A small admission fee is charged." Generally this means that admission fees are from $1 to $10 per person. The notation "Admission is charged" usually means that the fee is more than $10.

THE BRAZOS-REPUBLIC TRAIL

A train whistle blows steadily, and soon loudly, through the fragile darkness. Just before dawn a rooster begins its intonation, and moos soon follow. Days begin early in the country, breaking clean and fresh—the sky, grass, and picket fences seem unusually pure along central Texas's Brazos and Colorado Rivers, through a region spreading just to the east of the Balcones Escarpment and the state's fabled Hill Country. German, Scottish, and Czech immigrants made their way to new homes through this rolling corridor, toughing out a life that could become hazardous when conflicts with Mexicans and Native Americans arose. Here, dairy and cotton farmers and horse ranchers carved lives with their families and friends, thanks in part to their own determined spirit and that of the Texas Rangers.

It was through this part of the frontier, once called Tejas by the Mexicans and Indians, that pioneers crafted a republic, a sovereign nation that gave rise eventually to the Lone Star State. Today's explorers find great and lasting remnants of that period in peaceful towns that make wonderful discoveries on the way to someplace else and in a fine capital city whose enduring beauty and character make it a popular place for

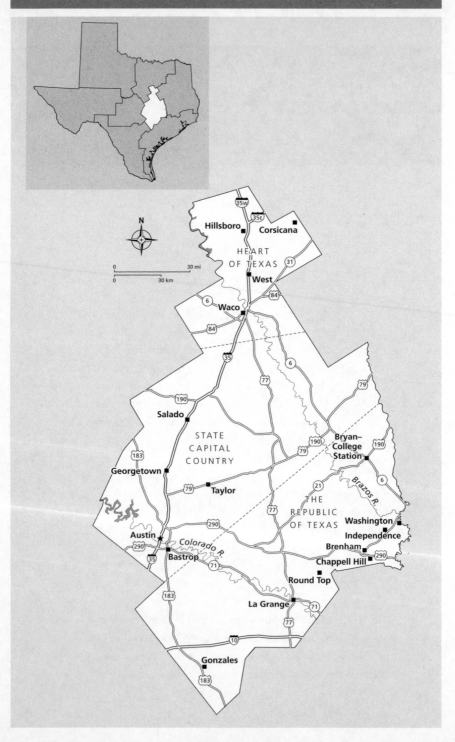

people who love art, history, rhythm and blues, comfort food, lakeside scenery, and even bats—yes, the nation's largest urban bat colony lives under the Congress Avenue Bridge spanning the Colorado River in Austin.

Heart of Texas

Hillsboro, resting at the center of Hill County, is a town of about 9,000, established as a trade center and county seat in 1853. People who've passed through remember most the *Hill County Courthouse,* built in 1890 to replace the original log cabin structure. The flamboyant, cream-colored design on the town square mixes styles to include classical revival, Italianate, and French Second Empire. A vintage *Saturday Evening Post* story called the courthouse "a monstrosity," while *Harper's* countered with a description declaring the ornate structure "like an outstanding cathedral." The courthouse was destroyed by fire on New Year's Day, 1993; however, the town and some of its powerful children—such as country singer Willie Nelson—rallied quickly to raise funds to restore the masterpiece to its original glory. Work was under way at once, and now the gorgeous creation of Texas limestone reigns over Hillsboro again.

Roughly a block north of the square, at the corner of N. Waco and West Paschal Streets, the old jail (1893–1983) is now the *Hill County Cell Block Museum*, (254) 582-2481. Inside find varied Native American artifacts. The museum is open April through October, Sat from 10 a.m. to 4 p.m. Admission is free. Five blocks north of the square on N. Waco Street, the Old Hillsboro Cemetery is covered with ancient cedar trees and filled with wonderful old headstones and monuments, marking those buried here from 1856 to 1940.

JUNE'S FAVORITE ATTRACTIONS

Ant Street Inn Brenham	**Lady Bird Johnson Wildflower Center** Austin
Armstrong Browning Library Waco	**McKinney Roughs** Bastrop
Festival-Institute Round Top	**Spoetzl Brewery** Shiner
Hill County Courthouse Hillsboro	**Star of the Republic Museum** Washington
Hudson's on the Bend Austin	**State Capitol Building** Austin

Two blocks from the square, the **1895 Tarlton House** (211 N. Pleasant St., Hillsboro; 254-582-3422; www.1895tarltonhouse.com) is a gorgeous Queen Anne–style Victorian home with 7 comfortable, thoughtfully appointed guest rooms. You'll be tempted to do nothing but sit in a rocker on the front porch and watch the world go by. You'll find plenty of stained glass throughout, as well as wireless connectivity. This is a great place for girlfriends' getaways and murder mystery weekends.

People also come to Hillsboro for a much more modern pursuit—finding deals at **Prime Outlets of Hillsboro,** at 104 I-35 Northeast, Hillsboro; (254) 582-9205; www.outletsathillsboro.com. The 50-plus stores here include Nike, Liz Claiborne, and Guess?, among other big names, all offering discounts from 20 to 75 percent off retail prices. The outlet center is open Mon through Sat 10 a.m. to 8 p.m. and Sun 11 a.m. to 6 p.m. Read more about Hillsboro at www .hillsborochamber.org.

Take a side trip to **Corsicana,** 41 miles east of Hillsboro on Highway 22. Although established in 1849, the Navarro County seat didn't see much action until oil was accidentally struck here in 1894 when the city was drilling for water. This set off quite a boom, and one of Texas's first refineries was built here in 1897. Today the city of about 23,000 is known far and wide as home to **Collin Street Bakery** (401 W. 7th Ave., Corsicana; 800-292-7400; www .collinstreet.com), the fruitcake company founded in 1896. Each year 1.6 million fruitcakes are shipped to every state in the US and to nearly 200 foreign countries. You can also find a 10-cent cup of coffee here. Open Mon through Sat from 7 a.m. to 5:30 p.m., and Sun noon to 6 p.m.

Get a little history lesson at Corsicana's **Pioneer Village** (912 W. Park Ave., Corsicana; 903-654-4846), where Navarro County's surviving historic structures, filled with heirlooms, artifacts, and family treasures, make up this living-history village. Grounds include a Peace Officer Museum, a Civil War Museum, the Lefty Frizzell Museum, various archives, an 1870 pioneer home, blacksmith shops, a general store, slave quarters, a barn, a carriage house, and an 1838 Indian trading post (the oldest structure in the park). Open Mon through Sat from 9 a.m. to 5 p.m. and Sun from 1 to 5 p.m. A small admission is charged; free for tots under 4 years.

Just 22 miles southwest of Hillsboro on Lake Whitney, find the beautiful **White Bluff Resort** (20022 Misty Valley Circle, off FR 933, Whitney; 888-335-8881; www.whitebluffresort.com). The inn, crafted from native limestone and rough cedar, rises over the glistening blue lake and has 47 rooms, some of which have gorgeous views of the rolling countryside and water. Or you can pick a one- or two-bedroom condo beside the golf course, complete with kitchen, washer-dryer, patio grill, and fireplace, or a rustic, 2-story cabin. In

JUNE'S FAVORITE ANNUAL EVENTS

South by Southwest Music & Media Conference
Austin, second and third weekends in March

Winedale Spring Festival
Round Top, third weekend in March

Wildflower and Bluebonnet Trails
La Grange, throughout March and April

Wildflower Tours
Brenham, Chappell Hill, and Round Top; throughout March and April

Texas Hill Country Wine & Food Festival
Austin, second weekend in April

Armadillo/Christmas Bazaar
Austin, early December

addition to golf, White Bluff offers a spa, as well as upscale dining (Black Angus rib eye, cedar-plank salmon) at the Lighthouse Restaurant.

As you return to I-35, bear in mind that the interstate can be particularly crowded, so allow plenty of time for your drive south. A few more miles south of Hillsboro along I-35, watch for exit 358 at the town of *Abbott* (birthplace of Willie Nelson). The beloved Turkey Shop has been replaced by *Up In Smoke BBQ* (on the east access road alongside I-35; 254-580-9644), a restaurant with roots in the Fort Worth area. The barbecue restaurant is kid-friendly and has free wireless service. It's open daily from 10 a.m. until 9 p.m.

Fifteen miles south—at the apex of the lines forming McLennan County— the tiny town of *West* on I-35 at FR 2114 is a town of 2,500 residents rich in Czechoslovakian heritage. Folks in north and central Texas know where West, Texas, is, but most people think we mean west Texas.

First and foremost, West is famous for Czech food, especially *kolaches*— thick, fruit-filled pastries—and homemade sausage. Travelers en route from Dallas or Fort Worth south to Austin and San Antonio invariably stop off in West to fill orders from friends back home who want plenty of kolaches. Consequently, the half dozen or so kolache bakeries on Main and Oak Streets always have pan upon pan ready to box, as well as frozen packages to go.

The *Village Bakery* (108 E. Oak St., West; 254-826-5151) is one of the town's original Czech bakeries, opened in 1952. Kolache fruit varieties include peach, apricot, blueberry, prune, apple, and several others, as well as sausage, or *klobasniki,* kolaches, by far the most filling. The bakery sells coffee, juices, and soft drinks, and a few tables inside serve those patrons who can't wait any longer to get that kolache fix.

Right on the interstate, however, there's another good place to stop for a quick bite of the local Czech culture. The *Czech Stop* (254-826-4161; www

.czechstop.net) on the access road on the east side of the highway (exit 353), has a convenience store, deli, and Shell station sharing a building with a sister business, Little Czech Bakery. The deli's big cases are filled with kolaches stuffed with fruit fillings, sausage and cheese, or sausage and sauerkraut. There are excellent sandwiches, too, from pastrami and Swiss on rye to egg salad or pimento cheese. You'll almost always find a long line here, attesting to the good food. The bakery next door has an even greater selection of pastries, but the Czech Stop is packed also with gifts and T-shirts; check out the ones in Czech.

If you happen upon West on Labor Day weekend, join in the celebration at *Westfest,* one of Texas's favorite parties. Held at the West Fair and Rodeo Grounds, at Main Street and FR 1858 (254-826-5058; www.westfest.com), the Saturday and Sunday affair features authentic Czech costume contests, folk dancing, and the music of a nuclear-polka group, Brave Combo. Count on plenty of kolaches, sausages, and other comfort food.

Shortly after heading south again on I-35 from West, start watching for FR 308, 10 miles south of West. You'll exit onto FR 308 and head southwest to reach the *Homestead Heritage Visitor Center* at Brazos de Dios; www.homesteadheritage.com. Stay on FR 308 for 3 miles, then turn north on FR 933 for 1½ miles, then turn west on Halbert Lane. This is the center of information for a small farming community where traditional crafts and arts are preserved and practiced. From time to time there are workshops for pottery throwing, basket weaving, soap making, woodworking, quilting, and spinning. At the visitor center, a 2-story, dogtrot-style cedar building, you'll find a deli, bookstore, and shop selling early Texas longleaf pine furniture, quilts, wrought-iron fireplace tools, pottery, and food items. Reach the visitor center at (254) 754-9600; it's open Mon through Sat from 10 a.m. to 6 p.m. Gifted woodworkers produce custom furniture true to that of the pioneer period at the *Homestead Heritage Furniture Shop* (254-754-9657; www.homesteadheritage.com).

Back on I-35, *Waco* is another 7 miles south. A city of 114,000 straddling the historic Brazos River, Waco is a place destined to be noted in history books as one with a diverse heritage. Although Waco remains reminiscent of its cotton-cattle-corn heyday, some people can't help remembering it for being the site of the tragic Branch Davidian episode in 1993.

Long populated by the Hueco Indians, from which the city took its name, Waco saw its first white explorers when a group of Hernando de Soto's men came through in 1542. Real civilization came when the Texas Rangers established a fort here in 1837, however. The town won the nickname Six-Shooter Junction later, when the Chisholm Trail was brought through the frontier post, but things have calmed down considerably, as the city is best known now for Baylor University and the Heart O' Texas Fair and Rodeo, held in early October.

Travelers enamored with Wild West history will love the **Texas Ranger Hall of Fame and Museum** (Fort Fisher Park, exit 335B off I-35; 254-750-8631; www.texasranger.org). Inside there's a replica of that 1837 Texas Ranger fort, as well as dioramas and displays detailing the history of the Rangers since Stephen F. Austin founded them in 1823. A firearms collection, Native American artifacts, and western art are exhibited here, headquarters for today's Company F of the Texas Rangers. Camping and picnic sites are available in the 37-acre park. Open 9 a.m. to 5 p.m. daily. A small admission fee is charged for ages 6 and up.

Waco's campiest attraction is the **Dr Pepper Museum** (300 S. 5th St., Waco; 254-757-1025; www.drpeppermuseum.com), housed in the original bottling plant for Dr Pepper, a favorite Texas soda pop. The fountain drink was originally mixed at the Old Corner Drug Store here in the 1880s, when R. S. Lazenby, a Waco beverage chemist and drugstore customer, took interest in the new soda. After working with the formula for two years, he sold it commercially, and the formula is virtually unchanged. The original 1906 bottling plant–museum is on the National Register of Historic Places and features a restored period soda fountain and much Dr Pepper memorabilia, as well as audiovisual enhancement. It's open Mon through Sat 10 a.m. to 4:15 p.m. and Sun noon to 4:15 p.m. A small admission fee is charged for ages 6 and up.

On the campus of **Baylor University**—chartered under the Republic of Texas in 1845, and now the world's largest Baptist university—is the marvelous **Armstrong Browning Library** (700 Speight St., Waco; 254-710-3566; www .browninglibrary.org). Inside find the largest collection of materials relating to Robert and Elizabeth Barrett Browning in existence, as well as 56 stained-glass windows depicting the famous pair's poetry. Open Mon through Fri from 9 a.m. to 5 p.m. and Sat from 10 a.m. to 2 p.m. Admission is free.

Sports-minded travelers will find the **Texas Sports Hall of Fame** (1108 S. University Parks Dr., Waco; 254-756-1633; www.tshof.org) of interest. Sports greats who competed on the fields, courts, and tracks of Texas are honored, including Shaquille O'Neal, Jackie Robinson, Jack Pardee, and "The Tyler Rose," Earl Campbell, whose high school letter jacket is featured here. There are auto racing uniforms worn by A. J. Foyt and Johnny Rutherford; racing silks; a crop and saddle blanket belonging to Willie Shoemaker; game jerseys worn by Nolan Ryan, Bob Lilly, Mean Joe Greene, and Roger Staubach; and Rogers Hornsby's 1926 St. Louis Cardinals uniform. Highlights from films of college and professional sports are shown in the museum's Tom Landry Theater. Open

Mon through Sat from 9 a.m. to 5 p.m. and Sun from noon to 5 p.m. A small admission fee is charged for ages 6 and up.

There are several more points of interest in Waco, including the *Cameron Park Zoo,* the splendid *Earle-Harrison House and Pape Gardens,* and the *Taylor Museum of Waco History.* For more information contact the *Waco Convention & Visitor Bureau* at (800) WACO-FUN or (254) 750-8696, or stop at the Tourist Information Center (take exit 335B off I-35); it's open Mon through Sat from 8 a.m. to 5 p.m. and Sun 9 a.m. to 5 p.m. Visit www .wacocvb.com.

Outdoorsy types can find Texas's oldest state park within close reach of Waco. *Mother Neff State Park,* a 259-acre spread in the scenic Leon River Bottom, was founded in 1916. Drive south from Waco on I-35 about 20 miles, then turn west on FR 107 and go another 13 miles. You'll see the park upon reaching Highway 236. There's good hiking in the park's Upland Hills and in ravines with shady rock cliffs. There's good fishing and picnicking here, and photographers frequently find dawn and dusk subjects in raccoons, white-tailed deer, roadrunners, and armadillos. Call the park at (254) 853-2389 or visit www.tpwd.state.tx.us.

Travelers who enjoy visiting historic cemeteries should make another little side trip from Waco to the town of *Moody,* 15 miles southwest via FR 2113. The *Naler Cemetery* sign bears the dates 1870–1924; the fence is interesting, too, with wiring attached at gateposts with cogs for tightening.

Another 55 miles south of Waco on I-35, *Salado* (suh-LAY-doe) is a bucolic, creek-side stop in Bell County. Although only 2,350 residents call Salado home, it's a well-known jumping-off point for travelers en route to Austin. It was founded on a tract of land along the Chisholm Trail, originally in a grant by the state of Coahuila, Mexico, in 1830.

Scottish colonizer Sterling C. Robertson brought settlers to the area in the 1850s, and it fast became a thriving settlement with the opening of one gristmill inside the town limits and seven others in a 9-square-mile area. After the

The Oldest Profession

The first legally regulated red-light district in Texas was, of all places, in Waco. It was also the second in the US, as Waco's leaders passed ordinances in 1889 that provided for the licensing of prostitutes and bawdy houses in a specified district called the Reservation or *Two Street.* The women working on Two Street were regularly examined by physicians, but their businesses were shut down after a campaign in 1917, and the last house burned in 1964.

railroad bypassed Salado near the end of the century, however, 40-year-old Salado College closed, and the town nearly disappeared. Today there are 19 state and 18 national historic markers in town.

The town was named for central Texas's Salado Creek, one of five creeks so named in Texas, and this creek was the state's first designated natural landmark. The lovely waterway is fed by springs that are the northernmost of the huge Edwards Aquifer, surfacing here on the Balcones Fault. Within a few minutes' walk along the creek, it's easy to see why the town has become a retreat for artists, writers, historians, and craftspeople.

Some important folks have passed this way—Gen. Robert E. Lee, Gen. George Custer, and Gen. Sam Houston all stayed at an inn now called the **Stagecoach Inn,** in a shady grove just east of the interstate on Main Street near Royal Street. In fact it was on the inn's front gallery that Sam Houston made one of his impassioned speeches, urging Texans not to secede from the Union.

The Stagecoach was the town's reason for surviving when times were toughest, and it's still a destination for travelers. The motel is a modern structure, but the restaurant is legendary, serving bounteous if unpretentious lunches for a moderate, fixed price, and enormous dinners; specialties include baked ham, fried chicken, roast lamb, orange roughy, and filet mignon. Lunch is served from 11 a.m. to 4 p.m., and dinner is from 5 to 9 p.m. Call (254) 947-5111 or visit their website at www .staystagecoach.com.

The **Central Texas Area Museum** on Main Street, facing the Stagecoach Inn, is busiest during the **Gathering of the Scottish Clans,** held annually in early November; it's open daily from 10 a.m. to 5 p.m. The building that holds the museum is well over a century old, and exhibits inside detail the history of central Texas. There's also the Wee Scots Shop inside, selling items from Scotland such as kilts and tartans. For information call (254) 947-5232 or try their website at www.ctam-salado.org.

After lunch or a look through the museum, wander a few yards north to the creek and follow the bank just a bit to the right. Until a flood in 2010 removed her from her perch, **Sirena,** a bronze mermaid, was a landmark sitting in a tiny inlet. At press time, she was still sitting in dry dock at her sculptor's studio, awaiting the reconstruction of the creek's passage through town. When she is returned to her rightful place, you'll once again see her exquisite and sad face as she eternally tries to remove a hook from her fin. The creek's

texastrivia

The Burleson County town of Caldwell, west of Bryan–College Station, hosts the annual **Kolache Festival** in September to celebrate Czech pastries and heritage.

grassy bank continues east and is traced by a road winding through **Pace Park,** a willow-shaded place to take a picnic and relax with a book.

Bed-and-breakfast accommodations in Salado have soared in number. Among the favorites is the **Rose Mansion** (254-947-8200 or 800-948-1004; www.therosemansion.com), an 1870 Greek Revival home in Victorian Oaks, just off Royal Street. In the main house there are 4 guest rooms, some of which have a private entrance, veranda, and/or fireplace; on the mansion's 2-acre grounds, lodging is also offered in comfortable, thoughtfully outfitted period cottages and cabins. Rates range from $80 to $160 and include a full home-made breakfast for two. An intimate retreat is **The Gazebo** (209 S. Main St.; 800-947-2175 or 254-947-7273; www.thegazebobedandbreakfast.com), a cozy guesthouse right on the river.

Among Salado shops to explore, see **The Apothecary** (209 S. Main St.; 800-947-2175; www.theapothecaryatsalado.com) for skincare products; **Coyote Glass Gallery** (26 Rock Creek Rd.; 254-947-4011) for handmade glass art, jewelry, and lamps; and **Horsefeathers** (600 N. Main St.; 254-947-3203) for home decor. For a complete listing call the **Salado Chamber of Commerce** at (254) 947-5040, or visit the website at www.salado.com.

texastrivia

The middle name of the father of Texas, Stephen F. Austin, was Fuller.

Georgetown, a charming town of 43,000, sits about 20 miles south of Salado on I-35 at Highway 29. The Williamson County seat is home to **Southwestern University,** Texas's oldest private institution of higher learning, founded in 1840. The university's gorgeous stone buildings, immediately east of the courthouse square on University Avenue, are positively European in architecture. The copper-domed county courthouse is its own masterpiece, and the square is lined with more than 50 Victorian-era buildings filled with gift shops, antiques stores, art galleries, and cafes. Some of the courthouse square shops to note are the **Windberg Gallery** (7100 N. I-35; 512-819-9463; www.windberg.com), offering American landscapes; the **Escape** (713 S. Main St.; 512-930-0052; www.shoptheescape.com), where contemporary arts and crafts made by Texas and US artisans are sold; and several antiques shops. Nearby, the **Inner Space Cavern** (4200 S. I-35; 512-931-2283; www.myinnerspacecovern.com) is a maze of fascinating underground rooms 80,000 years in the making. And right at the Georgetown exit off I-35, the **Mar-Jon Candle Factory** (4411 S. I-35; 512-869-1686; www.thecandlefactory.com) offers tours and a gift shop.

It's not unusual to find Austin-bound travelers staying overnight in Georgetown. When big Austin events, such as the springtime South by Southwest

Music Festival and football games at the University of Texas, claim most of Austin's lodgings, people find Georgetown a good option. A favorite is *San Gabriel House* (1008 E. University Ave.; 512-930-0070; www.sangabrielhouse .com), a renovated 1908 mansion by the university. For more information contact the *Georgetown Convention & Visitors Bureau* at (512) 930-3545 or (800) 436-8696; www.visitgeorgetown.org.

For a memorable barbecue experience, head east from Georgetown on Highway 29 about 17 miles until you reach Highway 95. Turn south on Highway 95 and continue 7 miles to *Taylor.* Your destination is *Louie Mueller BBQ* (206 W. 2nd St., Taylor; 512-352-6206; www.louiemuellerbarbeque.com), which was, in the 1940s, a tiny tin shack in an alley behind the Mueller family's grocery. They opened the barbecue joint in order to sell meats that didn't move in the store, but before too long another barbecue stand was needed as the farming community grew. In 1959 the third, and present, location opened, and Bobby Mueller took over the business in 1974 when dad Louie retired. Bobby's son, Wayne, took over upon Bobby's untimely passing in 2008, but the legacy remains well-tended. You'll see its long and beloved history on walls plastered with scads of newspaper and magazine articles from across the nation heralding the exceptional food, smoked daily on-site in what can only be called a rustic setting. Meals start at about $9. Open Mon through Sat from 10 a.m. to 6 p.m., "or until we run out of food," which may be as early as 3 p.m. on Fri and Sat.

From Taylor head west on US 79, which takes you back to I-35. From there it's 18 miles south to Austin.

State Capital Country

Just 28 miles south of Georgetown lies *Austin,* the capital city, seat of Travis County, and haven for 657,000 people who love to kick back. But the sun worshippers seen today around Barton Springs, the eternally cool spring-fed pool in Zilker Park, were not the first to find this a great place to hang around. Spaniards decided it was the best place to build a mission in 1730, and that was after Native Americans had been established here for centuries.

The 1800s saw the creation of the fledgling settlement named Waterloo, and new Republic of Texas president Mirabeau B. Lamar liked the place so much he moved the seat of government here. A few ego struggles moved the capital back and forth from the Houston area until 1844, and the town was eventually named for the father of Texas, Stephen F. Austin.

Since 1882, students of higher learning have found the *University of Texas*—with an enrollment today of around 50,000—and the Austin environs a place to stay beyond the traditional four years, thanks to numerous graduate programs and jobs in state government. Indeed, with hilly scenery, an easygoing lifestyle, a wealth of homegrown music, and abundant Tex-Mex eats, Austin is easy to love and hard to leave.

The *LBJ Library and Museum,* at 2313 Red River St., Austin, which is part of the university, is fascinating even for those who were not fans of the late President Lyndon B. Johnson. Great detail is used in chronicling his career, and personal items are quite interesting: There are early home photos and a fourth-grade report card showing excellent grades but a C in deportment. There are engagement photos of LBJ and Claudia "Lady Bird" Taylor, and there's an intriguing letter on Lady Bird Taylor's letterhead indicating her fear that Lyndon was thinking of a life in politics. The museum (512-721-0200; www.lbjlib.utexas .edu) is open daily from 9 a.m. to 5 p.m.

Just east of the interstate, the *French Legation Museum,* 802 San Marcos St., Austin, was regarded as ostentatious when built in 1841 for the French ambassador to the Republic of Texas. Today the French provincial cottage of Bastrop pine and French fitments seems modest, but it suited the arrogant Comte Alphonse Dubois de Saligny, if just for a short time. It was learned that the irritable chargé d'affaires held a fraudulent title, and that was after he'd shown great disdain for his Native American visitors and Austin neighbors. He passed most of his time in New Orleans, which he found much more enjoyable, and historians estimate he actually spent eight weeks at most in the Austin home.

Today the Daughters of the Republic of Texas operate the house-museum, situated behind grand iron gates atop a little hill and furnished with 19th-century antiques, a few of Saligny's belongings, and authentic items from a French Creole kitchen, such as copper pots and pewter tools. It's open Tues through Sun from 1 to 5 p.m. A small admission fee is charged. For details call (512) 472-8180 or visit them on the Web at www.frenchlegationmuseum.org.

A few blocks to the southeast, *Cisco's,* at 1151 E. 6th St. (512-478-2420), is a true Austin institution, especially at breakfast. The Mexican bakery and cafe has small-town friendliness for regulars and newcomers alike; the eye-opening dishes to look for are huevos rancheros and huevos *migas,* two sassy egg dishes. If you like something a bit heavier, order a basket of *picadillos,* which are homemade rolls stuffed with spicy beef. Lunches include traditional Mexican plates and chicken-fried steak; for a sweet, check out the bakery case in front. Note that Cisco's is a happy madhouse when the UT Longhorns have a home football game. It's open daily from 6 a.m. to 3 p.m.

Northwest of downtown, the *Elisabet Ney Museum,* at 304 E. 44th St. at Avenue H, Austin, awaits in one of the country's four existing studios of

How Sweet It Is

Next time you're in the grocery store buying ingredients for your favorite baked goodies, pick up flavoring from **Adams Extract Co.,** founded in 1909. The Austin-based
purveyor of good tastes produces 27 extracts, including the widely famous vanilla, as
well as Jamaican rum, butter, almond, peppermint, and lemon—and 95 seasonings.
Look for recipes at www.adamsextract.com.

19th-century sculptors. German immigrant Ney, a staunchly independent artist, came to the US in 1873 and built this studio in 1892, naming it Formosa
(meaning "beautiful") after her studio in Europe. Some of her work is displayed
here, while other pieces grace the Smithsonian National Museum of Art, various European palaces, and the Texas statehouse. Ney's friends and fans transformed Formosa into a museum soon after her death in 1907. It's been restored
but retains the rustic nature Ney loved. Art classes and audiovisual presentations are held here throughout the year. Visit the museum Wed through Sat
from 10 a.m. to 5 p.m. and Sun from noon to 5 p.m. Call (512) 458-2255 or visit
www.ci.austin.tx.us/elisabetney/ for information.

If you need to be refreshed, head west of downtown to 400-acre **Zilker
Park,** at 2100 Barton Springs Rd., home to the renowned **Barton Springs
Pool.** The 1,000-foot-long, rock-walled swimming hole—fed by Barton Springs,
the fourth-largest natural springs in the state—is an oasis, always a chilly 68
degrees. In warm weather the grassy, shady lawns sloping down to the pool
are covered by lounging or Frisbee-tossing sun lovers. Beyond the pool you'll
find the city's **Botanical Gardens,** the **Austin Nature and Science Center,** a
miniature train, canoe rentals, and 8 miles of hiking and biking trails. The park
grounds are open daily from 7 a.m. to 10 p.m. The pool is closed between late
January and mid-March; hours vary by season, but the website is updated annually with proper dates and hours; a small admission fee is charged. Call (512)
476-9044 or visit www.ci.austin.tx.us/zilker/ for pool and park information.

Right in the center of town on the UT campus, the **Harry Ransom
Humanities Research Center,** at 21st and Guadalupe Streets, has a remarkable collection of treasures. Visitors may view one of the nation's five complete
copies of the Gutenberg Bible, as well as the world's first photograph—shot
in 1826 by Joseph Niepce—in the fascinating Photography Collection, which
contains more than five million prints and negatives. The literary collection
includes autographed editions by Dylan Thomas and E. M. Forster, among
others; and the Hoblitzelle Theatre Arts Collection exhibits items ranging from
Harry Houdini's personal correspondence to some Burl Ives folk recordings.

The Ransom Center Galleries are open Tues, Wed, and Fri from 10 a.m. to 5 p.m.; Thurs from 10 a.m. to 7 p.m.; and Sat and Sun from noon to 5 p.m. The reading and viewing rooms are open Mon through Fri from 9 a.m. to 5 p.m. and Sat from 9 a.m. to noon. Call (512) 471-8944 or visit them on the Web at www.hrc.utexas.edu.

Within walking distance of the Harry Ransom Center, the **Blanton Museum of Art** (200 E. Martin Luther King Blvd. and Congress Avenue; 512-471-7324; www.blantonmuseum.org) is the university's fine arts museum and is counted among the top 10 university art museums in the nation. The permanent collection includes more than 17,000 works spanning the history of Western civilization, from ancient to contemporary periods. The country's largest and most significant collection of Latin American art and the 20th-century American art collection, which includes the Mari and James Michener Collection of American Paintings, are featured. The gallery is open Tues through Fri from 10 a.m. to 5 p.m.; Sat from 11 a.m. to 5 p.m.; and Sun from 1 to 5 p.m. Admission is free on Thurs and the galleries stay open until 9 p.m. on the third Thurs of every month; a small admission fee is charged otherwise.

Just south of the university, **Capitol Complex Visitor Center** (E. 11th and Brazos, 512-305-8400; www.tspb.state.tx.us) is well worth a visit. Built in 1857, the former General Land Office is the oldest government office building in Texas. Meticulously restored, it's now the Capitol Complex Visitor Center and Texas History Museum. Open Mon through Sat 9 a.m. to 5 p.m.; Sun noon to 5 p.m. Admission is free.

A few steps away, the **State Capitol Building** (11th and Congress Streets; 512-463-0063) is a glorious work of Texas pink granite. When the legislature is in session, onlookers can watch policy history in the making. Free tours are given Mon through Fri from 8:30 a.m. to 4:30 p.m., Sat from 9:30 a.m. to 3:30 p.m., and Sun from noon to 3:30 p.m.

texastrivia

The state capitol building in Austin, dedicated on May 16, 1888, is the tallest capitol in the nation, measuring 309 feet 8 inches from basement floor to the top of the Goddess of Liberty statue. That's about 7 feet higher than the National Capitol.

Just out of sight is the **Governor's Mansion** (1010 Colorado St., Austin; 512-463-5516; www.governor.state.tx .us/mansion), which was once the belle of Colorado Street. It has been the cherished home of every Texas governor since 1856. But, on June 8, 2008, a devastating fire ripped through the building, causing extensive damage to both the interior treasures and exterior beauty of this beloved landmark. As of press time, both the mansion and this block of Colorado Street are closed as efforts are underway to restore the building to its former glory. Be sure to visit the website to check on its progress as each phase of the restoration is completed. The tentative reopening will be sometime in 2012.

History buffs will be enthralled with the $80 million ***Bob Bullock Texas State History Museum*** (1800 N. Congress Ave., Austin; 512-936-8746 and 866-369-7108; www.thestoryoftexas.com). Surrounded by an exterior of six 11x16-foot concrete panels with sculpted bas-relief images that tell the story of Texas, the extraordinary museum is named for the beloved, late lieutenant governor. It houses three floors of exhibits that chart Texas's path. Find artifacts, photographs, art, an IMAX theater, and much, much more. Take extra film to document those sculpted panels, which portray a Native American leading a conquistador through the Palo Duro Canyon, a salute to the Alamo battle's purpose, and Texas-size achievements in the worlds of cowboys, trains, cotton, oil, and space exploration. Look for the smallest details, such as the horned toad near the conquistador's horse and the armadillo skittering out from a moon crater. Open Mon through Sat from 9 a.m. to 6 p.m. and Sun from noon to 6 p.m. Admission is charged.

Also downtown is the ***Mexic-Arte Museum*** (419 Congress Ave., Austin; 512-480-9373; www.mexic-artemuseum.org), which supports and promotes the Mexican/Latino art community. Exhibitions have shown the work of more than 5,000 artists, including Diego Rivera, Frida Kahlo, Juan Soriano, Jean Charlot, and others. Permanent exhibits showcase prints, photographs, textiles, masks, and artifacts. Open Mon through Thurs from 10 a.m. to 6 p.m. and Fri and Sat from 10 a.m. to 5 p.m.

The newest feature in the so-hot-again downtown is the new $300 million ***Austin City Limits*** venue, which matches, if not surpasses, its fancy attached neighbor, the new W Hotel. At the corner of W. 2nd and Lavaca Streets, you'll see a steady stream of evening traffic flowing up a wide staircase into what looks like nothing more than a tall black box. Upstairs, iconic 1970s lettering tells you you've reached Austin City Limits, now officially called ***ACL Live at The Moody Theater*** (310 W. Willie Nelson Blvd.; 512-225-7999). When Willie Nelson opened the venue with a two-night performance over Valentine's Day weekend 2011, crowds gawked at the chic but understated bar areas, including one exclusively serving Austin-based Tito's vodka, and whooped and hollered approval at the performance stage, whose corners sit no more than 75 feet from the most distant seat in the house. The new ACL accommodates 2,750 guests for its music shows and plays host, as well, to *Austin City Limits* tapings for KLRU, the local PBS television affiliate that has made a brand out of the broadcast for 36 years. Performing acts have included Janet Jackson, Bruce Hornsby, Blue October, the Moody Blues, Tony Bennett, and Jonny Lang and

George Thorogood, totaling roughly 60 to 100 concerts per year; KLRU will use the venue another 45 days per year, when tickets for tapings are free for an audience of about 800 people. To get those, you need to know someone or win a drawing at http://austincitylimits.org's blog. For the live concert schedule, visit www.acl-live.com.

A few blocks north, at the corner of 7th Street and Congress Avenue, *Art-house at the Jones Center* (700 Congress Ave.; 512-453-5312) has become the city's ultimate destination for contemporary art exhibits and events. Occupying an 1851 building previously housing a pharmacy, movie theater, and depart-ment store, the Arthouse recently reopened after tripling its space to nearly 21,000 square feet of galleries, a screening room, two studios, a mezzanine lounge, and a rooftop event space with BYOB Wednesday-evening gather-ings. Natural light and clever architectural innovations that utilize the building's bones offer artful appeal in which to enjoy a schedule of work from emerging and mid-career artists from around the world. Visit www.arthousetexas.org.

When downtown, make your way to dine at *Lamberts Downtown Barbecue* (401 W. 2nd St.; 512-494-1500; www.lambertsaustin.com). Located inside the historic Schneider Brothers Building, this chic but very comfortable dining spot will win you over with wood-smoked Wagyu beef ribs, prime rib, and coffee-rubbed brisket, as well as dry-aged rib eye steaks, Hawaiian ahi tuna, and desserts like Dr Pepper cake and fried blackberry pie. There's live music upstairs, too.

Another new downtown dining venue belongs to superstar chef David Bull, who earned his stripes as one of *Food & Wine*'s Best New Chefs in 2003 when he was executive chef at the Driskill Hotel in Austin. Now, he's carved three spaces out of one, all found on the ground floor of *The Austonian* (210 Con-gress Ave.; 512-827-2760), the residential tower at the corner of 2nd Street and Congress Avenue in the hopping downtown district nearest Lady Bird Lake and City Hall. The intimate, high-end dining room called *Congress* offers dinner in a 3-course ($65) or a 7-course tasting menu ($95, or $145 with wine pairings), Tuesday through Saturday evenings only. His brasserie-type *Second Bar + Kitchen* won us over with its casual-yet-tony approach to lounge dining, with fine wines on tap (an Enomatic system), beet and goat cheese salad, fried pick-les with gorgonzola cream, and seafood chowder with white beans and bacon among the delectable choices. Outdoor seating that offers a view of the capital, right up Congress Avenue. Bridging the two eating venues is *Bar Congress,* a smallish space for enjoying a cocktail with caviar or cheese before dinner or en route to the new Austin City Limits, two blocks away. www.chefdavidbull.com.

Right downtown, the *O. Henry Museum,* at 409 E. 5th St., occupies the quaint Victorian home briefly lived in by the master of short stories and surprise endings. His real name was William Sydney Porter, and he put out an extremely short-lived publication called the *Rolling Stone* from his Austin residence in the 1890s. The museum contains some of Porter's personal effects, including a yellowing original of his *Rolling Stone,* and various period pieces. Writing classes for adults and children are held here from time to time, and each spring brings the O. Henry Pun-Off, a good time for all. The home is open Wed through Sun from noon to 5 p.m. Call (512) 472-1903 for more information.

Head south from downtown by crossing **Lady Bird Lake** (formerly Town Lake) on the **Congress Avenue Bridge.** If you do so around dusk between March and October, you're likely to run into throngs of people hanging out to watch the millions of Mexican free-tailed bats that take flight from beneath the bridge in search of dinner each evening. In the booming area known as SoCo (South of Congress), just across the bridge, you'll find cool shops such as **Uncommon Objects** (1512 S. Congress Ave., Austin; 512-442-4000), a place to pick up a great birthday or wedding present or to furnish your home. The store stocks hundreds of pieces of handcrafted items, such as tables and chairs, candlesticks, and mirrors, as well as antiques from Mexico and the Southwest. Visit during the evening for First Thursday each month, when all SoCo stores open their doors for a street party.

The coolest digs in town can be found at the **Hotel San Jose** (1316 S. Congress Ave., Austin; 512-444-7322; www.sanjosehotel.com), a stylish inn carved from a 1930s tourist court that had gone to seed. The 40-room motel was turned into a model of retro refinement, with stained cement floors, comfy-modern furniture in the minimalist rooms, Indian cotton print spreads on thick platform beds, and butterfly chairs by the small, soothing pool. Potted cacti are everywhere, taking in the sun that peeks through handcrafted latillas and arbors along patios and walkways. Rooms come with high-speed Internet access, TV, phones, and clock radios with CD players. Guests can get same-day dry cleaning, on-site massage therapy, and beer and wine in the poolside bar after 5 p.m. Dog bowls and dog beds are provided at the front desk for your canine companions. Rates are about $95 to $375 and include a healthful continental breakfast. Some evenings feature dinner, too, and you can always find happy hour in the late afternoon.

The best downtown lodging of the independent sort is the lovely **Mansion at Judges' Hill** (1900 Rio Grande Ave., Austin; 800-311-1619; www.mansion atjudgeshill.com). A small luxury hotel with 48 rooms, this magnificent historic building is an easy walk to the capitol, Bob Bullock and Blanton Museums, and the Ransom Center. Packages can be crafted to include champagne, roses, and spa treatments. The on-site restaurant is one of the most coveted reservations in town.

To appreciate one of the state's finest sources of pride visit the **Lady Bird Johnson Wildflower Center** (4801 La Crosse Ave., Austin; 512-292-4100, www.wildflower.org), founded in 1982 by the late Lady Bird Johnson and called by *Texas Monthly* magazine her "visionary gift to Texas." Way back when her husband was still in the White House, Mrs. Johnson began her plan of beautifying America with roadside flowers. Her generous passion gave way to this extraordinary place, which remains the nation's only nonprofit organization committed to the preservation and reestablishment of native North American wildflowers, grasses, trees, shrubs, and vines in planned landscapes. Not only does the Wildflower Center maintain one of the largest collections of information about native North American plants for interested visitors, but it also makes information available to more than 20,000 members across North America as well as landscape professionals and gardeners around the world. The visitor's gallery, research library, and 232-seat auditorium all add to the educational experience of this unique facility.

The grounds are open Tues through Sat from 9 a.m. to 5:30 p.m. and Sun from noon to 5:30 p.m. The visitor's gallery is open Tues through Sat from 9 a.m. to 4 p.m. and Sun from 1 to 4 p.m. The store, Wild Ideas, is open Tues through Sat from 9 a.m. to 5:30 p.m. and Sun from noon to 4 p.m. The Wildflower Cafe is open Tues through Sat from 10 a.m. to 4 p.m. and Sun from

Austin Gone Batty

If Austin loves its wildflowers and live music, it's gone completely wild over its millions of nocturnal winged residents. A stupendous bat colony—now the largest in urban North America—roosting on crevices beneath the Congress Avenue Bridge over Lady Bird Lake has not only attracted a following of devoted observers, it's come under the watchful protection of Bat Conservation International (BCI).

From BCI, Austinites and visitors have learned that these gentle and incredibly sophisticated animals pose no threat to bat watchers—as long as no one tries to handle the bats. In fact on their evening flights from under the bridge, the Austin bats eat from 10,000 to 30,000 pounds of insects, including mosquitoes and numerous agricultural pests. Watching the nightly show of 1.5 million bats drag a flowing black curtain against the sunset is nothing less than spectacular; best viewing is from mid-March until early November, when the bats return to Mexico. As the nights become hotter and drier, the bats emerge earlier in the evening for food.

noon to 4 p.m. A small admission fee is charged. Children age 4 and under are admitted free.

Is it time yet to cool off again? If so, drive west from town on Highway 71 about 16 miles to FR 3238 and go south for 13 miles until you see *Hamilton Pool Nature Preserve,* a Travis County park on Hamilton Pool Road. This stunning, collapsed grotto has been a swimming hole since even old-timers can remember. There are 60-foot waterfalls cascading into the limestone-walled, jade green pool. County conservation authorities limit use to the first 75 carloads into the park, so it's wise to go early or call ahead to see if there's room; otherwise you'll be in line for a while. You can picnic and hike there and book a guided nature tour. Open daily from 9 a.m. to 6 p.m.; there is a small admission fee, visitors over 62 enter free. For details call (512) 264-2740; www .co.travis.tx.us/tnr/parks/hamilton_pool.asp

Because Austin calls itself the Live Music Capital of the World, you can count on finding dozens upon dozens of live music venues where you're likely to see groups you'll soon hear on the radio. To find out who's on stage when you visit, pick up a copy of the *Austin Chronicle,* an excellent alternative weekly, or check the weekend entertainment guide in the *Austin American-Statesman,* the city's daily newspaper. Almost any day of the week, the best acts are found at *Antone's* (213 W. 5th St., Austin; 512-320-8424; www.antones .net), also known as Austin's Home of the Blues; and at *Cedar Street* (208A W. 4th St., Austin; 512-495-9669), where martinis, imported cigars, and live jazz and swing are always served on the shady patio. The *Continental Club* (1315 S. Congress Ave., Austin; 512-441-2444) has become an exceedingly hip hangout and a place where the musical mix is decidedly eclectic. There might be a polka band on stage, or there might be a crooner singing the sort of lounge music that makes you crave a martini, shaken and not stirred.

To truly lighten up, unwind, and get centered, the destination of choice is the *Lake Austin Spa Resort* (1705 Quinlan Park Rd., Austin; 800-847-5637 or 512-372-7300; www.lakeaustin.com). A deluxe spa facility in a beautiful setting, the resort offers packages for three, four, or seven nights. Depending on your wants, your visit can include skin and body treatments; personal strength-training sessions; a nutrition consultation and healthy cooking classes; any assortment of fitness classes; body composition analysis; exercise options including kayaking, sculling, canoeing, and yoga; as well as meditation classes.

Widely regarded as one of the nation's finest spa retreats, LAS offers gorgeous suites, cottages, and rooms, many of which have private courtyards and/or porches with lovely views of the lake and hills. Landscaped gardens, a wonderful garden library, and the exquisite 25,000-square-foot Lakehouse Spa ensure comfort and restoration in one of the most unforgettable surroundings in Texas. Inquire about special seasonal offerings, which may include authors' forums, healthful gourmet cooking, and friends and mother-daughter programs. Three-night Spa Refresher stays, with a $330 spa allowance, starts at $1,925 per person, based on two people in a room.

Another spa stay to consider is at **Barton Creek Resort** (8212 Barton Club Dr.; 800-336-6158 or 866-572-7369; www.bartoncreek.com), also northwest of downtown Austin. The 4,000-acre luxury golf resort recently introduced Three Springs Spa, impressive for its wellness program and the serene room called Tranquility, built specifically to let guests gaze at the cavern wall discovered on the resort property.

Believe it or not, some people plan their entire visit in Austin around food. **Hudson's on the Bend** (3509 PR 620, Austin; 512-266-1369) offers an unequaled Hill Country setting where haute Texas cuisine includes water buffalo enchiladas, kangaroo loin marinated in orange and cilantro, and crepes filled with smoked lobster, shrimp, and scallops. Do call ahead for reservations and plan to spend at least $30 per person. Open for dinner Sun through Fri from 6 to 10 p.m. and Sat from 5:30 to 10 p.m.

Down-home food is found at **Stubb's Bar-B-Que** (801 Red River St., Austin; 512-480-8341; www.stubbsaustin.com), an outpost of a beloved Lubbock landmark housed within a historic brick building, offering a great deck under the stars. Beef ribs, brisket, chicken, coleslaw, pinto beans, new-potato salad, and cold beer spell success. Open Tues and Wed from 11 a.m. to 10 p.m., Thurs through Sat until 11 p.m., and Sun until 9 p.m. Meals are about $7 to $15. And at **Texas Chili Parlor** (1409 Lavaca St., Austin; 512-472-2828), you'll find the stuff legends are made of. This small, dumpy place is home to some pretty serious chili, rated X to XXX. You can get a bowl of chili or have it spread atop burgers or nachos. Clientele includes everyone from state politicos to university students and musicians. Meals start at about $5.

For more information on Austin, contact the visitor bureau at (800) 926-2282 or visit www.austintexas.org.

For some of the finest barbecue in Texas, head back east to town and follow US 290 across I-35 about 5 miles, then turn south on US 183, traveling 30 miles to Lockhart, seat of Caldwell County and home to just over 13,500 residents. **Kreuz** (pronounced krytes) **Market,** a veritable institution at its new location on US 183, is a cultural and gastronomical experience that will be long remembered.

Lines are long before the noon lunch hour, and steady streams of people file through the searing-hot, smoky pit room where your barbecue is cut to order by weight. They'll pile your request for smoked brisket, pork brisket, pork chops, or sausage onto brown butcher paper, along with a stack of white bread, which you then take over to a counter in the lunchroom to get "the fixin's," such as sliced onion, tomato, cheese, avocados, jalapeños, and pickles. If you ask for barbecue sauce, be forewarned that you may insult the proprietors—the meat is so tender and flavorful that none is needed. There are, however, bottles of hot pepper sauce on the tables for fire-eaters. Lunch is usually $5 to $10, plus cheap beer or soda. Kreuz's is open Mon through Sat from 10:30 a.m. to 8 p.m. Call (512) 398-2361 for details or visit www.kreuz market.com.

If it's a typically pretty day, get that barbecue to go. Head east 26 miles on FR 20 to Highway 71 and follow Highway 71 east 8 miles to **Bastrop,** where you can have a quiet picnic at **Bastrop State Park.** There, in 5,900 acres of rolling land studded with the mysterious "Lost Pines," is a tranquil and rich nature sanctuary along Lake Bastrop to be enjoyed for more than a mere day. Fishing, camping, hiking, golf, and nature study are big draws at the park, as are rustic but comfortable cabins. Find the park just a mile east of Highway 71's junction with Highway 21. Call (512) 321-2101; www.tpwd.state.tx.us

allnatural

Nature lovers will enjoy the *McKinney Roughs*, a blend of environmental laboratory and nature preserve found between Austin and Bastrop. The park was developed by the Lower Colorado River Authority in 1998 and offers an Environmental Learning Center. The park is at 1884 TX 71, just 8 miles west of Bastrop. Call (512) 303-5073.

The town of Bastrop is the Bastrop County seat and home to about 6,000 residents and several charming shops. The **Bastrop County Historical Museum** at 702 Main St., Bastrop, occupies the distinctive Cornelson-Fehr House, a Texas Historic Landmark and an 1850 structure resting on the site of a much older Spanish fort. Among miscellaneous and interesting manuscripts, pioneer collections, and Native American artifacts are silver spoons that are said to have been crafted from coins taken from Santa Anna at the Battle of San Jacinto. The museum is open Mon through Fri from noon to 4 p.m. and Sat and Sun from 1 to 5 p.m. A small admission fee is charged. Call (512) 321-6177 for information; www.bastropmuseumandvisitorcenter.org/.

East of Bastrop, the **Hyatt Lost Pines Resort** (512-308-1234; www.lost pines.hyatt.com) offers a vacation in itself. Lying adjacent to McKinney Roughs State Natural Area on the scenic Colorado River, the resort has lovely, comfortable rooms and more outdoor activities than you can imagine. You can opt for hiking, kayaking, river rafting, horseback riding, treatments at Spa Django, and sensational golf at the Wolfdancer Golf Club, or you can simply lounge by one of three swimming pools. There are three dining venues and two watering

Mystery Man

Sometimes people are not what they seem to be, even if they offer impeccable credentials. This was certainly the case with *Baron de Bastrop,* for whom the town 30 miles east of Austin was named. Claiming to be Felipe Enrique Neri, an important Dutch nobleman, the "baron" appeared in Texas in 1805; obtained a colony grant; established a freighting business; was named negotiator with the Mexican government for Stephen F. Austin's original Anglo-American colony; was elected representative to the Mexican state of Coahuila, which included Texas; and helped establish the port of Galveston. In reality, he was *Philip Hendrik Nering Bogel,* born in Dutch Guiana to ordinary Dutch parents. He moved to Holland, where he was a tax collector accused of embezzlement before fleeing to Texas for a life as an imposter. When he died in 1827, he didn't leave enough money to cover burial expenses, and there was still a reward offered in Holland for his capture. Interestingly, Bastrop was named for him a full decade after his death.

holes at the resort. Just be sure to go sit outside by one of the fire pits after the sun goes down for a little communion with nature under the stars.

If you decide to skip Bastrop, take US 183 south from Lockhart about 30 miles to *Gonzales,* appropriately nicknamed the Cradle of Texas Independence. Founded in 1825, Gonzales is the site where, a decade later, the first shot for Texas's independence was fired. The "Come and Take It" cannon, which fired that fateful shot on October 2, 1835, is displayed at the *Gonzales Memorial Museum,* on East Street at Lawrence Street, a grand structure built for the Texas Centennial and given to Gonzales by the state. Look on the town square for the *Gonzales Food Market* (311 Saint Lawrence St.; 830-672-3156; www.gonzalesfoodmarket.com), a timeworn, no-frills barbecue joint with very good lamb, beef, pork sausage, and chicken smoked over a combination of mesquite and oak.

Birders making the trek this way will want to stop at *Palmetto State Park* (north of Gonzales about 12 miles on US 183; 830-672-3266; www.tpwd.state.tx.us). Part of the Great Coastal Birders Trail, this 263-acre park is on the spring-fed San Marcos River and features natural artesian springs that have been thought for centuries to have healing powers. Numerous nature trails follow the steep banks of the river and wend through a palmetto swamp.

From Gonzales, make a worthwhile detour east via Alternate US 90, driving about 20 miles to *Shiner,* a tiny town in Lavaca County and home to the *Spoetzl Brewery.* This is where *Shiner Beer* is "brewed with an attitude," as the slogan goes. Shiner Bock and Shiner Honey Wheat have become extremely popular beers in Texas, and demand across the country is growing.

The brewery was founded by Kosmos Spoetzl, one of several German-Czech immigrants who came to this part of the state in 1909. Kosmos brought his Bavarian brewing recipes, and today the brewery produces Kosmos Reserve Lager in his honor.

Brewery tours, which end with complimentary tastings of fresh, cold beer, are given on weekdays at 11 a.m. and 1:30 p.m. or by appointment by calling (361) 594-3383. There's also the Spoetzl Brewery Gift Shop/Museum, where a video offers the history of the brewery. Find them on the Web at www.shiner.com.

The Republic of Texas

To explore deep into Texas's past, begin your journey by driving east on Highway 71, stopping just 32 miles down the road at the hamlet on the mighty Colorado River called *La Grange.* Seat of Fayette County and home to 4,500 residents, La Grange dates to 1831, when the road passing through was simply a buffalo trail. Historical markers abound—at the old railroad depot, the old county jail, the 1890s courthouse, the vintage Episcopal church—and the local historical route called Texas Pioneer Trail courses through town.

Of particular interest is *Kreische Brewery State Historical Site* and *Monument Hill,* 3 miles south of the town center and reached via a beauti-ful drive on Spur 92 (979-968-5658; www.tpwd.state.tx.us). Vestiges of a stone brewery and home erected by stonemason Heinreich L. Kreische, a German immigrant who arrived in 1840, mark the first commercial brewery in Texas and one that produced more than 700 barrels a year in its prime. Tours of the brewery and ruins are conducted on Sat and Sun at 2 and 3:30 p.m. A small admission fee is charged in addition to admission to Monument Hill, also part of the state park.

The latter is a resting place of the Battle of Salado martyrs and victims of the tragic Black Bean Episode of the Mier Expedition, all during the Mexican War. The dramatic monument is a 48-foot creation of stone, bronze, and poly-chrome. There's a visitor center as well as an interpretive trail, a nature trail, picnic sites, and a playground. The monument park is open daily from 8 a.m. to 5 p.m. A small admission fee is charged for adults; it's free for children. For more details call (979) 968-5658.

If it's spring, endless vistas of bluebonnets, orange and yellow Indian paintbrushes, and pink primroses will be your vivid companions as you con-tinue northeast on Highway 159 just 15 miles to *Round Top.* This wide spot in the Fayette County road seems small, with fewer than 100 residents, but it packs a cultural punch. The miniature town was once called Jones Post Office back in 1835, but its new name came from the Round Top Academy, which operated here from 1854 to 1867, with tuition costing $10 per semester.

Today, on what passes for a town square, there's **Royer's Round Top Cafe** (979-249-3611; www.royersroundtopcafe.com), a lively cottage setting for everything from rack of lamb and red snapper to fabulous homemade pies. Bordering the square's east side, **Henkel Square** is an impressive, growing collection of homes and buildings dating from 1820 to 1870. Furnishings and artistic decor are examples of the period's Anglo and German influences. The collection is administered by the Texas Pioneer Arts Foundation. Open Thurs through Sun from noon to 5 p.m.; a small admission fee is charged. Call (979) 249-3308 or visit www.texaspioneerarts.org for more information.

Five blocks north, on Highway 237, **Festival Hill** is the site of the **International Festival-Institute.** A concert weekend is scheduled monthly, and summer is devoted to popular performances by institute students with visiting orchestras and string quartets. Festival Hill is occupied by a marvelous array of restored period buildings; even if you're not planning to attend a concert, it's a gorgeous place to explore and photograph. For a schedule call (979) 249-3129 or visit www.festivalhill.org.

It's only a 4-mile drive northeast of Round Top on FR 1457 and 2714 to the **Winedale Historical Center,** a picture seemingly realized from *Grant Wood's American Gothic*. Perfectly restored farms, ranch houses, plantation homes, log cabins, smokehouses, and barns represent more of the Anglo and German heritage prevalent in Texas. The center is an extension of the University of Texas, and it's open for tours weekdays by appointment. On Sat tours run at 11 a.m. and 1 and 3 p.m.

Winedale's many events throughout the year include a summer Shakespeare Festival, Oktoberfest, Christmas open house, and spring craft exhibition. Some events cost a few dollars for admission, but others are free. Call (979) 278-3530 or visit www.cah.utexas.edu/ for complete information and appointments.

Lodging in and around Round Top has exploded in recent years. There are dozens of B&B choices within a few miles of the town square, ranging from restored period farmhouses to newer cabins and guesthouses built on area farms. Find the selection at www.roundtop.org. Be warned, however, that lodging is nearly impossible to find on antiques show weekends in late March/ early April and late September/early October, when thousands of dealers and buyers descend on this normally quiet burg.

From Round Top, drive north on Highway 237 about 8 miles and turn east on US 290, continuing 16 miles to **Brenham.** Yum—you've reached the home of the **Little Creamery, Blue Bell Ice Cream,** just 2 miles southeast on

Loop FR 577. *Time* magazine called it the best ice cream in the world, a small-town giant that now produces some 20 million gallons per year. Free tours and samples are given to visitors, who are also treated to a film and a look at production from an observation deck. For the seasonal tour schedule, call (979) 830-2197 or (800) 327-8135 or visit www.bluebell.com. A small admission fee is charged. Reservations are strongly recommended. It's closed on weekends.

Brenham, seat of Washington County—birthplace of the Republic of Texas—and home to 16,000 residents and plenty of antiques shops, is known also for sweetness of an altogether different nature. At *Ellison's Greenhouses* (2107 E. Stone St.; 979-836-6011; www.ellisonsgreenhouses.com), you'll find a floral operation so big and so impressive that the owners schedule guided tours. There's a gift and garden shop on-site. Brenham has numerous B&B offerings and antiques shops. For more information contact the *Washington County Convention & Visitor Bureau,* 314 S. Austin St., Brenham; (979) 836-3695 or (888) BRENHAM; www.brenhamtexas.com.

A moving picture of Texas's past is seen in *Independence,* just an 11-mile drive north of Brenham on FR 50. The Washington County settlement of 150 was founded in 1824 by one of Stephen F. Austin's original 300 families. A town square was designed for the Washington County seat, but Brenham won the hotly contested vote by just two.

Old Baylor Park, ½ mile west on flower-peppered FR 390, holds the ruins of Old Baylor University and the restored home of John P. Coles, the founding settler. Also on FR 390, you'll find the *Sam Houston Homesite,* noted by a granite marker. A few yards away, there's *Mrs. Sam Houston's Home*—one of the earliest surviving examples of Greek Revival architecture. Mrs. Houston bought it for herself and her eight children after her husband died in 1863. Sam Houston Jr., other Texas pioneers, and veterans of wars from the American Revolution to World War II are buried in the town cemetery.

It's but another 10 miles east on US 290 from Brenham to *Chappell Hill,* a charming Washington County township of 300 established in 1847 amid rolling pastures of horse farms, wildflowers, and twisting post oak trees. The town, filled with antiques shops, is close to *Washington-on-the-Brazos,* the legendary town where in 1836 the Texas Declaration of Independence was signed and where the constitution of the new Republic of Texas was drafted, also in 1836. From 1842 until 1846, Washington was also the capital of the republic, and the town prospered as a commercial center for the cotton-rich Brazos Valley.

Today that heritage is memorialized at the *Star of the Republic Museum at Washington-on-the-Brazos State Park,* on FR 1155, 18 miles north of Chappell Hill. The museum is indeed star-shaped, and its exhibits offer interpretation of Texas as a separate and exclusive nation as well as its journey to statehood. Seasonal exhibitions, audiovisual presentations, and demonstrations of early 19th-century life are often scheduled. The museum is open daily from 10 a.m. to 5 p.m. Call (936) 878-2461 for details or check www.starmuseum.org.

The state historical park, which underwent an extensive $6 million expansion, contains a portion of the historic town site; a reconstruction of Independence Hall; the home of Anson Jones, Texas's last president; an outdoor amphitheater; and a pecan grove doubling as a picturesque picnic area. Hours vary for the different sites, and special events are held on the Sunday closest to March 2, Texas's Independence Day. For information call (936) 878-2414 or visit www.tpwd.state.tx.us.

Just south of Chappell Hill sits *Texas Ranch Life* (866-839-2775; www.texasranchlife.com), a guest ranch on Lonesome Pine Ranch. Eight historic homes—all expertly restored—and two modern dwellings are situated on 1,600 rolling acres populated by native pecan trees and roamed by herds of longhorn cattle and buffalo. The homes offer something for everyone—a romantic escape or a place where girlfriends or a family can enjoy lots of space to hang together. While on the ranch guests can fish on any of 11 lakes, take riding lessons and head out on trail rides, participate in cattle roundups, enjoy hayrides and chuck wagon meals, hunt dove or quail (in season), go bird watching, or simply enjoy long, quiet walks. Breakfast is included.

From Washington-on-the-Brazos, head north on Highway 90 about 20 miles to the town of *Anderson,* a historic town of just 300, established in 1834 on La Bahia Road, the ancient Indian trail that stretched from Louisiana through Texas and was used by Spanish explorers. There are numerous charming buildings and homes from the post–Civil War and Victorian period, including the delightful 1891 Grimes County Courthouse. Don't miss an opportunity to see *Fanthorp Inn State Historic Park* (936-873-2633; www.tpwd.state.tx.us) in Anderson, a pre–Republic of Texas log inn built in 1834. It's said that Texas notables such as Sam Houston, Anson Jones, Jefferson Davis (who became president of the Confederacy), and generals Stonewall Jackson and Robert E. Lee stayed here. There are stagecoach rides on the second Sat of each month from 11 a.m. to 3 p.m.; a small admission fee is charged. The inn is open for tours daily. A small admission fee is charged.

From Anderson take FR 244 northwest about 10 miles to TX 30, then head west on Highway 30 another 31 miles to *Bryan–College Station.* Always referred to in hyphenated form, the attached cities spread over the gentle hills of Brazos County. Founded by Stephen F. Austin's colonists between 1821 and 1831, the duo has grown in leaps and bounds with Texas A&M University. Established in 1876 as the state's first public institution for higher education, in

1996 it became the school with the nation's largest undergraduate enrollment, claiming more than 50,000 students.

If the university is College Station's heartbeat, the university's magnificent heart and soul is the *George Bush Presidential Library Center,* dominating the west campus.

Reopened on its 10th anniversary after an extensive, 8-month, $8.3 million renovation, the 21,000-square-foot facility tells a compelling story of the 41st president of the US. Interactive exhibits show his courage and dedication through artifacts such as film, photographs, and documents enhanced by music, sound effects, interactive video, and computerization. War aficionados will be riveted by the World War II Avenger Torpedo Bomber display, while history buffs will be drawn to the 1947 Studebaker and a section of the Berlin Wall. You can sit in a replica of President Bush's Oval Office, walk through his Camp David office, and take part in a National Security briefing in the White House Situation Room. For more information and hours, call the center at (979) 691-4000 or visit the website http://bushlibrary.tamu.edu.

Also of significant interest on the Texas A&M campus is the *Sam Houston Sanders Corps of Cadets Center* (979-862-2862; www.aggiecorps.org/Corps Center/), which offers a look at the history and future of the illustrious Corps of Cadets. Bronzes of seven Aggie Medal of Honor winners and the Metzger Sanders Gun Collection are on permanent display here. The center is open Mon through Fri from 8 a.m. to 5 p.m. Open weekends only for special events. Admission is free.

In Bryan, which is immediately adjacent to College Station on the east, see the marvelous *Carnegie Center of Brazos Valley History* (111 S. Main St., Bryan; 979-209-5630). Built in 1903 with funds from the Carnegie Foundation, it is the oldest existing Carnegie Library in Texas.

For an indulgent afternoon head to *Messina Hof Wine Cellar* (4545 Old Reliance Rd., Bryan; 979-778-9463; www.messinahof.com). One of the most awarded premium wineries in Texas, Messina Hof produces numerous wines at its state-of-the-art winemaking facility. The visitor center, which includes a tasting room and deli, is housed in part of the reconstructed former home of Ambassador Williamson S. Howell and is filled with antiques and memorabilia. Next door is the Vintage House restaurant, which is open for lunch from 11 a.m. to 4 p.m. and from 5 p.m. until 9 p.m. Wed through Sat, and from 11 a.m. until 6 p.m. Sun. Call for the schedule of free tours and tastings daily at the winery. A pretty bed-and-breakfast with 10 private rooms is on-site, too.

For more information on Bryan–College Station, contact the Convention and Visitor Bureau at (979) 260-9898 or (800) 777-8292 or visit www.visitaggie land.com.

Other Places to Stay on the Brazos-Republic Trail

AUSTIN

Austin Motel
1220 S. Congress Ave.
(512) 441-1157
www.austinmotel.com
Dating from the late 1930s, this funky motel is pretty cheap ($80 and up) and has no two rooms alike in its rambling offerings. If possible get one poolside with two double beds, Saltillo tile floors, and a tiny refrigerator.

Woodburn House Bed & Breakfast
4401 Avenue D
(512) 458-4335
www.woodburnhouse.com
A 1909 home with many design details typical of plantation homes of the Old South, along with ornamental Victorian architectural details, this Hyde Park neighborhood jewel has undergone extensive restoration. Six bedrooms with private baths, phones, and data ports are offered, and a full breakfast is included.

BASTROP

Pecan Street Inn
1507 Pecan St.
(512) 321-3315
www.pecanstreetinn.com
This eclectic Queen Anne–Gothic home is nearly a

century old and is included on the National Register of Historic Places. Each of the 5 guest rooms, 4 of which have private baths, has a fireplace and a coffeemaker. The specialty breakfast dish is pecan waffles with Grand Marnier strawberries.

BRENHAM

Ant Street Inn
107 W. Commerce St.
(979) 836-7393 or
(800) 481-1951
www.antstreetinn.com
A sensational lodging that would impress even the most finicky traveler, this 14-room inn is owned by a former antiques dealer and a former teacher for *Southern Living* magazine's cooking school. Exquisite antiques, upholstery, bed linens, and attention to detail. Brenham Grill at the inn is a full-service restaurant.

CORSICANA

The Wicklow Inn
220 N. 14th St.
(903) 872-7311 or
(877) 694-5468
www.wicklowinn.com
This renovated 4-story mansion was built in 1898. Stays include a full breakfast.

GONZALES

St. James Inn
723 Saint James St.
(830) 672-7066
www.stjamesinn.com

This 1914 Greek Revival home has 3 floors, 9 working fireplaces, 5 guest rooms, 2 suites, 7 private baths, and period antiques. Guests are fed a full breakfast and can request candlelight dinners, too.

SHINER

Shiner Country Inn
1016 N. Avenue E
(Business US 90)
(361) 594-3335
www.shinercountryinn.com
This updated country motel has a particularly friendly spirit as well as in-room phones, high-speed Internet, and cable TV.

WACO

Judge Baylor House
908 Speight Ave.
(254) 756-0273
www.judgebaylorhouse
.com
There are 5 guest rooms available.

WHITNEY

Arrowhead Resort
Off Highway 22, 106 Arrowhead Rd.,
between Whitney and Lake Whitney Dam, near Hillsboro
(254) 694-3044
www.arrowheadatlake
whitney.com
Cabins, swimming pool, volleyball, trail rides, and lake sports.

Other Places to Eat on the Brazos-Republic Trail

AUSTIN

La Condesa
400 W. 2nd St.
(512) 499-0300
Not your ordinary Mexican joint, this stylish, colorful downtown favorite soothes with ceviches and thrills with grilled quail in green tomato marmalade, duck in Oaxacan mole, and hand-crafted cocktails.

Scholz Garten
1607 San Jacinto St.
(512) 474-1958
www.scholzgarten.net
Established in 1866, this beer garden calls itself the oldest tavern in Texas. Regardless, it's great fun.

Threadgill's
6416 N. Lamar St.
(512) 451-5440
www.threadgills.com
Need some comfort? Here's the place for fried Mississippi catfish, chicken-fried steak, meat loaf, mashed potatoes, and country vegetables. Meals start at about $9. (Another location is at 301 W. Riverside St., 512 472-9304.)

Wink
1014 N. Lamar St.
(512) 482-8868
http://winkrestaurant.com.
Intimate and very upscale, yet still informal, this ingredient-driven dining room features pure genius on a plate. The menu changes frequently but features local, sustainable, seasonal ingredients. Open for dinner Mon through Sat.

BRENHAM

Brazos Belle
Main Street in Burton
(16 miles west of Brenham via US 290)
(979) 289-2677
www.brazosbellerestaurant
.com.
An 1870s-era general store is now occupied by a comfortable, casual restaurant whose owner-chef is a French native and a former chef at the Four Seasons in Houston. Excellent choices include steak Delmonico and cassoulet with duck and sausage.

CHAPPELL HILL

Bevers Kitchen
Main Street
(979) 836-4178
www.bevers-kitchen.com
A cute, colorful country cafe, this great little find does good home cooking, from meat loaf to cobbler. Reservations are recommended.

GEORGETOWN

The Monument Cafe
500 S. Austin Ave.
(512) 930-9586
www.themonumentcafe
.com
Exceptional home cooking includes chicken-fried

Kobe steak, pan-fried pork chops, cheese enchiladas with two-alarm chili, and a massive breakfast menu.

ROUND TOP

The Oaks Restaurant
Highway 237 at Warrenton
(979) 249-5909
www.oaksfamilyrestaurant
.com
Informal, friendly family restaurant offers fried butterflied shrimp, burgers, steaks, baby-back ribs, and pizzas, as well as all-you-can-eat boiled shrimp on Sun.

SALADO

The Range at the Barton House
101 N. Main St.
(254) 947-3828
www.therangerestaurant
.com
Sensational fare offers a changing selection of thoughtfully prepared steaks, chops, and seafood. The delightful setting is an 1866 limestone house. Open for lunch and dinner Tues through Sat.

WACO

George's
1925 Speight Ave.
(254) 753-1421
www.georgesrestaurant
.com
Generations of Baylor alumni can attest to the worthiness of the burgers, chicken-fried steak, grilled chicken sandwiches, and exceptional cold beer at this casual hangout, just off the interstate.

THE GULF COAST

The lengthy, shimmering curve of seashore known as the Gulf Coast of Texas has long been a place of fascination for visitors. The Spaniards arrived in 1528, when Cabeza de Vaca shipwrecked just off Galveston Island; he was followed by conquistadors looking for fabled treasures in cities of gold, and although none was discovered, the Spanish priests established missions as necessary for colonization.

The French came, too, led by the explorer La Salle, who landed in 1685 at Indianola, which became a thriving port— German colonists came through here in the 1840s—but it's now only a ghostly stretch of sand. French buccaneer Jean Lafitte enjoyed a lucrative stay at Galveston Island from 1817 until 1821, when the US government ran him off for making moves on an American ship.

Significant milestones in American history came to pass on this shoreline: Texas's first oil well, the gusher Spindletop, blew in 1901 at Beaumont; NASA astronauts found a new home address in Houston's Lyndon B. Johnson Space Center in the early 1960s; and rock-and-roll legend Janis Joplin was raised in Port Arthur—if not for her, we might never have learned a great hum-along song, "Me and Bobby McGee,"

THE GULF COAST

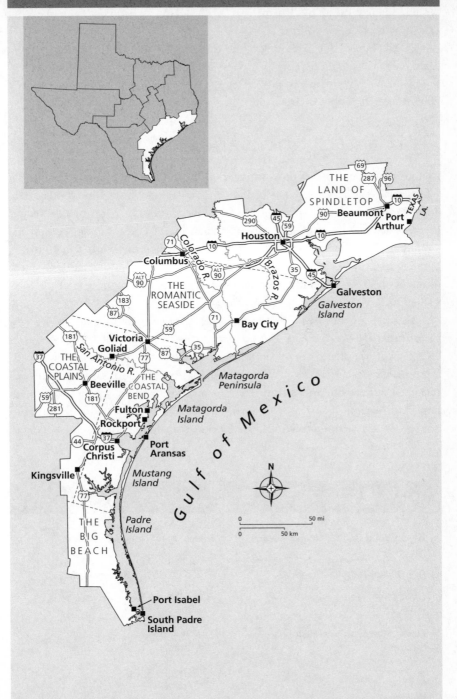

written for her by fellow Texan Kris Kristofferson, who hails from the Gulf Coast town of Corpus Christi.

The 624 miles of coastline you find on Texas's Gulf offer everything from a Mardi Gras to symphony concerts, deep-sea fishing to whooping-crane watching, weekends whiled away in Victorian mansions to gambling the night away aboard a Mexico-bound cruise ship. You may never want to go home.

The Land of Spindletop

As the state's rich forests unwind en route to the Gulf, the land turns to that which has seen massive bursts of industry yet still languishes in woodsy radiance. **Beaumont,** a city of about 115,000 connected to the Gulf by the Neches River, is a pulse point of this section, begun in 1837 as a lumber center that literally exploded onto the energy map in 1901, when the world's first gusher, Spindletop, erupted here. The little settlement of a few hundred suddenly grew to a city of 30,000—literally overnight—and became the birthplace of oil companies such as Exxon, Texaco, and Mobil.

To see just what Beaumont looked like at its moment of glory, pay a visit to **Spindletop–Gladys City Boomtown** (University Drive at US 69, 409-835-0823; www.spindletop.org). The whole place has been re-created, down to the post office, oil derricks made of wood, blacksmith shop, saloon, surveyor's office, photo studio, and so on. Here, too, is the 58-foot granite monument honoring Anthony F. Lucas's landmark well that blew in at 10 a.m. on January 10, 1901. The boomtown is closed Mon. A small admission fee is charged.

JUNE'S FAVORITE ATTRACTIONS

Bayou Bend Collection and Gardens
Houston

Big Thicket National Preserve

Discovery Green
Houston

Fulton Mansion State Historical Structure
Fulton

King Ranch
Kingsville

Padre Island National Seashore

Presidio La Bahía
Goliad

Rao's Bakery
Beaumont

The Strand
Galveston

Tarpon Inn
Port Aransas

A modern look at the complex petroleum industry is found at the ***Texas Energy Museum*** (600 Main St., Beaumont; 409-833-5100; www.texasenergy museum.org), touted by the Smithsonian Institution as being one of the world's finest. A remarkable parade of exhibits includes robotics and multimedia displays that simulate rig functions. Visit the museum Tues through Sat 9 a.m. to 5 p.m. and Sun 1 to 5 p.m. A small admission fee is charged.

Beaumont's other claim to fame is being home to Babe Didrikson Zaharias (1914–1956), undoubtedly the world's greatest female athlete, some say the most gifted of all American athletes. The ***Babe Didrikson Zaharias Museum*** (1750 I-10 East, Beaumont; 409-833-4622; www.babedidrikson zaharias.org/) offers tourists a chance to learn more about the woman who was a three-time basketball All-American, double Olympic gold-medal winner in track, and world-class golfer. A wealth of documents, awards, medals, and other memorabilia chronicle her illustrious career and life. The museum is home also to a good visitor center, offering travelers a variety of information on the area. The museum and center are open daily from 9 a.m. to 5 p.m.

As you'll find throughout the state, early industrialists built extraordinary, lasting structures that we're fortunate enough to enjoy today. Beaumont is no exception, offering sensational vintage architecture. One such place is the ***McFaddin-Ward House*** (1906 Calder Ave., Beaumont; 409-832-2134; www.mcfaddin-ward.org/). The 1906 Beaux Arts home is filled with the finery of its day and is open for touring Tues through Sat 10 a.m. to 4 p.m. and Sun 1 to 4 p.m. A small admission fee is charged. Call for reservations.

Beaumont's ***Fire Museum of Texas*** (400 Walnut St. at Mulberry Street, Beaumont; 409-880-3927; www.firemuseumtexas.org) is housed within an early 20th-century fire hall. The history of firefighting since 1856 is detailed with equipment, machinery, and memorabilia. Open Mon through Fri from 8 a.m. to 4:30 p.m. Admission is free.

A particular pride in Beaumont, understandably, is the ***John Jay French Museum*** (3025 French Rd., Beaumont; 409-898-0348), an exemplary 1845 home restored to its original Greek Revival grandeur. Inside, exhibits chronicle the lives of the French family. Discover more at www.jjfrench.com. Closed Sun and Mon. A small admission is charged.

> **texas**trivia
>
> The proverbial six flags that have flown over Texas include that of Spain, 1519–1821; France, 1685–1690; Mexico, 1821–1836; the Republic of Texas, 1836–1845; the Confederacy, 1861–1865; and the US, 1845–1861 and 1865 to the present.

One of the region's best-loved places for good food is **Rao's Bakery** (2596 Calder Ave., Beaumont; 409-832-4342; www.raosbakery.com), an institution since 1941. Open Mon through Fri for breakfast, lunch, and early dinner and Sat for breakfast and lunch, this is the go-to place for stuffed breakfast croissants and wraps, *kolaches*, and pecan sticky buns for breakfast and everything from quiche to tomato-mozzarella or Sicilian tuna sandwiches to gelato and fancy coffee drinks the rest of the day. If you simply want sweets, Rao's will load you up with Texas heritage apple pie, fudge-nut brownies, cream puffs, mousse cake, and crème brûlée.

In just a few minutes you can be out in the country enjoying several sites that define this southeasternmost corner of Texas. Head east from Beaumont on I-10 about 25 miles to the town of **Orange,** where the new **Shangri La Botanical Gardens and Nature Center** (2111 W. Park Ave., Orange; 409-670-9113; www.shangrilagardens.org) will awaken your sense of awe with the lushness of nature here along the Texas-Louisiana state line. There's a formal botanical garden with 350-plus plant species, as well as the Cypress-Tupelo Swamp, which you can tour in electric boats. A mile of boardwalk allows you to cross over wetlands.

While in Orange, make it a point to visit the **Stark Museum of Art** (712 Green Ave., Orange; 409-886-2787; www.starkmuseum.org), one of the most astounding, well-endowed small museums in the nation.

If you still yearn for more of the great outdoors, drive north to the Beaumont city limits, where the nation's biological crossroads—known best as the **Big Thicket National Preserve**—await. Spreading across seven counties, it's the only national preserve and the only place in the US where eight ecosystems coexist. Established in 1974, the Big Thicket National Preserve is the focal point of a tranquil, woodsy region with a deep heritage and plenty of recreational opportunities. Once an ancient, 3½-million-acre wild forest, it's now an inverted L–shaped, 84,000-acre ecological miracle struggling against the wrecking forces of human nature. The Big Thicket is a refuge for nature supporters who enjoy fishing, hiking, canoeing, and wildlife and wildflower watching. It's also a lab for naturalists and other scientists. The preserve is open daily, but hours vary by section and activity. For details contact the visitor center, 30 miles north of Beaumont via US 69 and FR 420 at (409) 951-6700, or visit their website www.nps.gov/bith.

One of the newest and more impressive distinctions related to Beaumont is its importance to the **Great Texas Coastal Birding Trail.** Conceived in 1993, the trail enables birders to get the best possible information about the millions of Neotropical migrant birds flying north to winter, most of them visiting the Texas coast from March through June. The trail includes more than 200 good

JUNE'S FAVORITE ANNUAL EVENTS

Janis Joplin's Birthday Bash
Port Arthur, mid-January

Mardi Gras
Galveston, weekend prior to Ash Wednesday

Oysterfest
Fulton, first weekend in March

Houston Livestock Show and Rodeo
Houston, first two weeks of March

Houston International Festival
Houston, mid-April

Great Texas Birding Classic
entire coast, mid- to late April

Gumbo Cook-Off
Orange, first weekend in May

Dickens on the Strand
Galveston, first weekend in December

birding sites along the 500-mile reach of coastline extending from Beaumont to Brownsville. Detailed information on the Great Texas Coastal Birding Trail is obtained from the Texas Department of Transportation's Travel Information office, (800) 452-9292, and from the Texas Parks and Wildlife Department (c/o Great Texas Coastal Birding Trail, 4200 Smith School Rd., Austin).

Just a 17-mile drive south of Beaumont via US 96, you'll find the waterside town of *Port Arthur.* Originally called Aurora in 1840, the town on the shore of coastal Sabine Lake, on the Louisiana state line, changed its name to honor the financier responsible for bringing the railroad to town. The memory of colorful daughter Janis Joplin is honored each year in January with a birthday celebration of concerts, and she's the focus of an exhibit on rock 'n' roll stars at the *Museum of the Gulf Coast* (700 Procter St., Port Arthur; 409-982-7000; www.museumofthegulfcoast.org). It's open daily.

The oil boom brought prosperity to this town, which has served as one of the state's melting pots. French, Dutch, and early American heritage can be seen in Port Arthur's architecture and museums. A place with a particularly eclectic flair is *Tex Ritter Park*—formerly called La Maison des Acadienne and Dutch Windmill Museum—(just north of town in Nederland; 409-723-1545), where the combined mix of exhibits includes a park dedicated to the memory of country singing star Tex Ritter; a 40-foot reproduction of a Dutch windmill; and a replica house of the French who were forced out of Nova Scotia by the British more than 200 years ago and wound up in Louisiana and Texas. From Mar until Sept the museum is open Tues through Sun 1 to 5 p.m.; after early Sept it's open Thurs through Sun 1 to 5 p.m.

Newest to this region is the *Golden Triangle Faith Trail,* which connects the myriad places of worship and spiritual enrichment that punctuate the landscape in and around three towns. The trail includes the magnificent *St. Anthony Roman Catholic Cathedral Basilica* (700 Jefferson St., Beaumont), dating from 1879; *Temple Emanuel* (1120 Broadway St., Beaumont), a copper-topped beauty built in 1923; *Buu Mon Buddhist Temple* (2701 Procter St., Port Arthur), with a 7-foot gilt-bronze Buddha statue and a lovely garden renowned for its varieties of lotus, water lilies, and bamboo; *First Presbyterian Church* (902 Green Ave., Orange), an exquisite pink granite building dating from 1912; and *Our Lady of Guadalupe Church and Shrine* (61st Street at 9th Avenue, Port Arthur), an imposing, modern church on the site of a parish dating from 1927. For greater detail on the Faith Trail, check with the *Beaumont Convention & Visitor Bureau* at (800) 392-4401 or visit www .beaumontcvb.com.

History lessons are fascinating at *Sabine Pass Battleground State Historic Site* (15 miles south of Port Arthur via Highway 87, or 34 miles south of Beaumont; 409-332-8820), which is slowly recovering from the devastation delivered by Hurricane Ike in 2008. The park is dedicated to the Confederate forces under Col. Dick Dowling, who managed a victory against staggering odds and much more powerful Union forces in an 1863 battle. In addition to a statue of Dowling, there are picnic areas and a boat ramp. The park is open daily 8 a.m. to 5 p.m.

While sailboarders and sailors are drawn to *Sabine Lake,* it's the camping, picnicking, nature study, and shell-collecting opportunities that make *Sea Rim State Park* a popular place. The state's only marshland park—spread over 15,109 acres—is 14 miles west of Sabine Pass on Highway 87. Interestingly, the highway splits the park into two separate parts, the southern being the Beach Unit, with stretches of sandy beach and a biologically unique spot where the salt tidal marshlands join the Gulf; and the northern section being the Marshlands Unit, where canoe trails and blinds are found. Bug repellent is a plus here, as mosquitoes can be vicious. Recovery work from the extensive damage left by Hurricane Ike in 2008 continues, but primitive camping, swimming, fishing, and seashell hunting has resumed. For information call the park at (409) 971-2559.

A trip to the nation's fourth-largest city, *Houston,* about 90 miles west of Port Arthur, can seem daunting; the key is to approach it simply by focusing on a handful of special places. Even though the entire metropolis sprawls across 500 square miles and is home to four million people, it is the city's individual elements that make it an intriguing whole.

Named, of course, for Sam Houston, the first president of the Republic of Texas, the town was founded in 1836, the year of the republic's birth. A city that boomed with the development of both the oil and the space-exploration industries, Houston has a surprising number of historical and natural attractions.

The first of these, appropriately, is **Sam Houston Park** (1100 Bagby St., Houston, 713-655-1912; www.heritagesociety.org), a 20-acre spread immediately west of downtown Houston containing an array of the city's first buildings, dating from 1823 to 1905. There's a small church, a gazebo, and an early commercial building. On-site there's the Heritage Society, with changing exhibits; and next door, the Long Row, a reconstructed office building, has a tearoom and gift store. Tours are offered daily, except Mon, Tues through Sat 10 a.m. to 4 p.m. and Sun 1 to 4 p.m. A small admission fee is charged.

In direct contrast to this historical park is a new and lively urban park called **Discovery Green,** situated smack in the middle of downtown Houston. Opened in spring 2008, the 12-acre park faces the George R. Brown Convention Center and is a boon for both leisure and business travelers, as it's just a short walk away from the basketball scene at Toyota Center and baseball games at Minute Maid Park.

Century-old live oak trees were natural assets around which designers built an expanse that includes the Great Lawn; grand-scale pieces of art; a big pond for boating; and green spaces occupied by a giant fountain (fun for kids to play in on warm days), dog fountains and runs, picnic grounds, a playground, an amphitheater, jogging trails, and places to play bocce ball, horseshoes, and croquet. The $122 million project includes restaurants such as the Grove, a Robert Del Grande operation that serves American rustic cuisine with lots of rotisserie specialties; the Treehouse, a supercasual drinks and snacks place; and the Lake House, a fast-casual spot serving burgers, hot dogs, salads, shakes, wine, and beer. *Green* is a keyword here, as all concessions are eco-friendly, utilizing all-biodegradable products. For more information visit www.discoverygreen.com.

History and art go hand-in-hand at the **Bayou Bend Collection and Gardens,** a division of the **Museum of Fine Arts** (1 Westcott Place, Houston; 713-639-7750; www.mfah.org), originally built as a residence in the 1920s for Will, Mike, and Ima Hogg, the children of former governor Jim Hogg. The paintings, furniture, ceramics, and silver housed here are among the finest collections of American decorative arts in the nation. Guided tours, lasting 90 minutes, are given Tues through Fri from 10 a.m. to 2:45 p.m. and Sat from 10 to 11:15 a.m. Or visit at your own pace Tues through Sat from 10 a.m. to 4 p.m. A small admission fee is charged. Children under 10 are allowed during audio tours only. Tour reservations are required.

Make it a point to visit the **Orange Show Center for Visionary Art** (2402 Munger St., Houston; 713-926-6368; www.orangeshow.org). Its late creator, Jeff McKissack, who hauled oranges during the Depression, began building this monument to the citrus fruit in 1954. Finally, in 1979, it was ready for folks to see. He was quoted as saying that he simply wanted "to encourage people to eat oranges, drink oranges, and be highly amused." What it is, is a patchwork, many-layered labyrinth of sculpture, wagon wheels, tractor seats, flags, tiles, wishing well, observation decks, and whirligigs. It must be seen to be believed. It's open Wed through Fri from 9 a.m. to 1 p.m. and Sat and Sun from noon to 5 p.m.—usually. It's best to call first. A small admission fee is charged.

You'll find one of the state's better examples of weird folk art at the **Beer Can House** (222 Malone St., Houston; www.orangeshow.org/beer-can-house), which was bought by the Orange Show Foundation in 2001. More than 50,000 aluminum cans and pop-tops decorate this little bungalow in a quiet, modest neighborhood. The work was a 25-year effort by the late John Mikovisch, who cut, flattened, and reshaped the cans to cover his house and to make mobiles and sculptures.

Perhaps the most sobering of Houston attractions is the **Holocaust Museum** (5401 Caroline St., Houston; 713-942-8000; www.hmh.org). Its exhibits and memorials provide testimonials of victims and survivors of one of the darkest eras in history. The museum also has an archives repository and an interactive learning center. Open weekdays from 9 a.m. to 5 p.m. and Sat and Sun from noon to 5 p.m. Admission is free.

Among Houston's profound wealth of arts is the **Children's Museum of Houston** (1500 Binz St., Houston; 713-522-1138; www.cmhouston.org), housed inside a structure designed by Robert Venturi. This is a great place for kids to explore science and technology, archaeology, agriculture, and the environment. The KID-TV studio features real sound and video production equipment. The courtyard has a greenhouse, pirate's ship, and Victorian playhouse. Open Tues through Sat from 9 a.m. to 5 p.m. and Sun from noon to 5 p.m. Admission is charged. Check out their website at www.cmhouston.org.

Other exceptional repositories of art are found at the **Menil Collection** (1515 Sul Ross St., Houston; 713-525-9400; www.menil.org) and the **Museum of Fine Arts** (1001 Bissonnet Dr., Houston; 713-639-7300; www.mfah.org). Complete information on these and all attractions is available from the **Houston Convention & Visitor Bureau,** 901 Bagby St., Houston; (713) 227-3100 or (800) 4-HOUSTON; www.visithoustontexas.com.

Shopping has become a prized pastime in Houston, with good reason—there are superb purchases to be made here that you won't find elsewhere. **310 Rosemont** in the **River Oaks Shopping Mall** (1965 W. Gray, Houston; 713-522-8133; www.rosemonthouston.com) is the destination for premium denim lines, plus late-night shopping with cocktails on the side. *Project Runway* fans are flocking to Chloe Dao's **Lot 8 Boutique** in **Rice Village** (6127 Kirby Dr.;

713-807-1565; www.lot8online.com) for hot cocktail duds and trendy daywear, plus an on-site hair salon. Although it's been around since 1883, **Hamilton Shirts** (5700 Richmond Ave., Houston; 713-780-8222; www.hamiltonshirts .com) is hot again, thanks to the young, fourth-generation owners of the haberdashery who have modernized the family business to make it more retail friendly. Charlie Wilson is among famous clientele who stop by (or visit online) to cherry-pick fabrics, cuffs, buttons, and cuts on lovely custom shirts, which are $200 to $400 each. If you have a minimum of $1,400 to spend, Alexandra Knight, former fashion editor at *Allure,* will hook you up with the sort of custom clutches and other accessories—sans hardware or logos—she designs for stars like Rachel Griffiths, Michelle Williams, Sandra Bullock, and Mary J. Blige. Houston local celebrities like Lynn Wyatt are frequently seen at Knight's atelier in the South Hampton neighborhood (by appointment only; 713-527-8848; www.alexandraknightonline.com).

When you're hungry, Houston will feed you well. Star chef Monica Pope offers a fun and fabulous version of all-natural barbecue at **Beaver's** (2310 Decatur St., Houston; 713-864-2328; www.beavershouston.com), a barbecue joint where thrills include spicy ground lamb wraps that incorporate almonds and dried fruit; fried pepperoncini stuffed with cream cheese and pork; and smoked brisket. Note: Truly good barbecue takes time, and Beaver's takes this rule seriously. No items on the "From the Smoker" menu are served from 3 to 5 p.m., which is when they pull out and prepare the barbecue that has been smoking all day. If barbecue is what you are craving for dinner, be sure to plan accordingly.

After a 7-year absence, **Armando's** in River Oaks (2630 Westheimer; 713-520-1738; www.armandoshouston.com) returns to rekindle a passion for Mexico City elegance. Here your palate will be pampered by ceviche, grilled snapper, *queso flameado* (spicy cheese), and dangerous margaritas.

The historic **Houston Heights** neighborhood is where you'll find **Sara's Bed & Breakfast Inn** (941 Heights Blvd., Houston; 713-868-1130 or 800-593-1130; www.saras.com). Originally a 1-story Victorian cottage, the home was later expanded and now contains 14 guest rooms and suites. Choices include rooms with twin, double, queen, or king beds, and one is a two-bedroom balcony suite with a kitchen. The breakfast, served in the garden room, consists of fruit, homemade breads, and juices.

A visit to the site where Texas finally won its long, tragically difficult fight for independence from Mexico means driving 22 miles east from the city center to La Porte, where **San Jacinto Battleground State Historical Park** (3800 PR 1836, Houston; 281-479-2421; www.sanjacinto-museum.org) is situated. Sam Houston and his army defeated the forces under Santa Anna in an 18-minute battle here in 1836, and markers on the battlefield detail positions and tactics of both armies. Rising from the park is the magnificent 570-foot *San Jacinto Monument,* honoring all who fought for Texas independence and particularly those at this site. The observation floor allows a view of the Houston Ship Channel and permanent mooring slip for the *battleship* **Texas,** the sole surviving dreadnought dating to before World War I. The *San Jacinto Museum of History* has exhibits covering 400 years of area history, as well as a theater showing "Texas Forever!", a multimedia presentation chronicling the events pertaining to the Texas Revolution and Battle of San Jacinto. You'll also find a gift boutique, picnic grounds, and concession stand in the park. It's open daily from 9 a.m. to 6 p.m. A small admission fee is charged only for the observation tower.

To gain deep, new appreciation for NASA and its work, pay a visit to *Space Center Houston* (1601 NASA Road 1, Houston; 281-244-2100; www .spacecenter.org), situated 20 miles south of downtown Houston at Johnson Space Center. The sensational new attraction is essentially NASA's visitor center, but the effect is marvelous. Upon arrival, visitors are briefed via continuous NASA update videos and firsthand greetings by Johnson Space Center engineers, scientists, and astronauts. There's a Space Shuttle Mock-Up with flight deck and sleeping quarters to examine; Mission Status Center, where you can see space flight and training activities; The Feel of Space, an interactive area where visitors can use computer simulation to land the shuttle or launch a satellite; two theater presentations, including one IMAX show; and a guided tram tour going behind the scenes at Johnson Space Center. It's open Mon through Fri from 10 a.m. to 5 p.m. and Sat and Sun from 10 a.m. to 6 p.m. Admission is charged. Visit their website at www.spacecenter.org.

Take time while you're in the NASA area to explore one of the more amazing tourist attractions to pop up in Texas. It's called *Kemah Boardwalk,* a creation on Galveston Bay in what was previously a quiet fishing village called *Kemah,* a Karankawa Indian word meaning "wind in the face."

Conceived and built by the owner of Landry's Seafood restaurants, Kemah Boardwalk is a sprawling arrangement of restaurants, amusement rides, landscaping with fountains and palms, and docks for visitors arriving by sailboat and yacht. The *Boardwalk Inn* is a 52-room hotel with a rooftop patio, suites, kitchenettes, retail shops, and plenty of dining.

One of the restaurants at the boardwalk is called *Aquarium,* where dining areas are surrounded by giant aquariums filled with fish from the Caribbean,

texas**trivia**

"Texas, Our Texas" was named the state song on May 23, 1929. It was submitted in March 1925 by William J. Marsh and Gladys Yoakum.

Batter Up

In Alvin, a town about 30 miles south of Houston at Highways 6 and 35, you'll find a statue of native Nolan Ryan, retired pitcher from the Texas Rangers, inductee to the Baseball Hall of Fame in 1999, and now owner and CEO of the Texas Rangers Baseball Club. Find the statue at City Hall and check out the **Nolan Ryan Foundation and Exhibit Center,** located at 2925 S. Bypass 35, Alvin; (281) 388-1134; www .nolanryanfoundation.org.

Hawaii, the South Pacific, and the Indian Ocean. Other dining spots include Landry's Seafood House; Joe's Crab Shack (you can't miss that EAT AT JOE'S sign); Cadillac Bar, a festive Mexican spot; and the Flying Dutchman, a favorite Kemah seafood spot for years.

Adjacent to **Kemah Boardwalk** is **Old Seabrook,** a cute cluster of antiques shops, seashell stores, a gourmet chocolate boutique, fine-art galleries, and more. For details on Kemah Boardwalk and Old Seabrook, contact the **Bay Area Houston Convention & Visitor Bureau** at (800) 844-5253 or visit their website, www.visitbayareahouston.com.

From Kemah or NASA it's a quick trip to **Armand Bayou Nature Center** (8500 Bay Area Blvd., Houston; 281-417-3818 or 281-474-2551; www.abnc.org), an unusual, 1,900-acre wildlife preserve encompassing forest, bayou, prairie, and marshland ecosystems. Choose one of several trails to hike or join up with a natural-history or boating tour. A re-created farmhouse recalls Victorian days and is designed to illustrate human-and-nature connections. Open Tues through Sat from 9 a.m. to 5 p.m. and Sun from noon to 5 p.m.

If this nature excursion leaves you inspired, you'll want to make time for an even greater communion with wildlife and the outdoors. This involves a journey west of Houston to the area of Eagle Lake, about an hour's drive west on I-10, then southwest on FR 3013 to Colorado County, near the river of the same name. First you'll find the **Attwater Prairie Chicken National Wildlife Refuge** (FR 3013, Eagle Lake; 979-234-3278; www.fws.gov). If you make your visit to the 8,000-acre reserve for the odd and endangered species between late February and early May, listen for the male's resounding mating call and watch the mates' ritualistic dance. The refuge is open daily from dawn until dusk.

If you're not heading to the beach, look northward for a place to be pampered. Just north of Houston on Lake Conroe, **La Torretta Lake Resort**'s Spa Terre has plenty of space—17,000 square feet, to be exact, with 20 treatment rooms—in which to indulge you. Attached to a 10,000-square-foot gym, with yoga, Pilates, and spin classes, the spa's specialties include the Milk and Honey

Body Wrap, including an exfoliating sugar scrub and Vichy shower; Balinese Massage, incorporating acupressure and rhythmic strokes to encourage relaxation; and the Essence of Thailand, a body massage and scrub combined with foot and facial massage. There's more, too: All spa guests can avail themselves of the *hamam,* the steam-eucalyptus bath said to boost circulation and rid the body of toxins. Packages at the all-suite resort can include golf and spa options. Just head to 600 La Torretta Blvd., Montgomery; (936) 448-3023, (877) 286-9590; www.latorrettalakeresort.com.

The Romantic Seaside

The utterly Victorian island-city known as **Galveston,** population almost 60,000, is roughly an hour's drive south from Houston via I-45. Plan to spend a few days here, because you'll be reluctant to leave.

Galvestonians lived lavishly in the mid-19th century: In 1858 alone they bought 23 grand pianos, almost $2,500 worth of silverplate, more than 3,600 gallons of French wine, and nearly 800 gallons of brandy.

Galveston was the largest city in Texas, the second-wealthiest city in the nation, and the busiest port in the Southwest. Cotton was king, ships called from around the world to the deep natural harbor, and deals were made by the hundreds on **The Strand,** the waterfront banking center dubbed the Wall Street of the Southwest and today's tourism magnet.

The opulent era of the island-city was characterized by full-scale mansions built by the local gentry; even an average family was housed quite comfortably in a pretty frame house profuse with gingerbread trim. These are generally viewed on walking and driving tours in the **Silk Stocking and East End Historical Districts.** Several homes are showcased annually during the first two weekends of May on the **Historic Homes Tour.** Brochures from the Galveston Visitor Center (2027 61st St. or 2215 Strand) have maps of these neighborhoods.

An abrupt and terrifying end to the glamour came upon the dawn of the 20th century: On September 8, 1900, a devastating hurricane claimed 6,000 lives and most of the city's structures, leaving Galveston in a deathly stillness. The event still ranks as the worst natural disaster in US history. To gain a deeper understanding of the devastation of the 1900 hurricane, see **The Great Storm** (Pier 21 Theater, Pier 21 at Harborside Drive, Galveston; 409-763-8808). The multi-image documentary experience lasts about 30 minutes and provides actual accounts from diaries and letters of survivors of the storm.

In reconstruction, a 4½-mile seawall was built, and for seven years silt was pumped onto the land to raise the city's grading. The resilience of

Galveston and its people was remarkable. Yet business moved in the meantime 50 miles north to Houston, and commerce on the Strand dwindled while countless stately Victorian homes lapsed into sickly states of disrepair. The Galveston Historic Foundation gathered its energy just in time, and wonderful vestiges of a golden era were saved from the wrecking ball in the 1970s.

The island city was hammered again, however, when Hurricane Ike swept in on September 13, 2008, damaging more than 75 percent of the island. Many businesses reopened within 6 months to a year, and cruise ships began sailing from the busy Galveston port again in 2009. Today you find a city that sparkles more than before, thanks to the hard work and diligence of its people.

texastrivia

From whence came the margarita? Published reports have credited a bar in Tijuana, Mexico, in 1930, and a hotel in Puebla, Mexico, in 1936. Another story says it came from a Galveston bartender named Santos Cruz, who made the drink in 1948 for singer Peggy Lee.

Ashton Villa, a redbrick Italianate mansion at 2328 Broadway, Galveston, was a primary salvage from threats of demolition in 1971. Built in 1859, the exquisite home is no longer a tour house but provides shelter to the *Galveston Visitors Center* (409-765-7834; www.galveston.com). The greatest of Galveston's historic structures, the *Bishop's Palace* (1402 Broadway, Galveston; 409-762-2475; www.galvestonhistory.org), has a prestigious reputation among architectural experts, who compare its ornate design to the Biltmore House in Asheville, North Carolina. Crafted from Texas granite, limestone, and red sandstone, the Bishop's Palace is the only Texas creation included on the list of 100 outstanding buildings in the US by the American Institute of Architects. Completed in 1893, its great pitched roofs, cupolas, gables, and cast-iron balustrades bear the mark of famed architect Nicholas J. Clayton. It's open for tours Memorial Day through Labor Day, Mon through Sat from 10 a.m. to 4:30 p.m. and Sun from noon to 4:30 p.m.; open daily noon to 4:30 p.m. the remainder of the year. Admission is charged.

The National Historic Landmark Strand District contains one of the nation's larger collections of restored Victorian buildings and is once again a vibrant and colorful mercantile center fixed within the old wharfside business zone. Great revelry invades during early spring for a massive Mardi Gras and again in December for a very British Dickens on the Strand celebration.

The *Mardi Gras Museum* (2309–2311 Ship's Mechanic Row, Galveston; 409-765-5930; www.mardigrasgalveston.com) helps you see how Galveston's Mardi Gras has become the third-largest in the nation, behind those in New Orleans, of course, and Lafayette, Louisiana. Costumes and historical memorabilia are displayed with models of the Arches created for Mardi Gras. There's a Mardi Gras gift shop here, too. Open Mon through Fri from 10 a.m. to 8 p.m., Sat from 10 a.m. to 10 p.m., and Sun from 10 a.m. to 6 p.m. Admission is free.

The 19th-century banking buildings and cotton warehouses along the Strand now hold a trove of shopping and entertainment. For a list of options, visit www.galveston.com.

Centerpiece for the *Texas Seaport Museum* is the **Elissa,** Texas's tall ship and another National Historic Landmark. The 1877 iron barque, built in Scotland, provides an exciting look at Galveston's seafaring past. The ship and adjacent museum, with superb exhibits and a dramatic film, are open daily from 10 a.m. to 5 p.m. at Pier 21, near the Strand at the foot of 22nd Street. For information call (409) 763-1877 or visit www.galvestonhistory.org/Texas_Sea port_Museum.asp/.

Three blocks from the Strand, the *Grand 1894 Opera House* is a distinctive, lavishly decorated theater whose stage has been graced by dignitaries from Anna Pavlova and John Philip Sousa to Hal Holbrook and Ray Charles. Found at 2020 Post Office St., the Grand continues to offer a full schedule of renowned entertainers. For information call (409) 765-1894 or (800) 821-1894 or visit www.thegrand.com.

One of the most popular Galveston attractions is *Moody Gardens* (1 Hope Blvd., Galveston; 800-582-4673 or 409-744-4673; www.moodygardens .com). Here a massive *Rainforest Pyramid,* undergoing a $25 million renovation at press time, houses thousands of exotic plants, birds, butterflies, and fish in a rather fantastic tropical setting with waterfalls, cliffs, caverns, wetlands, and forests. The on-site 3-D, 4-D, and Ridefilm IMAX theaters offer a selection of extraordinary multimedia films, while Palm Beach provides a white-sand beach with a blue lagoon, a 30-foot Yellow Submarine with octopus tentacle slides, a periscope, and water guns for kids. There's a fantastic penguin exhibit, too, which survived Hurricane Ike's devastation through a generous contribution of ice from donors from across the state. Open Sun through Fri from 10 a.m. to 6 p.m. and Sat from 10 a.m. to 8 p.m. Admission is charged.

texastrivia

Texas covers 275,416 square miles of land, inland water, and submerged tidelands to three leagues—enough to fit 15 of the 50 states and still have 1,000 square miles left over. The state extends 801 miles from north to south and 773 miles from east to west.

The island has 32 miles of beaches to explore, with *Stewart Beach* and *R. A. Apffel Park* among busy city areas with concessions, and *Galveston*

Island State Park (FR 3005 near 13 Mile Road; 409-737-1222), where people go for bird-watching, nature walks, and camping. Admission fees are charged at some beaches, and entry to the state park is $3 per person over 13 years of age. Be watchful on the sand at all beaches for tar deposits generated by offshore oil rigs, and jellyfish—two sure vacation dampers.

Old-fashioned rest and relaxation are obtainable in Galveston's several historic hostelries. *The Hotel Galvez,* a Spanish-style stucco mansion built in 1911 and recently spiffed up for its centennial, faces the gulf at 2024 Seawall Blvd., Galveston (409-765-7721 or 800-WYNDHAM; www.galveston.com/galvez/). *The Tremont House,* built in 1872 and located a block off the Strand at 2300 Ship's Mechanic Row, Galveston (409-763-0300 or 800-WYNDHAM; www.thetremont house.com/), has impressive and sophisticated appointments.

Charming and genteel bed-and-breakfast lodgings are numerous; for information contact the Convention and Visitor Bureau (409-763-4311 or 800-351-4237). Two bed-and-breakfast inns in Galveston are worth special mention. *The Victorian Inn* (511 17th St., Galveston; 409-762-3235; www.vicbb.com) is a beautiful 1899 home filled with period antiques. It has a particularly appealing second-floor suite, with a private veranda, king-size brass bed, and private bath with stained-glass window. All rooms have private balconies, and the third floor features a two-bedroom suite with a living room. Guests frequently wind up the day over a cup of tea on the veranda, after strolling home from a day of shopping and gallery browsing on the Strand. Breakfasts usually consist of fresh baked goods, granola, juices, and fruits.

There's also the *Coppersmith Inn* (1914 Avenue M, Galveston; 800-515-7444 or 409-763-7004; www.coppersmithinn.com), a Queen Anne mansion built in 1887 and outfitted with gingerbread trim; a double veranda; turret

Moody Gardens

It might seem easy to dismiss *Moody Gardens* in Galveston as a prettified theme park, but that would be doing a disservice to the respect this facility pays to nature. Kids love it because there is a world of hands-on stuff to do, and it gives little ones and grown-ups alike options—from swimming and playing on the sand to watching 3-D films.

Among diversions at Moody Gardens: a 10-story Rainforest Pyramid with an amazing bat exhibit; a blue lagoon and white sand at Palm Beach; an IMAX 3-D "Ridefilm" theater; the Aquarium Pyramid starring creatures from worldwide waters; a 4-D special-effects theater; and a very cool penguin exhibit with close encounters of the cute kind.

tower; winding staircase of teak, walnut, and curly pine; stained glass; fireplaces; and beautiful grounds with an herb garden. Among the guest rooms are Clara's Country Cottage, a private cottage nestled in the back garden; the Carriage House; and 3 main-house rooms, each with shared baths. Guests enjoy afternoon wine and cheese, elaborate breakfasts, and the option of dinner catered in guest rooms.

Dining has become a favorite reason to make escapes to Galveston. *Gaido's* (3828 Seawall Blvd., Galveston; 409-762-9625; www.gaidosofgalveston .com), founded in 1911, remains a place for good fried blue crabs, five kinds of baked oysters, and homemade pepper cheese bread. It serves lunch and dinner daily.

More contemporary is the very popular *Saltwater Grill* (2017 Post Office St., Galveston; 409-762-3474; www.galveston.com/saltwatergrill), with an open kitchen and chic decor. High marks go to Asian soba noodles cradling seared rare tuna and to the grilled red snapper draped in crabmeat. Prince Edward Island oysters are a big hit, too, at lunch and dinner. Very hip and casual is the *Mosquito Cafe* (628 14th St., Galveston; 409-763-1010; www.mosquitocafe .com), with a divine breakfast quiche of bacon and mushroom, and lunches of grilled shrimp salad. Weekend dinners are also a great idea. The oldest place in town, *Sonny's Place* (1206 19th St., Galveston; 409-763-9602) is also a hangout for the local medical students. Sort of a dive, Sonny's food is pretty cheap and good, the service can be a little surly, and the beer's cold. Try the oyster mug, an off-the-menu specialty of freshly shucked oysters with lots of cocktail sauce.

Diners swoon over the Central American ambience and menu at *Rudy and Paco* (2028 Post Office St., Galveston; 409-762-3696; www.galveston.com/ rudypaco). Empanadas (Latin turnovers) stuffed with spicy meats, hearts-of-palm salad, and grilled vegetables are all huge hits at lunch and dinner.

The Coastal Bend

The tricky aspects of following Texas's jagged coastline southward are fully realized on wildly meandering drives from Galveston Island down to the Coastal Bend. Travelers making just this journey will pass through Brazoria, Matagorda, and Calhoun Counties, skirting the coast's series of inward-jutting bays, driving 200 miles southwest on Highway 35.

Plan to spend time exploring *Matagorda Bay,* which was largely ignored by all but its residents before the 1995 discovery of La Salle's 17th-century shipwreck in these waters, roughly 100 miles north on the Texas shore from Corpus Christi. Nature lovers, however, are finding good reason to make their way here, thanks to that rarest of commodities on the coast—unspoiled, undeveloped waterfront. Word is starting to spread about the cool, 1,600-acre *Matagorda Bay Nature Park* (6420 FR 2031, Matagorda; 979-863-2603 or 800-776-5272, ext. 4740; www.lcra.org/parks/developed_parks/matagorda .html), a Lower Colorado River Authority operation that opened in 2007. As Matagorda County boasts the most coastal frontage of all counties along the Gulf of Mexico, this park gives you the best opportunity to experience the outdoors at its purest. When guests arrive they are greeted by one of the most remarkable pieces of sculpture found anywhere along the Texas coast. This 1-ton shiny scrap metal artwork, welded in the shape of a roseate spoonbill, was crafted by the Lower Colorado River Authority rail fleet and stands outside the park headquarters. Inside you can get information on the extraordinary bird watching to be done around here—some 230 different species were noted during the 2007 Audubon Christmas Winter Bird Count—and you'll find out about the wondrous monarch migration that comes through here in mid-spring.

On the park's long jetty pier, fishers show up around sunup to cast for saltwater cat, striped and speckled trout, and whiting. By midmorning, families are playing on the beach, and by afternoon the picnic tables and grills are busy. The most fun, however, is had on the monthly 4-hour, guided kayaking trips in the east bay's estuaries. After a few minutes of paddling instruction, you're off with guides, learning about the ecosystem, wetlands, and birds and looking in the shallow water for rays and other inhabitants.

Twenty miles inland at Bay City, the *Matagorda County Birding Nature Center* (TX 35, west of Bay City; 979-245-3336; www.mcbnc.org) is still another destination for birders and kayaking fans. The 34-acre refuge on the Colorado River covers former farmland with nature trails, butterfly and hummingbird gardens, deer habitats, waterfalls, flower gardens, and wildflower fields. There's a launch area for kayaking, and Kayaking 101 is typically offered in late spring.

For a good night's rest between all the encounters with nature, book a room at the historic *Stanley-Fisher House Bed-and-Breakfast* (107 Saint Mary's St., Matagorda; 979-863-2920; www.stanley-fisher.com). Built in 1832 by Samuel Rhodes Fisher, one of Stephen F. Austin's 300 colonists and one of the signers of the Texas Declaration of Independence, the imposing 4,000-square-foot, 2-story home has been restored by its new owners to show off intricate detail. Owners Peggy and Rik Stanley updated the home with modern, private bathrooms and central air; their ample hospitality includes lavish breakfasts.

A great detour en route south to Corpus Christi is found just shy of the LBJ Causeway, the portion of Highway 35 spanning *Copano Bay.* At the tiny unincorporated community of Lamar—it's too small even to be listed on the state highway map—you'll find PR 13, which leads to *Goose Island State Park* (361-729-2858), a 320-acre recreation area covering a little peninsula and an assortment of islands in the waters where Aransas, Copano, and St. Charles Bays meet. You can fish from a 1,620-foot lighted pier, bird-watch, take nature and wildlife walks, swim, and camp, and you'll have a chance to see a historical Karankawa Indian meeting site, the *Big Tree of Lamar.* This coastal live oak is possibly 2,000 years old and measures more than 35 feet around, 44 feet tall, and 89 feet at its crown span.

If you'd like to hang a while around Lamar, book one of four simple but comfortable cabins at the *Habitat* (164 4th St., Lamar; 361-790-3732; www .txhabitat.com). This quiet retreat sits beside a lovely pond, framed by palmettos, fan palms, live oaks, and little else. A kitchenette allows you to fix basic meals, and there's a screened porch where you'll want to have coffee in the morning and wine in the evening. Breakfast and snacks are included, and you're in easy reach of St. Charles Bay, Goose Island State Park, and the Aransas National Wildlife Refuge.

If you have plenty of time to spare, there's a great side trip inland nearly 60 miles to the town of *Victoria.* One of the first three towns incorporated by the Republic of Texas, Victoria's history dates to its 1824 founding by 41 Spanish families. Among the sites and sights is the *Texas Zoo* (110 Memorial Dr. in Riverside Park; 361-573-7681; www.texaszoo.org), a 6-acre spread with 200-plus animals indigenous to this area. In September the zoo hosts an annual South Texas Beautiful Burro Pageant, awarding prizes to the most beautiful, most congenial, best-dressed, and most obstinate burro. Open daily from 9 a.m. to 5 p.m. A small admission fee is charged.

There's also the *Nave Museum* (306 W. Commercial St., Victoria; 361-575-8228; www.victoriaregionalmuseum.com), a Greco-Roman–style building erected by the widow of artist Royston Nave to exhibit his Texas landscape and portrait paintings. Open Tues through Sun from 1 to 5 p.m. Admission is charged.

The *Victoria Convention & Visitors Bureau* (3404 N. Ben Wilson St.; Victoria, 361-582-4285 or 800-926-5774; www.victoriatexasinfo.com/) provides a good visitor guide and map to point you toward other interesting area attractions.

When you decide to head on down to the Corpus Christi area, you'll stay on Highway 35, cross the LBJ Causeway, and find yourself at the other end in the adjoining towns of *Rockport* and *Fulton.* Rockport, the Aransas County seat and home to a seaside art colony of about 4,700, is a quiet community fostering its cultural growth in places like the *Rockport Center for the Arts* (902 Navigation Circle, Rockport; 361-729-5519; www.rockportartcenter.com). The seaside arts center offers a main gallery for exhibition of invited and curated artwork, a pair of parlor galleries dedicated to member artists, and the

Victoria's Windmill

Unlike most of the windmills seen around Texas on farms and ranches, Victoria has a distinctive claim to a Dutch windmill. Located on Memorial Square in Victoria, it was built by two German immigrants, Fred Meiss Sr. and Otto Fiek, on a farm in the county around 1870. Made from hand-hewn logs and assembled with wooden pegs and homemade nails, it's thought that the windmill also contains machinery and mill-stones from a pre–Civil War windmill over in Goliad County. Interestingly, Henry Ford tried to buy the windmill in 1935 to exhibit at his Greenfield Village in Dearborn, Michigan, but the offer was declined. The Victoria Morning Study Club, a women's group, inherited the windmill and moved it to Memorial Square. See it at E. Commercial and De Leon Streets.

Sculpture Garden on Aransas Bay, where artwork includes *Lighthouse Fountain* and *Interlocking* by Jesus Moroles, *Rites of Spring* by Kent Ullberg, and *Return of Ancient Wisdom* by Leo Osborne. Closed Mon; free admission.

Barely 5 miles away in Fulton—also on Highway 35 and not far from the exotic-looking windswept leaning trees, twisted by constant winds—is the **Fulton Mansion State Historical Structure** (Fulton Beach Road at Henderson Street, Fulton; 361-729-0386; www.tpwd.state.tx.us). A 4-story showpiece dating to 1876, the innovative home was uniquely outfitted with central air-conditioning and hot and cold running water at its beginning. A French Second Empire garden design surrounds the 30-room mansion, which was restored by the state parks department. Visitors are asked to wear soft-soled shoes to protect the floors, and you're advised to call ahead in summer to find out if touring lines are long. The home is closed Mon; a small admission fee is charged.

Rockport and Fulton most often host nature enthusiasts visiting **Aransas National Wildlife Refuge** from November to March, prime months for viewing the rare whooping cranes, which numbered only 14 in 1941. The US and Canada have joined together in a sensational effort for more than 50 years to save these remarkable migratory birds, who journey annually from Canada in October and November to spend winter in these nesting grounds. The 55,000-acre asylum, home now to some 140 whooping cranes, is operated by the US Fish and Wildlife Service for protection and management of around 300 species of birds, including Canada geese, sandhill cranes, and pintail and baldpate ducks, as well as white-tailed deer, javelina, and raccoon. You can view the wildlife from an observation point or from one of several boat tours along the intracoastal canal from Rockport.

Information on the refuge, situated 37 miles north of Rockport and reached by car via Highway 35, FR 774, and FR 2040, is available by calling the visitor center at (361) 286-3559 or (361) 286-3533; the refuge is open daily from dawn to dusk, and the visitor center is open daily from 8:30 a.m. to 4:30 p.m. Boat tours departing Rockport cost about $20 to $25 per person; for a list of skippers, contact the **Rockport-Fulton Chamber of Commerce** at (361) 729-6445 or (800) 242-0071 or visit www.rockport-fulton.org.

Fourteen miles southeast of Rockport via Highway 35, **Port Aransas** can be reached via free ferry—which departs from a huge dock in Aransas Pass—operated 24 hours daily by the state highway department. For decades the little beach community fondly called Port A, at the northern tip of Mustang Island, has been a vacation spot where families spend days or weeks deep-sea fishing and body surfing in the Gulf and shell collecting on the hot sand. While it was once known as a lazy town, better access spurred the growth of multistory condos, beachwear boutiques, and nightspots.

Now as then, however, Port A, population 2,200, is a place meant for dawdling—if not feasting on fresh shrimp and crab, taking long walks on the shore, horseback riding, or Jet-Skiing. Children and grown-ups get a kick out of clinging to the rail and watching for porpoise acrobatics during the 5-minute ferry trip to the island. The other island access is at the southern end, where a highway connects Corpus Christi on the mainland to Mustang and to Padre Island, adjacent to the south.

At either end of the ferry run are several brightly painted shacks selling fresh seafood. Here people buy shrimp at bargain prices to cook for supper in their rented cottages or for icing down in a take-home cooler.

Port Aransas is also home to a free trolley system to cart you around town. The cute, vintage trolleys run continuously each day from 10 a.m. to 5 p.m., with pickup points including the Beach Access Road, the Birding Facility, the Marina, the Jetties, and Horace Caldwell Pier.

Mustang Island was one of Texas's barrier islands frequented by Jean Lafitte and his buccaneer buddies in the 1820s. Now and then island romantics, perhaps with the help of a little grog, set out in search of a legendary Spanish dagger that is said to mark the spot of a buried pirate treasure. The most common booty, however, is a wealth of sand dollars and varied seashells found just after high tide on the light brown sand. The island's 18 miles of beach are cleaned daily, and the tar deposits are usually fewer than those at Galveston. Cars are not given free rein of the beaches, as they were until the 1980s, but are limited to a narrow path alongside the dunes.

Crowds are naturally drawn to **Mustang Island State Park** (on Highway 361; 361-749-5246; www.tpwd.state.tx.us), almost 3,500 acres decorated with sand dunes, sea oats, and morning glory. The park, just 14 miles south of the town of Port A, has 5 miles of Gulf-front beach, and it offers camping, picnicking under arbors, a nature trail, a fish-cleaning station, and showers. The park is open daily from 8 a.m. to 10 p.m. for day use and at all times for campers. A small admission fee is charged. For a more private, open expanse of white sand, hop the Jetty Boat for an 8-minute ride to **San Jose Island** (Fisherman's Wharf, 900 Tarpon St., Port Aransas; 800-605-5448; www.wharfcat .com)—or, as the locals call it, St. Jo. The uninhabited beach reserve is known for excellent shelling along 21 miles of shoreline, and it's an ideal place to take a picnic, fresh water, and some fishing gear for a real getaway. The passenger-only ferry (you can take bicycles with you) operates 10 times daily from 6:30 a.m. to 6 p.m.; fares are $12 for adults and $6 for children.

Mostly, though, people come to Port A to see what they can find in the water. The town calls itself the place "where they bite every day," and fishing for redfish, speckled trout, flounder, and drum is free in the surf from the south jetty and the Station Street Pier. Group fishing aboard party boats such as the *Island Queen* gives anglers a chance to reel in bigger game fish for just $40 per person, which includes rod, reel, and tackle. Private charters, which can cost in the hundreds, go in search of tarpon, sailfish, marlin, kingfish, mackerel, bonito, red snapper, amberjack, barracuda, yellowfin tuna, wahoo, and shark. Call the chamber of commerce (361-749-5919 or 800-452-6278) for a list of charter companies or visit www.portaransas.org.

People who just want to look at sea life can go to the **University of Texas Marine Science Institute** (Cotter Street, opposite Port Aransas Park; 361-749-6729). The research facility has seven habitat aquariums as well as impressive shell displays. It's open daily from 8 a.m. to 5 p.m. during summer months and Mon through Fri from Sept through May.

Because travelers want to simply stay and stay once they've arrived in Port A, comfortable condos have become plentiful without being conges-tive—and most are reasonably priced. Some of the high-rises are a bit south of town, while many of the 2-story complexes are close to the commercial area, and everything's on the beach. Generally, condos are individually owned and well maintained and have large pools, tennis courts, cable TV, and landscaped boardwalks reaching across the dunes to the beach. For a step back in time, check out the **Tarpon Inn** (200 E. Cotter St., Port Aransas; 361-749-5555; www.thetarponinn.com), which has been beautifully updated. Originally built in 1886 by a boat pilot and lighthouse keeper who used sur-plus lumber from nearby Civil War barracks, the inn burned down and then its replacement was destroyed in a hurricane. Today's version is a renovation of the 1920 structure, and it remains popular with anglers. A list of noted guests includes Franklin D. Roosevelt, and the inn is included on the National Register of Historic Places.

For a complete listing of lodgings, including cottages, B&Bs, motels, and condos, contact the **Port Aransas Chamber of Commerce Tourist & Convention Bureau** at (800) 45-COAST or www.portaransas.org.

The **Crazy Cajun** restaurant (303 E. Beach St., Port Aransas; 361-749-5069; www.thecrazycajun.com) offers a Louisiana-style shrimp and crawfish boil: hot fresh shrimp, crawfish, stone crab claws, new potatoes, corn on the cob, and smoked sausage. The gumbo and sourdough bread are good, too. It's open Mon through Fri for dinner only, and Sat and Sun for lunch and dinner; closed Mon.

Other worthy Port A eating spots include **Shell's Pasta and Seafood** (522 E. Avenue G, Port Aransas; 361-749-7621), serving blue crab ravioli in red bell pepper cream sauce. Open daily, except Tues, for lunch and dinner; and **Pelican's Landing** (337 N. Alister St., Port Aransas; 361-749-6405), specializing in locally caught fresh fish, fresh-cut steaks, and music on the patio.

Just across Corpus Christi Bay, which laps at Mustang Island's western shore, is the same-name city with almost 300,000 residents. The Nueces County seat, **Corpus Christi** is reached on a half-hour drive inland from Mustang Island and is the most common arrival spot for travelers flying to Texas's Coastal Bend area.

Corpus is thought to have first hosted a European in 1519, when explorer Alonzo de Pineda made a visit. Today the city is separated from the Gulf by a lengthy seawall, which was designed by sculptor Gutzon Borglum of Mount Rushmore fame. Just a few years ago eight gazebolike *miradors*—Spanish for "lookouts"—were added to the seawall; the brilliant white miradors, capped by pointed, barrel-tile roofs and complemented by Victorian-style street lamps, function as both resting spots and wedding sites.

The shining star in Corpus remains the **Texas State Aquarium** (2710 N. Shoreline Dr., Corpus Christi; 361-881-1200 or 800-477-4853; www.texas stateaquarium.org), an outstanding aquarium featuring 250 species of aquatic plants and animals. Within you'll see that more than 350,000-plus gallons of seawater are required to support all the Gulf of Mexico life on exhibit, as well as an artificial reef created by the legs of an oil derrick, providing a home for rays, sharks, and tropical fish. Turtle Bend is a pool and beach area where several rare species live, including the endangered Kemp's turtle. Open Memorial Day through Labor Day weekend, daily from 9 a.m. to 6 p.m. The rest of the year it's open daily from 9 a.m. to 5 p.m. An admission fee is charged.

The ***Corpus Christi Museum of Science and History*** (1900 N. Chaparral St., Corpus Christi; 361-826-4667; www.ccmuseum.com) is home to the ships of Christopher Columbus. Today's discoverers can explore exact replicas of the *Niña, Pinta,* and *Santa Maria.* Explore a working shipyard, see a replica of Columbus's quarters, and go below the decks on the *Santa Maria.* Also find an armada of interactive exhibits that include the Smithsonian's **Seeds of Change,** commemorating the impact of Christopher Columbus's voyages, as well as science and natural history displays focusing on energy, birds, gems and minerals, and shells. The hands-on children's area has a shrimp boat, bird costumes, video phones, and more, while ***Reptiles of South Texas*** features a live alligator, and ***Shipwreck!*** is the award-winning story of the 1554 Spanish shipwreck off of Padre Island. Open Tues through Sat from 10 a.m. to 5 p.m. and Sun from noon to 5 p.m. Admission is charged; call for rates and packages.

Since 1992, when the World War II aircraft carrier ***USS* Lexington** opened as a museum in the port near the aquarium, naval history has been observed as never before on the Texas coast. Only the fourth carrier to make such a conversion, the *Lexington*—nicknamed the Lady Lex—was commissioned in 1943, participated in all major Pacific battles from Tarawa to Tokyo, collected 11 battle stars, and was the first to enter Tokyo Bay in September 1945. Among 16 decks to explore are the cavernous hangar area, where immense elevators carried fighters and attack planes from the landing deck for maintenance; and the landing deck, where volunteer guides—mostly retired naval officers—show center lines and arrest and catapult areas and explain the complications that go into running a small oceantop landing strip where planes land as often as every 30 seconds. The USS *Lexington* is open seven days a week from 9 a.m. to 5 p.m.; from Memorial Day through Labor Day, the museum stays open until 6 p.m. An admission fee is charged, and military discounts are offered. Call (361) 888-4873 or (800) LADY-LEX or try their website at www.usslexington.com.

Near the soaring Harbor Bridge, don't miss the ***South Texas Institute for the Arts*** (361-825-3500; www.stia .org), an austere white building whose interior is acclaimed for its huge picture window looking over the water. Traveling exhibits have included such varied works as those of Remington and Warhol. A major addition designed by Mexican architect Ricardo Legorreta features 13 rooftop pyramids and a noteworthy infusion of color and light. Open Tues through Sat from 10 a.m. to 5 p.m. and Sun from 1 to 5 p.m.; the museum also charges a small admission.

texastrivia

Texas is second only to Alaska in volume of inland water, with more than 5,175 square miles of lakes and streams.

Heritage Park (361-826-3410), on Bayfront, provides an opportunity to look at various historic homes all conveniently situated on a single block. The structures are among the best of old Corpus Christi, dating back to 1851. Among them are elaborate designs, such as the Colonial Revival Victorian Lichtenstein House and the ornate Queen Anne Sidbury House, as well as simpler cottages. The homes have been painstakingly restored and are open for tours.

Texas's oldest federal military cemetery is Corpus Christi's **Old Bayview Cemetery** (Ramirez Street at Waco Street), laid out by US army engineers while Gen. Zachary Taylor was encamped in Corpus Christi in 1815. Seven of Taylor's soldiers are buried there, as are many pioneer settlers, veterans of the American War of Independence, the Mexican War, Indian campaigns, and the Civil War. You'll find a Texas Historical Marker.

Learn still more about the city's early history at **Centennial House** (411 N. Broadway St., Corpus Christi; 361-882-8691), the oldest existing structure in Corpus Christi. Built in 1849–50, the spectacular building and Texas Historical Landmark served as a Confederate hospital, a hospital and officer's mess for the federal army, and a citizen's refuge during desperado and Indian raids during the 1870s. Open the first Sun of the month from noon until 4 p.m.

For a change of pace, there's the **Asian Cultures Museum** (1809 N. Chaparral St., Corpus Christi; 361-882-2641; www.asianculturesmuseum.org), focusing primarily on Japanese history, religion, and art. Exhibits feature Kabuki masks, shrine replicas, a large collection of costumed Hakata dolls, and a wonderful Buddha statue dating to the 1700s. Open Tues through Fri from 10 a.m. to 4 p.m. A small admission is charged.

Thrusting seaward from the huge seawall is the city marina, bustling within the shadows of tall downtown buildings. Watery diversions found in the marina vary from sailboat and sailboard rentals to fishing excursions. People arrive in droves in the afternoon to make cheap buys from fishermen of live shrimp and blue crabs. For information, visit www.corpuschristimarina.com.

Corpus Christi's status as one of the breeziest cities in the nation makes it a hot spot for those sailing and sailboarding fans. Sailboat regattas are held each Wednesday evening on Corpus Christi Bay. The variety of waterways, from open Gulf beaches to protected coves, including the Laguna Madre, Gulf of Mexico, Corpus Christi Bay, and Bird Island Basin, make this appealing to beginners and experts alike. Rentals and lessons are readily available.

Some places to consult are the **Corpus Christi Yachting Center** (at the marina on Cooper's Alley L-head, Corpus Christi; 361-881-8503; www .corpuschristiyachtingcenter.com), with services for beginner, intermediate, and advanced sailors, by captains licensed by the US Coast Guard, and **Wind & Wave Water Sports** (10721 South Padre Island Dr., Corpus Christi;

361-937-9283; www.windandwave.net), offering sailboarding lessons for beginner and advanced, individual or group instruction, as well as sailboard, surfboard, and boogie board and kayak rentals.

Fishing enthusiasts may call the **Corpus Christi Visitor Office** at (800) 766-2322 for information on charter companies, or visit www.visitcorpus christitx.org.

At the south end of town, Corpus Christi Bay meets Laguna Madre at the JFK Causeway, the connection to **Padre Island National Seashore.** The legendary narrow island extends 113 miles southward nearly to Mexico and is the longest of all barrier islands on the Texas coast. No commercial development is allowed on the 80-mile mid-island stretch, but National Park Service rangers provide information on camping and four-wheel-driving areas. Beachcombing and shell collecting are the national seashore's primary attractions, but federal law forbids taking flint points, coins, or anything that might be considered historical. Daily programs offered in summer by National Park Service rangers at **Malaquite Beach** include a 1 p.m. daily walk (and also at 11 a.m. on weekends). Rangers also conduct fireside talks at dusk on Friday and Saturday on a variety of island topics. For information call the National Park Service's Padre Island office at Malaquite Beach, (361) 949-8173. Or you can visit the website at www.nps.gov/pais.

The Corpus Christi area also features sites on the **Great Texas Coastal Birding Trail,** a $1.4 million effort with more than 300 marked spots along nearly 700 miles of coastline reaching from Beaumont to Brownsville. Some 500 species of birds have been documented on the isles of Texas, including sightings of brown pelicans, the rare masked duck, and the endangered whooping crane. Good birding information sources are the **Coastal Bend Audubon Society** (361-885-6203; www.coastalbendaudubon.org); the **Coastal Bend Sierra Club Group** (PO Box 3512, Corpus Christi 78404); and the state birding information center (888-TXBIRDS; www.texas.sierraclub.org).

Memories of fantastic fresh fish will linger if you dine downtown at **Water Street Seafood Company** (309 N. Water St., Corpus Christi; 361-882-8683; www.waterstreetco.com/corpus_christi/welcome2.html), open daily for lunch and dinner.

Another favorite for many years, **Snoopy's Pier** (13313 South Padre Island Dr., Corpus Christi; 361-949-8815; www.snoopyspier.com), is a waterside joint on Laguna Madre with excellent fried shrimp, oysters on the half shell, cheeseburgers, and ice cream. It's also cheap and open for lunch and dinner daily.

For more information log onto www.corpuschristicvb.com.

The Coastal Plains

An excursion from Corpus that won't easily be forgotten is the one to *Goliad,* a deeply historic spot northwest about 78 miles via US 181, US 77, and US 183. There you'll find the most fought-over and exemplary Spanish fort in Texas and the state's true birthplace. A metal plaque outside the heavy chapel doors at *Presidio La Bahía* seems to glow with the poignancy of the words it bears:

HERE FELL THE MEN IN MARTYRED DEATH TO GAIN THE FREEDOM AND INDEPENDENCE OF TEXAS; AND HERE FOR CENTURIES TO COME GENERATIONS OF MEN WILL GATHER IN REVERENCE AND APPRECIATION OF LA BAHIA'S GLORIOUS PAST.

The rough-hewn building dates to 1749 and is the nation's only completely restored inland fort. Among several important roles the presidio played is one from the Republic of Texas, one wrought with utter tragedy: The stillness of the tiny chapel here continues to emanate the desolation of Palm Sunday morning, 1836, when Col. James Walker Fannin and 352 Texas volunteers were held captive before being marched out and shot under orders of Mexican dictator Santa Anna. The death toll was twice that of the Alamo's.

The first flag of Texas independence, emblazoned with a bloody arm wielding a saber, is still flown here in remembrance of La Bahía's stature as the place where independence was first planned and where the Declaration of Texas Independence was signed on December 20, 1835. A museum in soldiers' quarters and officers' barracks details nine levels of civilization uncovered in artifacts, as well as artifacts from the revolution. Behind the presidio you'll find the Fannin Monument and Grave. The presidio, on US 183 about 2 miles south of Goliad, is open daily from 9 a.m. to 4:45 p.m. Admission is charged; call (361) 645-3752 or visit www.presidiolabahia.org for more information.

Across the San Antonio River from La Bahía rises the white-walled majesty of *Mission Espiritu Santo de Zuñiga,* once New Spain's finest outpost north of the Rio Grande. The mission is now contained within *Goliad State Historical Park,* also on US 183, just a quarter mile south of modern Goliad. Espiritu Santo functioned as a mission for 110 years and was the home of Texas's first large cattle ranch. Within the old mission building is a superb if small museum detailing Spain's attempt to colonize the New World.

The surrounding 180-acre park has wonderfully scenic shaded picnic and camping areas, interpretive nature trails, and river fishing. Across the highway, a junior-Olympic swimming pool is operated by the city of Goliad. Park admission is $3 per person; for information call (361) 645-3405.

The Goliad town square surrounds a grand limestone courthouse, built in 1894, and an enormous live oak known as the *Hanging Tree.* Court was held here during the mid-19th century, and the guilty were hanged, as many as five men at a time. Wonderful old Victorian and Texas pioneer buildings line the square. Nearby, at Franklin and Market Streets, *Fannin Park Plaza* contains a cannon from the revolution and a memorial to Fannin and his men.

If it's springtime, and especially in March, you'll want to make a detour from Goliad southwest on US 59 to *Beeville,* seat of Bee County, where wildflowers create a great big buzz in spring. A favorite route outlined in *Southern Living* magazine follows US 181 south from Beeville about 10 miles to the town of Skidmore, where you'll turn right on FR 797 and then loop into FR 1349 back to Beeville. Your drive's reward will be stunning vistas of tall, crimson Indian paintbrush next to purple-topped thistles, lemony blooms on prickly pear cactus, pink primrose and white prairie larkspur, burgundy-colored wine cups, and delicate crochet blankets of Queen Anne's lace.

From Goliad it's an easy, 95-mile path south via US 183 and US 77 to *Kingsville,* home of still more pure Lone Star heritage. Riverboat captain Richard King established the legendary *King Ranch* in 1853 in the southeast Texas coastal plains by purchasing Mexican and Spanish land grants totaling approximately 68,500 acres, originally naming it Rancho de Santa Gertrudes for the rare creek running through it. That the ranch succeeded in such an uninhabited place and time is as profound as the modern accomplishments that would come in the next dozen decades.

Ranch workers and King's family fought off armed attacks by Mexican bandits on numerous occasions; the towers from which guards kept watch remain the most notable design element on the ranch's oldest structure, a big white commissary built in the 1850s. Visitors straggled through the area without much regularity, but King and his wife, Henrietta, took in overnighters. One guest is said to have been Jesse James, who gave a gray stallion to King after the captain admired it; today, ranch lore holds that all gray horses are descendants of James's horse.

King brought some longhorn cattle to Texas from Mexico, luring entire Mexican villages to come along and work the livestock for room and board. Some of the descendants of these *kiñeos,* or king's men, continue to work for King Ranch today.

By the early 20th century, 1.2 million acres with departmentalized operations formed an empire that would be known worldwide as innovative in the cattle and horse industries. Today the spread measures 825,000 acres and reaches over Nueces, Kenedy, Kleberg, Brooks, Jim Wells, and Willacy Counties. Its fences, if placed in a straight line, would reach from the plains near Corpus Christi to Boston. The ranch is larger than the state of Rhode Island and home to 50,000 head of cattle, 1,000 horses, and 300 artesian wells reaching 600 feet or more into the earth.

Tours aboard minibuses take travelers around the Loop Road on King Ranch, through the brushy landscape, and guides point out the romantically named vegetation that characterizes this challenging corner of the world. The anaqua, or sandpaper tree, often grows up to 50 feet high, guides explain, and the sprawling, low-lying lantana brightens the terrain with a rainbow of colored flowers. In addition to persimmon, yucca, hackberry, and prickly pear, you'll find fragrant purple sage at home on the King Ranch range. Mesquite, that most defiant of Texas trees, gave the Kings plenty of problems, so a massive root-digging plow was invented expressly to clear mesquite from the King Ranch. One of the hostile, fanged machines is displayed with other model equipment near a cattle pen.

During the 12-mile tour, travelers can see where Santa Gertrudis cattle—the first beef breed developed in the US—are worked, as well as the horse areas, famous for having contributed to American quarter horse development.

A much-photographed building is the 1909 livery stable, a classic blend of western and Victorian influences. The only real disappointment is not being able to see the interior of the fabulous main house. A video of the interior is available to see or purchase at the *King Ranch Museum*. Birding tours are becoming extremely popular here. The scissortail flycatcher, whose males sport beautiful orange breasts, is one of 350 species living on the ranch. Call for tour rates and schedules. For details contact the King Ranch at (361) 592-8055 or (800) 282-KING or check www.king-ranch.com.

The adjacent town of Kingsville was created in 1904 when King's widow, Henrietta, deeded 853 acres of the ranch for a town to be built. An interesting stop after ranch exploration, it's home to the *Connor Museum*. Situated on the campus of Texas A&M–Kingsville, the Connor has a unique collection of horns, arrowheads, game trophies, spurs, and such that is strange and almost creepy, but a collection that's worth a stop. Also at the Connor, "The Living Mosaic" is a polished educational TV production illustrating the Texas coastal plain and its natural resources and history. The photography of plant and animal life, especially wildflowers, is nothing but stunning. Open Tues through Sat from 9 a.m. to 5 p.m.; call (361) 593-2810 for more information.

The *King Ranch Museum* (405 N. 6th St., Kingsville; 361-595-1881; www .king-ranch.com/museum.html), housed in a renovated 1907 icehouse, exhibits a wonderful, award-winning photographic essay by Toni Frissell depicting life on King Ranch in the early 1940s. Also of interest are fabulous collections of antique coaches, vintage cars, and saddles. Open Mon through Sat from 10 a.m. to 4 p.m. and Sun from 1 to 5 p.m. A small admission fee is charged.

The ***King Ranch Saddle Shop*** (6th and Kleberg Streets, Kingsville; 361-595-5761 or 877-282-5777; www.krsaddleshop.com) is the place to spend big dollars in a short time, although it takes a few hours to really see the spectacular inventory. A very sophisticated boutique, its pale hardwood floors and rough wood walls are adorned with artfully composed displays and beautiful Indian saddle blankets and rugs. Custom-made goods include leather backpacks, "gunpowder" shoulder or belt bags, antler candlesticks, Running W collector's china, a gift crate of mesquite, cactus and jalapeño jellies, and jewelry, including sterling-silver cuff links bearing the King Ranch's Running W brand against prickly-pear cactus.

The Big Beach

From Kingsville it's a little more than a 2-hour shot straight south to Texas's most famous spread of sand. To reach ***South Padre Island***, just follow US 77 down to Los Fresnos, then turn east on Highway 100, which ends at the state's southernmost beachfront.

The only reason to pause even for a moment before hitting the beach is to stock up on supplies in Port Isabel. Certainly there are legions of stores on the island, but you'll save money by shopping for groceries and fresh-caught fish in the placid little fishing village.

While you're at it, take note that the smallest state park in Texas is right here—the ***Port Isabel Lighthouse State Historic Park*** (Highway 100 and Tarvana Street at the Causeway; 956-943-2262; www.tpwd.state.tx.us). The only lighthouse on the Texas coast open to the public, it cast its light 16 miles out on the Gulf from its erection in 1853 until it was closed in 1905. Those in shape can scale the winding 70-plus steps to the top to gain a view of Port Isabel, the Causeway, South Padre Island, and the Gulf of Mexico.

Can't wait to get to the waves? Then head east, crossing the great blue Laguna Madre Bay on the ***Queen Isabella Causeway***, Texas's longest bridge, stretching just over 2½ miles. The center span rises 73 feet above the mean high tide, allowing ships heading to sea to pass below; its strength will withstand threefold hurricane-force winds.

The lower end of long, skinny Padre Island gained its name, South Padre, when the Mansfield Cut—about 35 miles north of this developed tip—was created by state engineers in 1964, chopping the island in two. ***Padre Island National Seashore*** (profiled in the Corpus Christi section) is north, and this megaresort area is south.

From a scattering of simple beachy bungalows in the 1960s grew a city of high-rise hotels and condominiums in the 1980s known for its powerful tourism magnetism. South Padre's 34 miles of coastline and beaches, music, volleyball, and dance clubs bring 125,000 college kids to the beach from more than 125 colleges and universities in the US and Canada during spring break, from early March to early April. Unless you're among this notorious crowd, it's best to visit South Padre Island any other time of the year.

Things are a bit saner during other periods of celebration, including the big *Windsurfing Blowout* in May; the *Rough Rider Regatta* in September; the *Texas International Fishing Tournament* in August; and *Christmas by the Seas* and *Island of Lights Festival* throughout December.

State and world fishing records are frequently set in South Padre's bay and Gulf waters—and no wonder, with the bounty of whiting, drum, flounder, trout, redfish, kingfish, wahoo, tuna, marlin, and sailfish here. Half-day and full-day trips in the Laguna Madre Bay and the Gulf of Mexico cost as little as $25 or as much as $1,000, depending on skill, budget, and how far offshore you venture. Find out more about conditions and booking a trip by visiting www .spadre.com/fishing.htm.

Fly-fishing in the clear, pale aqua Laguna Madre has become possibly the favorite pastime of all. Check into kayak and fly-gear rentals, as well as lessons, at *The Shop in Port Isabel* (318 Queen Isabella Blvd., Port Isabel; 956-943-1785; www.saltyflyshop.com). For a fly-fishing experience that includes lodging, contact the *Kingfisher Inn and Guide Service* (36901 Marshall Hutts Rd. in Rio Hondo; 956-371-8801; www.lagunamadre.net), which offers guided fishing trips and bed-and-breakfast stays on the Arroyo Colorado, about 45 minutes from South Padre Island.

The Laguna Madre Bay also is recognized as one of the world's top sailboarding destinations. The sailing season off South Padre runs from September through May. Water depth varies from 3 to 5 feet; daytime winds average 18 miles per hour. Novices and pros come to sail the bay, the Jetties, Boca Chica, and the Ditch. For complete information on conditions, accommodations, equipment, and rentals, contact the *South Padre Island Convention and Visitor Bureau* (600 Padre Blvd., South Padre Island; 956-761-6433 or 800-767-2373; www.sopadre.com).

Horseback riding is a great way to enjoy the beach. *Island Equestrian Center* (at Andy Bowie County Park, north of the city limits; 956-761-HOSS; www.horsesonthebeach.com) offers horse and pony rides on the beach daily, as well as guides and instruction.

An unforgettable experience is a dolphin tour with an outfit called *Colleys Fin to Feathers* (at Sea Ranch Marina, South Padre Island; 956-299-0629 or 956-761-7178; www.fin2feather.com). Guides Scarlett and George Colley have spent years cultivating a respectful relationship with several families of bottlenose dolphins in the Laguna Madre, and they'll share their friends with you in a most eco-conscious manner. The Colleys are also expert birders and can customize birding tours to suit all interests. They have opened the **Dolphin Research and Sea Life Nature Center** at 105 W. Pompano, South Padre Island (956-454-4799; www.spinaturecenter.com/). Birders can get information and maps there.

Nature lovers will enjoy visiting **Sea Turtle Inc.,** an endeavor begun years ago by the Turtle Lady, the late, beloved Ila Loetscher. Her successors continue to present shows on Tues and Sat to raise money for the preservation of the nearly extinct Kemp's ridley sea turtle and other endangered turtles. Several of the rehabilitating specimens are observed, and the staff offers information about these marine creatures. Visit Sea Turtle Inc. at 5805 Gulf Blvd., South Padre Island. Call (956) 761-4511 or visit www.seaturtleinc.com for a schedule. A small admission fee is charged.

The internationally acclaimed environmental artist simply known as **Wyland** picked the South Padre Island Convention Centre as his canvas for **Whaling Wall No. 53.** The giant mural, featuring a pod of orcas (commonly known as killer whales), covers three walls of the Convention Centre. The life-size whales are illustrated in full color and are accompanied by other local sea life. Wyland's purpose for painting giant murals—he plans 100 during his career—is to raise awareness of the dangers facing these wonderful creatures. In addition to his Whaling Walls, Wyland is recognized for his outstanding ability as a fine-arts painter and sculptor.

texastrivia

The largest county in Texas is **Brewster,** in west Texas, measuring 6,193 square miles, an area larger than the state of Connecticut. The smallest of the 254 counties is **Rockwall,** in north Texas, at 147 square miles.

Next to the Convention Centre and Whaling Wall No. 53, the **Laguna Madre Nature Trail** is a 1,500-foot boardwalk that extends across 4 acres of wetlands. Containing informative signs about dune systems and bird species that frequent the area, the nature trail provides visitors with the opportunity to observe many species of birds and other wildlife in their natural habitat. Both the Whaling Wall and the nature trail are always open to the public free of charge and can be accessed through the circle driveway leading up to the Convention Centre, located at 7355 Padre Blvd. at the north end of town.

The **University of Texas Pan American Coastal Studies Lab** (in Isla Blanca Park at the south end of the island; 956-761-2644; www.utpa.edu) has aquarium displays of fish and other marine life indigenous to the area as well as an extensive shell collection. It's open Sun through Fri from 1:30 to 4:30 p.m. Admission is free.

The area's largest nature exhibit is found at the **_Laguna Atascosa National Wildlife Refuge,_** a 45,000-acre federal preserve for wildlife and bird watching, located about 15 minutes away on the mainland across the Laguna Madre from South Padre Island. The largest protected area of natural habitat left in the Rio Grande valley, it's home to redhead ducks, snow geese, sandhill cranes, and white-tailed hawks, as well as ocelot, white-tailed deer, mountain lion, javelina, ground squirrel, long-tailed weasel, coyote, various snakes, and other animals and reptiles. The refuge is open daily from sunrise to sunset. The visitor center at the refuge is open from 10 a.m. to 4 p.m. A small admission fee is charged. For more information and detailed driving directions, contact the refuge at (956) 748-3607 or (956) 748-3608 or visit www.fws.gov/southwest/refuges/texas/laguna.html.

texastrivia

Clute, a coastal town in Brazoria County, celebrates the **Great Texas Mosquito Festival** annually in July. Special tribute is paid to Willie Manchew, "the world's largest mosquito."

Birders are flocking to a lovely retreat called the **_Inn at Chachalaca Bend,_** a small bed-and-breakfast lodge in the town of Los Fresnos, which is about 20 minutes from South Padre Island and convenient to Laguna Atascosa. Guests wake to the call of the wild chachalacas, native to south Texas and the nearby reaches of Mexico, which live on the grounds and wander between aged Texas ebony and honey mesquite trees. Nature lovers roam the walking trails to viewing platforms and towers and to butterfly gardens or sit by the outdoor fire pit to watch the soothing resaca, or oxbow, that feeds a nearby river flowing to the Gulf of Mexico. The renovated home features beautifully used mahogany and teak and holds seven lavishly decorated bedrooms, all with beautiful private baths. Elaborate breakfasts include salmon-ricotta frittata

The Aplomado Falcons' Comeback

Thanks to the Peregrine Fund's 1986 breeding program, **Aplomado falcons** are making a promising comeback at the **Laguna Atascosa National Wildlife Refuge.** Almost extinct since the end of World War II, the Aplomado are nesting at the refuge after being captured in Mexico and released in the south Texas sanctuary, where they are safe from the pesticides and loss of habitat that threatened their existence.

and apple soufflé. The inn is located at 20 Chachalaca Bend Dr., Los Fresnos (956-233-1180 or 888-612-6800; www.chachalaca.com).

There's so much good food on South Padre Island that it seems a shame to mention only a few restaurants. For excellent grilled shrimp and snapper, try ***Amberjack's Bayside Bar and Grill*** (209 W. Amberjack St., South Padre Island; 956-761-6500), open for lunch and dinner. For the island's own home brew, check out ***Padre Island Brewing Company*** (3400 Padre Blvd., South Padre Island; 956-761-9585), where the hot-hot chicken wings, beer-battered shrimp, snapper, and other fish are good.

As South Padre has boomed, so has its nightlife. Some of the most happening places include ***Kelly's Irish Pub*** (101 E. Morningside St., South Padre Island; 956-761-7571); ***Boomerang Billy's*** (2612 Gulf Blvd. at the Surf Motel, South Padre Island; 956-761-2420); and ***Blackbeard's*** (103 E. Saturn St., South Padre Island; 956-761-2962). All, by the way, are open during the day, too, if you need to relieve that sunburn.

Finding a place to stay on South Padre Island can be an overwhelming task, with more than 5,000 condos and hotel rooms to consider. For help with finding the condo or beach house you'd like, there are several reservation agencies on South Padre Island.

For a complete list of rental agencies and visitor information, contact the ***South Padre Island Convention and Visitor Bureau*** at (800) SO-PADRE or visit www.sopadre.com.

Other Places to Stay on the Gulf Coast

CORPUS CHRISTI

George Blucher House
211 N. Carrizo St.
(361) 884-4884
www.georgeblucherhouse.com
This stately 1904 home, one of the oldest in the city, is an elegant bed-and-breakfast with 6 guest rooms and private baths, and private phones, voice mail, TV/DVD, individual climate control, fine linens, and toiletries in each room. A full gourmet breakfast is included. Rates start at $120.

GALVESTON

Mermaid & Dolphin Bed & Breakfast
1103 33rd St.
(409) 762-1561 or
(800) 930-1866
www.mermaidanddolphin.com
An impressive 1866 home underwent extensive renovation to become this luxurious inn with 6 rooms and private baths, video and book libraries, bicycles, hot tub, spa massage therapy, happy hour in pub, and full breakfast. Rates are about $130 and up.

HOUSTON

Houstonian Hotel Club & Spa
111 N. Post Oak Ln.
(713) 680-2626 or
(800) 231-2759
www.houstonian.com
Sprawling over a woodsy setting near the Galleria

and Memorial Park, this exquisite lodging offers weekend golf packages and health club facilities from $200.

Other Places to Eat on the Gulf Coast

CORPUS CHRISTI

Taqueria Garibaldi
200 N. Staples St.
(361) 884-5456
Hearty, authentic Mexican breakfasts and lunches start at about $4.

GALVESTON

Cafe Michael Burger
11150 Termini San Luis Pass Rd.
(409) 740-3639
This madly popular burger joint offers the Michael Burger, a third-pounder with the usual trimmings; the Campeche, with jalapeños and picante sauce; the Jamaica Beach, with pineapple, jalapeños, and Swiss; and the Lichtenfeldt, with sauerkraut and Swiss. Open Wed through Sun for lunch and dinner.

Leon's World's Finest In & Out BBQ House
5427 Broadway
(409) 744-0070
www.leonsbbq.com
This old house serves well as a great barbecue joint, where you can have a brisket or sausage sandwich, or ribs, chicken, and other smoked meats by the pound or with turnip greens (this is the South, you know), coleslaw, potato salad, Leon's "rice stepped up" beans, green beans, and pies. Rum cake and sweet-potato pie are super desserts. Open daily for lunch and Fri through Sun for dinner (until 8:30 p.m.).

HOUSTON

Backstreet Cafe
1103 S. Shepherd Dr.
(713) 521-2239
www.backstreetcafe.net
Balancing acts include meat loaf with garlic mashed potatoes and roasted beet–goat cheese salad. Setting is a pretty, old house with a shady patio and overall comfort. Serves lunch and dinner; reservations are advised.

Churrascos
Shepherd Square at 2055 Westheimer Rd.
(713) 527-8300
www.cordua.com
Updated, stylish Latin dishes range from empanadas (savory turnovers) and quesadillas to yucca pancakes to grilled tenderloin with shrimp, jacketed with fried plantain. Open Mon through Sat for lunch and dinner; reservations are recommended.

SOUTH PADRE ISLAND

Sea Ranch
1 Padre Blvd.
(956) 761-1314
http://searanchrestaurant.com
This spot specializes in prime steaks and locally caught wild fish.

THE HILL COUNTRY

Visualize two-lane roads, twisting and climbing, leading to an antique borough here, a pioneer settlement there. Imagine hills, soft and scrubby, green valleys, limestone cliffs. Conjure up ranches and communities of German heritage, wineries and fields of wildflowers, sparkling rivers lined with cypress and oak.

Ah, the Hill Country realized. To some it's the state's greatest natural resource. No big cities, no bustle. Just cafes with country cooking, water for fishing and inner tubing, and old places with timeworn comfort.

Raised by the Edwards Plateau, the hilly region extends west from I-35, which follows the edge of the Balcones Fault. You can find this land of escape below US 190 and above US 90. Wander alone or take the whole family. But don't venture too far west of US 83, where the hills—and the Hill Country—taper off. Just go armed with plenty of film.

Spring—when Texas is blanketed in glorious wildflowers—is by far the most popular time to wander through the Hill Country. Experts at the Lady Bird Johnson Wildflower Center in Austin are deluged with calls every year in early March, when travelers are begging for information as to when the bluebonnets, the state flower, will sprout their colorful hats.

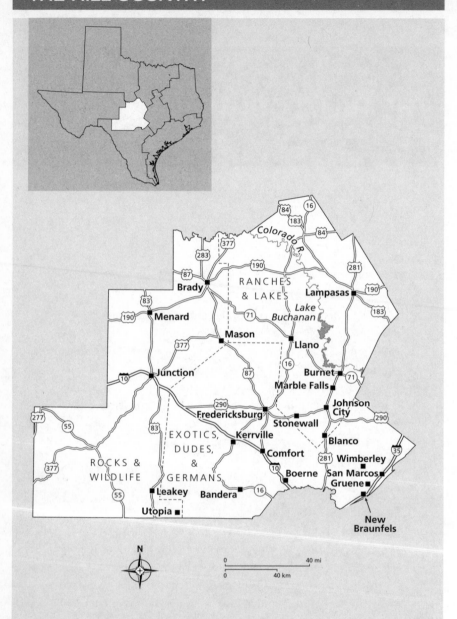

Colorado R.

84
16
183
283
377
190
84
87
281
Brady
RANCHES
& LAKES
Lampasas
190
83
Lake
Buchanan
183
190
Menard
71
Mason
Llano
377
Burnet
16
87
Junction
Marble Falls
71
10
290
Johnson
City
Fredericksburg
Stonewall
290
277
Kerrville
EXOTICS,
DUDES,
&
GERMANS
Comfort
Blanco
35
55
83
281
Wimberley
10
Boerne
San Marcos
ROCKS &
WILDLIFE
Gruene
377
Leakey
Bandera
16
55
New
Braunfels
Utopia

N

0   40 mi
0   40 km

These experts manage to patiently explain time and time again that everything depends on whether fall and winter rains reached the wildflower seeds after germination, whether sunshine followed, and whether Mother Nature decides to cooperate. In other words, blooming is just too hard to predict.

While there's no guarantee for abundant *Lupinus texensis* (the bluebonnet's proper name), you'll usually find plenty of opportunities to pose children amid the colored country fields for an Easter portrait. What the country's wildflower authorities will promise is that they'll pass along to you whatever bluebonnet and other flower information they have. Call the center at (512) 232-0100 or the highway department's hotline at (800) 452-9292 for information about the best highway routes in Texas for wildflower watching.

As the deeply blue carpet spreads northward from south Texas, we cross our fingers in hopes that the sapphire blooms—mixed in with the palette of Mexican hat, Indian paintbrush, black-eyed Susans, primroses, and hundreds of others—will make a timely appearance in the Hill Country for a scattering of festivals. The Hill Country's upper reaches, called the Highland Lakes for the 150-mile, sparkly string of seven lakes formed by the Colorado River, are particularly vibrant for two weeks in spring when the Highland Lakes communities throw out floral welcome mats during the annual bluebonnet celebrations.

From late March through mid-April, it's easy to spend a day or a weekend at a medley of arts and crafts fairs, featuring works by more than 500 artists in all, as well as related musical events, children's events, street parties, cook-offs, and fishing tournaments. Waterside pastimes—golf, tennis, and hiking among them—are handy, too, on cliff-lined lakes that offer more total shoreline than

JUNE'S FAVORITE ATTRACTIONS

Cooper's Barbecue
Llano

Enchanted Rock State Natural Area
near Fredericksburg

11th Street Cowboy Bar
Bandera

Fall Creek Vineyards
Tow

FR 337
Vanderpool

Luckenbach

Pedernales Falls State Park
near Johnson City

Vanishing Texas River Cruise
Lake Buchanan

Wimberley Pie Co.
Wimberley

Y.O. Ranch
near Kerrville

even the whole Texas coast. Stay the night at a lakefront resort, waterfront cabin, or bed-and-breakfast inn. Just pick your pace and do a self-guided tour aided by a free Bluebonnet Trail brochure and map. Call the chamber of commerce of any town the trail winds through, including Buchanan Dam, Burnet, Lampasas, Llano, Marble Falls, or Kingsland, or visit the umbrella website at www.highlandlakes.com.

Before you begin touring, you may want to note on your map the Hill Country's best lanes for spring wildflowers and year-round scenery. They include US 281 from Lampasas south to San Antonio; Highway 16 from Llano south to Medina; US 290 from Austin to west of Fredericksburg; Highway 71 from Austin northwest to Llano; Highway 29 from Burnet west to Llano; and Highway 46 from New Braunfels to just east of Bandera.

Ranches & Lakes

There's no better place to begin the Hill Country tour than in *Johnson City,* found about 50 miles west of Austin at the junction of US 290 and US 281. The seat of Blanco County, the town of only 932 residents and its nearby neighbor, *Stonewall* (just across the Gillespie County line, 16 miles west on US 290), lay in relative obscurity for a hundred peaceful years before one of the most colorful men in political history became president suddenly in 1963. Lyndon Baines Johnson was profoundly attached to his roots and made his family ranch in Stonewall, just 14 miles west of his Johnson City birthplace, the Texas White House.

The *Lyndon B. Johnson National Historic Park*, with units on US 281 in both Johnson City and Stonewall, and adjacent *Lyndon B. Johnson State Park* do a fine job of detailing the heritage of this larger-than-life figure and his land. The national park visitor center has a multimedia program on the illustrious LBJ and Johnson City history as well as a gift shop. There's also the president's boyhood home, a humble 1886 frame house where LBJ's parents moved in 1914; it's been restored and furnished to 1920s style.

The park's ranch unit spreads along the serene *Pedernales River* and is where LBJ retired. Since the passing of Lady Bird Johnson, scheduled bus tours onto the LBJ Ranch no longer are necessary. You can now pick up a free permit and CD at the LBJ State Historical Park Visitor Center and drive onto the ranch in your private vehicle and tour the ranch home, also called The Texas White House, for $2 per person.

While you're on the grounds, be sure to take photos of the cattle, family cemetery where LBJ is buried, and a reconstruction of the president's birthplace. Also on the site are a living historical farm; small church cemetery;

A Taste of the Grape

The tiny town of Stonewall, just outside of Fredericksburg, is home to four wineries. **Becker Vineyards** features a reproduction 19th-century German stone barn and more than 24 acres of grapevines producing chardonnay, cabernet sauvignon, ruby cabernet, and others. Located on Jenschke Lane, about 1 mile off US 290; (830) 644-2681; www.beckervineyards.com. **Grape Creek Vineyard** is known for its antique roses, gift shop, tasting room, and the only fully underground wine cellar in Texas. Find it on South Grape Creek, just west of Stonewall on US 290; (830) 644-2710; www.grapecreek.com. **Torre di Pietra** features a lovely tasting room and patio with live entertainment in the afternoon, a good gift shop, and comfortable couches for relaxing on before a fireplace. It is located on US 290 at Stonewall; (830) 990-9755; www.texashillcountrywine.com. For more information about these and all Hill Country wineries, visit www.texaswinetrail.com. Visit this site also to read about upcoming events—of which there are many—throughout the Hill Country wineries much of the year. You can plan entire weekends around these visits, so it's smart to consult the website frequently for new additions to the calendar.

two furnished, pioneer dogtrot-style houses; swimming pool; and tennis court spread about the parks, but its riverside picnic areas shaded by ancient live oaks provide unparalleled peace.

For details on the state park, call park headquarters at (830) 644-2252 or (830) 644-2241 or visit www.tpwd.state.tx.us. For national park information call (830) 868-7128 or visit www.nps.gov/lyjo/.

It's not just about history in Johnson City, however; here and there, you'll find various diversions, such as the ***Benini Foundation Galleries and Sculpture Ranch,*** immediately west of town (377 Shiloh Rd., Johnson City). Here's where you'll be able to view work by the Italian-born Benini, whose contemporary paintings and sculpture have been the focus of 160 one-man exhibitions around the world. He lives and works here, where the studios and galleries can be seen by appointment; call (830) 868-5244 or visit http://sculpturranch .com and www.benini.com. ***Chantilly Lace Country Inn*** (625 Nugent Ave., Johnson City; 830-660-2621; www.chantillylacesoaps.com) sits on 6 acres that include a lavender farm, of which you'll see plenty in this area these days. The handsome historic stone house holds 5 suites with king-size beds, private baths, refrigerator, microwave, and coffeepot; 2 suites have whirlpool tubs. There's a two-room cabin on the property that accommodates up to 4 guests. All stays include a big breakfast. The innkeepers also produce a line of all-natural soaps, as well. Lodging starts at $99.

Pedernales Falls State Park, about 10 miles east of Johnson City via FR 2766 (830-868-7304; www.tpwd.state.tx.us), is a stunning spread of nearly 5,000 acres of former ranch land with 6 miles of spectacular riverfront for tubing, swimming, fishing, hiking, and camping. The park is open daily and charges a small admission fee.

Another detour for naturalists is to *Westcave Preserve,* a 30-acre nature reserve northeast of Johnson City, near the Pedernales River. A Lower Colorado River Authority property, Westcave is first seen as upland savannah, replete with wildflower meadows, before it descends to a verdant canyon formed hundreds of centuries ago when a huge limestone cave collapsed. As you hike along, you'll find an amazing development: A spring-fed creek meanders for a while before sharply turning into a 40-foot waterfall spilling into a radiantly green pool. Sensational bird watching and wildflower spotting can be had in the preserve. Tours are given Sat and Sun at 10 a.m., noon, 2 p.m., and 4 p.m., weather permitting. No admission is charged, but contributions are welcome. You can reach Westcave by driving north on US 281 from Johnson City about 12 miles, turning east on RR 962, and continuing another 12 miles. For information call (830) 825-3442 or check www.westcave.org.

From Johnson City it's also easy to make a side trip to *Blanco,* south just 14 miles on US 281. A bucolic burg of the first order, this is the place to go to spend idle hours on the Blanco River banks. Named the Blanco County seat upon organization in 1858, the town of 1,200 lies about 45 miles north of San Antonio. A lovely little state park is in Blanco, too, offering nice riverside picnic spots.

The town's centerpiece is the old *Blanco County Courthouse,* a Second Empire design built in 1886 but then abandoned when the county seat moved

JUNE'S FAVORITE ANNUAL EVENTS

Bluebonnet tours
Burnet, Llano, Buchanan Dam, Lampasas, Marble Falls, and Kingsland; early April

Cowboy Capital Rodeo
Bandera, late May

Folk Festival
Kerrville, late May and early June

Harvest Wine Trail
Fredericksburg and area, early to mid-August

World Championship Barbecue Goat Cook-Off
Brady, early September

Oktoberfest
Fredericksburg, early October

Fall foliage
Lost Maples State Natural Area, early November

Wurstfest
New Braunfels, first two weekends in November

to Johnson City in 1890. After a recent impressive restoration effort, it is open to the public. For tour information call the Blanco Chamber of Commerce at (830) 833-5101 or visit www.blanco-texas.com.

Throughout the town, century-old limestone buildings are a testament to the German colony that settled in the river valley, and some of the best historic buildings line the courthouse square. Businesses here now include a covey of antiques shops with some funky collectibles; a tiny library; and a handful of cafes.

A funky, fun spot to grab a bite to eat in town is on the north side of the square and in a somewhat unlikely location. Inside the *Blanco Bowling Club Cafe* (310 4th St., Blanco; 830-833-4416), you can bowl a few frames and tuck into a fine, juicy burger, too. There's also mile-high meringue pie, as well as giant cinnamon rolls with coffee in the morning.

After your Blanco diversion, it's time to journey from Johnson City north on US 281 to the *Highland Lakes.* You'll first reach *Lake Marble Falls* in Burnet County, about 25 miles north of Johnson City. Overlooking the lake is a town of the same name, at US 281's junction with RR 1431, one of the Hill Country's most scenic highways. *Marble Falls,* with 6,500 residents, is home to *Granite Mountain,* situated just west on RR 1431, an 860-foot-tall dome of rusty-red granite sprawling across 186 acres. It's this rock source from which the spectacular state capitol in Austin was built more than a century ago. You can see it from the highway, but the quarry isn't open to the public.

texastrivia

Texas is the number one bird-watching destination in the US, and the Rio Grande valley is the number one bird-watching area in Texas. Some 465 species of birds, including 34 species found nowhere else in the country, have been spotted in Texas. Most can be found in the Rio Grande valley.

A good reason to stop in Marble Falls is to eat at the *Bluebonnet Cafe* (211 US 281, Marble Falls; 830-693-2344; www.bluebonnetcafe.net), a very popular country diner serving Texas and southern specialties, such as chicken and dumplings, cobbler, catfish, chicken-fried steak, steaks, and all-day breakfasts. It's open for breakfast, lunch, and dinner daily.

The best scenic drives from Marble Falls can easily fill a morning or afternoon. Try heading northwest on Highway 71 for a 32-mile jaunt to Highway 16; or go west on RR 1431, which unwinds 18 miles through the tiny towns of Granite Shoals and *Kingsland* before its intersection with Highway 29. This latter route follows the lakes trail, as the Colorado River meanders past dams creating Lake LBJ and then Inks Lake and *Lake Buchanan Dam.*

If you reach Kingsland during bluebonnet weekends, handcrafted items are exhibited and sold at the **Kingsland House of Arts and Crafts** (112 Chamberlain St., Kingsland; 325-388-6159; www.kingslandcrafts.com).

A turn-of-the-20th-century railroad hotel has been renovated and reopened as **The Antlers** (RR 1431 at Kingsland; 915-388-4411 or 800-383-0007; www.theantlers.com). First opened in 1901 by the Austin & Northwestern Railroad, the inn now offers 5 suites, each accommodating up to 3 people; one room for 2 people; and 8 cabins, housing between 2 and 10 people each, equipped with kitchens and porches. There are also restored train cars that you can stay in, each accommodating 4 guests. All lodgings have private baths; rates start at $140. The 15 acres of wooded grounds have nature trails, a fruit orchard, and 1,500 feet of waterfront on Lake LBJ.

Lake LBJ, immediately west of Lake Marble Falls, lies on the line shared by Burnet and Llano Counties and is probably the best liked of the Highland Lakes in terms of recreation and scenery. The 6,300-acre impoundment of the Colorado River is shielded from winds by tree-cloaked bluffs and granite cliffs and is consequently a big lake for waterskiing, sailing, Jet-Skiing, and fishing.

Some travelers who make Lake LBJ their destination settle in at **Horseshoe Bay Resort** (RR 2147 just west of US 281; 800-531-5105 outside Texas, 800-252-9363 inside Texas, or 830-598-2511; www.hsbresort.com). Guests stay in hotel-style rooms, condos, or town houses and spend time playing golf on three 18-hole courses. There's also a beach, marina, indoor and outdoor tennis, and stables, along with a selection of good dining and a deluxe Marriott Hotel (866-799-5384; www.horseshoebaymarriott.com). If you feel like some pampering, book a treatment at the resort's newly remodeled Bayside Spa and Fitness Center. Among them, the Essence of Hill Country Vineyards gives you a full-body exfoliation with cocoa extract, red wine grape body wrap, accompanied by a scalp massage and mini antiaging facial, and a light body butter application. Just to be sweet, the spa throws in wine-inspired locally handmade truffles. The Sweet Hill Country Escape includes the signature Sugar Honey Pecan full-body scrub, hydrating honey-based, glazed body wrap, scalp and foot massage, and a body butter massage all over. Either treatment is $190.

Your traveling path will likely take you from Marble Falls 12 miles north on US 281 to **Burnet** (pronounced BURN-it), seat of Burnet County and home to about 3,400 residents. Frontier Fort Croghan was established here in 1849, and the town grew up around it. Today Burnet—known as one of the most interesting geologic spots in the world—is a magnet for rock hounds as well as professional and amateur geologists.

Longhorn Caverns State Park (south on US 281, 5 miles to PR 4; 830-598-CAVE or 877-441-CAVE; www.tpwd.state.tx.us) is a remarkable, 11-mile underground maze of caves and passages a million years in the making. What's odd about this cavern is that it was the site of big speakeasy parties during Prohibition. On the first and second Saturday of each month, naturalists lead a program called Wild Cave Tours, which takes you on a 3-hour adventure, crawling and climbing and squeezing through small passageways where outlaw Sam Bass was said to have stashed $2 million. Other guided tours are offered daily, too. The snack bar and souvenir shop are better than some. Tour hours vary; admission is charged.

texastrivia

Guadalupe Peak, at 8,749 feet, is the state's highest mountain. That's more than 2,000 feet higher than North Carolina's Mount Mitchell, the highest point east of the Mississippi River.

Another Burnet stop is the *Fort Croghan Museum* (703 Buchanan Dr., Burnet; 512-765-8281; www.fort croghan.org). The museum offers more than 1,200 items pertaining to early central Texas history plus six pioneer cabins. Open Apr through Oct Thurs through Sat from 10 a.m. to 5 p.m. There's no admission, but donations are welcome.

Burnet's Bluebonnet Trail offerings in the spring wildflower months include a show from the *Burnet Creative Arts,* which includes original work by creators of ceramics, china paintings, oils, jewelry, stained glass, woodwork, weavings, and porcelain dolls. You'll find the show on Highway 29 at the Catholic Educational Building. Call the Burnet Chamber of Commerce for details at (512) 756-4297, or visit www.burnetchamber.org.

Just west of Burnet, head along 29 to Lake Buchanan and the *Canyon of the Eagles Lodge & Nature Park,* found on a 940-acre spread at the northern tip of the lake at the end of RR 2341, which you'll follow north from Highway 29 (800-977-0081; www.canyonoftheeagles.com). This nature lovers' retreat, with a 62-room lodge, is perfect if your interests include hiking, canoeing, kayaking, fishing, and birding. Newer offerings include kayaking and canoeing

Joy to the Fishes in the Deep Blue . . . Lake

Inks Dam National Fish Hatchery features scientific ponds in which thousands of fish are bred for stocking lakes across the nation. One of its functions is that of restoring Gulf Coast striped bass to the northern Gulf of Mexico. It's open weekdays from 8 a.m. until 4 p.m. and until noon on weekends and is located at FR 2342 at PR 4—look for signs—(512) 793-2474.

outings, along with nightly stargazing at the Eagle Eye Observatory. The long-popular *Vanishing Texas River Cruise* is boarded near the lodge; regularly scheduled tours take you on Lake Buchanan in fall and winter to look for great blue herons, osprey, red-tailed hawks, American white pelicans, and, with any luck at all, a bald eagle, roosting in trees along the shoreline or gliding over-head. In spring and summer the cruises give you a chance to see wildflowers, deer, and other samples of Mother Nature's gifts. To book cruises call (800) 4-RIVER-4 or log onto www.vtrc.com.

The lodge also schedules programs such as guided nature hikes, arts-and-crafts classes, cowboy poetry readings, and hayrides. Lodgings are very attrac-tive wood-and-stone cottages with tin roofs, rocking chairs on the porches, and quilts and Texas- and Mexican-made furniture in the rooms. The lodge serves inexpensive meals, as well as beer and wine. Call (800) 977-0081 to reserve or log onto www.canyonoftheeagles.com.

After the cruise continue on Highway 29 west to *Inks Lake State Park,* just an 8-mile reach from Burnet, (512) 793-2223; www.tpwd.state.tx.us. This 1,200-acre spread—one of the smaller but prettier lakes in Texas—is perfect for anybody who wants beautiful surroundings in which to read, sketch, or write postcards, and it affords camping, picnicking, fishing, and hiking. The park is open daily and charges a small admission. Inquire about canoe tours to the Devil's Waterhole.

Just 5 miles west of Inks Lake via Highway 29, across the line into Llano County, is the town of *Buchanan Dam* (pronounced buck-ANN'n), sitting on the lovely Lake Buchanan. Only 1,600 people call it home, but it's a busy place in mild weather and spring flower time. The 2-mile-long dam is a work of arches and is likely the largest multi-arch dam in the nation. Built in the 1930s, it holds the Colorado River and forms the highest and largest of the Highland Lakes. One of the better places to view the lake and dam is at the Buchanan Dam visitor center office, on Highway 29 in the observation building at the dam. Call the *Llano County Chamber of Commerce* at (512) 793-2803 or visit www.highlandlakes.com/Llano/ for more information.

From the town and lake, it's an easy, 14-mile side trip up to the town of *Tow,* on the lake's northwestern shore, to visit *Fall Creek Vineyards* (west on Highway 29, north on Highway 261, north on RR 2241; 325-379-5361; www .fcv.com). One of the more successful wineries in the state, Fall Creek offers an impressive visitor center, guided tours, a tasting room, Saturday wine lunches, and a gift shop. Admission is free, but hours vary.

From Buchanan Dam the Hill Country tour continues 17 miles west again on Highway 29 to *Llano,* seat of Llano County. Nearly 3,000 folks find Llano a comfortable place to live, and it's largely due to an undisturbed array of historic buildings. You'll want to explore the town one afternoon—it's easy to see on foot—to have a look at places such as the *Llano County Courthouse* (Main and Ford Streets), built in 1892; *Acme Dry Goods* (109 W. Main St., Llano), dating to the same time; the *Southern Hotel* (201 W. Main St., Llano), built in 1881 and housing a century-old hardware business; and the *Old Llano County Jail* (Oatman Street, northeast of the courthouse), today occupied by a museum. All details are available from the *Llano Chamber of Commerce* at (325) 247-5354 or www.llanochamber.org.

Llano is extremely popular with deer hunters in late fall and with rock hounds year-round. As the county is on the 1½-billion-acre *Llano Uplift,* described as a geological phenomenon, the ground is riddled with sensational finds of amethyst, azurite, dolomite, galena, garnet, quartz, serpentine, gold, and llanite, a brown granite with blue crystals and pink feldspar unique to this area.

People have been known to drive quite a way to eat Llano's barbecue. *Cooper's,* just west of Highway 16 on Highway 29 (604 W. Young St., Llano; 325-247-5713; www.coopersbbq.com), produces outstanding smoked ribs, brisket, pork, chicken, sausage, and *cabrito* (baby goat), with a fine pot of beans and savory barbecue sauce. It's open daily for lunch and dinner.

The wildflower period in spring signals a show and sale of paintings, sculpture, drawings, weavings, pottery, and more at *Llano Fine Arts Guild Gallery* (503 Bessemer Ave., Llano; 325-247-4839; www.llanofineartsgallery .org).

Llano is the best place to strike out for a side trip to *Colorado Bend State Park.* Reach it by driving north on Highway 16 for 16 miles, then, inside San Saba County, turn east on RR 501 for 15 miles. More out of the way than many parks, it can feel like a private Eden for travelers. Beautiful scenery unwinds along the banks of the Colorado River, where primitive camping sites, hiking trails, and picnicking areas are scattered. Anglers say the fishing is unsurpassed, and cave tours are offered on weekends. One is a walking tour through *Gorman Cave,* while the crawling tour explores smaller caves suited to the most dedicated spelunkers. Call for tour fees and times. The park is open daily and charges a small admission. For information call (325) 628-3240 or visit www .tpwd.state.tx.us.

Wine lovers will want to make time to visit *Alamosa Wine Cellars* (3 miles west of Bend via RR 580; 325-628-3313; www.alamosawinecellars.com). In recent years this small winery has produced some exceptional wines, including viognier, cabernet sauvignon, ruby cabernet, tempranillo, and syrah. Call ahead to find out when tours and tastings are offered.

Rocks & Wildlife

From Llano, point your car northwest on Highway 71 to **Brady.** It's a 54-mile drive to the seat of McCulloch County, home to 7,000 residents, and the town closest to the geographic center of Texas—hence the nickname, the Heart of Texas.

Any Texan who holds Lone Star foods near and dear to the heart can tell you Brady is the site of the **World Championship Barbecue Goat Cook-Off,** held annually on the Friday and Saturday before Labor Day. Don't laugh—the competition draws more than 100 teams from around the US and abroad. The weekend brings plenty of entertainment and unique contests, all held at Richards Park on Commerce Street, just west of downtown. Admission is free; for details call (325) 597-3491 or visit www.bradytx.com.

For a look into the past, check out the **Heart of Texas Historical Museum** (High and Main Streets; 325-597-0526), a converted old jail that rises 3 stories into the sky and resembles a castle. You'll see exhibits on area history and the background of the jail cells and gallows. Open Fri through Sun afternoons only; admission is free.

You're in barbecue country, remember, and the most popular place to go in town is **Hard Eight BBQ** (2010 S. Bridge St., Brady; 325-597-1936; www.hardeightbbq.com), specializing in giant smoked pork chops, sausage, brisket, and ribs.

Anyone who finds romance in history—and has a soft spot for animals—will want to stop in **Mason,** 28 miles south of Brady via US 377. The seat of Mason County—home to just 2,000—took its name from Fort Mason, built in the early 1850s as one in a chain of army posts established to protect against Indian attacks between the Red River and the Rio Grande.

Mason was unusual among Texas towns in that it endured an internal war in the 1870s when cattle rustlings and prejudices between German and Anglo settlers stirred up angry emotions; the upshot is that more than 10 men were killed in ambushes and lynchings before the Texas Rangers were summoned to reestablish peace in the community. For more information about the town, call the local chamber of commerce at (325) 347-5758 or visit www.masontx coc.com.

You can explore the fort and town history at **Fort Mason Officers Quarters** (Rainey and Post Hill Streets; 325-347-5758). Among the illustrious soldiers who were once stationed at the fort were George Armstrong Custer, Albert Sidney Johnston, and Robert E. Lee. Today's fort is a reconstruction on the original foundation, and a miniature of the fort is among the exhibits. The museum is open daily, but it's best to call ahead for hours.

If you read the book or saw the film *Old Yeller,* you probably never stopped crying long enough to wonder where its author, Fred Gipson, was from; Mason, it turns out, was his hometown. Gipson and other local notables are detailed in the local library, found at Post Hill and Schmidt Streets.

Rather unexpectedly you'll come upon the **Seaquist Home** (400 Broad St., Mason), a sensational, 3-story Queen Anne Victorian mansion. Remarkable are its 22 rooms, 15 fireplaces, beautiful wooden staircase constructed without nails, galleries wrapping around 2 stories on the exterior, and third-floor ballroom. The house was started in 1891, then renovated in 1919 by a Swede who made his fortune in boots. The home is not open to the public, but it is a wonderful example of Victorian architecture.

There's no shortage of down-home, country stays in the Mason area: There's **Bridges House Bed & Breakfast** (305 Broad St., Mason; 325-347-5151 or 800-776-3519) next door to the Seaquist Home, an 1884 home in a historic area with porches and lovely antiques, and **Hasse House** (east from town square 6 miles on Highway 29; 325-347-6463), a spacious place on a 300-acre working ranch.

Right in the middle of town is a particularly comfortable stay for just $60 to $70. The **Mason Square Bed & Breakfast** (236 Fort McKavett St., Mason; 325-347-6524 or 888-694-0111) is a 3-room inn with private bath, kitchenette, sunroom, and a balcony overlooking the town square, all above a law office. On the southeast corner of the square, **Santos Taqueria** (205 San Antonio St., Mason; 325-347-6140; www.santostaqueria.com) occupies a renovated filling station and has grown into one of the region's more popular eateries. It's open Thurs through Sun, offering full Mexican plates, nachos, salads, tacos, and wine and beer. Finally, rock hounds will be thrilled at the area's fantastic variety of minerals and rocks located in the geologic outcroppings. Specifically, blue topaz, the state gem—a rarity in North America—is found here. The public can hunt topaz at the **Seaquist Ranch** (325-347-5413; www.masontxcoc.com/topaz.html) just northwest of Mason. They charge fees but permit camping.

Continuing along the Hill Country trail, turn southwest on US 377 and go 39 miles through big deer-hunting country to **Junction,** the seat of Kimble County, home to about 2,600 people and more flowing streams than any other Texas county.

Most people who cite Junction as a destination do so for its wildlife watching and other outdoorsy pursuits. **South Llano River State Park** (4 miles south of town on US 377; 325-446-3994; www.tpwd.state.tx.us) is just the right place for these, as animals often seen here include white-tailed deer, wood ducks, fox squirrels, rock squirrels, javelina, and the Rio Grande turkey. The turkeys roost in bottomlands; this site is closed to visitors from October through

March. At the park enjoy camping, hiking, picnicking, canoeing, and inner tubing between wildlife sightings. The spring-fed river is simple pleasure itself. A small admission fee is charged.

Historians are wise to make two detours from Junction before exploring the remainder of the Hill Country. Thirty miles due north of Junction is the town of **Menard,** seat of Menard County, with a population of about 1,600. Established during the pioneer and cattle-driving days near the ruins of the 18th-century Spanish mission **Santa Cruz de San Saba,** Menard tells its story in a little county museum in the old train depot at 100 Frisco Ave. (325-396-2365).

Rather intriguing is the sight of ruins on the city golf course. There, by the eighth hole, are the ancient walls of the Spanish presidio built to protect the mission. The mission was attacked in 1758 by Comanche and other Native Americans; the presidio soldiers weren't numerous enough, and the presidio was abandoned in 1769. Learn details about the town and its annual outdoor musical drama in June by calling the local chamber of commerce at (325) 396-2365.

About 20 miles west of Menard, in the southwestern corner of Menard County, **Fort McKavett State Historic Site** (RR 864; 325-396-2358; www .tpwd.state.tx.us) presents yet another portrait of rugged Texas history. Established as Camp San Saba in 1852, the fort was one of the most important in west Texas pioneer history; 15 restored buildings include an officers' quarters, barracks, hospital, and a cluster of interpretive exhibits pertaining to military history and historic archaeology. From Memorial Day through Labor Day, the park is open daily from 9 a.m. to 6 p.m.; the balance of the year, it's open Wed through Sun from 8 a.m. to 5 p.m.

On the road again, prepare yourself for spectacular scenery. From Junction, take US 83 south, making a 57-mile journey to **Leakey** (LAY-kee), the Real County seat and a town of 400 tucked into an especially picturesque corner of the Edwards Plateau. About 12 miles shy of town, you'll be happy if you packed a picnic lunch, because there's a particularly good roadside park with superb scenery right there.

Although you won't see Comanches and Apaches living in the area around Leakey as did the Spanish explorers, you will find flocks of registered Angora goats from which area ranchers harvest mohair. This, too, is a popular hunting ground for white-tailed deer, mourning dove, quail, wild turkey, and javelina.

Consider taking a day or two to revel in the surroundings, putting your feet up at one of the comfortable retreats in this bucolic setting. Your dreams of rest and relaxation will be fulfilled at one of the cabins or private vacation homes booked through **Rio Frio Lodging** (throughout Uvalde Country; 830-966-2320; www.friolodging.com), which offers riverside abodes with fireplaces and full kitchens. At **River Haven Cabins** (RR 1120; 830-232-5400; www.river havencabins.com), the two-bedroom log cabins sitting on 6.5 acres along the Frio River are equipped with full kitchens, fireplaces, and satellite TV, and the grounds have barbecue pits, basketball goals, a playground, and picnic tables.

An appealing park in the area is **Garner State Park,** on the Frio River just inside Uvalde County, a 9-mile drive south of Leakey via US 83. Here the fun in warm weather is all about settling into a big inner tube and floating down the clear, cold Frio, surrounded by limestone shelves and shady cypress lining the way. Stone-and-timber cabins at the park offer a comfortable night's rest; call (830) 232-6132 or visit www.tpwd.state.tx.us for reservations. Other diversions include pedal boats, miniature golf, camping, hiking, fishing, and grocery facilities. (Note: Spring break crowds tend to be big and lively.) The park is open daily, and a small admission is charged.

If the park is full, check out **Neal's Vacation Lodges,** right on the Frio and near the park (830-232-6118; www.nealslodges.com). This collection of rustic cabins and motel-style kitchenettes—which also have televisions—has been a Hill Country favorite since opening in 1926. Also on-site are a grocery, laundry facility, country store, and cafe, the latter serving breakfast, lunch, and dinner. During the summer Neal's offers hayrides, along with inner-tube rentals and shuttles for floating the river.

From Garner State Park, your next destination is east on FR 1050—one you'll always remember for climbing views of bluffs and valleys and blooming cacti—15 miles to **Utopia,** an appropriately named town if ever one existed. The farming-ranching hamlet—population just 360—in Uvalde County was established on Sabinal Creek in 1852 and is a second home to hunters and campers; spring wildflowers and fall foliage bring plenty of fans, too.

Sparkling spring-water drinkers have likely heard of Utopia by now—the crystal liquid is bottled here and shipped around the world. Notice how at the post office, the general store, and the cafe, all those friendly people seem unusually happy? It must be the water.

Simple country cooking is the pride at **Lost Maples Cafe** (in the middle of town on RM 187; 830-966-2221). Chat with the local game warden, park rangers, neighboring farmers, and outgoing staffers over Frisbee-size pancakes or fresh, made-to-order chicken-fried steak, enormous baked potatoes, and barbecue.

People who want the restoration found in long, breathtaking drives come to the Leakey-Utopia area to see where the Frio, Nueces, and Sabinal Rivers etched vividly shaded canyons, from which hills and mesas rise between 1,500 and 2,400 feet. The specific drives from Leakey that attract photographers, painters, and other artists of the soul are FR 337 west to Camp Wood, past wooded rises and lonely, green valleys colored purple in spring with mountain laurel; and FR 337 east into Bandera County to **Vanderpool,** then north on Ranch Market 187.

Lost Maples State Natural Area is on every Texas fall foliage fan's list as a must-see, but be assured the park is roaring with beauty in all seasons. These bigtooth maples are said to be lost because they're far from any other stands of their kind, which are scattered over the western US and northern Mexico. The brilliant orange, red, and gold peak is usually in early November, and crowds tend to be staggering.

There are more than 90 plant families in the park, represented by more than 350 species. The bird population is healthy as well, with the golden-cheeked warbler among uncommon finds. Camping and hiking are the park's other big draws, and reservations are a good idea; call (830) 966-3413 or visit www.tpwd.state.tx.us. The park is open daily, and admission is charged.

The town of Vanderpool, population 20, is 4 miles south of the park on Ranch Market 187. You'll find accommodations here, including **Foxfire Cabins** (1 mile south of the park facing the Sabinal River; 830-966-2200 and 877-966-8200; www.foxfirecabins.com) offering log cabins.

Exotics, Dudes & Germans

From Vanderpool journey north on FR 187 for 19 miles to Highway 39, then eastward on Highway 39 for 26 miles, through the town of Ingram to the intersection of Highway 27; take this highway just another 7 miles east into **Kerrville,** the seat of Kerr County, the largest city in the Hill Country, and home to more than 21,000 people.

Easily the spiritual center of the Hill Country, Kerrville straddles the peaceful **Guadalupe River** and captures all that Texans treasure about this agreeable region—clean air, clear water, limestone bluffs, and pure repose. Kerrville owes its success to developer Charles Schreiner, who became a Texas Ranger at age 16 and later served as a captain in the Civil War, and whose grandson brought the Texas longhorn breed back from the brink of extinction.

An enduring foundation of the area, Schreiner's **Y.O. Ranch,** 26 miles west on I-10 and Highway 41, is a top working ranch and a top attraction in the state. Forty thousand acres remain of Schreiner's 550,000 acquired in 1880, and a Longhorn Trail Drive is still held annually one weekend in early May. There are herds and herds of longhorn, sheep, and goats, plus free-ranging animals from around the globe; this is considered North America's largest collection of exotic wildlife.

In all there are some 10,000 animals of 58 species, including wildebeest, oryx, addax, Japanese sika, aoudad, black buck antelope, ostrich, giraffe, zebra, and Watusi cattle, to name a few. The owner-family's conservation efforts are visible in the ranch's programs for children. Most day-trippers come for a tour or horseback ride and chuck wagon lunch. Summer afternoons are whiled away in a pretty swimming pool, and cattle drives can be arranged. Century-old log cabins and a former ranch home accommodate 35 overnight guests. For details and reservations call the ranch at (830) 640-3222 or (800) 967-2624 or visit www.yoranch.com.

You may spend a day seeing the Y.O.'s animals, but you won't want to miss a weekend in town, where culture and cowboys prevail. Kerrville's a bastion of artistic diversity, with folk music and folk-art festivals in May. For details contact the *Kerrville Convention & Visitor Bureau* at (830) 792-3535 or visit www.kerrvilletexascvb.com.

Kerrville is also home to possibly the nation's only museum dedicated to the work of a single group of living artists. The *Museum of Western Art* features the paintings and sculptures of about 30 members, some of whom are considered the country's foremost artists of Western American Realism. The building itself is wonderfully artful, incorporating light Mexican brick in bóveda domes that need no supporting forms or wiring. The museum charges admission and is just south of downtown on Highway 173; call (830) 896-2553 or visit www.museumofwesternart.org for more information. The museum is open Mon through Sat from 9 a.m. to 5 p.m. and Sun from 1 to 5 p.m. From Sept through May it's closed Mon.

For a lovely sunset drive, head west from Kerrville on *RR 1340,* which winds its way through the scenic communities of Ingram and Hunt. The ribbon of road twists and turns, repeatedly crossing the Guadalupe River, passing a scattering of summer cottages, boys' and girls' summer camps, and deer-hunting country. In the middle of one field, you'll see a Stonehenge replica, of all things.

There are three good places to find rest in Kerrville, starting with the *Inn of the Hills Resort* (1001 Junction Hwy., Kerrville; 830-895-5000 or 800-292-5690; www.innofthehills.com), a spreading complex with motel rooms, suites, and condo apartments. The 4 pools, pretty landscaping, games and activities for kids in summer, 3 restaurants, an exercise facility with sauna and whirlpool, bowling lanes, a putting green, bike and boat rentals, fishing in a stocked lake, and lighted tennis courts make this a full-service resort.

The *Y.O. Ranch Resort Hotel* (2033 Sidney Baker Blvd., Kerrville; 830-257-4440 or 877-977-3767; www.yoresort.com) is a charming hotel accented with western design. The huge lobby is lighted with chandeliers crafted from branding irons and is dominated by a bronze of a mounted cowboy working to bring a longhorn back to the herd. Room furnishings continue the theme.

Lazy Hills Retreat (west on Highway 27, just past Ingram; 830-367-1445; www.lazyhillsretreat.com) has shifted gears from a dude ranch offering to a family getaway destination with miniature golf, beach volleyball, kayaking, zip-line adventures, hiking and biking trail, and more in a beautiful hilly setting. The stone lodges have been spiffed up; rooms start at about $100 nightly.

Next stop after Kerrville is found north on Highway 16, 24 miles away in **Fredericksburg,** seat of Gillespie County. Texas's cache of German heritage is a miniature Bavarian treat with a proliferation of bed-and-breakfast lodgings, the backbone of Old World touring. In Fredericksburg, guests have the state's largest selection of places to spend rest periods off the road in quaint historic homes and inns, much more appealing to some than sleeping in cookie-cutter hotels.

Start your visit with a stop inside the *Fredericksburg Visitor Information Center,* 302 E. Austin St. (1 block off of Main Street; 888-997-3600 or 830-997-6523; www.visitfredericksburgtx.com). Here, you'll find information on Fredericksburg and the Hill Country, along with large public restrooms and plentiful parking, which gives you easy access to the National Museum of the Pacific War, across the street, and to Main Street shopping, dining, and entertainment. There's free wireless access at the visitor center, too.

If you haven't been to this burg recently, you'll have plenty of surprises in store. Yes, the deep German influence of its founders still prevails, but there's much more to this town than the sausage-beer-knickknack stop that became so popular in the early 1990s. Sure it's still a handy romantic getaway town, thanks to more than 350 guesthouses, but the level of sophistication that permeates the town today means that that signature "country-cute" appeal lingers only as a fading memory. Today you'll find a real wine country with requisite gracious dining to satisfy discerning palates, as well as galleries and shopping of a higher caliber than in the past. Travelers from the East Coast are finding this is an area for visiting and relocating, and developers have built million-dollar vacation homes on golf courses. In early summer you can wander the lavender trails, winding through farms blooming along the Pedernales River, and all spring and summer and parts of the fall, there are myriad weekend wine events hosted by area vineyards.

If you've come for the wine experience, you'll have plentiful ground to cover: There are nearly a dozen wineries in Gillespie County and another half-dozen within driving distance (consult www.wineroad290.com for details on these). On Main Street, you'll find 2 custom wineries (create your own labels and blends) and 4 tasting rooms, and there are 2 wine bars downtown. The Fredericksburg-based *Texas Wine Tours* lets you leave the driving to them when you sign up for half- and full-day winery tours (call 877-TEX-WINE or visit www.texas-wine-tours.com).

Descriptions of the numerous guesthouses vary widely, from tiny, cute places to larger, rambling Victorian homes in town, to remote cabins and historic stone buildings in the countryside. Some are luxuriously decorated and command higher prices. All include breakfast, of course, which can mean anything from breads, fruits, and juices left for guests to have when they choose to formal feasts served at a large dining room table. A good searchable database is found at www.visitfredericksburgtx.com. While in Fredericksburg take time to explore history a bit. The town was the 1885 birthplace of Adm. Chester W. Nimitz, commander in chief of the Pacific fleet during World War II. A tribute to him and other heroes of that war is found at the **National Museum of the Pacific War** (340 E. Main St., Fredericksburg; 830-997-8600; www.pacificwarmuseum.org). Now a museum of national standing, the complex began with an old hotel building that houses exhibits on Nimitz's life and the restored ballroom. The vastly expanded George H.W. Bush Gallery, now measuring 33,000 square feet and costing $15.3 million, opened more recently. Detail on the Pacific War is astounding, and the Pacific War education programs extend to include African Americans and Hispanic Americans serving there. Be sure to leave time to walk through the Japanese Garden of Peace. The museum is open daily; admission is charged.

Shoppers can spend considerable time (and money) at the 100-plus boutiques and stores along **Fredericksburg's Main Street,** which offer everything from books, candles, quilts, primitive antiques, bath goods, and herbal remedies to peach jam, wine, pewter mugs, dulcimers, jewelry, clothing, and fine art and folk art.

The Wine Trails

Of the 220 producing wineries in Texas, more than 50 are in the Hill Country/Central Texas region. Fredericksburg and Stonewall claim their fare share of those, and many more are in easy reach in towns like Johnson City, Mason, Comfort, and Sisterdale. In other words: There's a lot of wine to be tasted around here—and everyone seems to be on top of it.

You'll be wowed by swarming crowds at the **Becker Vineyards** (830-644-2681; www.beckervineyards.com) tasting room, but you won't be surprised that this spot in Stonewall, about 5 minutes east of Fredericksburg, has become a popular destination. Producer of some very nice wines, including a dandy viognier and best-selling chardonnay, Becker wines have been noted in the *Wine Spectator* and *Wine Enthusiast,* and they've been poured at at least two White House dinners in the past couple of years. You can learn more about the region's wineries at www.texaswinetrail.com.

Newer in the entertainment realm, the **Rockbox Theater** (109 N. Llano St.; www.rockboxtheater.com), just a block off Main Street, presents four live musical comedy shows every weekend in its 392-seat space. There's a new show each weekend, featuring music from the 50s, 60s, and 70s. At the **Fredericksburg Brewing Company** (245 E. Main St., Fredericksburg; 830-997-1646; www.yourbrewery.com), visitors tour the area's largest brew facility, housed in an 1890s rock building. There's a restaurant, lodgings, and a beer garden on-site, too.

Among favorite dining spots in Fredericksburg is **Navajo Grill** (803 E. Main St., Fredericksburg; 830-990-8289; www.navajogrill.com), a sophisticated sprawl of dining rooms inside a renovated cottage. For casual meals head to **Hondo's on Main** (312 W. Main St., Fredericksburg; 830-997-1633; www.hondos onmain.com) for grilled flat-iron steak, barbecued pork ribs, and mesquite-grilled burgers on sourdough buns. **Rather Sweet Bakery and Cafe** (245 E. Main St., Fredericksburg; 830-990-0498; www.rathersweetbakery.com) is the place for bacon-cheddar scones, brownies with praline topping, tomato-basil soup, curried chicken salad, portobello burgers, and omelets.

A favorite side trip from Fredericksburg is the jaunt to **Enchanted Rock State Natural Area,** 18 miles north of town on RR 965. The park surrounds an otherworldly, huge, monolithic dome of pink granite, rising 600 feet into the sky—a challenge perfect for ambitious hikers. Climb it if you have stamina, good athletic shoes, and the foresight to have arrived early enough to find a parking space inside the park, as the annual visitor count now tops 350,000.

Lincoln Street

One spring weekend I took my mom and her friends Vicki and Juanita on a girl-friends' getaway to Fredericksburg—a pastime that's now the most popular visiting demographic around town. We whiled away our days shopping—naturally—and wandering around the scenic countryside. In town we wound up an afternoon at what's become my favorite hangout—a place called **Lincoln Street,** a wine bar and market just off Fredericksburg's Main Street. Everyone gathers around a communal table, grabs comfy armchairs, or perches somewhere on the arbor-covered patio to kill an hour or two over wine from an impossibly diverse, global list. The staff exhibited infinite patience with our foursome as we mulled over the wine choices, all of which are available by the bottle for taking home, too. Ordering a cheese-olive board for two as a snack, we soon realized our enormous platter of exquisite edibles would render dinner plans completely unnecessary. We loved watching the locals drift in and out, some of them cowboys in hats and boots, dropping in for a glass of cabernet before heading back to the ranch. See more at www.lincolnst.com.

The surprising vegetation up top is as impressive as the views, particularly in the first light of day. On summer nights the huge rock creaks and moans as it cools down, an occurrence the Comanches understandably found to be of a powerfully spiritual nature. The park is open daily and charges a small admission; get details by calling (915) 247-3903 or visiting www.tpwd.state.tx.us.

For an explosion of color at any time of year, head to **Wildseed Farms,** 7 miles east of Fredericksburg on US 290 (800-848-0078; www.wildseedfarms .com). Wildseed Farms harvests up to 400,000 pounds of wildflower seeds annually and seems to be forever expanding its production. There are some 600 acres blooming in the Fredericksburg area, and the farm center allows visitors to see planting, harvesting, and flowers in various stages on 200 acres. The market complex, crafted from hand-cut Texas cedar and native stone, sells fresh-cut flowers, dried flowers, herbs, and hundreds of gifts pertaining to herbs and flowers. A beer garden offers refreshments, and a new pavilion with a butterfly house is in the works. A small admission is charged for a walk in the flower fields.

The most famous detour of all is **Luckenbach,** population 25, reached by driving 6 miles east of town on US 290, then turning south (right) on RR 1376; continue on this little road about 5 miles till you see signs. If you cross the creek, you've gone too far—maybe it's time to stop and ask directions, as signs to Luckenbach just don't last long, thanks to souvenir hunters.

"In Luckenbach, Texas, ain't nobody feelin' no pain" is how the song goes, and honestly, everybody feels fine when they're in Luckenbach because it's mostly a state of mind. It isn't even a town, but a little pocket of peace where the population is really just the number of people sitting around drinking longnecks on the porch of the eternally unpainted general store, playing dominoes, or pitching horseshoes. There's live music nightly in the dance hall, where you can join folks two-steppin' to the likes of Gary P. Nunn, who stops in occasionally to entertain the idea of going "home with the armadillo" in his song "London Homesick Blues."

An 1850 German settlement, Luckenbach was unremarkable for more than a century, with the exception of Jacob Brodbeck, who—years before the Wright brothers—invented an airplane powered with coiled springs. He abandoned the project after a discouraging crash in 1865.

Then in the 1970s humorist-writer and legendary Texas character Hondo Crouch invited like souls to share in Luckenbach's bucolic remoteness, laced

Make Your Own Way

When Waylon Jennings sang, "Let's go to Luckenbach, Texas, with Willie an' Waylon an' the boys," he knew instinctively how to get there. He had to, because there's no sign indicating where it is. The tiny burg of 25 people became so famous for its spontaneous concerts and parties in the 1970s that souvenir hunters kept swiping the signs. The highway department dutifully replaced them for years, just to have them stolen again and again. It finally gave up, deciding visitors who really wanted to find the place would do so. And they do.

with bluebonnets and pioneer flavor. This made it a place where "everybody's somebody," as prescribed by Waylon Jennings and Jerry Jeff Walker, in the song that propelled the tiny spot in the road into fame.

You can find great T-shirts, postcards (stamped with a Luckenbach postmark), jewelry, snacks, beer, and plenty of conversation in the general store; a barbecue stand next to the dance hall is generally open on weekends. For information call the general store at (830) 997-3224, or visit www.luckenbach texas.com.

From Fredericksburg the tour continues south on US 87 to **Comfort,** a 23-mile drive. Barely inside the Kendall County line, the borough of almost 2,400 was settled in 1854 by free-thinking German intellectuals, some of whom later joined Union forces in the Civil War; you'll see the Treue Der Union Monument, a tribute to them, on High Street between 3rd and 4th Streets.

Comfort is also known for being batty: The **Hygieostatic Bat Roost,** 1½ miles east on FR 473, was a 1918 experiment; more than 80 years later, the bats still use it. Sunset is the time to watch for them here and at the Old Railroad Tunnel, 14 miles north via FR 473 and Old Highway 9, where several thousand bats live in a tunnel abandoned in 1942.

Take a stroll down **High Street,** particularly the 800 block, to have a close-up look at one of the state's more complete 19th-century business districts still intact. The Chamber of Commerce office, at 7th and High Streets, (830-995-3131; www.comfort-texas.com), has free, helpful guides. Of particular interest to shoppers is **Comfort Common** (717 High St., Comfort; 830-995-3030), a bevy of antiques and gift boutiques in the old Ingenhuett-Faust Hotel, with a B&B on-site.

Within the lovely 1880 building remarkable for wide verandas that open onto a shady rear courtyard are 10 gorgeous suites and rooms, all with private baths and exquisite antique furnishings. Rates average $100.

Cozy sleepovers can be had, too, at **Meyer Bed & Breakfast** (845 High St., Comfort; 830-995-2304 or 888-995-6100; www.meyerbedandbreakfast.com), a historic little hostelry with a swimming pool and fishing behind the complex in Cypress Creek. The main building was a stage stop in Comfort's earliest days.

Do arrive in Comfort with an appetite, as the home cooking at ***Cypress Creek Inn*** (Highway 27 at the Cypress Creek Bridge; 830-995-3977) aims to fill you up with chicken-fried steak, sausage, liver and onions, fried chicken, or meat loaf. And please leave room for dessert—the pies are super. You can also get a great cappuccino, meat loaf sandwich, or fresh cookies at ***High's*** (726 High St., Comfort; 830-995-4995).

Camp Verde, west of Comfort 17 miles via Highway 27 and then RR 480, is barely a wide spot in the road. The community has only 40 residents but a Texas-size heritage. At its heart is ***Camp Verde General Store,*** in continuous operation since 1857 (intersection of Highway 173 and RR 480; 830-634-7722; www.campverdegeneralstore.com). Inside you'll find great souvenirs such as camel bells, T-shirts, gift baskets, Hill Country jams and jellies, wood carvings, books, and home decor items. For a snack pick up some homemade tamales, fried pies, jelly beans, or hard candies.

If you're ready to kick back at the ranch, head south on Highway 173, about 15 miles to ***Bandera,*** the Bandera County seat and home to a population of nearly 900, and growing fast. It claims the title Cowboy Capital of the World not just for its cattle-drive and ranching heritage but also for the record number of National Rodeo Champions who lived there or still do. And, what travelers most like to find, Bandera is home to seven terrific guest ranches.

Long before would-be dudes began showing up in Bandera, several hundred Comanches ambushed about 40 Texas Rangers here in 1841. Peace eventually prevailed, and settlers arrived in 1852, finding the cypress-and-live-oak–laden banks of the Medina River a good place to put down roots. The primitive countryside about 45 miles west of San Antonio still holds that

The Camel Corps

It is known as the ***great failed camel experiment.*** In 1856 the US Cavalry placed an outpost at ***Camp Verde,*** where Texas Rangers had already fought off Comanches in what was known as the Bandera Pass. Secretary of War Jefferson Davis chose the site for an Army experiment, using camels as pack animals. The idea was that the camel corps would be useful in communication and transportation through the arduous west to Fort Yuma, California. While there was some success, Confederate troops took over the fort in 1861, and many of the camels were allowed to wander off or simply die. At least one of the descendants of the camel corps lives at a ranch near Camp Verde, but visitors can see a camel theme in the Camp Verde General Store in the form of camel wind chimes and other gift items.

appeal, and vacationing cowboys and cowgirls have all the western-style fun they want.

The guest ranches each offer family lodging in bunkhouses or cabins, horseback riding and hayrides, trick-roping and snake-handling (!) demonstrations, rodeos, country-western dancing, chuck wagon meals on the trail, swimming, fishing, and inner tubing on the river. Some are more specialized than others, offering fitness programs, golf, and the occasional spa treatment.

Dixie Dude Ranch (9 miles south of town on RR 1077; 830-796-4481 or 800-375-9255; www.dixieduderanch.com) has been in the family for more than 50 years, and now the fourth generation is running the 800-acre spread. The place is nothing if not homey, and guests find themselves making friends from all over the globe during fried-chicken suppers, poolside cookouts, and Saturday-night barbecues. The ranch hands—especially good at matching riders with mounts—lead trail rides through a wild terrain, pointing out historic sites along the way.

Mayan Dude Ranch (1½ miles northwest of town via Main and Pecan Streets; 830-796-3312; www.mayanranch.com) is more like summer camp; it's an all-year affair for 100 or more guests of all ages. Days begin with cowboy-made breakfast on a trail beside the Medina River and usually continue in the saddle or in the Olympic-size pool. Nights are never dull—each one brings a different theme and activity, such as a Mexican fiesta, a ghost-town trip and steak fry, or a cocktails-barbecue-and-ice-cream party. The **Flying L Ranch** (1½ miles south on Highway 173; 830-460-3001 or 800-292-5134; www.flyingl .com) has cabins and condos, a water park, golf and tennis facilities, lots of nightly programs for family, along with horseback riding. There is a full-service restaurant, snack and coffee bar, and two watering holes on the premises.

If you're on your own for meals, the **OST**—named for the Old Spanish Trail, on which Bandera lies—(305 Main St.; 830-796-3836) will do you right with its chicken-fried steak, biscuits and gravy, Mexican food, and grilled steaks.

On Wednesday evenings, the **11th Street Cowboy Bar** (307 11th St., Bandera; 830-796-4849; www.11thstreetcowboybar.com) hosts steak night, in which you bring your own slab of meat—or chicken, fish, veggies skewers, or whatever you can pick up from the local grocery stores—and cook your own steak over one of several charcoal grills set up and readied for you. There are marinades and seasonings in a common pantry for all to use, and for $5 per person, you get a plate loaded with salad and sautéed veggies to augment your grilled item. Beer, wine, and soft drinks are sold, and a country band plays for your dancing pleasure. Most every other night, the bar's stage features a country band of local, regional, or national renown.

Even people just passing through Bandera should take just 30 minutes or so to have a peek at one of the funkier collections ever assembled: *The Frontier Times Museum* (506 13th St., Bandera; 830-796-3864; www.frontier timesmuseum.com) exhibits more than 40,000 items, including bottles from Judge Roy Bean's saloon; 500 bells from around the world; antique firearms and saddles; and spear- and arrowheads.

On Thursday, Friday, and Saturday, you can enjoy a wine flight and cheeseboard at *Mulberry's* (823 Main St., Bandera; 830-796-9463), a wine bar with a surprisingly good selection. A cigar shop and smoke room is adjacent.

Immediately southwest of Bandera is *Hill Country State Natural Area* (830-796-4413; www.tpwd.state.tx.us), reached by driving south of Highway 173 to RR 1077, which you'll follow to the west for 10 miles. This 5,370-acre spread—once the Bar-O Ranch—is cloaked with oak and juniper and offers 32 miles of trails shared by hikers, mountain bikers, and equestrians. The 23 marked trails are often used by trail-riding guests at the nearby guest ranches, as these pathways take in sensational springs, waterfalls, creeks, and hilly vistas. The park is absolutely primitive, so backcountry camping is the only option. The park is closed on Tues and Wed; entry is $3 per person over 12 years of age.

Another appealing place in the Bandera area is the *Hill Country Equestrian Lodge,* about 10 miles outside of town just off RR 1077 (830-796-7950; www.hillcountryequestlodge.com). Unlike the other guest ranches around, this one gives you a chance to take private riding lessons or even bring your own horse. Guests who don't want to ride can amuse themselves by hiking, birding, fossil hunting, mountain biking (bring your own wheels), or spending the day fishing, inner tubing, or kayaking on the nearby Medina River.

The lodge offers cabins crafted from native limestone and rough cedar, with fireplaces, sleeping spaces for 4 or 6 guests, one or two bathrooms, full kitchens, and great decks from which to watch the sun rise or set. Breakfast goodies are supplied for you to fix your own.

All details on lodging, dining, shopping, and other diversions in Bandera are easily obtained at the *Bandera Convention & Visitors Bureau* (Highway 16 South, a half-block from Main Street; 800-364-3833; www.banderacowboy capital.com).

If you drive about 15 miles northwest from Bandera on Highway 16 to the town of *Medina,* you'll be in the *Apple Capital of Texas.* Be sure to stop in the *Apple Store,* where you'll find delicious bakery goods, ice cream, coffee with apple strudel flavoring, apple jelly, cider, and saplings. Find it at *Love Creek Orchards* (14024 TX 16 North), which grows 11 apple varieties, lets you pick your own fresh fruit, starting with blackberries in May and June;

apples in July; and figs in August. Contact the store at (800) 449-0882 or visit www.lovecreekorchards.com.

After living the ranch life, it may be time to search for more of that German Hill Country; you can do that by driving east on Highway 46, 23 miles from Bandera to **Boerne** (BURN-ee), seat of Kendall County, with a population of about 5,000. The cerebral Germans who settled the town in 1851 named it for Ludwig Boerne, one of their fellow countrymen who was a political satirist, journalist, and refugee. You may run into day-trippers from San Antonio, just 30 miles southeast, while out browsing through the creaky old antiques shops—packed with great little finds—or at one of the pleasant restaurants in town.

You can't go hungry in Boerne, that's certain. A favorite is **Po Po Family Restaurant** (at I-10, 7 miles west of Boerne, at the Welfare exit; 830-537-4194; www.poporestaurant.com), in an old stone house and former dance hall decorated with an array of at least 1,000 china plates on the wall, serving solid American and southern fare. It's open daily for lunch and dinner.

The town's lodging of choice is **Ye Kendall Inn** (128 W. Blanco, Boerne; 800-364-2138 or 830-249-2138; www.yekendallinn.com). Opened in 1859 as a stagecoach stop for travelers heading west from San Antonio, this handsome landmark with state and national historical markers has 34 restored rooms, suites, and cabins. It's a showplace, with 22-inch-thick limestone walls and old-fashioned verandas, all sitting on 5-plus acres on the Cibolo Creek and the town's fairy-tale plaza. The Studio YKI is an on-site fitness studio and wellness center with cardio and strength-training equipment, Pilates classes, and personal training. Good dining is had at the inn's **Limestone Grille** (128 W. Blanco St., Boerne; 830-249-2138 or 800-364-2138), where steaks, seafood, and salads are good choices.

A special place to visit in Boerne is the **Kuhlmann–King Historical House** (402 E. Blanco St., Boerne; 830-249-2030). Built in the late 1880s by German physicist William Kuhlmann, the 2-story house offers a look into life in that period. The separate Archives Building houses historical documents of the area. Call for tour times. A $2 donation is welcomed. It's one of several sites listed on the town historical walking tour; visit www.visitboerne.org for the route and any other Boerne information.

Spelunkers will be happy to know that two caves open to the public are nearby. The larger is **Cascade Caverns** (3 miles south on I-10 to Cascade Caverns Road; 830-755-8080; www.cascadecaverns.com), fascinating for its 90-foot interior waterfall, crashing from an underground stream. Tours last 45 minutes; a nice park with campsites, picnic areas, dance pavilion, swimming pool, snack bar, and bunkhouses is outside the cave. Admission is charged; open daily from 9 a.m. to 6 p.m.

The smaller cave in the area is simply known as *Cave Without a Name* (FR 474 east 6 miles to Kreutzberg Road, 5 miles along this road to the cave; 830-537-4212; www.cavewithoutaname .com), so called because the 1939 contest held to give it a title was won by a local boy who declared the cave "too pretty to name." The cave, 98 percent still active, is enormous—it takes from about an hour to 90 minutes to tour— and is filled with stalagmites and stalactites, "soda straws," "strips of bacon,"

"gnomes," and all sorts of mushrooming formations. Open every day except Thanksgiving and Christmas. Check www.cavewithoutaname.com for maps, photos, and admission prices.

Guadalupe River State Park (Highway 46 and PR 31, 16 miles east of Boerne; 830-438-2656; www.tpwd.state.tx.us) occupies 1,900 acres where cypress, limestone bluffs, and natural rapids blend to make a place of beauty on the gracious Guadalupe River. Canoeing, fishing, hiking, camping, and nature study are all available. Open daily; a small admission fee is charged.

Just in case you haven't had enough of Texas's rich German heritage, more awaits in *New Braunfels,* a 43-mile drive east of Boerne on Highway 46. The seat of Comal County, New Braunfels has more than 27,000 citizens and a history that was almost very romantic.

The story goes that the town was settled in 1845 by a German prince and 200 immigrants; the prince named his establishment for the town in Germany where his castle stood. He was to build a new castle for his fiancée, Princess Sophie, but she refused to come to this rough, unknown land, so he returned home to marry her and never saw Texas again. This and the remaining history of New Braunfels are told at the *Sophienburg Museum*—named

Conserve History

Conservation Plaza is where you'll go in New Braunfels to see priceless historic structures, including the Lindheimer Home, the Rose Conservatory, the Church Hill School, the Jahn Cabinet Shop, the Buckhorn Barber Shop, and the Wagenfuehr Home. The local conservation society's work is also seen in the Baetge House, built 26 miles from town but dismantled and relocated in the downtown plaza to display its fine example of *fachwerk* (half-timbered) construction, done in 1852 by a German engineer.

for her anyway—at 401 W. Coll St., New Braunfels; (830) 629-1572; www .sophienburg.org.

One of the state's lovelier places to rest is the ***Prince Solms Inn*** (295 E. San Antonio St., New Braunfels; 830-625-9169; www.princesolmsinn.com), a luxury bed-and-breakfast hotel filled with antiques and housing a day spa. The historic ***Hotel Faust*** (240 S. Seguin St., New Braunfels; 830-625-7791; www .fausthotel.com) is restored and filled with antiques.

If you happen upon New Braunfels in the fall, plan to dance a polka and drink a stein or two to the oompah-pah in Wursthalle, as the town hosts well over 100,000 people each year at ***Wurstfest,*** an enormous German party held over the first two weekends in November. A generous schedule of events is always offered, as are food and drink. For details call (830) 625-9167 or (800) 221-4369 or check www.wurstfest.com.

For anyone looking for a little watery excitement, head north a couple of miles to the restored town of Gruene (north on I-35 to FR 306, west about 1½ miles to Hunter Road, then follow the signs). There, on the Guadalupe River, several river outfitters (call 830-625-2385 for a list) offer trips lasting anywhere from 3 to 5 hours. If it's late spring or early summer, the river will probably run high and fast, so do as the instructors say and paddle like crazy through the little rapids. If it's late in summer and there hasn't been much rain, you're likely to have a slow trip. For a lonely, peaceful trip, tackle the river on a weekday, when high-spirited rafters and tubers won't be clogging the waters.

While in Gruene, plan to spend time poking around ***Gruene Historic District,*** a quaint 1870s cotton-gin town containing what is now the oldest dance hall in Texas; restored buildings housing antiques shops, clothing boutiques, woodwork, leather goods, and pottery shops; a winery tasting room; and good restaurants, starting with the ***Gristmill*** (1287 Gruene Rd.; 830-625-0684; www.gristmillrestaurant.com), purveyors of excellent fried catfish, grilled chicken, steaks, burgers, and frosty margaritas. On weekend nights there's live music on the patio under the stars.

Next door to the Gristmill, ***Gruene Mansion Inn*** (1275 Gruene Rd., Gruene; 830-629-2641; www.gruenemansioninn.com) is a gorgeous Victorian home overlooking the Guadalupe River and operating as a bed-and-breakfast inn.

From New Braunfels head north on I-35 just 16 miles to reach ***San Marcos,*** seat of Hays County and home to nearly 42,000 residents. The headwaters of the San Marcos River are here, where Native Americans are thought to have lived some 12,000 years ago, making this one of the oldest continuously inhabited places on the continent. Springs forming the river come from the Edwards Underground Reservoir, pushing up through the Balcones Escarpment limestone at a rate of at least a million gallons daily.

Summer Fun

An oldie but goodie, **Schlitterbahn** is a splashy, 65 acre spread in New Braunfels. Known for German-like castles, waterslides, hot tubs, uphill water coasters, inner-tube chutes, and six water playgrounds, the park's newest attraction is Hans's Hideout, a 5-story water funhouse with a pirate theme. Yo-ho-ho and a stein of beer. Open all summer, Schlitterbahn is located at 400 N. Liberty St., New Braunfels; (830) 625-2351; www.schlitterbahn.com.

Aquarena Springs (512-245-7570; www.aquarena.txstate.edu) was long the primary reason folks visited San Marcos. In 1994, however, Texas State University in San Marcos—whose wonderful red-topped spires are seen on a hill above town—purchased Aquarena Springs and closed the resort. Today it's called *Aquarena Center,* a center for the study of endangered species and archaeological finds on this site. Visitors can still enjoy the beautiful springs, feed the ducks, walk the scenic grounds, tour an 1846 log home, and ride the famous glass-bottom boats or take a kayak tour. Admission to the grounds is free, but a small fee is charged for boat rides. Hours vary, so call ahead.

To see another set of Hill Country caverns, head to *Wonder World* (1000 Prospect St., San Marcos; 512-392-3760; www.wonderworldpark.com). There's a 120-foot-tall observation tower and tour of the million-year-old limestone cave. Hours and fees vary according to season.

Canoeing is a hugely popular activity on the fabulous San Marcos River. Outfitters include *T.G. Canoe Livery* (512-353-3946; www.tgcanoe.com). Floating the river on inner tubes is another great way to pass a warm day; call *Lions Club Tube Rental* in summer, (512) 396-LION; www.tubessanmarcos.com.

While it's not the typical off-the-beaten-path sort of place, it's hard to resist shopping at the *Prime Outlets at San Marcos* center (on I-35 at exit 200 in San Marcos; 512-396-2200; www.primeoutlets.com). Possibly the state's top outlet mall (and that's saying something), this is the place to find great deals on clothes, shoes, housewares, gifts, lingerie, and more. Stores with deep discounts here include Crate & Barrel, Coach, Neiman Marcus, Nine West, Sharif Collection, Guess?, Brooks Brothers, and Vitamin World.

There's plenty more good shopping and dining in San Marcos, as well as three historic districts to tour. For information contact the *San Marcos Convention and Visitor Bureau* at (888) 200-5620 or check the website at www.toursanmarcos.com. You can also stop at the tourist information center at 617 I-35; it's open daily.

From San Marcos you're in for a day in shopping heaven and a charming bed-and-breakfast night at *Wimberley,* a 15-mile drive west of San Marcos via RR 12. It's a small town—population 3,000—but its stature is large, indeed, among the enlightened.

Here's a mini-resort town that happens to rest between two of the prettiest little streams in Texas—the Cypress Creek and the Blanco River. It's a hub of shopping activity on weekends, when dozens of pottery studios, art galleries, antiques shops, and boutiques are open for business. The *Blue Hole,* on Cypress Creek, is one of the state's primo swimming holes, and most guests at resorts, ranches, and B&Bs spend a few lazy hours floating under the clouds.

If you're in the humor for shopping, Wimberley is a great place to exercise those credit cards. On the square, which isn't square-shaped at all, you'll find *Rancho Deluxe* (512-847-9570), selling curios and imports from Mexico and Guatemala. Check out the *Broken Arrow Rock Shop* (512-847-2282) for gems and minerals.

Wimberley has become a prime place to unwind with expert help. *Serenity Farmhouse Spa* offers a full menu of services, as well as dining and lodging (888-882-8985).

Sweet tooths will have a heyday at *Wimberley Pie Co.* (on RR 12 just south of the square; 512-847-9462; www.wimberleypie.com), where you'll be wowed by aromas of 70 or so pies baking at once. Pie varieties include buttermilk, black bottom cherry cheesecake, key lime, and pecan. It's open Wed through Fri from 9:30 a.m. to 5:30 p.m., Sat from 10 a.m. to 5 p.m., and Sun noon to 4 p.m.

7A Ranch Resort (1 mile west on River Road from RR 12; 830-847-2517; www.7aresort.com) has rustic cottages and lodges, river frontage, and a reconstructed pioneer village–amusement park.

The most popular lodging in town is probably *Blair House Inn* (100 Spoke Hill Rd., Wimberley; 877-549-5450; www.blairhouseinn.com). There are 3 rooms in the main lodge, 3 rooms in the Pond Cottage, 2 rooms in the Honeysuckle Cottage, and 3 individual Archangel Cottages, all of which are impeccably outfitted for a luxurious stay. The dining room serves elaborate breakfasts daily and 5-course feasts (by reservation only) on Saturday night. A cooking school and day spa are on-site, too. Rooms begin at $150.

A good night's rest is needed to prepare you for a drive on the *Devil's Backbone,* the wildly twisting RR 32, reaching from RR 12 immediately south of Wimberley almost 25 miles toward Blanco. This, a dramatically nicknamed route, is easily a contender for the state's most scenic drive, cutting a winding path along a sharp ridge through the hills; be on the watch early or late in the day for white-tailed deer. It's spectacular at any time, but with spring wildflowers or autumn foliage, it's the ultimate.

Other Places to Stay in the Hill Country

BANDERA

Rancho Cortez
872 Hay Hollar Rd.
(830) 796-9339 or
(866) 797-9339
www.ranchocortez.com
Half dude ranch and half fitness camp, this ranch south of town and next to a vast state park attracts couples and families from around the world. There's a pool, plenty of exercise and health-improvement options, and beautiful views.

Running R Ranch
9059 Bandera Creek Rd.
(830) 796-3984
www.rrranch.com
In addition to lots of riding opportunities from a well-tended stable, there are cattle drives in which guests participate. You can even bring your own horse here.

FREDERICKSBURG

Inn on Baron's Creek Spa & Conference Center
308 S. Washington St.
(830) 990-9202 or
(866) 990-0202
www.innonbaronscreek
.com
Close to Main Street, this resort has 89 suites,

including 6 on the creek. Serenity Spa is on-site, along with a fitness center. Spa package deals start at about $350.

Rose Hill Manor
Upper Albert Road
(877) ROSE-HIL
www.rose-hill.com
Elegant inn on a hilltop in the countryside east of town offers 4 large suites in the main house, as well as a scattering of private cottages on the grounds. A lovely restaurant is on-site as well. Rooms start at about $159.

NEW BRAUNFELS

Kuebler-Waldrip Haus B&B
1620 Hueco Springs Loop
(830) 625-8300 or
(800) 299-8372
www.kueblerwaldrip.com

SAN MARCOS

Crystal River Inn
326 W. Hopkins St.
(512) 396-3739 or
(888) 396-3739
www.crystalriverinn.com

WIMBERLEY

The Homestead Bed and Breakfast
RR 12 at Scudder Lane
(512) 847-8788
www.homestead-tx.com
Eight cottages on Cypress Creek in town are available.

Southwind Bed and Breakfast
2701 FR 3237
(512) 847-5277 or
(800) 508-5277
www.southwindbedand
break.com
Cottages with hot tubs are offered.

Other Places to Eat in the Hill Country

BANDERA

Dogleg Coffeehouse
315 Main St.
(830) 796-8080
Fresh coffee drinks and scones make this a good morning stop.

Pike's Place
167 Panther Ridge,
Highway 16, near Pipe Creek
(830) 535-4442
Lovely restaurant with farm-to-table offerings serves soups, salads, fresh fish, steaks, and gorgeous desserts.

FREDERICKSBURG

August E's
6285 US 290 East
(830) 997-1585
www.august-es.com
Asian pumpkin–asparagus soup, sushi, glazed grilled quail, and marinated salmon are typical offerings. Open for lunch and dinner; closed Mon.

Cabernet Grill
At Cotton Gin Village
Just south of Fredericks-
burg on TX 16
(830) 990-5734
Serving steaks and sea-
food, this restaurant offers
a Texas-only wine list.

The Peach Tree Tea Room
210 S. Adams St.
(830) 997-9527
www.peach-tree.com
This lovely shop offers
lunches of salads, soups,
sandwiches, pasta, and
desserts Mon through Sun
and more elaborate fare Fri
and Sat.

GRUENE

Janie's Table
1299 Gruene Rd.
(830) 629-6121
Barbecue, burgers, enchiladas, desserts, Texas wines,
and beer provide rib-
sticking pleasure at lunch
and dinner.

JOHNSON CITY

The Hill Country Cupboard
at the junction of US 290
and US 281
(830) 868-4625
www.hillcountrycupboard
.com
Specialties are plate
lunches and dinners, plus
fresh bakery goods.

KERRVILLE

Francisco's Restaurant
201 Earl Garrett St.
(830) 257-2995
Cilantro-lime chicken,
chipotle shrimp, pob-
lano pasta, and Veracruz
nachos are among special-
ties in this art-filled space in
a historic downtown building. Open for lunch and
dinner; closed Sun.

SAN MARCOS

Texas Reds Steakhouse
120 Grove St.
(512) 754-8808

WELFARE

Welfare Cafe
223 Waring Welfare Rd.
(830) 537-3700
Pork tenderloin in dried
cherry-molasses glaze,
chicken sautéed with
peaches, and crab cakes
with smoked-jalapeño
tartar sauce stand out.
Serving dinner only, Wed
through Sun.

WIMBERLEY

Cypress Creek Cafe
320 RR 12
(512) 847-2515
www.cypresscreekcafe
.com

SOUTH TEXAS

Resting beneath the Hill Country's lower reaches, San Antonio is indisputably the gateway to vast south Texas—often a lonely, wide open region. Long, unhurried drives impart views that must have been overwhelming to early settlers, so endless are the fiercely blue sky and the ferocious and scrubby land.

The Spaniards came to colonize the new land, doing so mightily in the San Antonio area with their missions, and other Europeans eventually followed. Fanning southward from the great Alamo City are settlements reflecting varied origins, from Alsatian to Polish and, of course, Hispanic.

Only a few communities in south Texas are heavily populated, but most towns have surprising depth of character. In between are protracted stretches of road, ranch land, and thickets of mesquite—a tough tree if ever one lived. For an hour or more you'll see nothing piercing the horizon other than clumps of cacti, fence posts, an occasional telephone pole, a very rare windmill, and that tenacious mesquite. For anyone who appreciates truly raw beauty, this might be heaven.

Along the Mexican border various small settlements still simmer with Texas's Old West heritage, and all are permeated

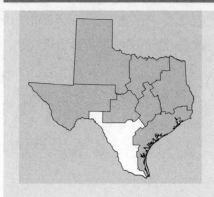

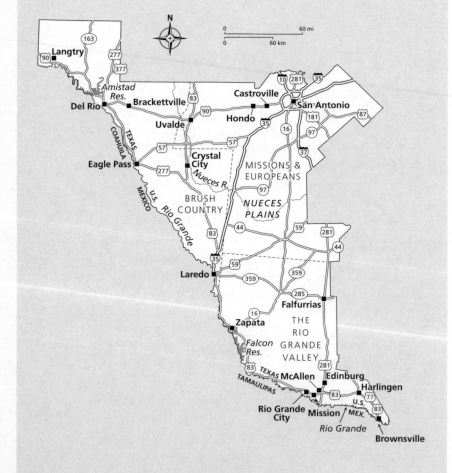

by a binational spirit that flows alongside the Rio Grande as it continues quietly and at length to the Gulf of Mexico. It's easy to picture, right there in your mind's eye, pioneer ranchmen of a century ago surveying the border, hoping somehow to tame a hopelessly wild land.

Missions & Europeans

Kaleidoscopic vistas of bluebonnets, Indian paintbrush, and other wildflowers frame US 281, Highway 16, and I-35 as you approach San Antonio in spring and summer, a subtle prelude to the year-round symphony of sights waiting in this cultural paradise. Get ready, because this vast storehouse of heritage and diversion knows how to entertain.

San Antonio, now the nation's seventh-largest city with 1.3 million residents, boasts healthy German and Native American influences, but Hispanic culture dominates the city. This Mexican-American accord will always be part of San Antonio, as the city was part of colonial or independent Mexico for nearly 150 years.

No written records tell us much of the area's early Native American period, but writings show that in the late 1690s resourceful Spaniards camped on the San Antonio River, which they called Rio San Antonio de Padua. Six Spanish missions were established in the early 1700s, but only five were successful. The first was Mission San Antonio de Valero in 1718, best known later under its nickname, *the Alamo.*

JUNE'S FAVORITE ATTRACTIONS

Casa de Palmas
McAllen

Fort Clark Springs
Brackettville

Institute of Texan Cultures
San Antonio

Lake Amistad
near Del Rio

Pearl Brewery
San Antonio

Seminole Canyon State Historical Park
Comstock

Southwest School of Art and Craft
San Antonio

Spanish Governor's Palace
San Antonio

Texas Iwo Jima War Memorial
Harlingen

World Birding Center
Mission

The Alamo mission doubled as a fort, where Davy Crockett, Jim Bowie, and William B. Travis were among the patriots who gave their lives for the Texas Revolution. For 13 days in late February and early March 1836, 187 men were surrounded and then crushed by the Mexican army. The would-be liberators managed to deplete Santa Anna's forces considerably before falling, enabling the Texans to win the Battle of San Jacinto and the revolution.

Heavy doors bearing bullet holes still front the Alamo, which sits before one of four Spanish plazas downtown, all connected by winding streets. Some people are disappointed to find the landmark to be such a small place, but its size doesn't diminish its significance. The Alamo, at 300 Alamo Plaza downtown, is open Mon through Sat from 9 a.m. to 5:30 p.m. and Sun from 10 a.m. to 5:30 p.m.; call (210) 225-1391 or visit www.thealamo.org for more information.

Behind the Alamo, in the elaborate RiverCenter Mall, there's an **IMAX Theatre** presenting an excellent, 42-minute docudrama entitled *Alamo: The Price of Freedom* on a 6-story-tall film screen. Historians double as actors in this production, telling a more factual story than the classic John Wayne movie version. For show schedule and ticket information, call (210) 247-4629 or (800) 354-4629 or visit www.imax-sa.com/movies/alamo/; an admission fee is charged.

Mission San Jose (6539 Mission San Jose Dr. at Mission Road, San Antonio; 210-932-1001), founded two years after the Alamo, is the most interesting of the four still functioning as churches. The mission, noted for its rare and opulent hand-sculpted rose window, is home each Sunday to a lively mariachi mass at noon. Today San Antonio is the only US city with as many missions within its city limits, and the five erected here comprise the **San Antonio Mission National Historic Park** (2202 Roosevelt Ave., San Antonio; 210-534-8833); missions are open daily in summer from 9 a.m. to 6 p.m. and in winter from 8 a.m. to 5 p.m. Visit www.nps.gov/saan for more information.

The Alamo Trolley offers a 1-hour narrated tour, stopping at the Alamo, HemisFair Park, Tower of the Americas, River Walk, La Villita, Market Square, San Fernando Cathedral, the Mission Trail, and the IMAX 3D Theatre. Your ticket (about $25) provides unlimited reboarding at the Alamo Trolley Hop Stops with your Hop Pass. You can buy tickets at the San Antonio Visitors Center on Alamo Plaza (210-247-0238; www.thealamotrolley.com).

The biggest of Texas's parties is **Fiesta San Antonio,** begun as a festival honoring visiting president Benjamin Harrison. Everyone had such a good time they didn't notice that the prez was a no-show, and the bash—now in its second century—is repeated annually. Fiesta, put on by some 50,000 residents, covers a 9-day period in the latter part of April and includes 150 events. Among the flashier are the Battle of Flowers Parade, the King's River Parade,

JUNE'S FAVORITE ANNUAL EVENTS

Texas Citrus Fiesta
Mission, late January

Charro Days
Brownsville, mid- to late February

Washington's Birthday
Laredo, second or third weekend in
February

Alamo Irish Festival
San Antonio, second weekend in March

Fiesta
San Antonio, mid-April

Texas Folklife Festival
San Antonio, second weekend in June

Candlelight Posada
McAllen, first weekend in December

Fiesta Night Parade, and A Night in Old San Antonio. There's also a king's coronation, Alamo pilgrimage, arts fair, and *charreada,* or Mexican rodeo. For information call the Fiesta office at (210) 227-5191 or (877) 723-4378 or visit www.fiesta-sa.org.

A rather bizarre cultural assemblage is that found at the **Buckhorn Saloon and Museum** (318 E. Houston St., San Antonio; 210-247-4000; www.buckhorn museum.com). See the museum's 118-year-old gallery of animal horns and antlers, plus hundreds of fish, bird, and large mammal trophies, combining to deliver visual overload. There's also a remarkable collection of antique and custom-made firearms, plus a wax museum that chronicles Texas history in figures from Cabeza de Vaca to Teddy Roosevelt. And finally, there's the pre-served San Antonio home of the writer O. Henry. Open daily from at least 10 a.m. to 6 p.m., some days to 8 p.m. (per manager's discretion). The museum charges admission.

Kids will find plenty to entertain them in San Antonio. For starters there's the **San Antonio Children's Museum** (305 E. Houston St., San Antonio; 210-212-4453; www.sakids.org). This entertaining, hands-on museum appeals to kids ages 2 to 10 and makes learning fun with all kinds of interactive educational exhibits. Closed Mon, the museum charges admission.

HemisFair Park (Alamo Street, I-37, Durango, and Market Streets) is home to the 750-foot Tower of the Americas, the symbol built for the 1968 World's Fair. A glass elevator whisks you to the top in less than a minute, and the sky-high restaurant makes one revolution per hour. On the ground there's a pleasant configuration of walkways, ponds, and waterfalls.

The park is home to the **Institute of Texan Cultures,** by far one of the nation's superior ethnic history museums and now associated with the

Texas Ghost Town

About an hour southeast of San Antonio in Karnes County lies the ghost town of *Helena,* population 35. Established in 1852 near the famed Chihuahua Trail and the Indianola–San Antonio Road, the rowdy frontier town saw plenty of shoot-outs—one too many, it seems. When 20-year-old Emmett Butler, an area resident, was killed during a saloon gunfight in 1884, his wealthy rancher father, Col. William Butler, vowed to kill the town that killed his son. By donating land miles away, he persuaded the railroad being built across south Texas to bypass Helena. Helena lost its county seat status, and the townsfolk moved away. The old courthouse, a post office, and a jail can still be seen.

Smithsonian Institution. Exhibits focus on the people of 26 ethnic and cultural groups of Texas; the multimedia show and museum store are also superb. Open Tues through Sat from 9 a.m. to 5 p.m. and Sun from noon to 5 p.m. Admission is charged. Call (210) 458-2300 for information or check www.texan cultures.utsa.edu.

From the HemisFair area, head west to **Market Square** (514 W. Commerce St., San Antonio; 210-207-8600; www.sanantonio.gov/marketsquare/), a re-created Mexican *mercado*. Time and money easily disappear among the bustle of mariachis, whir of margarita machines, and come-ons from vendors in hundreds of booths packed with arts, crafts, jewelry, and produce and other foods.

While you're there, **Mi Tierra** (210-225-1262; www.mitierracafe.com) is the place to find good Tex-Mex eats 24 hours daily—and the bakery case is where you'll satisfy that sweet tooth.

Near Market Square see what the National Geographic Society once called one of San Antonio's most beautiful buildings. The **Spanish Governor's Palace** (105 Plaza De Armas, San Antonio; 210-224-0601) was the former home of officials who governed the Spanish Province of Texas; over its entrance is the original keystone on which is carved the double-headed eagle of the Hapsburg coat of arms and the inscription in Spanish, "finished in 1749." Distinguishing features include the period furnishings and a spacious cobblestone patio with fountain and luxurious foliage. Open Mon through Sat from 9 a.m. to 5 p.m. and Sun from 10 a.m. to 5 p.m. A small admission fee is charged.

An extraordinary source of pride for more than 70 years is the **Witte Museum** (3801 Broadway St., San Antonio; 210-357-1866; www.wittemuseum .org). The exciting regional museum features history; science; the humanities; hands-on exhibits of Texas history, natural science, and anthropology;

changing exhibits; and family programs. Permanent exhibitions include *Texas Wild: Ecology Illustrated,* focusing on the ecological diversity of the state's seven natural areas. Recent additions to the Witte include the *H-E-B Science Treehouse,* a 4-story building full of multiple-level hands-on exhibits that make all kinds of scientific stuff a real treat for kids to explore. You'll also want them to have a look around *Ancient Texans,* a place to see pictographs from Native Americans of the Lower Pecos region, and *Unwrapping the Past,* an archaeological display that includes an Egyptian mummy. A walk-through diorama re-creates the south Texas thornbrush and its wildlife, including javelina, armadillo, and the endangered jaguar. The museum also includes an EcoLab of live Texas animals, an outdoor Butterfly and Hummingbird Garden, and five restored historic homes. The museum is open Mon through Sat from 10 a.m. to 5 p.m. (9 p.m. on Tues) and Sun from noon to 5 p.m. Admission is charged for visitors ages 4 and older.

History buffs will enjoy the **Texas Transportation Museum** (11731 Wetmore Rd. in McAllister Park; 210-490-3554; www.txtransportationmuseum.org), filled with antique pedicabs, horse-drawn and gas-powered vehicles, three model railroads, and technology and physics displays. Train rides are offered on Sunday afternoon from 1 to 3 p.m. with donation. The museum is open Thurs from 9 a.m. to 4 p.m. and Sat and Sun from 10 a.m. to 5 p.m. A small admission fee is charged.

Art is another of San Antonio's considerable strengths. The **McNay Art Museum** (6000 N. New Braunfels at US 81, San Antonio; 210-805-1754; www.mcnayart.org) is the former estate home of Marian Koogler McNay and now repository of Impressionist and post-Impressionist paintings (van Gogh, Monet, Picasso, Matisse, O'Keeffe, Goya, Renoir, and Bourdelle), early New Mexican arts and crafts, plus gothic and medieval collections and one of the nation's largest theater-arts collections. A highlight of the McNay is its charming patio and gardens and the excellent museum store. Open Tues through Sat from 10 a.m. to 5 p.m. and Sun from noon to 5 p.m. Donations are accepted.

The **San Antonio Museum of Art** (200 W. Jones Ave., San Antonio; 210-978-8100; www.samuseum.org) is housed inside the remarkable former Lone Star Brewery's castlelike building. Art collections range from ancient art to the most contemporary, including magnificent Greek and Roman sculpture and Latin American folk art. The Asian section has been expanded to include Asian sculpture as well as Chinese, Japanese, and Korean art. The museum is listed in the National Register of Historic Places. Open Tues from 10 a.m. to 8 p.m., Wed through Sat from 10 a.m. to 5 p.m., and Sun from noon to 6 p.m. A small admission fee is charged.

Two galleries worth seeking out are the *Blue Star Contemporary Art Center* (116 Blue Star St., San Antonio; 210-227-6960; www.bluestarart.org) and *ArtPace* (445 N. Main St., San Antonio, 210-212-4900; www.artpace.org). Blue Star is a very stylish, contemporary gallery in a fashionably renovated warehouse area, featuring such works as mixed-media paintings, papier-mâché sculptures, and videos. It's open Wed through Sun from noon to 6 p.m. Housed inside a renovated 1920s auto dealership, ArtPace features contemporary art that ranges from hand-tinted photos to mixed media from international artists. This gallery is open Wed through Sun from noon to 5 p.m.

The *Southwest School of Art and Craft* (300 Augusta St., San Antonio; 210-224-1848; www.swschool.org) occupies a former girls' school established by the Ursuline Order. The old convent and beautiful courtyard are the settings for classes, workshops, exhibitions, special events, and a restaurant. Artistic craftpersons create, exhibit, and sell a variety of items on-site, from weaving and macramé to pottery and wood carvings. Numerous classes are offered on a year-round schedule. Gallery hours are Mon through Sat from 10 a.m. to 5 p.m. and Sun from 11 a.m. to 4 p.m. Admission is free.

Just south of downtown, the *King William Historic District* (on and around King William Street; www.kingwilliamassociation.org) is a trove of wonderful mansions built by the city's German gentry. Walking and cycling this area on spring or fall days is a pleasure that will be long remembered, but you can have a look inside, too. The *Steves Homestead* (509 King William St., San Antonio; 210-227-9160; www.saconservation.org/tours/steves.htm) is a century-old Gothic Revival mansion on the San Antonio River containing period antiques owned and maintained by the San Antonio Conservation Society; a small admission fee is charged, and the home is open daily from 10 a.m. to 4:15 p.m.

haveaseat

Texas has everything else, so why not a *Toilet Seat Art Museum*? It's in San Antonio and contains the work of Barney Smith, who has painted more than 400 toilet seats for display in his garage. Inspired by his various journeys throughout the world, the artist opens his exhibit space when he's home. Call for directions and hours, (210) 824-7791.

Make it a point to visit *Guenther House* (205 E. Guenther St., San Antonio; 210-227-1061 or 800-235-8186; www.guentherhouse.com) in the King William Historic District. Inside you'll find historic items related to the development of Pioneer Flour Mills, an impressive collection of Dresden plates, a gift shop, and a restaurant. Museum and gift shop hours are Mon through Sat from 9 a.m. to 4 p.m. and Sun from 8 a.m. to 3 p.m. The restaurant is open from 7 a.m. to 3 p.m. daily. Admission is free.

The city is chock-full of art galleries, clothing boutiques, gift shops, craft markets, and the like. Those accessible on foot are found on the flagstone banks lining the **River Walk,** or **Paseo del Rio,** sitting beneath street level downtown and following the river's twisting contours. Arbors of palms, olive trees, cottonwoods, cypress, and willows shade sidewalk cafes, and pots of flowers are set between doors to shops, galleries, boutiques, hotels, bistros, and watering holes. Beware that crowds on weekends can be crushing.

River barges cruise the Paseo's 21 blocks, allowing visitors to review the retreats, unique retail shops, restaurants, and nightclubs. This 35 to 40-minute historical tour can be reserved by calling the Rio San Antonio River Cruise Tours at (210) 244-5700 or (800) 417-4139; www.riosanantonio.com. Special breakfast, lunch, or dinner cruises can be arranged, as well.

La Villita Historic Arts Village (418 Villita, facing the Convention Center, San Antonio; 210-207-8610; www.lavillita.com) is an unusual arts-and-crafts community adjacent to the River Walk. Working artists in 26 shops as well as three restaurants and a post office are within. You're likely to find irresistible creations such as Oaxacan rugs and Peruvian tapestries at Village Weavers; mixed-media paintings at Artistic Endeavors; stoneware and porcelain pottery at the Village Gallery; colorful Oaxacan animal sculptures at Casa Manos Allegres; and all manner of supplies at Bonsai Arbor. You'll also find the Old San Antonio Exhibit (located in Bolivar Hall), housing a small collection of art objects and artifacts relevant to San Antonio's earliest days. Open daily; admission is free.

The River Walk has recently expanded to include the deftly and extensively renovated **Pearl Brewery** (200 E. Grayson St.; 210-212-7260; www.atpearl .com), complex, which is reachable by river taxi, too. Found about a mile and a half due north of the Alamo, on what is called the Museum Reach of the San Antonio River, the Pearl sits along riverfront with a landscaped park, amphitheater, plentiful shopping, and dining and cultural experiences. Among favorite destinations at Pearl, the **Culinary Institute of America** (312 Pearl Pkwy.; 800-285-4627; www.ciachef.edu/sanantonio)—this is only the second outpost opened outside of New York—offers day, weekend, and weeklong cooking programs, along with its 2-year schedule for professional chefs. There's also an **Aveda Institute,** where you can enjoy a makeover, and a fabulous Saturday farmers' market, too. Among restaurants not to miss, **La Gloria** (100 E. Grayson St.; 210-267-9040; www.lagloriaicehouse.com) brings the best dishes from the heart of Mexico; and **Osteria Il Sogno** (200 E. Grayson St.; 210-223-3900) will spoil you for antipasto forever. Leave time to shop at **Melissa Guerra Tienda de Cocina** (200 E. Grayson St.; 210-293-3983; www.melissaguerra.com), a spectacular kitchenware store. Find more detail by going to www.atpearl.com.

San Antonio's sightseeing and shopping are nothing if not exhausting, so it's probably time to check into the ***Menger Hotel*** (204 Alamo Plaza, San Antonio; 210-223-4361 or 800-345-9285; www.mengerhotel.com), outfitted with the Alamo Plaza Spa, where an old-fashioned 2-hour treatment includes steam bath, sauna, and herbal scrub. The Menger, next door to the Alamo, was a splendid hotel at its 1859 opening, and its claim to fame is that Teddy Roosevelt came to this wild and raucous city and this very hotel in 1898 to recruit his Rough Riders—or so the story goes. It's still a good hotel with choice rooms in the older section, and the bar has a friendly, comfortable feel.

Travelers will have to look long and hard to find better Mexican food anywhere else. The first of two favorites is ***Los Barrios*** (4223 Blanco St., San Antonio; 210-732-6017), a delightful family operation with hearty Mexican and South American dishes of beef, chicken, and soups. Open for lunch and dinner daily, prices start at about $12. More elaborate in decor and menu, ***La Fogata*** (2427 Vance Jackson at Addax Street, San Antonio; 210-340-1337; www.lafogata .com) continues to pull people in droves to its rambling patios and its unbeatable chiles rellenos, flaming cheese, enchiladas, and possibly the best salsa anywhere. Open for lunch and dinner daily, meals average about $10 to $12.

Keep in mind that the Alamo City grows ever more popular: Polls conducted by a national travel magazine show San Antonio ranking consistently in the top 10 favorite US destinations. Between 10 and 11 million people visit annually, so don't think you can just show up and get a room in the central area without a reservation.

Easily one of the most beautiful lodgings in all of San Antonio—and there are plenty of them—is ***Beckmann Inn and Carriage House*** (222 E. Guenther St., San Antonio; 210-229-1449 or 800-945-1449; www.beckmanninn.com). Right in the heart of the King William Historic District and listed among the city's historic landmarks, the home was built in 1886 by Albert Beckmann for his bride, Marie Dorothea, daughter of the Guenther Flour Mill family, on the mill grounds. Immediately winning is the wraparound porch, where wicker furniture is perfect for enjoying a cup of tea or coffee. Design includes a rare burl pine front door, wood mosaic floor imported from Paris, and beveled glass windows. One of three guest rooms in the main house has a fireplace, and all have private baths. The carriage house features 2 private suites, each with sitting room and private bath. Gourmet breakfasts typically include juices, hot entrees, fresh fruit, and coffee cake. There is a two-night minimum stay on weekends.

Just as luxurious is the ***Oge House*** on the River Walk (209 Washington St., San Antonio; 210-223-2353 or 800-242-2770; www.ogeinn.com). Located in the King William Historic District, this gorgeous and extensively refurbished 1857 home is packed with period antiques and offers 9 rooms, many with fireplaces.

A relatively quiet River Walk lodging is the ***Hotel Havana,*** a 1914 downtown national historic landmark, recently renovated by the owners of the Hotel San Jose and the Saint Cecilia in Austin. Period Cuban music seeps from unseen speakers throughout the vintage-chic, 27-room hotel, whose design features hardwood floors, high ceilings, Persian area rugs, and a dark, sexy bar. A restaurant is on-site, as well. Find this hideout at 1015 Navarro St., San Antonio, (210) 222-2008; www.havanasanantonio.com.

Complete information is offered by the ***San Antonio Convention and Visitor Bureau,*** (210) 270-6700 or (800) 447-3372; a handy visitor center is situated steps from the Alamo at 317 Alamo Plaza, San Antonio. It's open daily from 8:30 a.m. to 6 p.m. Call (210) 207-6748 or visit the website at www.visit sanantonio.com.

Head to ***Castroville,*** 20 miles west on US 90, a town of just more than 2,500 in Medina County. It became the Little Alsace of Texas after founder Henri Castro brought a band of Alsatian settlers with him from that region of France. It's the only Alsatian community in the country, and it has clung tightly to its heritage; it's a lucky visitor who comes across descendants of those settlers, especially those who can speak the original, unwritten dialect, which is more German than French.

For a look into Alsatian history, visit ***Mount Gentilz Cemetery*** (US 90 and Alsace Street), also called Cross Hill. Here you'll have a far-reaching view of the Medina Valley, and you can see the burial spot of Amelia Castro, Henri's wife.

Also see ***St. Louis Catholic Church*** (US 90 and Angelo Street), built in 1868–70 next to the colonists' original chapel, constructed in 1846. The big, 3-story building is the ***Moye Center,*** a convent erected in 1873 for the Sisters of Divine Providence.

Travelers will be pleased to find the Alsatian community's ***Landmark Inn State Historic Site*** (Florence and Florella Streets, Castroville; 830-931-2133; www.visitlandmarkinn.com), a hotel on the San Antonio–El Paso road when built in 1863; it's said that Robert E. Lee was among its guests. Now it's the only historic inn run by the state, which restored it to a 1940s look. A visitor center and an old gristmill are here, too.

simplybatty

Although everyone expects Austin to hold this honor, it's actually a spot about 20 miles north of San Antonio that is home to the world's largest bat colony. Austin is the largest urban colony. The ***Bracken Cave Colony*** is a population of some 20 to 40 million bats, thought to be the largest congregation of mammals anywhere, eating some 250,000 pounds of insects nightly during summer months.

Continue west from Castroville on US 90, traveling another 20 miles to **Hondo,** which became the seat of Medina County after the Southern Pacific Railroad bypassed Castroville in the 1880s. Today it's a community of 6,000 known best for attractions of the four-legged kind.

Much older and far more exotic, **dinosaur tracks** cast in stone are easily viewed in Hondo Creek's bed, almost 24 miles north of town via FR 462. Scientists speculate these were made by 15-ton, 40-foot herbivores called trachodons.

Forty-two miles farther west on US 90, **Uvalde,** seat of the same-named county and home to 15,000 residents, is known as the crossroads of two roads spanning the whole country—US 90 and US 83—and a fat little pocket of Old West and US history.

In the 1880s, J. K. King Fisher and Pat Garrett—two unforgettable lawmen of their day—lived in Uvalde. Fisher was an outlaw who became a deputy, though some said he was both at the same time, and Garrett was the man who killed Billy the Kid in nearby New Mexico in 1881.

Uvalde's John Nance Garner served as vice president of the US from 1933 to 1941; his life is chronicled in detail at the **Garner Museum** (333 N. Park St., Uvalde; 830-278-5018). Garner went to Congress in 1903 during Teddy Roosevelt's administration, served as Speaker of the House, and stayed in Washington, serving as the number two man under FDR. It's said that his signature Texan candidness earned him the nickname "Cactus Jack." The museum is housed in his former home, a beautiful building; Garner died shortly before his 99th birthday and was buried at the west end of **City Cemetery** (on US 90 West). The museum is open Tues through Sat from 9 a.m. to 5 p.m.

Take time to look at **Uvalde Grand Opera House** (104 W. North St. at N. Getty Street, Uvalde; 830-278-4184). A building befitting its name, this 2-story creation seated 370 patrons and is now partially occupied by a museum. Open Mon through Fri from 9 a.m. to noon and 1 to 5 p.m., Sat from 10 a.m. to 3 p.m. Admission is free.

With big skies and pretty rivers nearby, Uvalde's fine for hanging around for a couple of days. Several options for lodging are available just 24 miles north via US 83 in Concan. Check with the Uvalde Convention and Visitor Bureau at 300 E. Main Ave., Uvalde. Call 800-5-UVALDE or visit www.visit uvalde.com for details.

Brush Country

From Uvalde, proceed 40 miles west on US 90 to reach **Brackettville,** seat of Kinney County. Be assured that this is the epitome of isolation: There's only one other town in the county.

You'll see a familiar sight here, and maybe it will seem like a mirage: The Alamo right here in Brackettville's **Alamo Village** is the one from the 1959 John Wayne movie, not the one in San Antonio. That's because an entire set had to be built for the epic film—it's still one of the larger and more thorough sets ever built in this country—and this lonesome land provided ideal scenery. Adobe craftsmen from Mexico created the Alamo replica, which continues to overlook a complete frontier village straight out of the 19th century. Rounding out the village are a cantina and restaurant, stage depot, jail, bank, livery, and trading post. In summer there are musical shows and melodramas, often interrupted by Old West gunfights. The village is open Thurs through Sat, 10 a.m. to 3 p.m., except December 21 to 26. Call (830) 563-2580 or visit www .alamovillage.com for details.

On the town's eastern edge on US 90, find **Fort Clark Springs,** a resort resting on old Fort Clark, one of the country's best-preserved cavalry posts. Built in 1852 to protect settlers against Indians and banditos, the fort is famous for having been the training ground for 90 years for several infantry units, including the Ninth and Tenth Infantry's black Buffalo Soldiers and almost all of the army cavalry units. Others stationed at Fort Clark included generals George S. Patton Jr. and George C. Marshall. Historic buildings remain, some of which have been restored. The Old Guardhouse contains a small museum, and the resort offerings include a motel in old limestone barracks; two restaurants; a large spring-fed pool; tennis courts and golf courses; and a fitness center. Call (800) 937-1590 or (830) 563-2493 or visit www.fortclark.com for details.

At **Seminole Indian Scout Cemetery,** 3 miles south of town on FR 3348, you'll find the burial sites of several scouts hired by the army to help in campaigns against the warring Apaches. These Seminoles were descended from escaped Georgia slaves who intermarried with Florida Native Americans and moved west. Four of those buried here received the prestigious Congressional Medal of Honor, and some of the Seminole offspring still reside in Brackettville, working at ranching or farming.

From Brackettville, keep steady on US 90 another 32 miles to **Del Rio,** the seat of Val Verde County and nicknamed "Queen of the Rio Grande." In this corner of dry, hot south Texas, Del Rio is a blessing, as it rests atop bubbling San Felipe Springs, the outlet of an underground river pouring forth 90 million gallons of crystal-clear water daily. That's why you see so many ranches around—the irrigation opportunity is abundant for those prospering in sheep and Angora goat ranching nearby.

One look at the ornate, gothic 1887 **Val Verde County Courthouse** is to understand the wealth and depth of history in this town. Stop by the Del Rio Chamber of Commerce (1915 Avenue F, Del Rio; 830-775-3551; www.dr

George West

Leaving San Antonio, the land flattens out considerably and reveals a thick carpet of mesquite, prickly pear, and occasional lechuguilla. Cruising past Three Rivers, a jumping-off spot for the oasis that is Choke Canyon State Park, stop some 80 miles south of the Alamo at *George West,* the seat of Live Oak County and birthplace of legendary writer J. Frank Dobie, resting along the Nueces River. On the courthouse lawn you'll see Geronimo, a rather mangy stuffed version of the 2,200-pound steer who had his own pasture on the giant local ranch. Since 1927, Geronimo has displayed his 9-foot, 6-inch horn span behind glass in his own small stone building; he left, however, for a time in 1976 when he went with an Americana tour to Moscow. Just outside of town, in the median along a four-lane stretch of US 281, is the biggest live oak in this part of the state, surely thousands of years old.

chamber.com) and pick up the detailed walking guide and map of 34 historic homes, buildings, and sites, many dating to a romantic, if tumultuous, time in Texas history.

Another gaping surprise out here is *Lake Amistad,* home of *Amistad National Recreation Area,* 10 miles northwest of town via US '90. This 67,000-acre, vividly blue impoundment on the Rio Grande is a perfect example of the unity enjoyed today between Mexico and the US, and particularly Texas. As the US shares the river with Mexico, it also shares the dam creating the mesmerizing binational lake, which stretches 75 miles upriver and offers 1,000 miles of shoreline. Fishing permits are offered by both countries, and there are dozens of other diversions, including camping, boat rentals, picnicking, and bow hunting. The dam is topped by a 6-mile road that connects the lake's two sides. For information contact the National Park Service office on US 90 West, just at the Del Rio city limits, at (830) 775-7491.

One of the best hideouts in south Texas is *Laguna Diablo Resort,* found about 20 minutes northwest of Del Rio on the Devil's River arm of Lake Amistad (830-774-2422 or 866-227-7082; www.lagunadiablo.com). The humble lodge is made up of several native rock and rough-wood apartments with either one or two bedrooms, full-size kitchens, bath and living areas, barbecue grill, all kitchen utensils, and linens. Try to get a unit with a big porch overlooking the water. It's not a fancy place, but it's clean and the setting is magnificent.

Another look into history is discovered at *Val Verde Winery* (100 Qualia St., Del Rio; 830-775-9714; www.valverdewinery.com), Texas's oldest winery, begun in 1883 by Italian immigrant Frank Qualia. It's still in the same family, whose members offer free tours of the vineyards, storage vats, aging room, and bottling processors. Among eight wines made here, one is the Lenoir, the first wine produced more than 110 years ago. Tasting and buying opportunities follow the tour. It's open Mon through Sat from 10 a.m. to 5 p.m.

Set aside ample time for two outstanding side trips from Del Rio, which can be done on the same drive northwest of the city along US 90. The first stop is **Seminole Canyon State Historical Park,** 45 miles from Del Rio and about 9 miles past the village called Comstock. The rugged setting of desert and canyons showcases a collection of Indian paintings and pictographs thought to be more than 8,000 years old. Look in Fate Bell Shelter, just below the park's interpretive center, for the most brilliant pictographs. Discoveries of other human artifacts—possibly 12,000 years old—and the drawings have combined to give scientists some ideas of daily life all those millennia past, which are illustrated in a life-size diorama at the visitor center. Call to inquire about ranger-led tours, usually offered on weekends. The park is open daily from 8 a.m. to 10 p.m. and at all times for campers. Admission is $2 per person 13 and older; call (432) 292-4464 or visit www.tpwd.state.tx.us.

The second side trip from Del Rio is **Langtry,** only 20 miles beyond Seminole Canyon on US 90, still in Val Verde County. The desperately lonely Wild West outpost was founded in 1881, when the railroad came through, representing the junction of eastbound and westbound construction. How the town's name came about is still up for debate: Some historians believe that the civil engineer, a man called Langtry, who directed a crew of Chinese railroad laborers, is the source, but romantics stick with the story of Judge Roy Bean, who said he named the town for his favorite actress, the Jersey Lily, Englishwoman Lillie Langtry.

Worth the trip alone, the **Judge Roy Bean Visitor Center** is the preserved site of the infamous, unforgettable Law West of the Pecos, whose 1880s rule was a masterful blend of wit and bravery. Travelers find the rustic saloon, courtroom, and pool hall that was Bean's, along with a visitor center staffed by counselors and stocked with loads of free brochures, maps, guides, and varied information. Outside there's a cactus garden with indigenous southwestern plant life. Open daily from 8 a.m. to 5 p.m., the center's phone number is (432) 291-3340.

Notice on your way to Langtry, about 18 miles east of town, there's a terrific **Pecos River Canyon scenic overlook,** offering a stunning view of the formidable canyon. This is an ideal place to stretch your legs, and a picnic area is right there if you've brought lunch along.

texastrivia

In 1900 Texas had 26 wineries; only one of those remains operational today: **Val Verde Winery** in Del Rio outlasted the Prohibition era.

From Del Rio, you can begin making tracks to the southeast along the Rio Grande, traveling 56 miles on US 277 to **Eagle Pass,** the seat of Maverick County and home to 20,650 residents. An early US settlement during the Mexican War, it's where the government founded Fort Duncan in 1849 and remains a gateway to Mexico today.

Have a look into that window of history at the **Fort Duncan Museum** (on Bliss Street between Monroe and Adams Streets; 830-758-1445), housed in the old headquarters. There are archaeological exhibits, as well as details on the Kickapoo tribe nearby, and 11 surviving buildings. The history told here is of the post's closing in 1900, then reopening in 1916 during the Mexican Revolution, and its use as a World War I training base. Among famous officers who spent time here were Phil Sheridan, James Doolittle, and Matthew Ridgway. Open Mon through Sat from 1 to 5 p.m.

From Eagle Pass, travel 50 miles east on US 277 and east on FR 191 to **Crystal City.** It may seem odd, but this seat of Zavala County and town of 8,000 is home to a big **statue of Popeye the Sailor,** found in front of city hall on the square. Well, it's not so strange after all—this town calls itself the Spinach Capital of the World for its huge production of spinach. Look also for farmers selling watermelons, tomatoes, onions, carrots, and peppers from their pickup trucks.

It's 92 miles straight south on US 83 from Crystal City to **Laredo,** seat of Webb County, with more than 175,000 residents. Rich in history and culture, Laredo is the place for more of that beloved binational experience. Since its founding by Don Tomás Sánchez, a captain in the Spanish colonial army, on May 15, 1755, Villa San Agustín de Laredo has served as everything from a raiding site for Lipan Apaches and Comanches, a cattle and sheep ranching community, and an outpost for the expanding New Spain to capital of the Republic of the Rio Grande and an international commerce center.

Here you'll find numerous historic neighborhoods and buildings. While you're looking around downtown, be sure to pay attention to **San Agustín Plaza,** bordered by Grant, Zaragoza, Flores, and San Agustín Streets; here you'll see the beautiful **St. Agustín Church,** a Gothic Revival masterpiece, and several remarkable buildings in designs ranging from Mexican colonial and Mexican vernacular to Victorian and neoclassical revival, dating from the 1700s.

Facing the plaza, **La Posada Hotel** (1000 Zaragoza, Laredo; 956-722-1701 or 800-444-2099; www.laposadahotel.com) occupies the former Laredo High School, built in 1916. The hotel is nothing short of lovely, with an exquisitely blue-tiled pool surrounded by a lush courtyard. The food is fair to good in the hotel's restaurants, the best being the **Tack Room,** upstairs in an adjacent building that was once the town's telephone exchange. You'll find big steaks, spareribs, chicken, and fish on the menu.

Laredo's supply of Mexican food will keep your motor running. Start your day with a blast at *Las* Cazuelas (303 Market St., Laredo; 956-723-3693). Be bold and have a breakfast taco packed with stewed meat, potato and eggs, or avocado. Soups are excellent at lunch. Open daily from 6:30 a.m. to 2:30 p.m.

If you happen upon Laredo in February, you may be in for a real treat during *George Washington's Birthday Celebration,* a two-week party held annually since 1898. The fiesta includes parades, pageants, fireworks, dances, a jalapeño festival (one contest challenges brave souls to gobble as many jalapeños as possible in 15 minutes!), carnival, *charreada* (Mexican rodeo), and an occasional bullfight.

The Rio Grande Valley

Back on the road, it's another 49 miles south on US 83 to *Zapata,* seat of Zapata County and home to 4,800 Texans. Named in honor of Antonio Zapata, the renowned Mexican pioneer and tough Indian fighter, the town is mostly a supply point for outdoor enthusiasts embarking on an adventure at *Falcon State Park* (28 miles south on US 83, FR 2098, and PR 46; (956) 848-5327; www.tpwd.state.tx.us). The shores of the enormous international lake, impounded on the Rio Grande, offer more than 500 acres for camping, picnicking, fishing, and swimming. There are groceries at the park, too, as well as a snack bar. Admission is $2 per person; the park is open daily.

From Zapata, it's 51 miles south on US 83 till you reach *Rio Grande City,* seat of Starr County, with a population of nearly 12,000. The town came about in 1848 when Gen. Zachary Taylor established Fort Ringgold, which was named for Maj. David Ringgold, the first army officer killed in the Battle of Palo Alto, opening the Mexican War. The fort remained active until 1944 and was home to Col. Robert E. Lee when he commanded the Department of Texas prior to the Civil War.

Travelers will want to pause in Rio Grande City just to stay at *La Borde House* (601 E. Main St., Rio Grande City; 956-487-5101), the 1899 home and border mercantile built by a French merchant and riverboat trader who had the house designed in Paris, then refined by San Antonio architects. Renovated about 30 years ago, the home was made into a hotel and contains sublime Victorian furniture and antiques. With shaded verandas, courtyard, patio, parlor, guest rooms, and restaurant, it's the rare showplace along this part of the Rio Grande.

Continuing south on US 83 just 12 miles, watch for FR 886, which you'll turn right onto for 2 miles until you reach the Rio Grande and a sight found nowhere else on a US border. The *Los Ebaños Ferry* is a wooden, two-car ferry hand pulled by a Mexican staff using ropes. Rumors of its replacement by a bridge seem to be unfounded, as it was recently restored to prime condition. Its operation is from 8 a.m. until 3:30 p.m. daily, but service suspends during the month of April, when irrigation in the Rio Grande valley brings the water level too high in this area for the ferry to run. Fares are $2.50 per vehicle and 50 cents per pedestrian. For details, call (956) 485-2855.

Another 14 miles south on US 83, **Mission** is an 1824 settlement where the Rio Grande valley's famous citrus industry was begun, possibly by the original priests. Today the town of 45,000 in Hidalgo County is Home of the Grapefruit, specifically the famous Texas ruby red. Mission is not only the citrus center but also the state's poinsettia center and home of the nation's only all-poinsettia show, held annually in December. Most Texans—and all Rio Grande valley residents—will also proudly tell you that Mission is the birthplace of Tom Landry, the first (and 30-year) coach of the Dallas Cowboys. See his mural on a building downtown at Conway Avenue at Tom Landry Street.

Should you join other Winter Texans for a January stay in the valley, rest up for the more than 70-year-old **Texas Citrus Fiesta,** held the last week of the month all over the area. The bash consists of a grand parade, barbecue cook-off, carnival, dances, citrus judging, arts and crafts show, sporting events, and a spectacular citrus products costume style show. For information call the **Mission Chamber of Commerce** at (956) 585-2727 or (800) 580-2700, or visit www.missionchamber.com.

La Lomita Chapel (on FR 1016, 3 miles south of town) was first an adobe way station dating to 1865 for Oblate padres traveling on horseback upriver from Brownsville. The present, rebuilt version, erected in sandstone in 1889, is a tiny structure with original floors, rough beamed ceilings, and an outdoor beehive oven. It sits in a 7-acre park with picnic areas, barbecue grills, restrooms, walkways, and historic site signs.

For still more outdoors, head for **Bentsen–Rio Grande Valley State Park** (6 miles southwest on US 83, FR 2062, and PR 43; 956-585-1107; www.tpwd.state.tx.us), 760 acres of land along the Rio Grande with excellent bird watching, especially for the Audubon's oriole, hooded oriole, zone-tailed hawk, and redeye cowbird. At the park office, pick up lists and booklets on these, as well as mammals, herbs, plants, butterflies, and other flora and fauna to be seen on nature trails. Camping, picnicking,

texastrivia

The south Texas town of Luling hosts an annual **Watermelon Thump** in June, a 4-day festival celebrating the annual crop and the traditional thumping to test the melon's readiness.

and boating are options, too. The park is open daily. A small admission fee is charged.

The Bentsen–RGV park also functions as the headquarters for the wonderful **World Birding Center,** the most exciting nature facility to open in south Texas. The spectacular new buildings, along with exhibits, trails, bird-viewing blinds, and bird-feeding and watering stations, cost roughly $7 million. You'll find more great birding information than you ever thought possible, as well as a good gift shop and snack bar. Read more at www.worldbirdingcenter.org.

McAllen, 10 miles east along US 83, also lies in Hidalgo County and is home to 106,000 residents. The hub of activity in the lower Rio Grande valley, McAllen appeals to retirees from the Midwest and Canada who spend entire winters here in the subtropical environs.

McAllen International Museum of Art & Science (1900 Nolana St., McAllen; 956-682-1564; www.imasonline.org) has a wonderful Mexican folk-art mask and textile collection, as well as contemporary American and regional prints, sculptures, and oils from 16th- to 19th-century Europe. Open Tues and Sat from 9 a.m. to 5 p.m., until 8 p.m. Thurs, and Sun from 1 to 5 p.m. A small admission fee is charged.

The citrus season lasts from October through April; to pick some citrus for yourself or buy your own crates, head over to **Bell's Farm to Market** (116 S. Ware Rd., McAllen; 956-630-1015 or 800-798-0424; www.bellsfarm.com), a great place to buy fruits to be shipped home. Gift packs are sold, and an adjacent garden center offers exquisite tropical foliage.

If you find yourself in McAllen around the holidays, try to catch the lovely **Candlelight Posada,** typically held the first full weekend in December in Archer Park. You'll see traditional Christmas entertainment and caroling in the burnished glow of luminarias, and you'll be moved by the beautiful Mexican posada, or candlelit posada, that represents the journey of Mary and Joseph as they look for a place to rest so that the Christ child can be born. For details contact the **McAllen Convention and Visitors Bureau** at (956) 682-2871 or visit www.mcallen.org.

Close to downtown and the lovely Casa de Palmas hotel you'll find an exquisite Mexican dinner at **Costa Messa Restaurant** (1621 N. 11th St., McAllen; 956-618-5449; www.costamessarestaurant.com). Painted in serene shades of blue and coral, the dining room is a relaxing place in which to feast on grilled steak with enchiladas, seafood soup, and an excellent chile relleno stuffed with shredded beef. Don't miss the appetizer of grilled onion with bacon and jalapeño. Open for lunch and dinner.

A side trip to take if you have a free morning or afternoon—and if it's not too awfully hot—is to **Santa Ana National Wildlife Refuge** (US 83 east to

Alamo, south on FR 907, 7 miles to US 281, and east to the entrance; 956-784-7500; www.fws.gov/southwest/refuges/texas/santana.html). Here 2,000 acres of subtropical foliage provide a habitat for an astounding variety of bird species, some of which aren't found elsewhere in the US. The species list of nearly 400 can be picked up at the visitor center, and three nature trails are offered. In the winter a tram tour is available. Trails are open daily from sunrise until sunset, and the visitor center is open daily from 9 a.m. to 4:30 p.m. Admission is free, but tram tours, which run Thurs through Mon, cost $3 for adults and $1 for children. Note: Use insect repellent before going out on trails.

texastrivia

McAllen in the Rio Grande valley is called the **Square Dance Capital of the World.** Each fall some 10,000 square dancers swing their partners during winter months in the warm climate.

Head north of McAllen 8 miles on US 281 to **Edinburg,** the Hidalgo County seat, on Saturday night to see a proud Texas tradition, the rodeo. The **Sheriff's Posse Rodeo** is a weekly offering, with cowboys demonstrating calf roping, bull riding, and quarter horse racing. The rodeo arena is 2 miles south of town on US 281. Admission is free.

Just a couple of miles east of McAllen via US 83, the San Juan exit delivers you to the doors of the **Shrine of La Virgen de San Juan del Valle** (US 83 and Raul Longoria Road; 956-787-0033; www.olsjbasilica.org/web/home). This impressive church was built to the tune of $5 million—mostly paid for by small contributions—after the elaborate 1954 original was destroyed when a plane was deliberately crashed into it. The wooden La Virgen statue wasn't harmed, and now it has a special place at the center of a 100-foot wall. Open daily from 6 a.m. to 8 p.m.

texastrivia

Country-western musician and singer **Freddie Fender** was born Baldemar G. Huerta in San Benito.

It's but 30 miles east from McAllen on US 83 to **Harlingen,** a town of nearly 80,000 in Cameron County named for a city in the Netherlands. The town was called Sixshooter Junction for a wild time around 1910 and the Mexican Revolution, when frequent bandit raids necessitated the peacekeeping efforts of the Texas Rangers and mounted patrols from US Customs. The National Guard was eventually brought in to help the Rangers when, it's said, there were more firearms than citizens in town.

A somewhat unexpected treat is found at Harlingen's **Marine Military Academy and Texas Iwo Jima War Memorial** (320 Iwo Jima Blvd.,

Harlingen; 956-423-6006). The Public Affairs Office will tell you if any parades or activities are scheduled that offer the chance to see a US Marines–style private academy at work. On the campus is the original working model for the Iwo Jima Memorial bronze statue at Arlington National Cemetery, donated to the academy by sculptor Dr. Felix W. de Weldon in 1981. The figures are 32 feet high, the M-1 rifle is 16 feet long, the flagpole is 78 feet long, and the canteen could hold 32 quarts of water. The pole flies a cloth flag. The Marine placing the flagpole in the ground was Corp. Harlon Block from nearby Weslaco, who was later killed in battle.

Good Harlingen eats, such as hearty dishes of smoked pork, beef ribs, hot Polish sausage, chicken, and turkey, are served at *Lone Star* (4201 Business Highway 83, Harlingen; 956-423-8002). It's open daily for lunch and dinner, and prices start at about $8. If your mouth waters for huge platters of fajitas, however, head to *Los Asados* (210 N. US 77/Sunshine Strip, Harlingen; 956-421-3074). Just south of Harlingen in San Benito, try *Longhorn Cattle Company* (3055 W. US 83, San Benito; 956-399-9151 or 956-399-4400). Smoked beef brisket, sweet pork ribs, and all the fixin's are served while you watch longhorn cattle graze out in the pastures. Open for lunch and dinner Tues through Sun; prices start at about $8.

The final leg of the valley tour is a 26-mile stint south from Harlingen on US 83/US 77 to *Brownsville,* seat of Cameron County and city of 140,000 Texans. While it's a pleasant place near the ocean and a popular gateway to Mexico, Brownsville's past is tumultuous.

In 1846 President James K. Polk ordered Gen. Zachary Taylor to build a fort at this spot, and the Mexicans understood this to be an act of veiled aggression. Soon the Mexicans invaded Texas here, igniting the Mexican-American War, which counted among early casualties a Maj. Jacob Brown, for whom the fort and city were eventually named. Two important battlefields are found near town, the first being the *Palo Alto Battlefield,* north of town at FR 1847 and FR 511, home to a small but beautiful new visitor center (956-541-2785, ext. 233; www.nps.gov/paal). The other is *Resaca de la Palma Battlefield* on FR

The End of the Road

Highway 4 leads east from Brownsville in a slightly curving path 24 miles to the Gulf of Mexico. *Boca Chica* is the name given to the end of the road, where motorists will find a stop sign at the point where the road ends, meeting the sand. There's the beach, period. Apparently the stop sign is meant to keep you from driving straight into the ocean.

1847 between Price and Coffeeport Streets; a leader in this battle was 2d Lt. Ulysses S. Grant.

Another significant battle site—this in the Civil War—is **Palmito Ranch Battlefield,** about 14 miles east of downtown via Highway 4. The fight was won by Confederate forces who hadn't heard that Lee had surrendered at Appomattox a month earlier. When the Rebels learned of the South's concession, the victors were taken prisoner by the prisoners.

For a much more modern and nature-oriented attraction, look no further than the **Gladys Porter Zoo** (at Ringgold and 6th Streets; 956-546-2177; www.gpz.org). Widely considered one of the top 10 zoos in the nation, this one is special for having no bars or cages. Animals in the 31-acre spread are kept separated by moats and waterways and have room to roam. There are some 1,800 birds, mammals, and reptiles representing five continents. A children's zoo offers petting opportunities and an animal nursery. There's a half-hour, narrated tour aboard a miniature train on Sunday. Open Mon through Fri from 9 a.m. to 5:30 p.m. and Sat and Sun from 9 a.m. to 6 p.m. Admission is charged.

A favorite for Philly cheesesteak sandwiches is **Cobbleheads Bar and Grill** (3154 Central Dr., Brownsville; 956-546-6224; www.cobbleheads.com), open for lunch and dinner daily. For the most authentic tacos anywhere, check out **El Pato** (1631 Price Rd., Brownsville; 956-541-0241; www.elpato mexicanfood.com), where fillings inside soft tortillas include spicy, stewed beef; potatoes; chicken; cheese; avocado; beans; and *chorizo,* a spicy Mexican sausage.

If you've a hankering for some crashing waves, head just 22 miles east of town on Highway 4 to **Brazos Island State Park,** also known as Boca Chica. There's nothing but ocean and a little swatch of sand—it's completely undeveloped, and no facilities are available, so take your own water, drinks, ice chest, snacks, towels, and sunblock. If you're so inclined, feel free to swim, camp, surf, picnic, hunt for seashells and sand dollars, or just stroll the dunes. For Gulf fishing, there's a ½-mile-long stone jetty at the northern end of the beach.

Other Places to Stay in South Texas

BROWNSVILLE

Residence Inn
3975 N. Expressway 83
(956) 350-8100
On the north end of town, this nonsmoking hotel has suites with kitchens. There's a hot breakfast buffet daily and a social hour Mon through Thurs.

DEL RIO

Amistad Lake Resort
US 90 West
(830) 775-8591
www.amistadlakeresort
.com
This renovated lodge suits anyone who wants to be on the water. There's a restaurant, bar, and swimming pool on-site, and some of the 40 rooms have kitchenettes.

LAREDO

La Quinta Inn
3610 Santa Ursula Ave.
(956) 722-0511
This 152-room place has a pool; breakfast is included.

MCALLEN

Renaissance Casa de Palmas
101 N. Main St.
(956) 631-1101
This Texas Historical Landmark has 165 rooms and a bar, restaurant, and sauna.

SAN ANTONIO

The King William Manor
1037 S. Alamo St.
(800) 405-0367 or
(210) 222-0144
www.kingwilliammanor
.com
An 1892 Greek Revival home and adjacent 1901 guesthouse in King William District offer 11 guest rooms with Victorian antiques and reproductions. Full breakfast is included.

Mokara Hotel and Spa
212 W. Crockett St.
(866) 605-1212
www.mokarahotels.com
A truly luxurious offering, the swanky spot with 99 rooms and suites offering a fabulous spa and good dining right on the River Walk was previously the Watermark Hotel and Spa.

Other Places to Eat in South Texas

LAREDO

Charlie's Corona
3902 San Bernardo Ave.
(956) 725-8227
Longtime town favorite, this is the place for garlic-slathered steak with grilled onions and chicken-fried steak in rich gravy. Open for lunch and dinner; closed Sun.

SAN ANTONIO

Aldaco's
100 Hoefgen St.
(210) 222-0561
www.aldacos.net
Dine under the stars or inside the hacienda setting on lovely soups, homey tacos *al pastor,* and baked vegetable chile relleno. Great margaritas, plus cooking classes. Open for lunch and dinner; closed Sun.

Biga on the Banks
203 S. St. Mary's St.
(210) 225-0722
www.biga.com
Biga features upscale fusion (Asian–southwestern–New American) dishes. Steaks, fish, chops, vegetables, salads, and soups receive thoughtful treatments and preparations that command medium to high prices for dinner, Mon through Sat.

Boudro's
421 E. Commerce St.
(210) 224-8484
www.boudros.com
Possibly the best restaurant along the River Walk, this one does wonderful blends of southwestern and Cajun influences in seafood, beef, soups, salads, and fowl. Open for lunch and dinner; the average meal costs $10.

Josephine Street Cafe
400 E. Josephine St.
(210) 224-6169
www.josephinestcafe.com
An unpretentious favorite for years, this restaurant's

menu offers great steaks, shrimp, and chicken, while the bar is legendary. Open for lunch and dinner Mon through Sat; meals average $10.

Liberty Bar
1111 S. Alamo St.
(210) 227-1187
www.liberty-bar.com
Longtime favorite for salads, soups, steaks, seafood, pasta, and fowl. Open daily for lunch and dinner; prices start at about $12.

UVALDE

Evett's Barbecue
301 E. Main Ave.
(830) 278-6204
A local favorite for smoked brisket and barbecue sand-wiches. Open Tues through Sat for lunch and dinner.

Rexall Drug and Soda Fountain
201 N. Getty St.
(830) 278-2589
The place for old-fashioned burgers, shakes, and malts. Open for lunch and early supper; closed Sun.

THE PINEY WOODS

East Texas's Piney Woods region defies so many myths held by those who don't truly know Texas: It's generously green, frequently hilly, and always lush. There are majestic millions of acres of forest—four national forests, to be exact. Rich in ancient pines, cypress, and plenty of hardwoods, this is where Texans make annual pilgrimages in autumn to see fall blazing in its radiant glory. And in spring, country paths in and out of the forest lands are sensational with brilliant explosions of magenta azaleas, frilly pink and white dogwoods, and evening primroses blooming across wild fields in lavender profusion. Amid the legions of trees pushing skyward are lakes and more lakes, small places and big spreads of water, where lifelong lake residents share space and stories of honey holes with anglers hoping to catch even a little one—shimmering lakes where sailing and waterskiing and watching sunrises are the most important events that occur in a day, places where time-less Native American legends tell of the Great Creator's work in watery, woodsy artistry.

Everything in the Piney Woods seems fresh and new, though the area has history dating to Texas's origins as a republic and as a state. Vestiges of the life of Sam

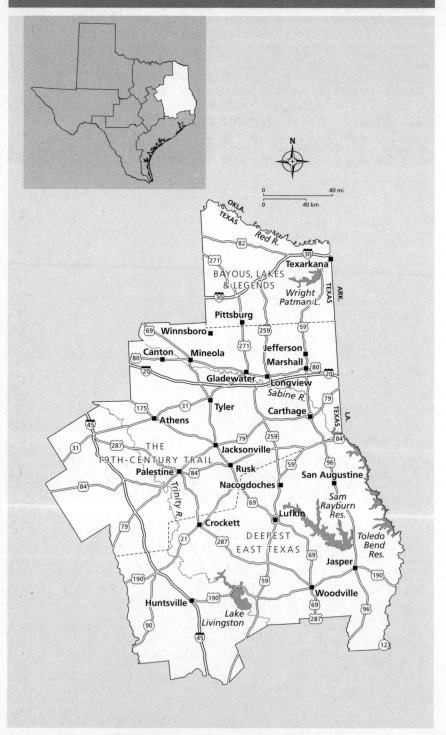

THE PINEY WOODS

OKLA.
TEXAS
Red R.
82
271
Texarkana
BAYOUS, LAKES
& LEGENDS
30
Wright
Patman L.
TEXAS
ARK.
Pittsburg
69 Winnsboro
259
59
Jefferson
271
Canton
80
Mineola
Marshall
80
20
20
Gladewater
Longview
Sabine R.
79
175
31
Tyler
Carthage
45
Athens
TEXAS
LA.
31
287
84
THE
19TH-CENTURY TRAIL
79 Jacksonville
259
96
Palestine
84
Rusk
59
San Augustine
84
Nacogdoches
69
Trinity R.
79
Crockett
Lufkin
Sam
Rayburn
Res.
21
287
DEEPEST
EAST TEXAS
69
Toledo
Bend
Res.
190
59
Jasper
190
Huntsville
190
Woodville
96
90
Lake
Livingston
69
287
45
12

N

0   40 mi
0   40 km

Houston—whose later years were spent serving his adopted, beloved Texas—are found here, and the state university in Nacogdoches, a wonderful Piney Woods town, is named for the Father of Texas, Stephen F. Austin. A healthy population of Native Americans, the people of the united Alabama and Coushatta nations, lives on a reservation near one of the state's great pioneer living-history museums. Travelers to the Piney Woods can ride restored 19th-century railroads or buy baskets that have been made here for more than 100 years and pottery that has been crafted by generations of the same families, families that helped

texas**trivia**

From late February into early March, the prettiest blooms in East Texas are those at **Mrs. Lee's Daffodil Garden,** a 28-acre bright yellow sweep of blooms on a 900-acre farm just outside of Gladewater (call for directions; 903-845-5780; www .daffodilgarden.com).

settle the region. There are no amusement parks or major league athletic teams or 4-story shopping malls in the Piney Woods, but you will find a rose garden with 500 varieties that supplies a third of the nation with its commercial roses; the state's antiques capital; Victorian mansions made over into bed-and-breakfast homes, some rumored to be staffed by resident ghosts; and towns offering the World's Richest Acre, the nation's first drill team, a biblical airplane, and some of the best fried alligator tail you could ever hope to savor. That's just a small taste of the Piney Woods.

Deepest East Texas

Begin this journey in **Huntsville,** an hour north of Houston, the Walker County seat and home to 35,000 east Texans. Settled in a very pretty setting of rolling, forested terrain at I-45 and US 190, Huntsville was founded as a trading post in 1836, the same year Texas won its independence from Mexico. Now home to Sam Houston State University (SHSU), the city is better known as the place to learn more about the life of Sam Houston himself. The **Sam Houston Memorial Museum Complex** (on the SHSU campus at 1836 Sam Houston Ave., Huntsville; 936-294-1832; www.samhouston.org) is a 15-acre spread that belonged to the Texas hero and now holds two of his homes, the furnished Woodland Home and the Steamboat House, the latter of which was the site of his death in 1863. Other buildings there include a law office, kitchen, and blacksmith shop displaying, among other things, some of Houston's possessions, as well as Mexican items taken at the defeat of Santa Anna at San Jacinto. Pack a lunch for this visit, as the grounds have a spring-fed pond with picnic

JUNE'S FAVORITE ATTRACTIONS

Come Together Trading Company Canton	**Oak Grove Cemetery** Nacogdoches
The Country Tavern Kilgore	**Old Port Caddo Canoe Company** Caddo Lake
Kiepersol Estates Tyler	**Stillwater Inn** Jefferson
Municipal Rose Garden Tyler	**Texas Basket Company** Jacksonville
New Zion Missionary Baptist Church Barbecue Huntsville	**Texas State Railroad** Rusk and Palestine

facilities. Open Tues through Sat from 9 a.m. to 4:30 p.m. and Sun from noon to 4:30 p.m. Free admission.

There's no better testimony to Houston's huge bearing on Texas than the enormous, 67-foot-tall *statue of Sam Houston,* dedicated in October 1994. Called *A Tribute to Courage,* it's the world's tallest statue of an American hero. Made from 30 tons of concrete and steel, artist David Adickes created the monument from his life-size (6-foot, 6-inch) model, which is seen in the library at Sam Houston State University. See Big Sam at 34000 US 75, off I-45 at exit 109. There's a visitor center with a gift shop; it's open Mon through Fri from 10 a.m. to 5 p.m., Sat from 10 a.m. to 5 p.m., and Sun from 11 a.m. to 5 p.m. Call (936) 291-9SAM for more details.

You can visit Houston's burial site at Oakwood Cemetery, Avenue I and 9th Street. *Sam Houston's Grave and National Monument* is marked by a tomb bearing Andrew Jackson's sentiment, "The world will take care of Houston's fame." Always open, there is no admission charge.

An entirely different kind of attraction is found at the *Texas Prison Museum* (1113 12th St., Huntsville; 936-295-2155; www.txprisonmuseum.org), where exhibits include the history of the Texas prison, with Bonnie and Clyde's rifle collection; Old Sparky, the electric chair; relics from the Carrasco prison siege; memorabilia from the famous, defunct Texas Prison Rodeo; and music and art projects by inmates. Open Mon through Sat from 10 a.m. to 5 p.m. and Sun from noon to 5 p.m. A small admission fee is charged.

Some say the best barbecue in the state is had at *New Zion Missionary Baptist Church* (2601 Montgomery Rd., Huntsville; 936-294-0884), a shade-tree barbecue stop of sorts. Sausage, chicken, brisket, and ribs are smoked on-site and served from 11 a.m. until 7 p.m., Thurs through Sat. Don't overlook the buttermilk pie.

To begin your tour of Texas's thick forest country, drive east on US 190 just 2 miles from Huntsville, and you're in *Sam Houston National Forest* (936-344-6205; www.fs.fed.us/r8/texas/). Covering 160,000 acres in Montgomery, San Jacinto, and Walker Counties, this forest contains 27 miles of the 140-mile *Lone Star Hiking Trail.* To reach this National Recreation Trail, find the trailhead off FR 1725 just northwest of the town of Cleveland on the forest's southern edge. For a map see the forest ranger's offices either at Cleveland or at New Waverly, 13 miles south of Huntsville. There is a $3 parking fee per vehicle. Also in the forest, *Stubblefield Lake* is on the West Fork of the San Jacinto River about 12 miles north and west of New Waverly; there you can go camping ($12 per night) and picnicking.

From the forest head east on US 190; you'll immediately see *Lake Livingston,* 52 miles long and lined with 452 miles of wooded shoreline with every sort of recreation. The 640-acre state park on the east shore of the lake offers campsites, screened shelters, group trailers, boat ramps, a store, floating docks and gas docks, showers, and hiking-nature trails. Fishing, swimming, and waterskiing are the most popular pastimes on the lake. For details call the state park at (936) 365-2201 or visit www.tpwd.state.tx.us. Admission is $3 per person for day users and $2 per person for overnight users 13 and older. Groceries, restaurants, and all supplies are available in the town of Livingston, the Polk County seat, 7 miles east of the park.

About 40 miles east of Lake Livingston, watch for *Heritage Village Museum* (right on US 190; 409-283-2272; www.heritage-village.org). This

JUNE'S FAVORITE ANNUAL EVENTS

First Monday Trade Days
Canton, weekend prior to first Monday of each month

Heritage Festival
Nacogdoches, third weekend in March

Dogwood Trails Festival
Palestine, third and fourth weekends in March and first weekend in April

Azalea and Spring Flower Trail
Tyler, first weekend in April

Historic Pilgrimage
Jefferson, last weekend in April and first weekend in May

Tomato Festival
Jacksonville, mid-June

Great Texas Balloon Race
Longview, last weekend in July

reconstructed pioneer village contains old shops, homes, and vehicles, while photographs, documents, maps, and other aids show the difficult lives of early settlers. A log cabin built on this site in 1866 still has its peg windows and wooden door hinges. Also on the site is a rebuilt 1911 Cherokee church, which was moved from the Cherokee Dies community, northwest of Woodville, in 1990. Open daily from 9 a.m. to 5 p.m.; admission is charged.

Don't miss the chance to eat at the nearby *Pickett House* (409-283-3371), a re-created boardinghouse with family-style offerings including fried chicken, chicken and dumplings, homegrown veggies, stone-ground corn bread, and homemade preserves. Hours vary according to season, so call ahead.

If that's not enough food for you, note that you're in superior home-cooking country. Just another 2 miles from the Pickett House east on US 190 is the community of *Woodville,* where you can pick up US 69 and follow it 8 miles south to the village of Hillister and its restaurant, *The Homestead* (409-283-7324). This restored 1912 house behind a white picket fence has a certain rustic charm, with its hardwood floors and walls, and rugs, wallpaper, and furniture from the period—but atmosphere isn't the main appeal of The Homestead. The cornucopia of country cooking is simple, including smothered or baked chicken, steaks and roast beef, fish and ham, plus irresistible desserts. Be advised that reservations are a good idea at this small place, which serves Fri and Sat from 5 to 9 p.m. and Sun from 11 a.m. to 3 p.m.

Spend a little time moseying around Woodville, a town of about 3,000 residents and the Tyler County seat, 90 percent of which is covered in forest. This is another good jumping-off place to explore the Big Thicket National Preserve (see Gulf Coast chapter) and a pleasant place to hunt for antiques.

Back near Lake Livingston, *Davy Crockett National Forest* is 11 miles west from the lake on US 190, then north on FR 356, 12 miles northwest to Sebastopol, where you'll pick up FR 355 and go 14 miles north. This forest, like the other three national forests in Texas, was ravaged early in the 20th century yet has made remarkable recovery in its hardwood and pine populations. The Davy Crockett is 161,000 acres in Houston and Trinity Counties, containing the Big Slough Canoe Trail and Wilderness Area on the Neches River, and the Four C Hiking Trail, a 19-mile path linking the Neches Bluff and Ratcliff Lake. That lake has camping, picnicking, and swimming areas, plus screened shelters and canoe rentals. For maps and facilities go to the ranger station at Ratcliff (936-655-2299; www.fs.fed.us/r8/texas/) on FR 227 just off Highway 7, or Apple Springs (936-831-2246), in the forest on Highway 94.

While you're in the neighborhood, make a detour to the town of *Crockett,* about 10 miles west of Davy Crockett Forest via Highway 7. Naturally the town—the Houston County seat—was also named for the Alamo hero, and

Bizarre Texas Stuff

A plague known far too well among most Texans is that of the fire ant. But the good folks in Marshall exhibit a perverse but contagious sense of humor with their annual *Fire Ant Festival*, held the second weekend every October in honor of the insidious little insect with a burning bite. Some 50,000 celebrants have been known to gather on and around the downtown courthouse square to join in the zany festivities. Among the events are fire ant costume contests, fire ant calling contests, a chili cook-off (recipes must call for the inclusion of one fire ant), a giant parade, and much more.

it's said he stopped en route to the Alamo to camp at the springs found at the intersection of Highways 7 and 21, now marked by a historical plaque. Spend some time poking around the quaint town, filled with more antiques shops.

At the *Texas Forestry Museum* (1905 Atkinson Dr., Crockett; 936-632-9535; www.treetexas.com) in *Lufkin,* 12 miles east of the forest on Highway 94, the state's lumber industry is detailed, as well as the impact the forestry-products business has had on the region. Also there's a moonshiner's still, a fire lookout tower, a blacksmith's forge, and a logging train. Open Mon through Sat from 10 a.m. to 5 p.m. and Sun from 1 to 5 p.m. Admission is free, but donations are welcome.

From Lufkin head 22 miles southeast on US 69 to the *Angelina National Forest,* a 152,000-acre preserve spreading across Angelina, Jasper, Nacogdoches, and San Augustine Counties and wrapping itself around vast *Lake Sam Rayburn.* The lake, exceptionally popular with bass and catfish anglers, has 560 miles of shoreline with numerous marinas and campgrounds. The pine-and-hardwood land gives shelter to deer, squirrel, and turkey, some of which can be seen on the Sawmill Hiking Trail, a 5½-mile path following the Neches River and stretching from Bouton Lake Park to the Old Aldrich Sawmill and Boykin Springs. Along the way you'll find ruins of an old tram line, logging camps, and bridges. Several parks line the lake, offering various concessions. For maps and information, as well as ranger-led activities, check at the ranger office next door to the Texas Forestry Museum in Lufkin (listed earlier); call (936) 639-8620.

After a day on Lake Sam Rayburn, you can rest easy at a pleasant little inn in *Jasper,* 15 miles south of Angelina National Forest via Highway 63. Jasper has several unique gift shops and an outstanding art gallery downtown. The *Belle-Jim Hotel* (160 N. Austin St., Jasper; 409-384-6923; www.belle-jim.com) is right there, too; the 1910 structure offers private baths and homemade breads for breakfast. There's a cafe on-site, too, that offers weekday lunches of soups, salads, and sandwiches.

From the Angelina forest, head for the **Sabine National Forest** by following Highway 147 to its intersection with Highway 103, which leads east to this last of Texas's four national forests. At nearly 158,000 acres, covering ground in Jasper, Sabine, San Augustine, Newton, and Shelby Counties, the Sabine hugs the 65-mile-long **Toledo Bend Reservoir,** which Texas shares with Louisiana. Along the lake, in the shade of southern pines and hardwoods, are seven different parks with offerings ranging from picnicking, camping, and swimming to boating areas and nature trails.

Fishing on Toledo Bend is a big attraction to anglers in search of bass, catfish, bluegill, and crappie. Check at the ranger offices for maps, concessions, and activities in Hemphill, in the forest on Highway 87 (409-787-2791; www .toledo-bend.com).

San Augustine is conveniently found just 8 miles west on Highway 21. A town of nearly 3,000, San Augustine is known as the Cradle of Texas and was settled officially in 1832, although it was a community on the Spaniards' Old Road to San Antonio, also called El Camino Real, even earlier. Because a mission was established here in 1716 (and abandoned just 20 years later), San Augustine claims to be the oldest town in Texas. Important historical residents included Sam Houston, who was a San Augustine resident while seeking the republic presidency, and J. Pinckney Henderson, Texas's first governor.

Although much of the town burned in 1890, there are some good sites still standing, such as the **Ezekiel Cullen House** (207 Congress St., San Augustine; 936-275-5110; http://visit.sanaugustinetx.com/homes/cullen.html). The home belonged to a judge and Texas House of Representatives member who fought for public-school lands funding. This Greek Revival house was built in 1839, given to the Daughters of the Republic of Texas by Cullen's family, and is headquarters for an annual tour of homes in April. Call ahead for hours and admission fees.

From San Augustine continue your tour for 36 miles on Highway 21 to **Nacogdoches** (NACK-ah-DOE-chez), the town generally credited with being the oldest in Texas. The settlement is historically believed to have had hospitable Native Americans—the Caddo people—when the Spaniards came through en route to Mexico, probably around 1541 or 1542. The first permanent European settlement, however, is dated at 1716, when Father Margil founded the Mission of Our Lady of Guadalupe of Nacogdoches; it was abandoned in 1773, when the settlers were ordered to move to San Antonio.

Several weren't happy and moved back with Antonio Gil Ybarbo to Nacogdoches; in 1779 he laid out the town and built a stone house and trading post there, which survives as the **Old Stone Fort,** the town's most heritage-packed site. An exact replica of Ybarbo's structure sits today on the Stephen F. Austin State University Campus, at Griffith and Clark Streets (936-468-2408; www.sfasu .edu/stonefort/). Its long and colorful history includes its service as a fort and a prison, as well as government headquarters during many attempts to establish the Republic of Texas; its function as offices for the first two newspapers published in Texas; and the place where Jim Bowie, Thomas Rusk, Sam Houston, and Davy Crockett were administered the oath of allegiance to Mexico. Nine different flags have flown over the fort, including those from three failed revolutions. Now a museum, the Old Stone Fort offers exhibits detailing this tumultuous past and the people who left an indelible mark on the republic and the state. Open Tues through Sat from 9 a.m. to 5 p.m. and Sun from 1 to 5 p.m. Admission is free, but the museum welcomes donations.

Nacogdoches is fairly flooded with historic sites directly related to the Republic of Texas. One that must not be missed is the **Sterne-Hoya House** (211 S. Lanana St., Nacogdoches; 936-560-5426; www.ci.nacogdoches.tx.us/

texastrivia

The first oil well was drilled in Texas in 1886 near Nacogdoches. By 1928 Texas was the leading oil-producing state in the US, a position that's never been relinquished.

departments/shmuseum.php), built in 1828 by Adolphus Sterne, a prominent landowner who raised $10,000 to outfit a volunteer company to serve in San Antonio. Sam Houston was baptized there in the Roman Catholic faith in 1833 as Mexican law required at the time to become a Texas citizen. Today the home is a memorial library and museum of Texas history since colonization. Open Tues through Sat from 10 a.m. to 4 p.m. Admission is free.

Nearby **Oak Grove Cemetery,** at Lanana and Hospital Streets, is where four of the signers of the Texas Declaration of Independence are buried. One is Thomas Rusk, secretary of war in the republic, San Jacinto hero, commander-in-chief in Sam Houston's army, and one of the first US senators from Texas. Another is William Clark, the great-grandfather of this author's maternal grandmother. The cemetery is always open, and there is no admission charge.

Today Nacogdoches—seat of the same-named county—is home to nearly 29,000 residents, some of whom have worked to make a success of several worthy downtown antiques shops, as well as the showplace known as **Millard's Crossing,** at the north end of town (6020 North St., also US 59 North, Nacogdoches; 936-564-6631; www.millardscrossing.org). Numerous 19th-century homes and commercial buildings have been relocated here in a village setting. Among them is the first Methodist parsonage (1900) and its chapel

(1843); a rustic stone-and-log cabin (1830); and the Millard-Burrows House (1840), graced with enormous holly bushes and an iron fence with fleur-de-lys detail. Tours are given Mon through Sat from 9 a.m. to 4 p.m. and Sun from 1 to 4 p.m. Admission is charged. For all Nacogdoches information, call (888) 653-3788 or visit www.visitnacogdoches.org.

Do plan to relax for a few days at the ***Llano Grande Plantation Bed and Breakfast,*** a complex of three historic homes sheltered deep in the woods immediately south of town. The centerpiece is the Tol Barrett house, a pioneer farmhouse dating to 1840, named for its original owner, the oilman credited as being the first to drill a producing well west of the Mississippi. It's rustic, but most guests find it comfortable. Its front is framed by myriad wildflowers, and the interior is filled with period pieces. Guests cook their own breakfasts of venison sausage and homemade breads (in the stocked kitchen, of course) in this private house; other guests stay in one of the two other lovingly restored houses, within walking distance of the Tol Barrett. Guests find their hosts to be hospitable and friendly historians. Reservations and directions must be obtained in advance by calling (936) 569-1249. Visit the website at www.llano grande.com.

Another countryside retreat is ***Pine Creek Lodge,*** 8 miles west of Nacogdoches via FR 225 and FR 2782 (936-560-6282; www.pinecreeklodge.com). The Pitts family has owned the hilly, 140-acre farm near Lake Nacogdoches off and on since before World War II and developed it into a bed-and-breakfast in 1995. Rustic buildings contain a total of 17 guest rooms filled with handmade furniture, and each has a king-size bed, sitting area, small refrigerator, private bath, and a basket of candies and fruit. There are terry robes for guests to wear to the hot tub, and a swimming pool is on-site. A full breakfast buffet is offered daily in the main lodge, where guests are welcome to borrow videos and help themselves to popcorn, coffee, tea, and hot chocolate. The on-site Creekside Restaurant is open Thurs through Sat from 6 p.m. to 8 p.m.; it's BYOB for now. Visit their website at www.pinecreeklodge.com.

The 19th-Century Trail

From Nacogdoches head west on the very scenic Highway 21—once the famed El Camino Real—25 miles to the town of Alto, where you'll head north on US 69 for 12 miles to reach ***Rusk.*** More than 5,000 people live in the Cherokee County seat, cited for having the nation's longest footbridge, measuring 546 feet, located in Footbridge Garden Park, 1 block east of the town square on E. 5th Street. The town was also the birthplace of Jim Hogg and Thomas Mitchell Campbell, the first and second native-born Texans to serve as governor.

Most visitors come to Rusk with a single purpose, that of riding the **Texas State Railroad,** which has one of its two depots here. The parkland surrounding the train terminal here is spread with 100 acres of pines and hardwoods. Not only can you catch the scenic train ride here, but you can camp, hike on trails, picnic, rent paddleboats and rowboats, turn the kids loose in a playground, play tennis, and cast for catfish, bass, and perch in the 15-acre stocked lake. The park is 2 miles west of town on US 84; call (888) 987-2461 for information.

The Texas State Railroad, formerly an operation of the state parks, came under private ownership in 2007. Established in 1881, it's an antique train that transports passengers along 26 miles of track between Rusk and **Palestine.** Passengers ride in vintage coaches powered by antique steam engines through gorgeous forestlands, decorated with pink and white dogwood blooms in spring and rust, scarlet, and gold tapestries in fall. There's a snack bar aboard the train and short-order restaurants at both terminals. The train trip is exceptionally popular, and reservations are a must. The train operates year-round. Call (888) 987-2461 in advance for reservations, schedules, and fares, or see the monthly train schedule online at www.texasstaterr.com.

In Palestine, the Anderson County seat and home to 18,000 Texans, your sightseeing opportunities are varied. The **Howard House Museum** (1011 N. Perry St., Palestine; 903-729-5094) has been established in an 1851 home and offers a doll collection, an array of antique photos depicting early residents and events, and good period furniture. The home is shown by appointment but is usually open during Palestine's **Dogwood Trails Festival,** a popular event among Texans from around the state, as it is a prime opportunity to see the delicate pink and white blooms cover the forests in a dainty blanket. The event is usually held in late March and early April and features tours of historic homes, a parade in historic downtown, an arts and crafts festival, a chili cook-off, a community theater play, trolley tours, and a car show. The festival has a link on the Palestine Convention and Visitor Bureau website at www .visitpalestine.com.

A great reason to hang around Palestine a little while longer is to dig into one of the choice Black Angus steaks served at the **Ranch House** (305 E. Crawford St., Palestine; 903-723-5400). A rustic, upbeat place where you can toss your peanut shells on the floor, the Ranch House also does a good job with grilled chicken and fish. Find it opposite a great stretch of antiques shops.

Once back in Rusk via the Texas State Railroad, you can continue your journey by driving north on US 69, 14 miles to **Jacksonville,** another Cherokee County town. Known 50 years ago for its abundant tomato crop, the modest city of 12,000 residents today is known for baskets. The **Texas Basket**

Company (100 Myrtle Dr., Jacksonville; 903-586-8014; www.texasbasket.com) is one of a handful of such companies still in operation in the nation. Established in 1924, this outfit still uses original equipment to make baskets crafted entirely from wood cut within 200 miles of town, including sweet gum, black gum, birch, hackberry, elm, cottonwood, and sweet bay. Between 6,000 and 10,000 baskets are produced daily for shipment to all 50 states, as well as to Canada, Germany, and Puerto Rico. Visitors can watch craftspeople at work, and most will want to spend some shopping time in the large store, stocked with thousands of baskets in every imaginable shape and size. Open Mon through Sat from 8 a.m. to 5 p.m. Admission is free.

While you're in Jacksonville, be sure to eat at *Sadler's Kitchen* (402 E. Rusk St., Jacksonville; 903-589-0866), which, Tues through Fri, is a good place to lunch on anything from deluxe sandwiches and salads to pot roast and grilled chicken. But on Friday and Saturday nights, it's open for lovely dinners of pecan-crusted rainbow trout and shrimp with spinach fettuccine. The restaurant doubles as an antiques shop, too. Closed on Mon. For more information about Jacksonville, call the chamber of commerce at (903) 586-2217 or visit www.jacksonvilletexas.com.

Travelers who enjoy a leisurely drive filled with exquisite scenery will rejoice in the countryside surrounding Jacksonville. Take a picnic to *Love's Lookout Park,* on the roadside 5 miles north of town on US 69. Or just take a few soft drinks and soak in the hilly vistas of forest and water on FRs 747 and 2138 wrapping around Lake Jacksonville.

For a lake of greater import, follow US 175 from Jacksonville 17 miles west to Frankston and catch Highway 155 north, which crosses *Lake Palestine,* a 25,500-acre impoundment on the Neches River in this rolling timberland. Anglers especially will want to spend time here, as the lake is known for record catches, such as a 12-pound striper bass and a 12-pound largemouth bass. Waterskiing is popular here as well. Marinas and campgrounds surround the lake, as do numerous catfish restaurants serving up the freshest local catches.

texastrivia

Produce is popular here: East Texas hosts festivals for the tomato in Jacksonville, the hot pepper in Palestine, and the yam in Gilmer.

From the east side of Lake Palestine, continue north on Highway 155 another 13 miles to *Tyler,* the Rose City of Texas. The Smith County seat, Tyler has more than 83,000 residents. After the Civil War, nurserymen found the sandy soil and rainfall ideal for growing fruit trees and roses. The fruit trees became diseased before the turn of the 20th century, however, and the rose business

Wide World of Wildlife

In Tyler your kids will enjoy seeing **Brookshire's World of Wildlife Museum and Country Store** (1600 W. Southwest Loop 323 at the Old Jacksonville Highway, Tyler; 903-534-2169; www.brookshires.com/museum/). One section features stuffed and mounted critters from Africa and North America, including some 250 specimens of animals, reptiles, and fish. The Country Store illustrates the kind of marketplace found in east Texas in the late 1920s, complete with products and fixtures. A 1926 Model T Ford delivery truck and an antique fire truck are on-site, too. Closed Sun and Mon. Admission is free.

carried these growers happily into the 1900s. Today more than a third of the nation's commercially grown rosebushes are raised within a 50-mile radius of Tyler.

Visitors revel in the glory found at Tyler's **Municipal Rose Garden** (420 Rose Park Dr., Tyler; 903-531-1212; www.cityoftyler.org), where more than 30,000 rosebushes in 500 varieties fill a 14-acre park—making it the country's largest municipal rose garden. The blooming season peaks in mid-May and continues through November. The garden is open daily, 24 hours a day. Admission is free.

This huge rose business gives rise to the **Texas Rose Festival,** a giant celebration held every October, complete with the crowning of a Rose Queen, a rose show featuring more than 100,000 roses, and parades, balls, antiques shows, crafts fairs, and more. Call the chamber of commerce at (903) 592-1661 for details, or visit www.texasrosefestival.com.

Tyler is well known for its **Caldwell Zoo** (2203 Martin Luther King Dr., Tyler; 903-593-0121; www.caldwellzoo.org), begun in 1938 as a backyard menagerie. Today it's a 35-acre spread with wonderful, lush settings for elephants and giraffes, birds, bears, alligators, flamingos, and numerous ducks from around the world. There's a monkey island, an aquarium, and a native Texas exhibit. Open daily from 9:30 a.m. to 6 p.m. A small admission fee is charged.

Should you find yourself in Tyler and starving for performing arts, check out the schedule at the **Cowan Center** on the University of Texas/Tyler campus (3900 University Dr., Tyler; 903-566-7424; www.cowancenter.org). Typical playbills include the Vienna Boys' Choir, the Russian National Ballet, and Hal Holbrook in his Mark Twain show.

You also might consider a visit to the **Tyler Museum of Art** (1300 S. Mahon St., Tyler; 903-595-1001; www.tylermuseum.org). Exhibits featured here have included one on Latin American textiles and another entitled *Self-Taught Artists of the Twentieth Century*. Open Tues through Sat from 10 a.m. to 5 p.m. and Sun from 1 to 5 p.m. Admission is free.

The sweetest place to stay in Tyler is the ***Rosevine Inn*** (415 S. Vine Ave., Tyler; 903-592-2221; www.rosevine.com). A 1930s-style home in a bricked-street area becoming well-known for good antiques shops, the inn is surrounded by a white picket fence with well-manicured grounds. The interior is thoughtfully decorated, its cozy corners and comfortable rooms scattered with antiques and country decor. Each of the 6 rooms has a private bath, and there's a hot tub on the patio. Breakfasts are gourmet affairs.

Another excellent choice is the ***Woldert-Spence Manor*** (611 W. Woldert St., Tyler; 903-533-9057 or 800-WOLDERT; www.tylertexasinn.com), an 1859 home built by a German immigrant and civil engineer. The home has been added on to over the years, and today it's an elegant inn with original stained-glass windows, chandeliers, several porches and fireplaces, and 5 guest rooms. A full breakfast is served on antique china. (You can tour the house on the website.)

Tyler's selection of good eating places has grown at a surprising rate. For traditional southern breakfasts and juicy burgers, try ***Cox's Grill*** (706 W. Front St., Tyler; 903-593-8940). Or you can dine at the place the locals prefer for steak and seafood, ***Bernard Mediterranean Cuisine*** (212 Grande Blvd., Tyler; 903-534-0265; www.bernardsintyler.com), where specialties include baked brie, crab cakes, tortellini, and rib eye Provençale.

Tyler is a central location for various east Texas side trips. One to keep in mind is a jaunt to ***Edom,*** 15 miles west of Tyler via Highway 31 and FR 279. A tiny artists' enclave, Edom has become known for its extraordinary annual arts and crafts show held in September, with juried works drawing artists from around the nation. Several artists—mostly crafters of pottery, leather, and brass—keep shops in town right on the main street, which is FR 279. These shops don't keep regular hours, so you will have to take your chances. Next to one row of shops on the road is ***The Shed,*** a simple country cafe serving huge lunches and dinners, with specialties such as pork chops, chicken-fried steak, catfish, and enormous coconut, banana cream, and chocolate pies. The cafe's phone number is (903) 852-7791, or you can visit the website at www .theshedcafe.com.

Slightly southeast of Tyler, near the burg of Bullard, ***Kiepersol Estates*** (21508 Merlot Ln., Tyler; 903-894-3300; www.kiepersol.com) has become a popular destination for weekend escapees from Dallas, Houston, and Louisiana. Doing quadruple duty as an elegant B&B inn, restaurant, winery, and cattle business, this impressive operation offers 5 lush suites with private porches and hot tubs. The restaurant offers fancy preparations of duck, sea bass, lamb, and hand-cut steaks, along with a tempting wine list. Reservations should be made well in advance.

Another option is an excursion to **Kilgore,** 25 miles east of Tyler via Highway 31. Crude, classics, and kicks aren't what most people expect in an east Texas town of 11,000. Home to the **World's Richest Acre,** Kilgore has the mammoth success of the Great Texas Oil Field discovery in 1930 to thank for its prosperity, but the community is best known as giving the world its most famous classical pianist, Van Cliburn, who now resides in Fort Worth; it's also responsible for the phenomenon known as the drill team.

> # warbetween thestates
>
> In the spring of 1864, a place called **Camp Ford** had a stockade holding some 6,000 Union troops, making it the largest prisoner-of-war compound west of the Mississippi. You can see a historical marker noting the place in a rest area on US 271, about 2 miles northeast of Tyler.

First the oil business: Head to the corner of Main and Commerce Streets, a small area with one life-size derrick and 23 miniderricks representing the oil boom days when more than a thousand wells were jammed into the downtown area and 24 wells, claimed by six different operators, were crowded onto a 1-acre site, creating the World's Richest Acre, which produced more than 2.5 million barrels of crude oil.

To see the industry explained in an interesting manner, visit the **East Texas Oil Museum** (Henderson Boulevard at Ross Street on the Kilgore College campus, Kilgore; 903-983-8295; www.easttexasoilmuseum.com), and see how a town grew from 800 to 8,000 residents in 24 hours. There's a working oil rig out front, with a 70-foot wooden derrick, steam boiler, rotary table, and draw works. A realistic model of a 1930s street is created inside, complete with a car stuck in the mud, board sidewalks, post office, barbershop, general store, sounds of a thunderstorm building overhead, and music from a period radio. Firsthand accounts of boomtown existence can be heard through headphones; a 15-minute film of actual footage is shown in a "town theater," with the theater rumbling during a gusher; and an elevator takes riders to the center of the Earth. This just scratches the surface of the museum's offerings; see for yourself Tues through Sat from 9 a.m. to 4 p.m. (Apr through Sept, Tues through Sat from 9 a.m. to 5 p.m.) and Sun from 2 to 5 p.m. A small admission is charged.

For something radically different, and certainly more frivolous, walk down the street a block to the **Rangerette Showcase,** also on the Kilgore College campus, at Broadway and Ross Streets (903-983-8265; www.rangerette.com). In this little corner of east Texas is yet another worldwide attention getter, born 10 years after the oil boom began. The Kilgore Rangerettes formed their first high-kick line in 1940, and the showcase tells the story of this famous precision-and-drill dance team of Kilgore College. Some may say it is sexist, but many will argue it's just Texas camp. Red Grange called them the "sweethearts of the nation's gridiron," and they perform annually on New Year's Day at the Cotton Bowl halftime, their painted red lips matching their shirts, contrasting with little blue skirts and white boots and cowgirl hats. The group responsible for putting showbiz on the football field is chronicled through an assemblage of displays with historical films and videos and decades of newspaper clippings illustrating the team's global reach. The showcase is open Mon through Fri from 9 a.m. to 4 p.m. and Sat from 10 a.m. to 4 p.m. Admission is free.

Even if these attractions don't draw you to Kilgore, the **Country Tavern,** on Highway 31 just on the western outskirts of town, probably will. Most patrons are from all over Texas, and many will argue that this unassuming beer joint serves the best pork ribs in the state. A jukebox and dance floor are good for dancing the Texas two-step, and blue-jeaned waitresses are good for friendly local color. For more than 30 years, this place has served up the biggest platter of ribs in memory, with sides of tasty potato salad, onions, and pickles. Open Mon through Sat for lunch and dinner, the tavern's phone number is (903) 984-9954, or visit www.countrytavern.com.

Still another side trip from Tyler is **Mineola** (minny-OH-lah), north 27 miles on US 69. An impressive collection of antiques shops brings folks to Mineola, but it's the **Munzesheimer Manor** (202 N. Newsom St., Mineola; 903-569-6634; www.munzesheimer.com) that makes them stay. The remarkable 1906 home—with stained-glass windows, seven fireplaces, wraparound porch, and footed tubs—has been thoroughly restored and decorated with English and American antiques. It's a huge, comfortable home with 7 guest rooms, perfect for settling in with a cup of tea and a good novel. Breakfasts during the week are continental, while weekends are full affairs with such treats as fresh berries and German pancakes.

Munzesheimer Manor isn't the only B&B to note in Mineola, however. Another wonderful place is the **Lott Home Cottages** (311 E. Kilpatrick, Mineola; 903-569-0341; www.lotthomecottages.com), a 1918, 2-story southern home with suites in cottages, private baths, porches with rocking chairs, antiques, bicycles, and TVs.

Amid Mineola's antiques shops, a wonderful find is **Kitchen's Hardware & Deli,** at the corner of Pacific and Broad Streets. Part museum and part retailer, the vintage store has old auger bits and ancient tools on display, as well as new stuff, ranging from plumbing supplies and Case knives to American flags and Marshall pottery. In front there are some picnic tables where you can lunch on the deli's roast beef sandwiches, German sausage plate, homemade chili, or specials such as corn bread, beans, and greens. Or get an old-fashioned root beer float to go.

While you're in the area, drive 10 miles north from Mineola on Highway 37 to the town of Quitman, home to **Governor Hogg Shrine** (903-763-4045). Formerly a state park, this city-owned park with three museum buildings is named for Rusk-born James Stephen Hogg, who served as governor of Texas from 1891 to 1895. The honeymoon cottage of Hogg and his bride, Sallie Stinson, is on-site, as is the Miss Ima Hogg Museum, named for their daughter.

About 14 miles east of Mineola on Highway 49, find **Pine Mills Pottery** (5155 FR 49, Mineola; 903-857-2271; www.pinemills.com), a studio and gallery showing and selling some exceptional work by artists Gary C. Hatcher and Daphne Roehr Hatcher. It's generally open daily from 10 a.m. until 5 p.m., but it's wise to call in advance to be sure.

Fishing enthusiasts will want to linger in this area, as 27,000-acre **Lake Fork** (fewer than 10 miles west of Quitman, via Highway 182) is where record-setting bass are caught annually. The lake is surrounded by marinas where you'll find good fishing guides, while Lake Fork Lodge (at the intersection of Highways 17 and 515, Alba; 903-473-7236; www.lakeforklodge.com) offers everything including comfortable rooms, hot tubs, a game room, bass boats, licensed guides, dog kennels, fishing pier, and full breakfasts with your stay. Your next destination is **Canton;** head west of Tyler 40 miles on Highway 64, and you'll wind up directly at the Van Zandt County Courthouse Square, just a few yards beyond your actual destination, **First Monday Trade Days.** If you arrive early and are lucky, you may be able to find a parking spot on the square or nearby, then just walk the block east to the 100-acre fairgrounds, where some 5,000 vendors are spread out with their goods for sale. This, of course, occurs the Friday, Saturday, and Sunday preceding the first Monday of each month. Since the middle of the 19th century, country folks have been traveling here to buy and sell everything from kitchenware, clothes, farm equipment, furniture, and toys to baby carriages, jewelry, homemade jellies and jams, and books. Collectors of Depression glass, quilts, iron beds, and china find this a great place to hunt bargains. Food booths are set up everywhere, too, selling burgers, barbecue, pastries, and cold drinks. It's a colorful experience well worth taking in, even for visitors who aren't in the market to buy anything. Trade Days gates open at 7 a.m. and close at dark; for information call the chamber of commerce at (903) 567-2991 or visit www .firstmondaycanton.com.

But even if you reach Canton on a non–First Monday weekend, there's good reason to slow down and look around. The town has a growing farmers' market, a water park called Splash Kingdom, golf courses, an alligator-wildlife park, Christmas tree farms, regularly scheduled bluegrass music festivals, and much more. Check with the *Canton Visitors Bureau* by calling (877) 462-7467 or visiting www.visitcantontx.com.

Right on the town square, a store you wouldn't necessarily expect to find is one of the more original of its kind in the Piney Woods. *Come Together Trading Company* (116 E. Dallas St., Canton; 903-567-1133; www.cometogether trading.com) promotes fair-trade practices by stocking merchandise made in developing African countries. Messenger bags, yoga bags, purses, satchels, clothing, accessories, jewelry, baskets, and kitchenware are among the goods.

Across the street, *Canton Square Bakery and Cafe* (105 S. Buffalo St., Canton; 903-567-4630) makes a darn fine hamburger, along with a lot of other big sandwiches, salads, and pastries. It sounds crazy, but the signature item is the Nut Job, a burger slathered with peanut butter—and it's really very good. Open for breakfast and lunch, Tues through Sat.

From Canton head south on Highway 19 almost 30 miles to the town of *Athens,* known to masters of American food trivia. Proof that Athens is birthplace of the hamburger is found on a historical marker on the north side of the Henderson County Courthouse Square, next to the 1927 First National Bank Building. It explains that on this site in the late 1880s, a cafe owner named Fletcher Davis (1864–1944) created the first hamburger sandwich. He took his invention to exhibit at the 1904 St. Louis World's Fair, in fact. Family members and local friends, as well as the resources of the McDonald's Hamburger University, support this story.

Athens has become nationally famous in the past couple of years for its proximity to *Black Beauty Ranch* (18 miles east of town off Highway 31, via FR 1803 and County Road 3806; 903-469-3811; www.blackbeautyranch.org). Open to the public only for special events (check their website for listings), the ranch is a setting for modern-day miracles in the form of a 1,620-acre refuge for abandoned and abused animals of all sorts, from chimpanzees, burros, and elephants to dogs, cats, and horses. Founded in 1979 by the late author Cleveland Amory and the Fund for Animals, the ranch is operated as a nonprofit facility supported primarily by donations. Today, several hundred animals are guaranteed a healthy, safe home for their lifetimes at this extraordinary sanctuary. Call ahead to have a guide show you some of these wonderful, living stories.

In Athens be sure to take the kids to visit the *Texas Freshwater Fisheries Center* (5550 Flat Creek Rd., Athens; 903-676-BASS; www.tpwd.state.tx .us), a 106-acre operation of the Inland Fisheries Division of the Texas Parks and Wildlife Department. Here you'll learn about the "sharelunker" program, designed to increase the production, size, and quality of Florida largemouth bass in Texas waters.

The massive visitor center—named for Athens native Edwin L. Cox Jr., a former chairman of the Parks and Wildlife Foundation of Texas, rancher, and conservationist—presents an introduction to this intriguing aquarium and hatchery complex, which houses some 300,000 gallons of fishy representatives of more than 40 species from the state's freshwater streams, ponds, and lakes. Among hundreds of things to see (and often, to catch) are some of the heftiest largemouth bass in the world and the American alligator. The fisheries center is open Tues through Sat from 9 a.m. to 4 p.m. and Sun from 1 to 4 p.m. Admission is charged.

About 30 miles north on Highway 155 and then 10 miles east on US 80 is the *Antiques Capital of East Texas,* seen on the map as *Gladewater,* a town of 6,500 in Gregg County. It is home to more than 250 antiques dealers scattered around in 16 antiques malls and 16 individual shops. Most of the shopping is concentrated in Gladewater's vintage downtown area, all within easy walking distance from one point to another.

Slow down long enough to enjoy lunch at *Glory Bee Baking Co.* (111 N. Main St., Gladewater; 903-845-2448), a good place for soups, salads, sandwiches, and rich desserts; it's also open for dinner on Saturday. From Gladewater continue to *Longview,* 13 miles east on US 80. The unassuming town of 73,000 is the Gregg County seat and has a heritage of railroad, agriculture, lumber, and oil businesses that left it somewhat undistinguished. This has changed, however, as the popularity of the *Great Texas Balloon Race* has skyrocketed. For a 3-day weekend in mid-July, hundreds of brightly colored hot-air balloons can be seen scattered throughout the sky in early morning or evening as pilots from around the nation compete in tests of skill. The contest involves a pilot's ability to maneuver the balloon between points and drop a marker on a designated target—all of which is determined by the winds. Besides the flights, there are on-ground events during the festival, such as arts and crafts fairs, aircraft exhibits, evening concerts, and other fun for spectators. The party is held at the Gregg County Airport; information is available from the chamber of commerce by calling (903) 237-4000 or visiting www.greattexasballoonrace.com. Admission is free, but parking fees are charged.

If you've worked up an appetite, head for *Bodacious Barbecue,* at 227 South Mobberly and five other locations in Longview (903-753-8409), an east Texas institution famous for its chopped-beef sandwiches as well as sliced beef brisket, ribs, and spicy links. Open Mon through Sat 10 a.m. to 7 p.m.

With bellies full, try to find the strength to push on to **Marshall,** 23 miles east on US 80. The Harrison County seat, with almost 24,000 residents, has a deep southern heritage imbued with plantations and Civil War history—in fact, more than 150 historical markers are found throughout Harrison County. So strong is its legacy that newsman Bill Moyers, Marshall's favorite son, hosted a PBS broadcast titled "Marshall, Texas, Marshall, Texas" in his *A Walk Through the 20th Century with Bill Moyers.*

People whose artistic tendencies run toward throwing clay may have already heard about Marshall's famous retailer, **Marshall Pottery,** an old-fashioned business that celebrated its centennial in 1995. Found at 4901 Elysian St., Marshall, the pottery is the largest manufacturer of red clay pots in the nation, but it retains every bit of its friendly country charm. Master potters—some of whom are third- and fourth-generation potters—can be observed at their craft, some painting the cobalt blue decoration commonly seen on the glazed bowls, pitchers, mugs, and dinnerware. These items are all for sale and are always reasonably priced. Under the same roof are 20 shops with savings on baskets, silk flowers, linens, candles, and other decorative housewares. Outside, a "seconds" yard is filled with slightly misshapen or barely chipped pottery—look for real steals here on many things that don't appear to be damaged at all. Marshall Pottery is open Mon through Sat from 9 a.m. to 6 p.m. and Sun from 10 a.m. to 6 p.m. Admission is free. Call (903) 938-9201 or check www.marshallpottery.com for more information.

Artistic expression of a different nature is in the **Michelson Museum of Art** (216 N. Bolivar St., Marshall; 903-935-9480; www.michelsonmuseum .org), a small treasure house of works by Impressionist painter Leo Michelson (1887–1978). His work is also displayed in museums in Baltimore, Jerusalem, Paris, San Diego, and Tel Aviv, among others. Traveling exhibits fill the gallery as well. Open Tues through Fri from noon to 5 p.m. and Sat and Sun from 1 to 4 p.m. Admission is free.

Winter is prime time for visiting Marshall, when the town lights up like a Christmas tree—literally. The **Wonderland of Lights** is focused on the historic county courthouse, which is covered with 4.5 million tiny white lights, and area businesses and homes are aglow as well, from Thanksgiving until New Year's Day. For information on special events, call the chamber of commerce at (903) 935-7868 or (800) 953-7868 or visit www.visitmarshalltexas.org.

Look in Marshall's beloved Ginocchio Historic District for the **Three Oaks Bed and Breakfast** (609 N. Washington Ave., Marshall; 903-935-6777 or 800-710-9789; www.threeoaks-marshall.com). The 1895 historic landmark offers 4 guest suites decorated with antiques, each with its own private bath and free wireless access. A full breakfast is included. Music fans will find a worthwhile detour 31 miles south of Marshall, via US 59, in the town of **Carthage.** In the summer of 1998, Panola County residents welcomed the new **Texas Country Music Hall of Fame** at the **Tex Ritter Museum** (300 W. Panola, Carthage; 903-693-6634; www.carthagetexas.com/HallofFame/museum.htm). The first inductees were the late Jim Reeves, whose nearby grave is noted with a Texas Historical Marker, as well as Gene Autry and Tex Ritter. The museum is filled with honorees' guitars, stage clothing, gold records, and photographs. Hours vary according to season, so call ahead.

Bayous, Lakes & Legends

From Marshall you need travel only 14 miles northeast on Highway 43 to find one of the state's greatest natural assets, **Caddo Lake.** The only lake in Texas not created artificially, the 35,400-acre lake is characterized by seven-century-old cypress trees draped in an ethereal manner with heavy curtains of Spanish moss. The effect nature has wrought is one of haunting beauty, appropriate for a place whose creation is a mystery. One legend holds that the reservoir was formed when a resident Caddo Indian chief was warned by the Great Spirits to move his people to higher ground or watch them die in a terrible earthquake and flood. It seems he ignored them and chose to take his warriors hunting; they returned to find that a mighty shake had occurred and their village had been replaced by a huge lake. Some part of the story could be true, as recorded history shows that an earthquake in 1811 in New Madrid, Missouri, is estimated to have had a force that would register 8.9 on today's Richter scale—and it's possible that that tremor created a logjam in the Red River that dammed Caddo Lake, lapping a bit across the Louisiana state line.

Naturally, photographers and painters are captured by Caddo's ancient beauty, best seen on boat tours led by lake experts. These sloughs and canals are terribly confusing to anyone unfamiliar with its shrouded paths, but the fishing and wildlife watching are far too wonderful to pass up. Inquire about guides at **Caddo Lake State Park** on Highway 43 by calling (903) 679-3351 or visiting www.tpwd.state.tx.us.

At the state park, on FR 2198, just 1 mile east of Highway 43, several rock cabins—which have been completely remodeled and updated—are available for rental, but they are reserved for weekend stays up to 90 days ahead, so call the state park early or try for a weeknight stay. Shaded by towering pines near the water, these are nice places to kick back for a while. Canoe rentals are offered in the park, as are camping, fishing, hiking, picnicking, and nature study. One of the canoe outfitters to try is **Old Port Caddo Canoe Company** (903-679-3073; www.oldportcaddo.com). Note that it is closed on Tues and Wed.

Adjacent to the park is the tiny community of *Uncertain*—and no one's certain how the name came about. One theory is that when the hamlet was contemplating incorporation, a poll was taken to choose a town name, and "Uncertain" was frequently listed on the third-choice line. Of one thing you can be sure, there is a cluster of little businesses offering rustic accommodations, marina and fishing guide services (helpful in navigation and landing big catfish and bass), cafes, and good humor. Among those offering accommodations are *Shady Glade* (903-789-3295) and *Uncertain Inn* (FR 2189, on the lake; 903-789-3292). You'll find these and many more at www.cityofuncertain.com.

If you don't sign up for a fishing tour, be sure to book a ride on the *Graceful Ghost* with *Caddo Lake Steamboat Company* (903-789-3978 or 888-325-5459; www.gracefulghost.com), a southern-style paddle-wheel boat operating from Uncertain. Tickets are $20; call well in advance for a schedule and reservations.

A little side trip into history from Caddo is a short drive away at *T. C. Lindsey and Company General Store,* found by following FR 134, 13 miles east in the town of Jonesville. In business since 1847, it's still a family-owned, no-frills country store. With high ceilings and creaky wooden floors, this general store is obviously the real McCoy. Shelves are stacked with groceries, fabrics, and feed, while a room off to the side is now a makeshift museum. You'll find farm tools, old hunting traps, horseshoes, massive iron skillets, and other relics from another time. Glass cases in front hold antique eyeglasses, glass bottles, toiletries, and household items used by our grandparents and great-grandparents. Snacks, candies, cold drinks, and slices from a massive wheel of cheese will tide you over until supper. The store is open Tues through Sat from 8 a.m. to 4 p.m. Admission is free; call the store at (903) 687-3382.

From Caddo Lake your next destination could be the old bayou town of *Jefferson,* a town packed with charm and romance, 13 miles west of the lake on FR 134. The Marion County community of 2,200 is rapidly growing in stature around the state for its perfect balance of historical preservation and hospitality.

A good place to call home during a few days of relaxation and exploration is the *Excelsior House* (211 W. Austin St., Jefferson; 903-665-2513; www.the excelsiorhouse.com). The second-oldest hotel in Texas, the Excelsior has been in continuous operation since 1858 and has hosted dignitaries such as Ulysses S. Grant, Rutherford B. Hayes, W. H. Vanderbilt, Oscar Wilde, and Lyndon B. and Lady Bird Johnson. A beautiful place with ornate furniture and heavy, baroque French frames around paintings, crystal chandeliers, Oriental carpets, a grand piano, Italian marble mantels, and pressed-tin ceiling, it's a showplace as well as a delightful setting in which to have a plantation breakfast—by reservation, of course. The 14 rooms and suites are in demand on weekends, so call ahead or try for a midweek visit.

The Excelsior's 1961 restoration spurred revitalization throughout the town, which had fallen into a quiet decline after its riverboat days were long past. In the 19th century, steamboats churned the waters of the Big Cypress Bayou from Jefferson, via Caddo Lake and the Red River, all the way south to New Orleans. Today's visitors can still tour the bayou aboard the *Jefferson Bayou Tours,* an open-air boat departing Jefferson Landing four times daily in spring, summer, and fall for 1-hour, narrated tours. Call (903) 665-2222 for hours and rates, or visit www.jeffersonbayoutours.com.

Another way to see the water and woodsy environs is aboard the *Jefferson and Cypress Bayou Railroad,* a narrow-gauge railroad powered by an antique steam locomotive winding along the bayou on a scenic, 5-mile route; this is another great way to gain an overview of the town. Tours are offered on weekends. Call (866) 398-2038 for details and schedule updates, or visit www .jeffersonrailway.com.

For more background on the town and area, head for the *Jefferson Historical Society Museum* (223 W. Austin St., Jefferson; 903-665-2775; www .jeffersonmuseum.com), where history lessons are made fun. Housed in a former federal courthouse and post office (1888), this big red gem of the past contains three floors of the historical society's collected memories. More than 30,000 visitors come annually to see the dress Lady Bird Johnson (from nearby Karnack) wore to a state dinner for the West German chancellor; sterling silver flatware that belonged to Whistler's mother; and personal belongings of Sam Houston and Annie Oakley. Open daily. Admission is charged.

For a great, fresh lemonade or scoop of ice cream, visit *City Drug & Old Fashioned Soda Fountain* (109 W. Lafayette St., Jefferson; 903-665-2521 or 800-287-0378), where books and all sorts of souvenirs and gifts are sold.

Dozens of antiques shops are found along the brick streets of downtown in historic commercial buildings. Some beautiful 19th-century homes are open for tours year-round, while eight homes are chosen annually to be on show during the *Jefferson Pilgrimage,* held the first weekend in May. The weekend features not only the homes but also the *Diamond Bessie Murder Trial,* a wonderful melodrama based on the story of a former prostitute who was thought to have been murdered by her rich diamond-merchant husband. For pilgrimage information contact the chamber of commerce, (903) 665-2672, or the Jessie Allen Wise Garden Club, event hosts, at the Excelsior Hotel, (903) 665-2513, or visit www.theexcelsiorhouse.com/tour.htm.

Among the finer B&Bs in the state is *McKay House* (306 E. Delta St., Jefferson; 800-468-2627 or 903-665-7322; www.mckayhouse.com). The antebellum

June's Texas Anecdotes

Luck rode shotgun with me the day I wheeled into Jefferson in search of a great slice of pie. It was a weekend, and it turns out that's when you're most likely to get a taste of the *Hamburger Store*'s famous lemon meringue pie. Rarely do I find a version that approximates the rich, dreamy one we loved eating at my grandmother's house, but the one at this Jefferson landmark comes startlingly close. One bite and I was deep into the whole swooning-moaning routine, with some eye rolling on the side. That's because this creamy lemon filling absolutely captured that ideal balance of sweet and sour, with a beautifully burnished, picture-perfect meringue on top. Most days you can tuck into a piece of the Hamburger Store's glorious three-berry pie made with blackberries, raspberries, and strawberries, and you can count on finding apple-caramel-nut, Nuts About Fudge, chocolate meringue, and coconut meringue pies every day. Be prepared to go into full swoon. Visit www.hamburgerstore.com to read the menu.

home, built in 1851, bears state and national historical markers. Each of the 7 guest rooms has a private bath, Victorian nightgowns and sleep shirts, and bath goodies. The "gentleman's breakfast" is always something special. Featured in *Vacation* magazine as "One of the Ten Most Romantic Inns in America," McKay House is extremely popular, so make reservations early.

Jefferson's dining options are numerous. Lunch at the *Hamburger Store* (101 Market St., Jefferson; 903-665-3251) means good burgers, taco salads, fries, and homemade fruit pies. A lively spot for nachos and beer is *Auntie Skinner's River Boat Club* (107 W. Austin St., Jefferson; 903-665-7121; www .auntie-skinners.com), while the town's most elegant dinners of grilled veal chop, red snapper, and dessert soufflés are served at *Stillwater Inn* (203 E. Broadway St., Jefferson; 903-665-8415; www.stillwaterinn.com).

For complete details on Jefferson, call the Marion County Chamber of Commerce at (903) 665-2672 or (888) 467-3529 or visit www.jefferson-texas.com.

For a detour into curiosity, take an hour's drive north from Jefferson on US 59 to *Texarkana,* sometimes called the State Line Cities, as it's part Texas, part Arkansas—hence, the name. Of particular interest here is the *Perot Theatre* (at 221 Main St., Texarkana; 903-792-4992), an Italian Renaissance theater opened as the Saenger in 1924. Seating 1,600 patrons, it was among the most famous showplaces in a four-state area in its heyday. In the late 1970s, Texarkana native Ross Perot donated $2 million to restore the theater to its former magnificence with glistening chandeliers, royal blue and gold interiors, and marble floors. A symphony series, plays, musicals, and pop music concerts are staged here from September through May. Tours are by reservation, depending on scheduled events.

Most unusual in Texarkana is the ***Bi-State Justice Center*** (100 N. State Line Ave., Texarkana; 903-798-3504), a building straddling the Texas-Arkansas line and, therefore, shared by two cities, two counties, and two states. It is thought to be the world's only post office and federal building with a state line bisecting it. As was appropriate, the building was crafted from both Texas pink granite and Arkansas limestone. The building is open Mon through Fri from 8 a.m. to 5 p.m.; tours are free and by appointment.

Once you've laid eyes on the ***Mansion on Main*** (802 Main St., Texarkana; 903-792-1835; www.mansiononmain.com), you won't want to leave Texarkana anytime soon. Built in 1895, the inn is found in the downtown historic area and bears a state historical marker. The front exterior is noteworthy for 14, 2-story columns that came from the Mississippi Exhibit at the St. Louis World's Fair in 1904. There are 6 guest quarters, including the Butler's Garret and the Penthouse Suite, all with private baths and antique furnishings. A full southern breakfast is served.

From Jefferson there is still much to be seen in the way of outdoor beauty. To sample this bounty drive west from Jefferson on FR 729 for 17 miles and you'll find yourself at the shores of shimmering ***Lake o' the Pines,*** surrounded by lush hardwoods and pines, a scene that's splendid in autumn, as the leaves make quite a show of changing to crimson, burnt orange, and amber. The lake is 18,000 acres, with excellent fishing for largemouth, white, and spotted bass; swimming, waterskiing, and sailing are favorites here, too. Campsites abound, as do picnic areas and nature trails. The Army Corps of Engineers, at (903) 665-2336, offers more information. For more information about all services and attractions, visit www.lakeothepines.com.

About 10 miles north of the lake via US 259, the town of ***Daingerfield,*** Morris County seat and home to 2,500 Texans, offers supplies, groceries,

Take Flight

The modest town of Pittsburg is regionally famous for possessing the ***Ezekiel Airship,*** a replica of a 1902 flying craft that, while undocumented, is said to have been airborne a year before the Wright brothers made their first flight. Its inventor was an inspired, sometime-Baptist preacher who took his idea of an airship from the prophet Ezekiel, who described in the Bible an apparatus that flew. The preacher raised $20,000, sold stock in his company, and built his ship. Unfortunately it was destroyed during shipment to the St. Louis World's Fair in 1904. The 26-by-23-foot replica was for many years displayed at a restaurant in Pittsburg. Now it's on view at the ***Depot Museum,*** 204 W. Marshall St.; (903) 856-0463; www.pittsburgtx museum.com.

lodging, and an excellent array of cheesecakes and other sweets at Main Street Bakery. Check out other available attractions at the chamber of commerce, 102 Coffey St.; (903) 645-2646; www.daingerfieldtx.net.

At *Daingerfield State Park,* immediately east of town on Highway 11, 550 acres of pine-blanketed land surround a lovely, 80-acre, spring-fed lake. Photographers have traveled from around the state to capture the color riot in autumn, and spring's demonstration is just as dramatic, as redbuds, dogwoods, and wisteria explode in shades of pink and purple. Hiking trails, fishing, camping, cabins, playgrounds, and picnic areas make this a place to stay for more than a day. For information and reservations call the park office at (903) 645-2921 or visit www.tpwd.state.tx.us.

From Daingerfield, travel west 16 miles on Highway 11 to *Pittsburg,* the Camp County seat and home to 4,000 residents. Its economy is based on a significant poultry business—Pilgrims Pride alone produces more than 600 million pounds of chicken yearly.

The chicken business may be big here, and there is a Spring Chick Festival held in Pittsburg in late April, but the primary food found here is the *Pittsburg Hot Link.* The not-too-spicy sausage made from beef and pork is, appropriately, served up hot at the *Pittsburg Hot Links Restaurant* (136 Marshall St., Pittsburg; 903-856-5765; www.pittsburghotlink.com). Patrons place their orders at the counter in back, ordering by the link or choosing from other specialties, such as beef stew, chili, burgers, or chicken-fried steak. The restaurant is open Mon through Sat from 8 a.m. to 6 p.m.

Before heading back to your cabin at Daingerfield, your campsite at Lake o' the Pines, or your cozy corner in Pittsburg, consider another detour, this time to *Winnsboro,* a pleasant hamlet just 22 miles west of Pittsburg on Highway 11. There's another pretty lake here for a dip in summer, but the primary attractions come after the weather begins changing. Fall foliage is a cause for big celebrations, hence the *Autumn Trails Festival,* held every weekend in October. The chamber of commerce hosts an antique car show and a homes tour; driving maps to see the best in fall's color parade are offered, too. And the Christmas season brings folks from all over east and north Texas to choose a special tree from one of the several area Christmas-tree farms; hot apple cider is a bonus offered by the farmers

timber

The Piney Woods reaches southward from the Red River to within 25 miles of the Gulf Coast and receives about 40 to 55 inches of rainfall each year. With millions of acres of pine forests, the Piney Woods is the source of nearly all of Texas's larger commercial timber productions.

while customers find the prettiest evergreen. For details contact the chamber of commerce at 100 E. Broadway Ave., Winnsboro, or via (903) 342-3666; www .winnsboro.com.

One of the finest, most praised bed-and-breakfast inns in the state happens to be in Winnsboro. **Thee Hubbell House** (307 W. Elm St., Winnsboro; 903-342-5629; www.theehubbellhouse.com) is an 1888, 2-acre plantation estate containing a mansion that has 5 luxurious guest rooms and suites and a wonderful carriage house with 6 guest rooms. All have private baths, and all stays include a full plantation breakfast in the mansion.

Other Places to Stay in the Piney Woods

ATHENS

Sleepy Hollow Ranch Bed and Breakfast
about 16 miles southeast via US 175 and FR 2588
(903) 675-1776
www.sleepyhollowranch bedandbreakfast.com

CROCKETT

Warfield House
712 E. Houston Ave.
(936) 544-4037
www.warfieldhouse.net

JEFFERSON

Breckenridge Garden Cottages
502 Houston St.
(903) 665-7738 or
(800) 665-7758
www.breckenridgegc.com
Small garden cottages with kitchenettes afford lots of privacy.

Falling Leaves Bed and Breakfast
304 Jefferson St.
(903) 665-8803
www.fallingleavesinn.com
Antiques fill 4 guest rooms.

Old Mulberry Inn Bed and Breakfast
209 Jefferson St.
(903) 665-1945
www.oldmulberryinn.com

The Claiborne House and Touch of Class Day Spa
312 S. Alley St.
(903) 665-8800 or
(877) 385-9236
www.claibornehousebnb .com
This restored 1872 home has rooms with private baths named for poets Browning, Yeats, Tennyson, Wilde, Dickinson, and Keats. Ask about the Jacuzzi tubs and king-size beds.

NACOGDOCHES

Hardeman Guest House
316 N. Church St.
(936) 569-1947
www.hardemanhouse.com

Stag Leap Retreat
Route 3
Box 1267, TX 75964
(936) 560-0766 or
(936) 715-9477
www.stagleap.com

UNCERTAIN

Hodge Podge Cottages
Route 2
Box 55B, TX 75661
(903) 789-3901
www.hodgepodgecottages .com

Spatterdock
Route 2
Box 66B, TX 75661
(903) 789-3268
www.spatterdock.com
Three guesthouses—one with 3 bedrooms and 2 baths, one with 4 bedrooms and 3 baths, and one with 1 bedroom and bathroom. All have fully equipped kitchens. The hosts offer fishing and hunting guide services, too.

Other Places to Eat in the Piney Woods

JEFFERSON

The Bakery and Restaurant
201 W. Austin St.
(903) 665-2253
Draws a great breakfast crowd for raisin bread done french toast–style, coffee, and chat.

Lamanche's Italian Restaurant
124 W. Austin St.
(903) 665-6177

NACOGDOCHES

Mike's BBQ House
1622 South St.
(936) 560-1676

TYLER

Southern Magnolia
3307 Chandler Hwy.
(903) 596-8847
Remodeled old cottage serves baked chicken with dressing, meat loaf, chicken salad, and freshly baked pies.

Sonoma Grill
5875 Old Bullard Rd.
(903) 534-9779
www.sonomagrilltyler.com

NORTH TEXAS

North Texas mirrors the Lone Star State's uncanny ability to wear a vast number of different hats. Denying any one classification or description, the region exhibits a broad range of personalities. Big D, as Dallas is proudly called in the Southwest, was built largely from the fruits of the oil and cattle industries and is known as well as a major fashion, electronics, and motion pictures center. Further, Dallas boasts having more restaurants per capita than any other city in the nation, and the city joins Fort Worth in being home to teams competing in every professional sport. Together the two are called the Metroplex. Fort Worth, 30 miles east, is also called Cowtown, and it is famous for a curious mix of Wild West and world-class fine arts. In addition, Fort Worth has a restored stockyards area where Butch and Sundance hid out and where today you can "scoot a boot" in the world's largest honky-tonk.

Travelers to the north Texas region find that in perfect balance to this unusual cosmopolitan–Wild West mix are the small towns where a simpler way of life is still valued. Communities that gave the world such dignitaries as Sam Rayburn and Dwight D. Eisenhower are special places that continue to

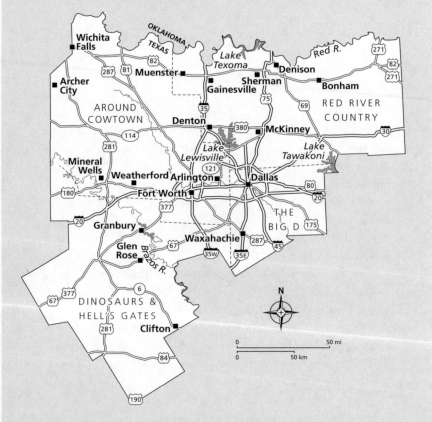

Wichita
Falls

OKLAHOMA

TEXAS

Red R.

271

82

Lake
Texoma

Denison

82

271

Muenster

Sherman

Bonham

Archer
City

Gainesville

RED RIVER
COUNTRY

AROUND
COWTOWN

75

69

Denton

380

McKinney

30

114

Lake
Lewisville

Lake
Tawakoni

281

Mineral
Wells

121

Weatherford

Arlington

Dallas

80

180

Fort Worth

20

377

THE
BIG D

20

Granbury

175

Glen
Rose

67

Waxahachie

287

45

Brazos R.

35W

35E

67

377

6

DINOSAURS &
HELL'S GATES

N

281

Clifton

0   50 mi

84

0   50 km

190

live in yesteryear, where historic houses and pretty lakes—instead of shopping malls and symphonies—are the draws.

Exotic wildlife ranches, a quiet Norse community, a rustic ranch where city folks can play cowpoke for a day, an ancient riverbed where dinosaur tracks are plainly visible—these are the places where people go to escape e-mail and voice mail.

Red River Country

Oldest town in the Red River Valley and home to more than 9,900 residents, the Fannin County seat of **Bonham** was settled in 1837 by a former Arkansas sheriff who brought settlers to a land grant he received from the Republic of Texas. The community was eventually named for James Butler Bonham, the Alamo's courageous messenger, whose statue stands before the courthouse.

But Bonham's greatest claim to fame is Sam Rayburn, the political legend who spent 49 consecutive years, or 25 terms, in the US House of Representatives—17 of those as Speaker of the House. Mr. Sam, as he was fondly called, is remembered at the **Sam Rayburn Library** (800 W. Sam Rayburn Dr., Bonham; 903-583-2455), which holds an exact replica of his Capitol Hill office, with all furnishings. A host of his memorabilia is displayed here, including a gorgeous white marble rostrum that was used by every House speaker from 1857 until 1950. Other interesting artifacts are a collection of political cartoons, gavels, and a 2,500-year-old Grecian urn Rayburn received from the Athens

JUNE'S FAVORITE ATTRACTIONS

Acton State Historic Site
Acton

Amon Carter Museum
Fort Worth

Cafe Modern
Fort Worth

Hall of State
Dallas

Inn on Lake Granbury
Granbury

Lake Mineral Wells State Park
Mineral Wells

Rangers Ballpark
Arlington

Rough Creek Lodge
Glen Rose

Sixth Floor Museum
Dallas

Wildcatter Ranch
Graham

Palace Guard. The library was donated to the University of Texas, whose students come to use it for research. It's open Mon through Fri 8 a.m. to 5 p.m. and Sat 1 to 5 p.m. Admission is free.

Rayburn, who was born in Tennessee in 1882, moved to Texas with his parents in 1887. The **Sam Rayburn House,** 1 mile west of town on US 82 (903-583-5558; www.thc.state.tx.us or www.visitsamrayburnhouse.com) is a 14-room home he built for his parents in 1916. Modest but comfortable, it's been restored, along with the grounds, to the look it had upon his death in 1961. It's open Tues through Sat from 8 a.m. to 5 p.m. Admission is free. Rayburn's funeral was attended by President Kennedy, Vice President Johnson, and former presidents Truman and Eisenhower; Rayburn is buried in Bonham's **Willow Wild Cemetery,** on W. 7th Street at Highway 121. The large monument there bears the impression of a gavel and the simple epitaph, MR. SAM, 1882–1961. The cemetery is never closed, and no admission is charged.

If you happen onto Bonham in October, see if you're in time for the **Fannin County Fair,** a wonderful tradition more than a hundred years old, with livestock shows, baking and other homemaking contests, a carnival, and entertainment. For more information, call the chamber of commerce at (903) 583-4811 or visit www.bonhamchamber.com.

Also in Bonham see the **Fannin County Museum of History** (1 Main St., Bonham; 903-583-8042), housing pioneer furniture, tools, vintage clothing, toys, Native American artifacts, and photographs depicting life in one of the counties of the Republic of Texas. A genealogical and historical library and the Red River Valley Art Gallery are also located here. Open Apr 1 through Sept 1, Tues through Sat from 10 a.m. to 4 p.m. The remainder of the year, it's open Tues through Sat from noon to 4 p.m. Admission is free.

From Bonham follow US 82 west 15 miles, then head north on US 69 another 13 miles to **Denison,** a town of nearly 23,000 in Grayson County. It's best known for being the gateway to **Lake Texoma,** created from the mighty Red River by the building of Denison Dam, the nation's largest rolled earth-fill dam upon its completion in 1944. The enormous reservoir on the Texas-Oklahoma line covers 89,000 acres and has 50 parks, more than 100 picnic areas, and plenty of recreation facilities along 580 miles of shoreline. Travelers come from a three-state area to the resort hotels and motels and marinas surrounding these waters, and anglers spend time on the lake catching record black bass, striper bass, crappie, and lunker catfish. Many of today's vacationers head for the 14-mile Cross Timber Hiking Trail that hugs the water. Stop by the **Denison Chamber of Commerce** at 313 W. Woodward St. for specific information, call (903) 465-1551, or visit www .denisontexas.us.

JUNE'S FAVORITE ANNUAL EVENTS

Southwestern Stock Show and Rodeo
Fort Worth, mid January through early February

Irish Festival
Dallas, first weekend in March

New Vintage Wine and Art Festival
Grapevine, mid-April

Main Street Arts Festival
Fort Worth, third weekend in April

National Polka Festival
Ennis, late April

Scarborough Renaissance Festival
Waxahachie, late April through early June

Mayfest
Fort Worth, first weekend in May

Concerts in the Garden
Fort Worth, early June through early July

Cowboy Gathering
Fort Worth, last weekend in October

State Fair of Texas
Dallas, late September and early October

Lake Texoma has dozens of places to stay right at the water's edge. The nicest of all is *Tanglewood Resort* (903-786-2968 or 800-833-6569; www .tanglewoodresort.com), where accommodations range from hotel rooms to master suites complete with kitchens. Rates are about $100 to $325.

Interesting that the same year the dam was completed, Denison's most famous son became an all-time American hero. Five-star general and two-term US president Dwight D. Eisenhower is remembered at the *Eisenhower Birthplace* at 208 E. Day. The 2-story frame house saw the birth of the great soldier and leader on October 14, 1890, and it's been restored to that period. The family moved a short time later to Abilene, Kansas, but there is an Eisenhower family quilt displayed in the bedroom where Ike was born. His large bronze statue makes a great place for souvenir photos of the family. People interested in taking the "Ike Hike" on the 10-acre reserve should make reservations. Open Tues through Sat from 10 a.m. to 4 p.m. and Sun from 1 to 5 p.m. A small admission fee is charged. For information call (903) 465-8908 or visit www.visiteisenhowerbirthplace.com.

Don't miss Denison's charming *Red River Railroad Museum* (101 E. Main St., Ste. 120, Denison; 903-463-6238). The small museum inside the vintage railroad station is the official repository of historical records and artifacts of the Katy Railroad Historical Association and will delight any train buff. Open Mon through Sat from 10 a.m. to 1 p.m. and from 2 to 4 p.m. Admission is free. Right across the street check out the marvelous inventory at Katy Antique Station (104 E. Main St.).

Sherman, 9 miles south of Denison on US 75, is the Grayson County seat and a city of 35,000 people. Settled in 1846, it was named for Sidney Sherman, a Battle of San Jacinto leader and hero credited with the well-known cry "Remember the Alamo! Remember Goliad!" To see some of the lovely homes and buildings from Sherman's late-19th-century boom, grab a map from the chamber of commerce (307 W. Washington St., Sherman; 903-893-1184), which covers places dating from 1883.

Among buildings of special note in Sherman's downtown are the *Museum of American Victorian Furniture* (201 E. Lamar St., Sherman), housed in a historic church building; *Kelly Square* (115 S. Travis St., Sherman), a 3-story complex of antiques shops, art galleries, and charming cafes in the gorgeous Kelly Building, built in 1915; and the *C. S. Roberts House* (915 S. Crockett St., Sherman), an Eastlake-style home built in 1886 and maintained today by the Sherman Preservation League.

Many of Sherman's beautiful Victorian homes and buildings—there are 33 on the downtown walking map, for starters—are open to the public during the city's Preservation League Tour of Homes in April and the Pilgrimage of Homes in December. Contact the chamber of commerce for details at (903) 893-1184.

Austin College (900 N. Grand, Sherman; 903-813-2000) is the oldest college in Texas operating under an original charter. Several firsts include being the state's first college to grant a graduate degree, the first to start a law school, and the first to have a national fraternity. A bell hanging in the chapel was a gift from Sam Houston, one of the first trustees of the college. Plays and concerts are staged by the theater and music departments, and monthly art exhibits are held.

For still another look at history, stop in at the *Sherman Museum*, formerly the *Red River Historical Museum* (301 S. Walnut St., Sherman; 903-893-7623; www.theshermanmuseum.org), which occupies a wonderful 1914 Carnegie Library building, listed on the National Register of Historic Places. Among exhibits are a room of furnishings and artifacts from Glen Eden, the main house of a grand Red River plantation that was dismantled upon the creation of nearby Lake Texoma; a 1900 country store; and an excellent collection of World War II aircraft models. Open Tues through Sat from 10 a.m. to 4 p.m. A small admission fee is charged.

Now you may want to head west on US 82, stopping 33 miles down the road at *Gainesville,* the Cooke County seat and home to 15,500 people. Some of their ancestors were forty-niners headed to California during the gold rush, and some of these were freethinkers in their day: When most Texans wanted secession in the 1860s, Cooke County folks were against it, and some of them created a secret society supporting the Union.

The surrounding area is now renowned for its rich quarter horse ranches, seen on country drives from town. Downtown, however, is a charming, bricked square with its 19th-century appeal intact, augmented by a cluster of antiques shops, one of which contains a cute little tearoom.

Stop in at the local chamber of commerce (101 S. Culbertson St., Gainesville; 940-665-2831 or 888-585-4468) and pick up a driving tour map of historic Gainesville. There are 34 homes and buildings on the map, including some beautiful homes dating from the 1880s.

Chances are you'll want to spend time exploring the town square, whose centerpiece is the majestic *Cooke County Courthouse,* a 4-wing, 4-story limestone work with a polygonal art-glass dome, built in 1910. Look for remaining detail work, such as the mosaic tile in the entryway at Otis Furniture on the west side of the square.

As you make your way around the square, some things to note are the office of KXGM-FM radio, an oldies station on the west side of the square with outdoor speakers to let shoppers hear hits by the Monkees and other groups; Watts Bros. Pharmacy, an old-fashioned drugstore with Elizabeth Arden makeup and a soda fountain, established in 1915, on the northwest corner of the square at Commerce and California Streets; and Val's Antiques, also at Commerce and California Streets, occupying the ground floor of an old brothel and calling itself "the best little antique house in Texas."

Other antiques shops are Miss Pittypat's, on the north side of the square on California Street, and Carousel Antique Mall, on the east side of the square on Dixon Street. A nonantiques shop that's especially appealing is Bella Matiz (on the square's north side, on California Street), a purveyor of southwestern art, furniture, and jewelry.

Right on the courthouse square, find a pleasant diner called the *Fried Pie Co. & Restaurant* (corner of Commerce and Main Streets). Framed stained glass is hanging in the window, and a huge chandelier hangs from an original pressed-tin ceiling. Burgers, club sandwiches, and a salad bar are offered, and delicious slices of homemade fried pies—including peach, cherry, coconut, Dutch apple, and apricot—are $1.35.

One of the most interesting detours in this part of the state is the one to *Muenster,* about 14 miles west of Gainesville via US 82. In this minute German town, you'll easily find the *Center Restaurant & Tavern* (right on US 82; 940-759-2910; www.thecenterrestaurant.com). It's open for breakfast, lunch, and dinner daily from 6 a.m. to midnight; specialties are outstanding pork schnitzel, German potato salad and sauerkraut, homemade sausages, and apple strudel.

On the way to or from Muenster, slow down in the small town of *Lindsey,* about 3 miles west of Gainesville on US 82. Have a look inside *St. Peter's*

Church, ornately adorned with frescoes, stained-glass windows, and carved altars, imparting a distinctly European look. Much of the work was done by Frie- dolin Fuchs, a Swiss national who was stranded in Texas during World War I.

Before heading away from Gainesville, make a detour 5 miles north of town on I-35 to the Texas Travel Information Center. Here you can pick up hundreds of pieces of free literature, such as state highway maps, colorful guides, and brochures pertaining to every city and nearly every town in Texas. The travel counselors at these centers are especially helpful. Open daily from 8 a.m. to 5 p.m.

If German fare doesn't grab you, and the idea of fantastic barbecue piques your interest (and taste buds), you'll want to head for *Tioga,* south from Gainesville on I-35 for 10 miles, then east on FR 922 for 17 miles. Another supertiny town, this one is on the old M-K-T rail line and is in the heart of that rolling, multimillion-dollar horse ranch country.

The object of this drive is to have a lunch or dinner that will remain long in your memory at *Clark's Outpost* (on US 377 at Gene Autry Lane, Tioga; 940-437-2414; www.clarksoutpost.com). Looks can be deceiving, and this little brown roadhouse appears to be leaning a bit to one side, but the interior is warm and homey, as is the service. Find smoked brisket, ribs, turkey, and river trout, plus lots of vegetables, great barbecue sauce, and sensational homemade pies. The walls are covered with photos of championship horses from nearby ranches, as well as celebrities—supermodel Christie Brinkley has been among them —who love this Texas chow. It's open Mon through Thurs from 11 a.m. to 9 p.m., Fri and Sat to 9:30 p.m., and Sun to 8:30 p.m.

From Tioga drive about 20 miles south on US 377—skirting scenic Lake Ray Roberts—to US 380, and go west about 7 miles to *Denton,* seat of the county bearing the same name and home to 80,000 residents. Besides being home, too, to the University of North Texas, Denton is the site of Texas Wom- en's University (TWU), where you'll find *Little Chapel in the Woods,* at Bell and University Streets. Designed and built in 1939 by noted architect O'Neil Ford, it's considered one of the country's finer architectural achievements. Art melds with nature, as the stained-glass window (designed by students) depicts *Woman Ministering to Human Needs.* Open daily from dawn to dusk (call ahead for Saturday and Sunday hours of operation). For more information call (940) 898-3644.

Also on the TWU campus, in the TWU Administration Conference Tower (117 Bell Ave., Denton; 940-898-3644), the *DAR Museum* houses the inaugural gowns of the first ladies of Texas. The only one of its kind in existence, the collection features either the original garments or faithful copies. Open Mon through Fri from 8 a.m. to 5 p.m. and by appointment. Admission is free.

Denton's appealing courthouse square earned the town a national desig-
nation as a Main Street City. Inside the elaborately designed Denton County
Courthouse, built between 1895 and 1897, is the county's ***Courthouse-on-the-
Square*** museum (110 W. Hickory St., Denton; 940-349-2850). Exhibits tell the
story of the county's history and 19th-century life with a period country kitchen,
farm tools, antiques, textiles, branding irons, guns, dolls, and folk art. Open
Tues through Fri from 10 a.m. to 4:30 p.m., and Sat from 11 a.m. to 3 p.m.
Two blocks away is the Victorian ***Bayless-Selby House,*** open Tues through
Sat from 10 a.m. to noon and 1 to 3 p.m. Admission to both museums is free.

Check out ***Evers Hardware Store*** (109 W. Hickory St., on the south
side of the courthouse square, Denton). Measuring 25 feet wide, the front of
the store is exactly as it was at its opening in 1885. You'll find the merchandise stacked floor to ceiling, with clerks using old rolling ladders to get to top
shelves. Open Mon through Sat from 8 a.m. to 5:30 p.m.

Shops and sites worth a look on the square include ***Recycled Books,
CDs, and Records,*** a 3-story treasure trove in the old 1901 opera house on
the northeast corner at 200 N. Locust St.

There's a lot of dining right on the square, as well. ***The Loop Hole*** (119
W. Hickory St., Denton; 940-565-0770) has a menu written in pseudo-legalese,
with appetizers called arraignments, and so on. ***Denton County Hamburger
Company*** (113 W. Hickory St., Denton; 940-383-1022) is a quick place to grab
a cheeseburger with fries.

Just a block south of the square, ***Sweetwater Grill and Tavern*** (115 S.
Elm St., Denton; 940-484-2888) does a dynamite job with grilled vegetable
sandwiches, grilled shrimp over greens, toasted tomato salsa, and bountiful
burgers with elaborate toppings.

If you are looking to spend time exploring the ***Oak-Hickory Historic
District,*** which offers several buildings to be seen on a walking tour as well
as a handful of good restaurants and bars, contact the Denton Convention
and Visitor Bureau for information at (940) 382-7895. Stay overnight with the
Heritage Inn Bed and Breakfast Cluster, which includes the ***Redbud Inn***,
the ***Magnolia House***, and the ***Pecan House***, with 11 rooms in all. Take the
Redbud Inn for example. A 1910 Tudor Revival home, this B&B offers 5 guest
rooms, each with claw-foot tubs and antique beds, 7 blocks north of the courthouse. A full, homemade breakfast is served in the dining room. Call (940)
565-6414 or (940) 382-7895 or check www.theheritageinns.com.

Let's hope it's time to eat again, as this ranch country has plenty of good
eats to share. From Denton head 4 miles west on US 380, then take FR 156
south another 4 miles to the hamlet of ***Ponder,*** home to an excellent steak
joint called ***Ranchman's Cafe,*** right on FR 156 (940-479-2221; www.ranchman

.com). A legendary favorite of north Texans, this family place serves a mean steak dinner. The St. Louis beef is cut when you order your steak, cooked exactly to order, and served with salad and baked potato—if you had the foresight to call ahead and reserve your very own spud. Do not, under any circumstances, get too full for dessert: Ranchman's is famous for its homemade pies and cobblers, good enough alone to draw people from Fort Worth and Dallas, both an hour away. The cafe is open Sun through Thurs from 11 a.m. to 9 p.m. and Fri and Sat from 11 a.m. to 10 p.m.

A different side trip from Denton is to the town of **McKinney,** a straight shot east of Denton on US 380 about 30 miles, then south on Highway 5 about 2 miles. The Collin County seat has been revived in recent years, with a terrific courthouse square surrounded by delightful shops. The Victorian buildings have been renovated and now offer a full day of shop and cafe browsing.

The favorite dining and lodging spot in McKinney today is the elegant **Grand Hotel** (107 N. Kentucky St., McKinney; 214-726-9250; www.grandhotel mckinney.com), housed in a lovely 1880s building downtown. There are 14 luxurious suites, and the on-site restaurant, Rick's Chophouse, is earning raves for its aged steaks. Local history is detailed at the **Collin County History Museum** (105 N. Chestnut St., McKinney; 972-542-9457; www.collincounty history.org), in a 1911 building.

Get a complete guide to the town from the **McKinney Chamber of Commerce** by stopping by 1801 W. Louisiana St., McKinney; calling (972) 542-0163 or (888) 649-8499; or visiting www.visitmckinney.com. More than 60 specialty and antiques shops, boutiques, galleries, and cafes are listed.

The Big D

The way to **Dallas** is easy from McKinney: Drive 35 miles south on US 75 and you're there. Stay on I-35 all the way into the city and watch for I-30 East, which you'll be upon when you see downtown and the unmistakable **Reunion Tower**—that big silver ball atop a tall tower. Take I-30 East, avoiding morning or evening traffic hour if possible, and continue a short distance to the exit for **Fair Park.** Follow the directional signs a few blocks until you reach entrances on Parry Street or Cullum Boulevard.

Inside the park your destination is the **African American Museum** (3536 Grand Ave., Dallas; 214-565-9026; www.aamdallas.org), a $6 million storehouse/showcase of ethnic artifacts. The only one of its kind in the entire Southwest, the grand building of ivory-colored stone with a huge rotunda and four vaulted galleries contains a library and research center, as well as remarkable changing exhibits that typically include the work of 19th-century black masters: wood carvings, contemporary paintings, photography, and sculpture. The museum is open Tues through Fri from noon to 5 p.m., Sat from 10 a.m. to 5 p.m., and Sun from 1 to 5 p.m. Admission is free, except for groups of 10 or more ($2 adults, $1 children).

Nearby are other important buildings worth a look. For example, the **Hall of State** (3939 Grand Ave., Dallas; 214-421-4500; www.hallofstate.com) is one of the fantastic art deco buildings erected for the 1936 Texas Centennial exhibition held at Fair Park. Inside find heroes of Texas's fight for independence honored in bronze, including William B. Travis, Gen. Sam Houston, and Stephen F. Austin. Several fascinating murals illustrate the state's history from the pioneer period to the centennial year. The hall is open Mon through Sat from 9 a.m. to 5 p.m. and Sun from 1 to 5 p.m. Admission is free.

For radically different entertainment in spring, summer, and early fall, make a detour by heading east again on I-30 about 10 miles to I-635, which you'll take south 3 miles to the Military Parkway exit. Just ahead on the right you'll see a big, covered arena, home to the **Mesquite Championship Rodeo** (1818 Rodeo Dr., Mesquite; 972-285-8777; www.mesquiteprorodeo.com). Since 1958 cowboys and cowgirls have considered this a top place to make a name at bull riding, calf roping, and steer wrestling, and spectators have been ever enthusiastic. A barbecue pavilion offers supper—that's what dinner is called in many parts of Texas—at 6:30 p.m. on performance nights. The rodeo is staged for 6,000 fans every Fri and Sat night from June through Aug at 8:30 p.m. Admission is charged.

texastrivia

Ennis, about 35 miles south of Dallas, hosts the **National Polka Festival** every May.

Another attraction that's been a favorite for several generations of Texans is found back in downtown Dallas at the **Farmers' Market,** a rich country tradition deep within the heart of the nation's eighth-largest city. Head back to town on I-30 West and take the downtown exit marked Pearl Street. You'll find the 10-block, open-air market at 1010 S. Pearl St., best if visited early in the day. Some farmers personally bring their produce from around the state, while other vendors are locals who buy from farmers or wholesale nurseries and then sell to the public. Even if you're not in need of fresh fruits, vegetables, herbs, flowers, or plants, the sensory experience is pure invigoration—be sure to load the camera. The market is open daily from 7 a.m. to 6 p.m. Call (214) 939-2808 or check www.dallasfarmersmarket.org for more information.

Next stop is also downtown, at the **Belo Mansion** (2101 Ross Ave., Dallas). This extraordinarily opulent house was designed by noted architect

Herbert Green and completed in 1900. It's the only residence still existing in the city's Central Business District and was home to Col. Alfred H. Belo, founder of the venerable *Dallas Morning News*. Belo died in 1901, and the family retained ownership of the building, leasing it out as a funeral home from 1926 until 1977, when it was purchased by the Dallas Bar Association. Now open as the Dallas Legal Education Center, it's available for free tours by appointment; just call (214) 220-0239.

Barely a block away, the **Dallas Museum of Art** (1717 N. Harwood St., Dallas; 214-922-1200; www.dallasmuseumofart.org) is a vast facility with collections including pre-Columbian, African, and decorative arts. Upstairs at the museum, an elegant restaurant called **Seventeen Seventeen** (214-880-9018 or 214-922-1200) offers lunch and dinner selections including lobster, pasta, roast lamb, Vietnamese chicken salad, and incredible desserts.

Speaking of food, there are close to 100 excellent, nonchain restaurant offerings just north of the museum in the Uptown neighborhood. Breakfast, lunch, and dinner are wonderful at **Breadwinners** (3301 McKinney Ave., Dallas) and **Dream Cafe** (in the Quadrangle at 2800 Routh St., Dallas). Lunch and dinner at **Cafe Express** (3230 McKinney Ave., Dallas) means roasted chicken and vegetable sandwiches and salads piled high with grilled fish or meat; **Mattito's** (3011 Routh St., Dallas) is the place for fancy versions of Tex-Mex favorites; **Arcodoro/Pomodoro** (2708 Routh St., Dallas) is well loved for upscale pizza and pasta; and **Abacus** (4511 McKinney Ave., Dallas) is among the top pan-Asian restaurants in town, thanks to owner-chef Kent Rathbun.

Also in this area, **Hotel St. Germain** (2516 Maple Ave., Dallas; 214-871-2516; www.hotelstgermain.com) is a spectacular small hotel inside what was a fashionable home when built in 1909. The boutique hotel has won several industry awards for its luxurious lodgings and exceptional restaurant. There are 7 suites, with turn-of-the-20th-century French antiques, private baths, fireplaces, cable TV, Jacuzzi tubs, and expensive toiletries. There's 24-hour concierge, butler, and room service.

texastrivia

Bonnie Parker was an honor student in west Dallas before going on, with her partner Clyde Barrow, to become one of the country's most famous criminals.

Guests choose to have breakfast either in the dining room, the courtyard, or their suites.

A few blocks west of the Dallas Museum of Art find the **Dallas World Aquarium** (1801 N. Griffin St., Dallas; 214-720-2224; www.dwazoo.com), a spectacular offering. Bearing the look of a small European museum, it showcases a 65,000-gallon array of saltwater marine life including sharks, sting-rays, and reef fish in a reconstructed coral reef ecosystem. Then there are tropical blackfoot penguins in their own terrarium world. A restaurant, called the Eighteen-O-One, is open daily for lunch and Sunday brunch. A second restaurant, Cafe Maya, is open for lunch and dinner. The aquarium is open daily from 10 a.m. to 5 p.m. Admission is charged.

Among your downtown destinations should be **Old Red,** the imposing red sandstone building that originally was Dallas County's courthouse when erected in 1892 at the corner of Main and Houston Streets. It's quite a spectacle in all its Richardsonian Romanesque glory, complete with scary gargoyles scowling down at you from the corners. This is a great photo opportunity for anybody with a zoom lens.

Right in front of the courthouse, bounded by Houston, Commerce, and Elm Streets, is **Dealey Plaza,** a small and very scenic little park with a reflection pool, trees, and a statue honoring early *Dallas Morning News* publisher and civic leader George Bannerman Dealey. Since November 22, 1963, however, Dealey Plaza has been known as the place where President Kennedy was assassinated. No matter the time of day or night when you visit, you won't be alone: Decades after the tragedy people of all ages and nationalities still show up to look around, perhaps wondering if some answer could ever be known.

The life, death, and heritage of President Kennedy are detailed in an educational and historical exhibit across the street from the park, **Sixth Floor: John F. Kennedy and the Memory of a Nation** (411 Elm St., Dallas; 214-747-6660; www.jfk.org), a remarkable museum on the sixth floor of the former Texas School Book Depository from which Lee Harvey Oswald allegedly shot the president. Opened in 1988, the exhibit contains historic pictures, artifacts, 40 minutes of documentary films, and an award-winning audio tour. Open daily from 9 a.m. to 6 p.m. Admission is charged.

Don't dare leave downtown Dallas without visiting the retail institution **Neiman Marcus** (1618 Main St., Dallas; 214-741-6911; www.neimanmarcus .com). The original and still-flagship store is mecca for serious shoppers, and it's just fun to look around even for those who aren't into spending sprees. Take a trip up to the top floor for lunch in the venerable Zodiac Room, where chicken salad and popovers with strawberry butter have been in style since the 1950s.

One of the coolest lodgings to open in Dallas in recent years is the **Belmont Hotel** (901 Fort Worth Ave., Dallas; 866-870-8010; www.belmontdallas .com)—although it's not entirely new. This laid-back, mid-century–modern hotel was opened in 1946 just east of downtown, and it got new life recently

Take a Tour on the Darker Side of Dallas

Dallas's legends are the stuff of infamy, to be sure. If your sightseeing tastes run a little to the dark side, the **Dallas Historical Society** has tours tailor-made for you. Twice a year you can join in the "JFK Tour: Following in the Steps of Lee Harvey Oswald," which traces the presidential assassin on his route through downtown on November 22, 1963, to his boardinghouse, the theater where he was captured, and the basement where he was killed while in custody. Another pick of the criminal type is the "Legend of Bonnie & Clyde Tour," which takes you to the places where the young outlaws worked, hustled, staged gunfights, and were buried. For more information call (214) 421-4500, ext. 104, or visit www.dallashistory.org.

with a magnificent renovation. There are 68 supercool rooms and suites in 4 buildings, along with a swanky lobby lounge and a fabulous restaurant called Smoke (www.smokerestaurant.com).

Dallas's supply of art galleries, theaters, and concert halls is enormous. For a timely schedule of events, pick up free copies of the alternative weekly, the *Observer* and the *Met*. For a complete guide to all attractions, stop by the **Dallas Convention and Visitor Bureau,** located downtown at 325 N. St. Paul St., Ste. 700; or call (214) 571-1000 or go to the website at www.visitdallas.com to request a visitor kit.

Before leaving the Dallas area, consider a worthwhile side trip. Head exactly 30 miles due south of Dallas on I-35 to **Waxahachie,** the Ellis County seat and home to 21,000 citizens. Waxahachie (WOCKS-uh-hatch-ee) is a charming Victorian town built on the rich cattle and cotton businesses here at the turn of the 20th century. Some 170 of the original, ornate homes with extensive gingerbread detail survive, giving the community its "Gingerbread City" nickname. For a map of historic places on both walking and driving tours, ask at the chamber of commerce, 102 YMCA Dr., Waxahachie; (972) 937-2390; www.waxahachiechamber.com.

You won't dare miss the **Ellis County Courthouse,** easily the most fabulous of all Texas's many magnificent courthouses. Located at Main and College Streets, the 1896 masterpiece is noted for a spectacular clock tower, balconies, arches, and gargoyles. An intriguing story that's survived the past century says that one of the artisans brought from Italy to craft the stonework became enamored with a Waxahachie beauty and modeled the lovely face above the east entrance after her; she did not return his love, however, and in his anger he created monstrous faces on the rest of the detail.

Waxahachie's celebrated Victorian veneer has appealed to Hollywood in a big way: Among the excellent films shot here are *Places in the Heart, Tender Mercies, The Trip to Bountiful,* and *Bonnie & Clyde.* A brochure outlining the movie sites is available from the chamber of commerce.

If you're looking for a good lunch, you'll find it at the ***Dove's Nest*** (105 Jefferson St., Waxahachie; 972-938-3683; www.thedovesnestrestaurant.com), immediately south of the courthouse square in what was a hardware store, built in 1913. More sophisticated than most places in a town of this size, this charming dining room is a pleasant spot for enjoying gourmet pizzas, antipasto platters, chicken-apricot salad, and a Reuben sandwich. The restaurant is open Mon through Sat for lunch.

You'll need the sustenance for all the shopping to be done here on the courthouse square, home to dozens of antiques shops stocking antique and vintage furniture in European, American, Texas, and country designs; Depression glass; fine china; crystal; linens; pottery; lamps; books; dolls; toys; and pictures.

Overnight stays in Waxahachie are luxurious at the ***Chaska House*** (716 W. Main St., Waxahachie; 972-937-3390 or 800-931-3390; www.chaskabb.com), with 5 antiques-filled rooms and nearby guest cottages. The town's architecture is exhibited in grand style annually on the first Saturday and Sunday in June during the ***Gingerbread Trail.*** The special tour showcases several homes, the courthouse, two museums, and a fine auditorium. For information and tickets call the chamber of commerce at (972) 937-2390 or visit www.waxahachie chamber.com.

Another annual event that brings throngs to Waxahachie is ***Scarborough Renaissance Festival,*** a re-created 16th-century English village spread over 35 acres of open countryside. It's an impressive production, consisting of more than 400 actors and musicians portraying royalty, peasants, jesters, knights and ladies, and minstrels. Among activities and entertainment are jousting competitions, juggling, sheep dog demonstrations, magic, and comedy shows. Arts and crafts—some of which aren't entirely Old World—are available, as are all kinds of foods and drink. The fair is held on eight weekends from late April until mid-June. Admission is charged. Call (972) 938-3247 or visit www.srfestival .com for details.

Don't fill up on the fair's junk fare, however, because you don't want to miss ***Catfish Plantation*** (814 Water St., Waxahachie; 972-937-9468; www.cat fishplantation.com), which reopened after renovations due to a 2003 fire. The delightful 1895 house is said to be haunted, but that seems to simply enhance the good dining experience found here. Besides the signature fresh catfish, enjoy sweet-potato patties, fried corn, fried chicken, black-eyed peas, bread pudding in rum sauce, and cobbler. It's open Wed through Sat from 11 a.m. to 9 p.m. and Sun from 11 a.m. to 8 p.m.

Around Cowtown

From Waxahachie your destination is **Arlington**, a fast-growing place of more than 330,000 residents that has the highest average income per household in the state. You'll find it by traveling 42 miles northeast via US 287.

The stunning **Rangers Ballpark**, home to the Texas Rangers Baseball Club, is situated on I-30 at the Pennant Drive exit. This masterpiece is crafted from the popular Texas pink granite and redbrick to look like a vintage stadium from baseball's glory days in the 20th century. The stadium boasts multiple tiers as well as friezes around the facade detailed with Texas longhorns and Texas Rangers, the lawmen, and an interior hall of fame honoring baseball greats. The ballpark has restaurants, sidewalk cafes, bars, various shops, and other kinds of businesses—even a dentist. Around the stadium an expansive park includes Little League fields, picnic areas, a riverwalk, and an amphitheater.

The ballpark is also home to the **Legends of the Game Baseball Museum and Learning Center** and the **Sports Legacy** art gallery. The history of the game is detailed in an assortment of exhibits, and shoppers can find tons of souvenirs at the adjacent **Grand Slam Shop**. All admissions are free, but call ahead for hours, game times and tickets, and information, (817) 273-5600 or visit www.rangers.mlb.com.

Next door, NFL owner Jerry Jones built a $1 billion home for his football team. **Cowboys Stadium** hosted the 2011 Super Bowl and is a venue for all kinds of events, from monster truck pulls to major rock and country music concerts, along with football games galore. Find the stadium at 900 E. Randol Mill Rd. in Arlington; call (817) 892-4161 or visit www.stadium.dallascowboys .com for tour information.

Less than 10 miles east of Arlington in the town of Grand Prairie, visit **Lone Star Park** (Belt Line Road, just north of I-30, Grand Prairie; 972-263-RACE; www.lonestarpark.com). Here you'll find world-class thoroughbred and quarter horse racing at the state's top Class 1 track. The Post Time Pavilion is a 36,000-square-foot simulcasting facility with a Las Vegas–style race book, sports bar, and restaurant. Live racing is seen from a multilevel, 280,000-square-foot grandstand with European-style paddock.

And north about 5 miles from Arlington on Highway 360, the **American Airlines C. R. Smith Museum** (Highway 360 at Highway 183; 817-967-1560; www.crsmithmuseum.org) is a hugely impressive tribute to the history of flight. Among attractions is a film called **Dream of Flight,** which introduces the exhibits; a pre–World War II DC-3, the 1940 *Flagship* **Knoxville**; histori-cal photos and equipment; and a fine museum store with books, toys, videos, models, and travel gifts. The museum is open Thurs through Sat from 10 a.m. to 6 p.m. Admission is free.

From the American Airlines museum, your destination is 10 miles north to *Grapevine,* at the intersection of Highways 360 and 114. The town's roots date to negotiating days between Native Americans and settlers; in fact it was the site of an 1849 treaty signing by Gen. Sam Houston. Don't let its chain restaurants and close proximity to DFW Airport fool you; Grapevine, which boasts a National Register Historic District, is rich with Texas heritage. Pick up a walking-tour guide and list of historic sites at the *Grapevine Convention and Visitors Bureau* in the old Wallis Hotel Building (1 Liberty Park Plaza, Grapevine; 817-410-3185 or 800-457-6338; www.grapevinetexasusa.com) or at the visitor center in the Grapevine Depot (707 S. Main St., Grapevine).

> ## texastrivia
>
> *Big Tex,* the official greeter at the State Fair of Texas, was intro-duced at the 1952 fair. He stands 52 feet tall; boasts a 30-foot chest; and wears a size 90 shirt, size 70 boots, and a 75-gallon hat. The inseam on his western-style jeans measures 15½ feet.

The train depot is one end of a popular daily route made from Fort Worth by the *Grapevine Vintage Railroad* (see page 171). The *Grapevine Heri-tage Center* (817-410-3126) is here, too, with a museum containing castings of dinosaur footprints found at nearby Lake Grapevine. The Heritage Center is home to a blacksmith shop, a railroad foreman's house, and an artisan's shop where old arts and crafts, such as rug hooking, quilting, wood carving, chair caning, and boot making are taught and practiced.

Grapevine's entertainment includes the Grapevine Opry and other musical events at the *Palace Theatre* (300 S. Main St., Grapevine). Shopping includes the *British Emporium* (130 N. Main St., Grapevine; 817-421-2311), *Tolbert's Texas Trading Co.* (311 S. Main St., Grapevine; 817-442-8688), and *Off the Vine* (336-A S. Main St., Grapevine), where wines and wine-related gifts are sold. Next door to Off the Vine, Into the Glass is an excellent wine bar with an inspired menu.

The wine business is booming in suitably named Grapevine. Among sev-eral wineries in town are *Delaney Winery & Vineyards* (2000 Champagne Blvd., Grapevine; 817-481-5668); *La Buena Vida Vineyards* (416 E. College St., Grapevine; 817-481-WINE); and *La Bodega Winery and Tasting Room* (inside Terminal 2-E, facing Gate 6, Dallas/Fort Worth International Airport; 972-574-1440). Call for tasting and tour times and for fees. Also check in with the **Texas Wine and Grape Growers Association** at 1 Liberty Plaza in Grapevine, or call them at (817) 424-0570, to learn more about Texas's wine industry, now second in the nation behind California.

Stop for a bite to eat along the main drag in Grapevine at **Tolbert's Chili Parlor** (423 S. Main St.; 817-421-4888), **Big Fish** (414 S. Main St.; 817-481-2010), **Main Street Bread Baking Co.** (316 S. Main St.; 817-424-4333), or **Weinberger's Delicatessen** (601 S. Main St.; 817-416-5577).

It's time for a megadose of enjoyable culture, so head on into **Fort Worth,** taking Highway 121 south to Highway 183. Stay on 183, then take I-30 west and exit at University Drive, heading north on that street less than a mile to the **Cultural District,** a highly unusual place where four unforgettable, very independent museums are clustered within a 5-block area.

From University Drive, turn left at the Lancaster Avenue light and you'll quickly see the **Kimbell Art Museum** (3333 Camp Bowie Blvd., Fort Worth; 817-332-8451; www.kimbellart.org). Designed by the famous architect Louis Kahn, the museum was founded by industrialist and entrepreneur Kay Kimbell, who left a wealth of art and money to begin the nation's second-richest privately endowed museum, surpassed only by the Getty in Malibu, California. Within the beautifully vaulted, gray-white building are vast galleries filled with paintings by El Greco, Velázquez, Rembrandt, Cézanne, Picasso, and others, plus varied pieces of pre-Columbian art. World-class exhibits make appearances here on worldwide tours; for information call the museum or check out the website. Architect Renzo Piano has designed the museum expansion building scheduled to open in 2013.

The Kimbell is open Tues through Thurs and Sat from 10 a.m. to 5 p.m., Fri from noon to 8 p.m., and Sun from noon to 5 p.m. Admission is free. There's an excellent lunch cafe inside the museum, the Kimbell Buffet, which is open Tues through Sun.

Just a block west, the **Amon Carter Museum** (3501 Camp Bowie Blvd., Fort Worth; 817-738-1933; www.cartermuseum.org) is known for its outstanding collection of western art, particularly by Frederic Remington and Charles M. Russell, willed to the city along with a foundation by millionaire Amon G. Carter, the founder of the Fort Worth Star-Telegram and dedicated promoter of Fort Worth. An extensive renovation and expansion in 2002 has only improved the museum's stature, long ago established by its collection, which includes works by such noted American artists as Winslow Homer, Grant Wood, and Georgia O'Keeffe. A sensational bookstore is found here, too. Open Tues, Wed, Fri, and Sat from 10 a.m. to 5 p.m., Thurs from 10 a.m. to 8 p.m. and Sun from noon to 5 p.m.; tours are given at 2 p.m. daily, except Mon. Admission is free.

Fort Worth's beloved *Museum of Science and History* (1600 Gendy St., Fort Worth; 817-255-9300; www.fwmuseum.org) reopened in 2009 with an entirely new building. A place of great discovery for kids, it holds ample appeal for adults, too, in exhibits that explore natural history, space, regional culture, and much more. There's a planetarium on-site, as well as an IMAX theater. Open daily.

Among the newer arrivals in the Cultural District is the *National Cowgirl Museum and Hall of Fame* (Montgomery at Harley Streets, Fort Worth; 817-336-4475; www.cowgirl.net), a spectacular, 33,000-square-foot space that honors legendary women whose work epitomized the pioneer spirit of the American West. Among the many honorees are trick riders and rodeo stars, as well as Patsy Cline, Dale Evans, Georgia O'Keeffe, and Laura Ingalls Wilder. A research library is on the premises, and there's a fabulous gift shop. The museum charges admission. Open Mon through Thurs from 9 a.m. to 5:30 p.m., Fri and Sat from 9 a.m. to 8 p.m., and Sun from 11:30 a.m. to 5:30 p.m.

Also relatively new to the district is the magnificent new home of the *Modern Art Museum of Fort Worth* (3200 Darnell St., between University and Arch Adam Streets, Fort Worth; 817-738-9215 or 866-824-5566; www.the modern.org). Designed by Japan's Tadao Ando, the nation's second-largest modern art museum is also the oldest art museum in Texas (formerly located on Montgomery Street). This $60 million, 53,000-square-foot masterpiece of stone, steel, and glass is breathtaking, and possibly even more impressive than the wealth of art inside. Find works by Andy Warhol, Henry Moore, Jackson Pollock, and many others. The museum's *Cafe Modern* is also a stunner, both with an exceptionally interesting menu and a setting in an elliptical space that seems to float over the museum's shimmering pond. Closed Mon, the museum charges a small admission fee.

The entire Cultural District is electrified from mid-January until early February when the *Southwestern Stock Show and Rodeo* is held at *Will Rogers Coliseum,* facing the Carter and Kimbell Museums at 3301 W. Lancaster Ave., Fort Worth (817-871-8150; www.fwssr.com). This terrifically Texan event—which includes the world's largest indoor rodeo—celebrated its centennial in 1996. Annual attendance is edging close to one million, with attractions ranging from shows of more than 15,000 animals; livestock auctions; and sales of every sort of western wear, western art, Texas souvenirs, and food to pig races, goat-milking contests, and a carnival. Rodeo tickets sell out early, so order in advance if possible. A small admission fee is charged for the grounds.

Because so many people make an entire day of touring museums in the Cultural District, it's a good thing there are lots of places to have a great meal within walking distance. Inside the Kimbell Art Museum, there's The Buffet, an upscale place for lunch Tues through Sun and dinner on Fri. Visit *Lanny's Alta Cocina Mexicana* (3405 W. 7th St., Fort Worth) for an upscale meal that incorporates Mexican ingredients and Mediterranean cooking techniques, open Tues through Sat for lunch and dinner; *Saint Emilion* (3617 W. 7th St., Fort Worth) for an elegant, country French dinner Tues through Sat; or *J&J Oyster Bar* (612 University Dr., Fort Worth) for good fish at lunch and dinner daily.

Barely a 3-minute drive south of the Cultural District, find the *Fort Worth Zoo* (1989 Colonial Pkwy., Fort Worth; 817-759-7555; www.fortworthzoo.org), widely rated among the top five zoos in America. Exceptional natural habitats for hundreds of animals plus nature shops and cafes are on the grounds. A miniature train is in the adjacent park, taking a tour alongside the Trinity River. The zoo is open weekdays from 10 a.m. to 5 p.m. and Sat and Sun until 6 p.m. A small admission fee is charged.

Across the street from the zoo, *University Park Village* (on University Drive just south of I-30) is an upscale complex featuring stores such as Anthropologie, lululemon, Talbots, The Apple Store, Williams-Sonoma, Pottery Barn, Victoria's Secret, Bath and Body Works, Nine West, Ann Taylor, Francesca's, and Starbucks Coffee. Good restaurants here are Blue Mesa and La Piazza.

Now head downtown to *Sundance Square* (the center is at Main and 4th Streets), which is undoubtedly the envy of all Texas's other larger cities. This superb and extensive renovation of beautiful Victorian buildings has revitalized downtown Fort Worth to an extraordinary extent. Day and night, the 14-block area with redbrick streets is bustling with folks visiting museums, dining, shopping, and attending plays, concerts, and movies. Special architecture to note is at the Knights of Pythias building—the first such temple ever built—at 315 Main St.

The Circle Theatre (230 4th St., Fort Worth; 817-877-3040), *Casa Mañana* (109 E. 3rd St., Fort Worth; 817-332-2272), and the *Jubilee Theater* (506 Main St., Fort Worth; 817-338-4411) offer plays and musicals. Newest is the phenomenally grand *Nancy Lee and Perry R. Bass Performance Hall* (4th and Calhoun Streets, Fort Worth; 817-212-4325 or 877-212-4280; www.basshall

Vestiges of the Wild, Wild West

Every year on February 8, folks gather outside the *White Elephant Saloon* in the Fort Worth National Historic Stockyards District to see a reenactment of what's said to have been the last gunfight in Fort Worth. Legend holds that in 1887, town marshal Jim Courtright shot gambler Luke Short outside the White Elephant. Seems like a good reason for an annual party.

.com), the premier performing space for Fort Worth's opera, symphony, ballet, and national touring productions. If you want to catch up on current movies, there's the Sundance 11-theater complex, at 3rd and Houston Streets, and the Palace, at 3rd and Calhoun Streets, with nine more screens. Next to the Palace find a cavernous, 2-story Barnes & Noble bookstore, which also has a Starbucks Coffee inside.

Sundance Square museums include the beautifully expanded and remodeled **Sid Richardson Collection of Western Art** (309 Main St., Fort Worth; 817-332-6554; www.sidrmuseum.org), with western masterpieces by Charles Russell and Frederic Remington, and **Fire Station No. 1** (203 Commerce St., Fort Worth; 817-255-9300 or 888-255-9300), home to a permanent exhibit called *150 Years of Fort Worth Museum*. And you can't miss the **Chisholm Trail Mural** (on the Jett Building at 400 Main St., Fort Worth), a wonderful, enormous artwork honoring the Fort Worth portion of the Chisholm Trail cattle drives from 1867 to 1875.

For cool lodging in Sundance Square, there's **Etta's Place** (200 W. 3rd St., Fort Worth; 817-255-5760 or 866-355-5760; www.ettas-place.com), a bed-and-breakfast inn named for the Sundance Kid's schoolteacher-girlfriend. All 10 guest rooms are done in period style, with Texas antiques and reproductions, and come with fresh flowers, candies, and cookies. All have private baths with lotions and bath toys. Breakfast is an elaborate 3-course event, complete with sterling silver, china, and crystal. Hosts will assist with theater and dinner reservations.

texastrivia

NASCAR's *Texas Motor Speedway* in Fort Worth, which opened in 1997, has seating for 150,061. That makes it the second-largest sports facility in America.

The beautiful **Tarrant County Courthouse,** 100 Weatherford St. at Main Street, is at the north end of Sundance. The 1893 Renaissance Revival architecture is worth a good look, crafted again from marble and that wonderful Texas pink granite.

The list of Sundance Square's dining options grows all the time. A big favorite is **Reata** (310 Houston St., Fort Worth; 817-336-1009; www.reata.net), where you can dine on enchiladas and steaks. **Taverna** (450 Throckmorton St., Fort Worth; 817-885-7502; www.tavernabylombardi.com) is popular for focaccia, wood-oven pizza, and Italian wines. **Piranha Killer Sushi** (335 W. 3rd St., Fort Worth; 817-348-0200) makes a mean Caribbean conch salad, as well as a dramatic spider roll.

Restaurants in or within 3 blocks of Sundance Square with lively bar scenes include **8.0** (111 E. 3rd St., Fort Worth; 817-336-0880); the **Flying**

Culture Clash

Several summers ago, a friend from New York called to say that a chum from England was making his first cross-country trek through America. Our New York friend was calling pals all over the States to ask if we would show the Englishman around our towns. Happy to oblige, we received the Brit on a hot August evening and immediately took him for a Mexican-food feast. The place we chose was a little family operation in Fort Worth's historic *Stockyards District,* right on Exchange Avenue, the main thoroughfare. A very good sport, he seemed to genuinely enjoy the spicy salsa, the sizzling fajitas, and the cold Texas beer we ordered. But as he looked out the window next to our table, he looked perplexed. Finally he asked, "Is there a costume party of some sort?" We looked but had no idea what he meant. "Well," he elaborated, "what about all these chaps wearing hats and boots and those big belt buckles?" I told him those were cowboys, probably heading to one of the dance halls or saloons up and down Exchange. "Real cowboys?!" he asked. Yep, the very thing. Our New York friend called us several weeks later to report that after visiting New York, Atlanta, Chicago, Fort Worth, San Francisco, and Los Angeles, our English friend said his favorite stop was our very own Cowtown.

Saucer Draught Emporium (111 E. 4th St., Fort Worth; 817-336-7468); the *Pour House Sports Grill* (209 W. 5th St., Fort Worth; 817-335-2575; www .pour-house.com); *Razzoo's Cajun Cafe* (318 Main St., Fort Worth; 817-429-7009); and *Mi Cocina* (509 Main St., Fort Worth; 817-877-3600).

About 3 miles north of downtown Fort Worth via N. Main Street, the *Stockyards National Historic District* supplies a full day or night of history and fun. The district's main intersection is N. Main Street and Exchange Avenue, and the visitor center kiosk (817-625-9715; www.fortworthstockyards .org) is on E. Exchange Avenue between the White Elephant Saloon and Stockyards Station.

In the Stockyards you can visit *Billy Bob's Texas* (Rodeo Plaza, Fort Worth; 817-624-7117; www.billybobstexas.com), the "world's largest honky-tonk," where top country performers often include Willie Nelson, George Jones, Pat Green, Merle Haggard, Patty Loveless, Trisha Yearwood, and Jerry Jeff Walker. There are two dance floors, 40 bar stations, gift shops, and live bull riding inside, too.

At *Cowtown Coliseum* (121 E. Exchange Ave., Fort Worth, 817-625-1025), home of the world's first indoor rodeo, there's a professional rodeo and Wild West Show every Saturday from April through September. Next door at the Livestock Exchange Building (817-625-5087), built in 1904 as offices for livestock traders, you'll find the *Stockyards Collection Museum,* which chronicles the importance of the Stockyards to Fort Worth's history.

Right across the brick street in **Stockyards Station** (817-625-9715), sou-venirs, gifts, clothing, artwork, food, and drink are found in 30 shops and restaurants in what was once the Stockyards's hog-and-sheep pens. It's also a depot for the **Grapevine Vintage Railroad** (call 817-625-RAIL or visit www .gvrr.com to get a schedule), a vintage 1896 steam engine making daily excur-sions to nearby Grapevine (using diesel engines).

Wandering down Exchange Avenue you'll find the **White Elephant Saloon** (817-624-8273; www.whiteelephantsaloon.com), a century-old barroom named "One of the Best 100 Bars in America" by *Esquire* magazine. It offers cold beer and margaritas, live music, a lively dance floor, and a breezy beer garden. Across the street from the White Elephant, the historic **Stockyards Hotel** (109 E. Exchange Ave., Fort Worth; 817-625-6427; www.stockyardshotel .com) is a charming 1907 hotel with 52 rooms with period decoration. Just another block west, find **Miss Molly's Hotel** (109½ W. Exchange Ave., Fort Worth; 817-626-1522; www.missmollyshotel.com), a bed-and-breakfast inn in a restored 1910 building with 8 guest rooms.

Plenty of good eating goes on in and around the Stockyards area. For an excellent steak and fabulous bottle of wine, with a rattlesnake appetizer and a jalapeño margarita, visit **Lonesome Dove Western Bistro** (2406 N. Main St., Fort Worth, 817-740-8810); for Mexican fare try **El Rancho Grande Restau-rante** (1400 N. Main St., Fort Worth; 817-624-9206); **Joe T. Garcia's Mexican Bakery** (2122 N. Main St., Fort Worth; 817-626-5770); and **Joe T. Garcia's Mexican Dishes** (2201 N. Commerce St., Fort Worth; 817-626-4356).

The **Fort Worth Convention and Visitor Bureau**'s office is right in Sundance Square at 415 Throckmorton St., Fort Worth; (817) 336-8791. Call the events hotline, (817) 332-2000, to hear an update of current happenings. You can also visit the website at www.fortworth.com.

From Fort Worth head west on I-30, then US 180, for about 30 miles to **Weatherford.** The seat of Parker County, Weatherford was established in 1855 and grew in 1857 when the Butterfield Stage was routed through town. Hundreds of lives were lost, however, as pioneers warred with Native Ameri-cans in 1877. One of the lasting monuments to the late 19th century is the Parker County Courthouse, at the center of town on US 180. Made of locally quarried limestone in 1884, the richly Victorian building cost $55,555.55 to construct.

Three blocks east of the courthouse, you'll find a flurry of activity once a month when **First Monday Trade Days** is in progress. Thousands of folks buying and selling junk, antiques, farm animals, puppies, and food converge for the Friday, Saturday, and Sunday prior to the first Monday of each month. Across the street, the stucco Weatherford Public Market is a 1932 WPA building housing an open-air farmers' market, where produce, plants, honey, seeds, jams, and peanuts are sold by the bushel.

Stroll down to the **Weatherford Public Library** (1214 Charles St., Weatherford) and see a **life-size bronze of Peter Pan** out front. The sculpture honors Weatherford's late daughter, Mary Martin, who originated the role of Peter Pan in the Broadway musical. The library's Heritage Gallery houses costumes, photos, sheet music, and other mementos belonging to the actress.

Other important sites include a Queen Anne Victorian home at 202 W. Oak St., which was the boyhood home of former US Speaker of the House Jim Wright; and the Greenwood Cemetery, at Front and Mill Streets. Here you'll find a state historical site, the grave of Oliver Loving, known as the Dean of Texas Trail Drivers, whose story inspired the Pulitzer Prize–winning novel, *Lonesome Dove,* written by Texan Larry McMurtry. Loving died after being wounded by Native Americans during a trail drive with his close friend Charles Goodnight; Goodnight, along with Loving's son, returned his body more than 600 miles to be buried, as he had wished, in Weatherford.

texastrivia

The small town of Olney, northwest of Fort Worth in Young County, hosts an annual **One-Arm Dove Hunt** in September. An event of international repute, the hunt attracts arm and hand amputees for two days of fun and fellowship.

There are pleasant antiques shops, as well as homegrown cafes offering Texas and southern specialties, barbecue, pizza, and Mexican food.

For information on lodging, dining, historic sites, antiques, and the wonderful Parker County Peach Festival, held every July, contact the **Weatherford Chamber of Commerce,** 401 Fort Worth St., Weatherford 76086; call (817) 596-3801 or (888) 594-3801; or visit www.weatherford-chamber.com.

Dinosaurs & Hell's Gates

From Fort Worth the next destination is **Granbury,** a charming 1800s town that was restored in the 1970s to its original Victorian glory. You can reach Granbury by driving south 30 miles from Fort Worth on US 377; note, however, that a slight but most worthy detour can be found 5 miles shy of Granbury. **Acton State Historic Site** is just 2 miles away on FR 4, which intersects US 377. The Acton Cemetery holds a lovely monument to Elizabeth Crockett, widow of Alamo hero Davy Crockett, who moved here after he was killed. The statue rising above her grave shows her with her hand to her brow, watching and hoping he will come home. If you arrive during spring, the cemetery—and all this countryside—will be blanketed in vibrant bluebonnets.

Continue then to Granbury, following signs directing you to the historic downtown, which has been listed on the National Register of Historic Places. The town, after its 1890s heyday, fell into a decline but was grandly resuscitated by a town project in the 1970s that became a model for all Main Street renovation projects in the state. The town of 5,700 is the Hood County seat and a charming escape for a day, but most people stay at least a weekend.

The centerpiece of the square is the *Hood County Courthouse,* built in 1890 and containing its original Seth Thomas clock; past that is *Granbury Opera House,* 116 E. Pearl St., built in 1886 and a very popular stage for a variety of musical productions from February through December. For show information and tickets, call (817) 573-9191.

Off the north side of the square, the *Hood County Jail,* 208 N. Crockett, Granbury (817-573-5135), is an 1885 Old West jail crafted of hand-hewn stone. Used as a jail for 90 years, it's now home to the chamber of commerce, but visitors are welcome to look at the old cellblock and hanging tower. The newest and most impressive place to rest your weary bones in Granbury isn't exactly new. The former Doyle House, a historic cottage a couple of blocks from the square and one of the early bed-and-breakfast homes in town, has been extensively renovated and remodeled to become the exquisite *Inn on Lake Granbury* (877-573-0046; www.innonlakegranbury.com), with a scenic bluff-top setting on the lakeshore. It's as comfortable as it is stylish: Each room features a mix of pine, red oak, and maple, as well as elegant linens on a fancy pillow-top mattress, and the baths offer a lovely mix of granite, marble, and tile. The common area has a fireplace, leather couch and chairs, and a help-yourself area with coffee and pastries in the morning and wine and snacks in the afternoon. Outside the back door there's a gorgeous salt-water swimming pool with a waterfall and rock-and-pine landscaping. You can gaze at the lake poolside, or walk down the live oak–shaded lawn to a boat dock. There's an elaborate breakfast, served in a large detached dining room, which typically includes a pancake casserole with sausage and maple syrup, southwestern hominy, eggs with chives, fresh fruit, thick-cut bacon, and blueberry cobbler.

It's an easy walk from the inn to the most popular eatery in town, *Babe's Chicken Dinner House,* found on one corner of the square (114 W. Pearl St., Granbury; 817-573-9777; www.babeschicken.com). Thick, crunchy crust cloaks the chicken at this landmark, where family-style servings include chicken, mashed potatoes, creamy corn, salad, and biscuits with sorghum syrup on the side.

Granbury is known by north Texas weekend explorers for its abundance of reasonably priced antiques stores, tearooms offering wonderful lunches, and bed-and-breakfast lodgings. To get a list, a few good maps, and information, contact the **Granbury Convention and Visitor Bureau** at 116 W. Bridge St., Granbury 76048; call 817-573-5548 or 800-950-2212; or visit www .granburytx.com.

The **Brazos River** cuts its path diagonally across north and central Texas and in Granbury is impounded to make the 8,700-acre **Lake Granbury** that nearly wraps around the city. There are more than 100 miles of shoreline with parks, swimming beaches, and marinas.

From Granbury follow Highway 144 south for 17 miles and you'll find the bucolic town of **Glen Rose.** Founded in 1849 as a trading post, it is now the Somervell County seat and home to 2,000 people. From the 1920s through the 1930s, however, this was a thriving health resort for people who came to sanitariums here to take the rejuvenating waters. One still standing has been transformed into a lovely place to stay: the **Inn on the River,** at 205 SW Barnard St., Glen Rose (254-897-2929 or 800-575-2101; www.innontheriver.com), an extravagantly renovated and decorated 19-room bed-and-breakfast lodge. Built in 1919, the inn backs up to the serene Paluxy River and is a romantic place to spend the weekend. Gourmet breakfasts and dinners are offered to guests, and sometimes to nonguests, by reservation only.

If you're feeling flush, book a night or two at **Rough Creek Lodge** (County Road 2013, Glen Rose; 800-864-4705; www.roughcreek.com), a resort that melds adventure with luxury on the 11,000-acre Chalk Mountain Ranch, about 20 minutes south of Glen Rose. Hang out in your fabulous room or suite or in one of the new cottages, but don't skip the many activities offered here, including a rock-climbing wall, a 200-foot zip-line, a bungee trampoline, a family pool complex, a kids' ranch, a petting corral, horseback riding, a full-service spa, ATV riding, shooting clays, archery, and seasonal bird hunting. Exceptional dining comes from chef Gerard Thompson's kitchen, which offers three meals daily. Ask about family rate packages and good deals in the hottest part of summer.

Glen Rose is best known, though, for something much older—actually prehistoric. **Dinosaur Valley State Park,** 4 miles west of town on FR 205 (254-897-4588), is the site of the best-preserved dinosaur tracks, some experts say, in the world. In the solid limestone bed of the Paluxy River, just above its confluence with the Brazos River, the unmistakable prints have been found to be those of the sauropod, a gargantuan creature that ate plants, measured longer than 55 feet, and weighed more than 30 tons. Other tracks have indicated that the duck-billed dinosaur and the theropod also lived in this area. Near the river, a fenced-off area contains two life-size models of the T. rex and the bronto-saurus, fiberglass models left over from the Sinclair Oil Corporation's dinosaur exhibit at the 1964–1965 New York World's Fair. The park is about 1,500 acres and offers a wild but enchanting shrubby terrain of bluffs and water, ideal for picnicking, camping, and hiking. A dinosaur exhibit at the visitor center is open daily from 8 a.m. to 5 p.m. Park admission is $5 per person.

North Texans also come to Glen Rose at the end of September for a **blue-grass festival** hosted by Oakdale Park, on Highway 144 about 3 miles south of US 67 (254-897-2321). There are camping facilities, cabins, a swimming pool, and a pavilion here, as well.

Three miles southwest of town via US 67 is the fascinating, renowned **Fossil Rim Wildlife Center** (254-897-2960; www.fossilrim.org). More than 1,000 endangered animals from five continents call this 3,000-acre conservation cen-ter home. There's a 9-mile driving tour through the ranch, where visitors see animals roaming at will, among them the white rhino, cheetah, gray zebra, and wildebeest. The scenic overlook near the route's end is an excellent place for photos and reflection, and a restaurant, petting zoo, nature-hiking trail, riding stables, and picnic areas are close by. The ranch is open daily from 9 a.m. to 2 hours before sunset. Admission is charged.

The ranch also offers the **Foothills Safari Camp,** a wildlife safari provid-ing guests with tents and weekend dinners. Five rooms are also available at the lodge. For inquiries and reservations call (254) 897-2960.

From Glen Rose depart on Highway 144 heading south 23 miles, pick up Highway 6 in the town of Meridian, and follow it south another 12 miles. This places you at the tiny community of **Clifton,** settled in 1854 on the banks of the pretty Bosque (BOS-Kee) River, today the largest town—with about 4,000 residents—in Bosque County. Fishing is a popular pastime here on the Bosque River and nearby at Lake Whitney.

Scandinavian traditions are still observed in Clifton by descendants of the original Norwegian settlers. To see the terrain of this heritage, drive into what's known as Norse Country, along FR 219 west from town and FR 182 north from town. Tours can be arranged through the **Clifton Chamber of Commerce,** (254) 675-3720. The Norse church, sitting alone in the countryside, is really special.

To explore more of this Norse community, check out the **Bosque County Memorial Museum,** at Avenue Q and W. 9th Street (254-675-3720; www.bosquemuseum.org), a small but informative place with exhibits detailing the founding and growth of the Norse Capital of Texas. You'll see excellent examples of "rosemaling," the Norwegian craft of painting or carving intricate floral detail on all sorts of wooden furnishings. The museum is open Tues through Sat from 10 a.m. to 5 p.m. No admission is charged, but donations are gratefully accepted.

Your next destination from Clifton takes you along some roughly scenic prairie and ranch land, gently rolling into the west. Drive north along Highway 6, 36 miles to the town of **Hico** (HY-koe), stopping for a robust breakfast, lunch, or dinner at the **Koffee Kup Family Restaurant,** at the intersection of Highway 6 and US 281 (254-796-4839; www.koffeekupfamilyrestaurant.com). Don't try to resist the extraordinary meringue pies—it's impossible. If you have time, poke around the little town of Hico. There's good shopping for cool jewelry, clothing, and vintage western boots at **Western Otter** (118 N. Pecan St., Hico; 254-796-4775; www.westernotter.com); for home furnishings, jewelry, books, and gifts at **Blue Star Trading** (112 S. Pecan St., Hico; 254-796-2828; www.bluestartrading .com); and for lovingly crafted sweets at **Wiseman House Chocolates** (406 Grubbs St., Hico; 254-796-2565; www.wisemanhousechocolates.com).

From Hico drive north on US 281 for 47 miles, touring through more rolling, tree-dotted ranch country, until you arrive in **Mineral Wells,** a pretty old town of nearly 17,000 in Palo Pinto County, a wonderful place to pause in your approach to west Texas. Here's another town that saw a boom—this one in the 1880s—thanks to its mysteriously healing waters. Since no one could explain why this mineral-laden water, which didn't have an appealing scent, would make people feel better, it became known as Crazy Water, and everything in town was named similarly, such as the Crazy Hotel, the Crazy Park, and a radio show called *The Crazy Gang*.

Lions, Tigers and . . . Bats, Oh My!

In 1987 Amanda Lollar rescued an injured Mexican free-tailed bat (the state's official flying mammal) on her way to her furniture store. Since then she liquidated her business and turned it into the state's only permanent sanctuary for nonreleasable bats, and she became a state-licensed wildlife rehabilitator. She runs **Bat World Sanctuary** (217 N. Oak St., Mineral Wells; 940-325-3404; www.batworld.org), where she provides a home to up to 15 bat species, including orphaned bat pups, bats used in lab research, wild bats with permanent injuries, and bats confiscated from the illegal pet trade. Inside you can see several wire-mesh cages with bats hanging upside down from special roosts that she designed and her father built. Lollar says she can tell by the bats' eyes or facial expressions if they're feeling sick, and she has inspired her town to go batty, too. More than 100 bat houses are up on buildings and poles in Mineral Wells; the police department added a roost to its building and painted "Bat Cops" on it, while the bank's bat roost is labeled "Nite Depository." Lollar has also penned two books, *The Bat in My Pocket: A Memorable Friendship*, and *The Crazy Water Town That Went Batty.*

The boom was highlighted by the building of the elaborate, luxurious Baker Hotel in 1929, but the Depression ended the boom, and today the grand Baker Hotel—which was a copy of the famous Arlington Hotel in Hot Springs, Arkansas—stands deserted. Nevertheless, it's a great photo site rising above the skyline in the middle of town.

A charming, relaxing place to spend a night or two is **Silk Stocking Row Bed & Breakfast** (415 NW 4th St., Mineral Wells; 940-325-4101; www.silk stockingbb.com), found inside a fastidiously restored 1904 home. Five guest rooms each have a private bath, TV, and king, queen, or twin beds. A full gourmet breakfast is included with your stay.

If a cheap meal is up your alley and you enjoy an old-fashioned pool hall spirit, by all means drop into **Woody's** (6105 Highway 80, Mineral Wells; 940-325-9817). A Mineral Wells legend, this little hole-in-the-wall offers a darned good burger from an old griddle, along with an ice-cold beer.

On beautiful west Texas days, when the sun's out and the rivers aren't too low, you should think about taking a little canoe excursion on the beautiful Brazos River. **Rochelle's Canoe Rentals** (Highway 4 at the Brazos River; 940-659-3341 or 940-659-2581; www.rochellescanoerental.com) is a friendly outfit that will charge you $30 per canoe, and they'll pick you up at a designated spot.

Hikers and rock climbers will want to spend at least a day at **Lake Mineral Wells State Park** (Highway 180, 3 miles east of town; 940-328-1171; www.tpwd.state.tx.us). Crowded with trees and rocks, this scenic spread with a 650-acre lake is popular with nature watchers, too, in search of white-tailed deer, raccoon, and armadillo. The park is the western terminus of the outstanding **Rails-to-Trails pathway,** a 22-mile connection of Mineral Wells and Weatherford, built on an old rail bed and opened in 1997 for hikers, cyclists, and horseback riders to enjoy.

Another great place to spend a few days in this area is at **Possum Kingdom Lake State Park,** reached by driving west of Mineral Wells on US 180 for 38 miles until you reach the settlement of Caddo. Then head north 17 miles on PR 33, which ends at the park entrance; the park's phone is (940) 549-1803 and the website is www.tpwd.state.tx.us. Near the entrance look for some not-too-shy longhorn cattle; they are part of the official state herd.

The massive lake, a 22,000-acre reservoir formed by damming the beautiful Brazos River, has depths up to 150 feet and the clearest water in the Southwest, making it a popular site for scuba diving, waterskiing, and sailing. An extraordinary cliff formation on the southwestern end of the lake is called **Hell's Gates;** it's a great photography subject and is magnificent at sunset. Campsites, cabins, marinas, and cafes sit around the 300 miles of shoreline, but the state park's offerings are generally the best. Sitting on the south shore, the 1,500-acre park has superb hiking trails, nice if small beaches, shady and scenic campsites, a playground, canoe rentals, simple cabins, a small store, a long and lighted fishing pier, and countless good places for bank fishing. (*Note:* At press time, wildfires had ravaged homes near Hell's Gate. While construction endures on rebuilding this area, some roads may be blocked.)

A resort on the eastern shores of Possum Kingdom is called *The Cliffs* (940-779-4040 or 888-843-2543; www.thecliffsresort.com). You'll find it along Highway 16, south of PR 36. There guests can choose between lodge and condo accommodations and take advantage of the resort's 18-hole, championship golf course; health and beauty spa; tennis and swim center; full-service marina; and private, white-sand beach. There are plenty of kid-friendly programs, too, at the Cliffs.

There are modest, old-fashioned lake retreats in the form of cabins and apartments on Possum Kingdom, too. Call the *Possum Kingdom Lake Chamber of Commerce* at (940) 779-2424 for information.

About a half-hour drive northwest of Possum Kingdom Lake, you'll find one of the most appealing retreats to open in Texas in the past few years. *Wildcatter Ranch* (on Highway 16; 888-462-9277; www.wildcatterranch.com) sits on 1,500 acres about 20 miles from the lake and just 7 miles southeast of Graham, the Young County seat. It's a delightful destination for families and couples in need of a getaway in the hilly, rocky countryside, and you'll find yourself wishing for more than a weekend to squeeze in all the fun offered at the ranch. There's hiking, mountain biking, canoeing, horseback riding, tank fishing, sand volleyball, fossil hunts, cow-pasture golf, birding, scavenger hunts, hayrides, archery, skeet shooting, and ATV touring, and you can also watch the wranglers work their cattle dogs. Or, if you'd rather, you can just book a massage, followed by a poolside siesta. Ranch cook Bob Bratcher spoils guests with his grilled salmon in barbecue sauce, smoked pork ribs, and T-bone steaks. Sweet dreams are guaranteed in your plush room, with a remote-controlled fireplace and DVD player, and you can relax on your private porch with rocking chairs.

After hanging around the ranch awhile, head north to *Archer City* and Wichita Falls. From Possum Kingdom or Wildcatter Ranch, head north on TX 16, pass through Graham, and drive about 30 miles north of Graham until you reach US 281. Follow US 281 north another 7 miles to Windthorst, deep in dairy country, then turn west on Highway 25 and travel 11 miles until you reach Archer City.

You've arrived in the hometown of author Larry McMurtry, who penned the Pulitzer Prize–winning *Lonesome Dove,* as well as *Terms of Endearment* and *The Last Picture Show,* which was filmed in this very burg. Archer City has but 2,000 residents, but thanks to McMurtry, it is prospering.

McMurtry owns and operates **Booked Up** (216 S. Center St., Archer City; 940-574-2511; www.bookedupac.com), the nation's largest collection of antiquarian books, found in four stores around the Archer County Courthouse square. The buildings are clearly marked in front: No. 1 holds tomes of African-American studies, law and true crime, sports, first editions, and more; No. 2 contains art, military, photography, and children's books; No. 3 has books on classical studies, fiction before 1925, and foreign books; and No. 4 ranges from books on books, anthropology, archaeology, dance, and drama to journalism and medicine.

It's a fascinating place and well worth the trip alone.

Archer City is also home to the old movie house that inspired *The Last Picture Show*. The **Royal Theater,** sitting on one corner of the Archer City town square, was rotting away when locals pitched in to raise money for its restoration. Today the Royal is home to occasional musical performances—often hosted by groups such as the Late Week Lazy Boy Supper Club and the Texasville Opry—and other performing arts. Find out more by calling (940) 574-2489 or visiting www.royaltheater.org.

The favorite Archer City lodging is the **Lonesome Dove Inn** (225 W. Main St., Archer City; 940-574-2700; www.lonesomedoveinn.com), McMurtry's 7-room bed-and-breakfast lodging in a large, Georgian-style home.

Now turn north on Highway 79, and 25 miles later you'll find yourself in **Wichita Falls,** a city of a little more than 100,000 with an oil-boom heritage, situated on the Wichita River, nearly right on top of the Texas-Oklahoma state line.

Among many historic sites is **Kell House** (900 Bluff St., Wichita Falls; 940-723-2712; www.wichita-heritage.org), the early 20th-century home of a city founder who entertained lavishly. The restored home features original period furnishings, a baby grand player piano, 7 fireplaces, and hand-stenciled decorations. Open Tues, Wed, and Sun from 2 to 4 p.m. A small admission fee is charged.

City with a Storied History

An astoundingly ordinary-looking town of about 1,800, *Archer City*—roughly 85 miles north of Albany—is quite a bit more than it seems. Thanks to native son Larry McMurtry, author of *Lonesome Dove, Terms of Endearment, The Last Picture Show,* and other novels, Archer City isn't in danger of disappearing, as other rural Texas towns are. Archer City has been used as the filming location for *The Last Picture Show* (1971) and its sequel, *Texasville* (1989), Hollywood's versions of McMurtry's stories. In addition, McMurtry established Booked Up, in Archer City, a bookstore offering the largest collection of antiquarian books in the US. Over the years the author has collected the rare, odd, and out-of-print books carried in this store. Find it in several renovated buildings along Main Street.

At the ***Wichita Falls Museum of Art at Midwestern State University*** (2 Eureka Circle, Wichita Falls; 940-692-0923; www.mwsu.edu/wfma/), a permanent collection of pre–American Revolution prints are exhibited, and there's a planetarium and a discovery room for kids on-site. Open Tues through Fri from 9:30 a.m. to 5 p.m. and Sat from 10:30 a.m. to 5 p.m. A small admission fee is charged.

texastrivia

Thousands of cyclists from across the US converge in Wichita Falls, northwest of Fort Worth, in late August every year for the *Hotter 'n Hell Hundred*—to ride 100 miles at the hottest time of the year.

Overnight guests in Wichita Falls can choose from a number of hotels and motels, or they can stay in an elegant, Prairie-style home built in 1919, ***Harrison House*** (2014 11th St., Wichita Falls; 940-322-2299; http://hhbb.3hndesigns.com). Inside are 4 guest rooms with shared baths; a full breakfast is included with your stay.

Some of the more popular chow palaces in Wichita Falls are the ***Bar-L*** (13th Street at Travis Street, Wichita Falls; 940-322-3400), a down-home beer-and-barbecue joint that counts McMurtry and sportswriters among its fans; ***El Gordo's*** (513 Scott St., Wichita Falls; 940-322-6251), a friendly, fattening Mexican-food spot; and ***McBride's Land & Cattle*** (501 Scott St., Wichita Falls; 940-322-2516).

Other Places to Stay in North Texas

DALLAS

Hotel Crescent Court
400 Crescent Ct.
(800) 654-6541 or
(214) 871-3200
www.crescentcourt.com
Elegant, Turtle Creek–area lodging with excellent restaurants, shopping, and sensational spa.

Magnolia
1401 Commerce St.
(214) 915-6500 or
(888) 915-1110
www.magnoliahoteldallas
.com
This first-class hotel is in a renovated 1922 office building and has rooms, suites, dry-cleaning service, and exercise room.

FORT WORTH

Ashton Hotel
610 Main St.
(817) 332-0100
www.theashtonhotel.com
Fort Worth's first boutique hotel is a lovely place for both business and pleasure travelers, smack in the middle of downtown. Elegant

trappings, nice bar, and restaurant downstairs.

Azalea Plantation Bed and Breakfast
1400 Robinwood Dr.
(800) 687-3529 or
(817) 838-5882
www.azaleaplantation.com

Texas White House
1417 8th Ave.
(817) 923-3597 or
(800) 279-6491
www.texaswhitehouse.com
One of Fort Worth's historic landmarks, the 1910 Colonial Revival home is often the site of weddings and receptions. Three guest rooms have period decor and private baths with lotions, bubble bath, thick

towels, and (on request) feather beds.

GRANBURY

Arbor House
530 E. Pearl St.
(800) 641-0073
www.granbury-bed-and-breakfast.com

Other Places to Eat in North Texas

DALLAS

Cafe Madrid
4501 Travis St.
(214) 528-1731
www.cafemadrid-dallas.com
Dallas's original tapas bar does a fabulous potato omelet, grilled pork loin, marinated squid, cheeses, and more.

Javier's
4912 Cole Ave.
(214) 521-4211
Real Mexican food—meaning from Mexico's interior—includes steak, roasted chicken, fish, and enchiladas with earthy chile treatments. Open for dinner nightly; prices start from about $20 per meal.

Snuffer's
3526 Greenville Ave.
(214) 826-6850
Laid-back bar and grill popular for its cheeseburgers, cheese fries, big beers, and convivial atmosphere.

Sonny Bryan's
Locations all over
(214) 357-7120 for the 2202 Inwood Rd. location
Possibly the best smoked brisket and ribs anywhere in north Texas. Open for lunch only, seven days a week; meals start at about $5.

DENTON

Hannah's Off the Square
111 W. Mulberry St.
(940) 566-1110
www.hannahsoffthesquare.com
Exquisite steaks, intriguing vegetarian options, fancy sandwiches, and posh desserts make this perfect for dates, families, or business folks.

FORT WORTH

Carshon's Delicatessen
3133 Cleburne Rd.
(817) 923-1907
The only kosher-style restaurant in town; the sandwiches and pies are outstanding. Open Tues through Sun for lunch. Meals start at about $5.

Lambert's Fort Worth
2731 White Settlement Rd.
(817) 882-1161
www.lambertsfortworth.com
Lots of Texas flavors in oak-smoked meats and fire-grilled steaks, fish, and fowl. Cool place to have drinks and appetizers and hear music, too. Open for lunch and dinner daily.

Paris Coffee Shop
700 W. Magnolia Ave.
(817) 335-2041

Railhead Smokehouse
2900 Montgomery St.
(817) 738-9808
This is the best place in town for smoked ribs, pork, chicken, and cold schooners of beer. Open Mon through Sat for lunch and dinner; meals start at about $5.

MINERAL WELLS

Baris Pizza & Pasta
2805 Highway 180 West
(940) 325-0333

Longhorn Bar and Grill
3501 US 180 West
(940) 325-9882

WEATHERFORD

Fire Oak Grill
114 Austin Ave.
(817) 598-0400
Favorites include pecan-crusted trout and pork tenderloin in Dr Pepper sauce.

Mesquite Pit
1201 Fort Worth St.
(817) 596-7046
A big favorite for barbecue and grilled steaks.

THE TEXAS PANHANDLE

Romance and longing? For the Texas Panhandle? Why not? The pioneers who settled here came with a dream that—with plenty of muscle and heart—they made come true. Although the earth and the elements had their hard edges, the South, Staked, and High Plains also offered sweet repose. Anyone who read the Pulitzer prize–winning *Lonesome Dove* will have a sense of déjà vu upon arrival. The *Llano Estacado* (Staked Plains) stretch north toward the Cap Rock Escarpment, later yielding to the High Plains.

The 16th-century Spanish conquistadors were enamored with the endless grasslands and countless buffalo of the Panhandle, as were the Apaches, who were followed by the war-loving Comanches and young American pioneers, determined to find a future. Some would-be gold rushers jumped off the Fort Smith–Santa Fe Trail in the Panhandle, and ranchers came sometime after the Comanches were conquered and sent to the Oklahoma Territory. By 1888 33 ranches spread to occupy a land the size of Ireland.

Yucca plants shoot sharply skyward, nettles sprout white blooms, and challas burst with pink blossoms after a rainy spring. It's not unusual to drive an infuriatingly straight

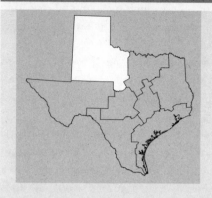

highway, then find it inexplicably winding and climbing a bluff before the monotonous view suddenly falls off into a green-and-red valley blanketed in yellow flowers. Purple-red fireweels scale rocky hillsides that are also lined by paths etched by the collared lizard, whose skin ranges from neon green to dusty yellow. Watch out for bushes with 3-inch thorns, but rest assured it's okay to eat the tart sumac berries—Native Americans made their version of Kool-Aid from the stuff.

Barbed-wire fences—which originated on ranches in this region—stretch for thousands of miles, attempting to corral this great openness. The sky grows larger every day. A few of the scarce trees have elongated, gnarled arms that surely were loved by those who administered outlaw justice. And hilly rises where there were once no trees are now populated by the tenacious mesquite.

Just a few years after the buffalo hunters and ranchers came to Texas a century ago, the Native Americans and buffalo had been exterminated. Indeed, Panhandle cattle-empire builders were successful in their work; for a period, there were three cows to every person. Poking around the same plains today, it's easy to trace history. Little has changed, for one matter, and the region's children are accomplished at preservation and continuation, for another. You'll come away wondering why all westerns aren't filmed here—it's so utterly Texan that other places in the state seem almost fraudulent by comparison.

Fandangles & Rattlesnakes

Most likely your Panhandle tour will pick up where our north Texas trail left off. But whether you're approaching the northwest section of Texas from Possum Kingdom Lake, just west of Fort Worth, or coming directly from the Dallas–Fort Worth area, you'll want to follow US 180 west from the Metroplex. First stop is *Albany,* seat of Shackelford County and home to 1,900 Texans, 120 miles west of Fort Worth on US 180.

Albany earned the handle "the home of the Hereford" for being the place where the favorite cattle breed was introduced in Texas's young days. The western heritage associated with the town endures: Hereford and other cattle represent some 90 percent of Shackelford County's agriculture business; historians point out that one of Albany's more famous sons was Edwin Dyess, for whom the Air Force base at Abilene is named; and one of its more infamous guests was prisoner John Selman, who later killed gunman John Wesley Hardin in El Paso.

First stop on the Albany tour is the *Old Jail Art Center,* S. 2nd Street near Walnut Street (325-762-2269; www.theoldjailartcenter.org), which has achieved status as one of the finer small art museums in the Southwest, having gained a great deal of stature since its 1980 opening. Several wings have been added to

JUNE'S FAVORITE ATTRACTIONS

Allen Family Style Meals
Sweetwater

Historic Downtown
Canadian

Buffalo Gap Historic Village
Buffalo Gap

Old Jail Art Center
Albany

Cadillac Ranch
Amarillo

Palo Duro Canyon State Park
Canyon

Caprock Canyons State Park
Quitaque

Panhandle Plains Historical Museum
Canyon

Fort Phantom Hill ruins
near Abilene

Perini Ranch Steakhouse
Buffalo Gap

the original structure, which was built in 1877. Some of the masons were paid by the stone, and their initials are visible on many of the large rectangles of stone. The jail once housed the keeper's office, cells, and exercise room, also known as a runaround. Today it contains the remarkable pre-Columbian collection donated by a Mineral Wells resident. Of note are the Chinese terra-cotta tomb figures, dating to 206 BC, and a Buddhist prayer book from Cambodia dating to the 16th century.

In the several new wings added to the jail are such interesting items as art deco doors from the Old Town Drug Store; an exceptional jade and amethyst collection; Picasso drawings; Italian ballroom chairs; and small Henry Moore bronzes. There also are exquisite furnishings, such as a grand piano crafted from tiger-eye oak in 1895. The museum's courtyard is a pretty place for reflection and for the myriad parties held there. Commanding attention in the center is a blockish contemporary windmill carved from native stone by artist Jesus Morales. The museum is open Tues through Sat from 10 a.m. to 5 p.m. and Sun from 2 to 5 p.m. Admission is free.

Just a block away in the City Park on S. Main Street at S. 1st Street, the *Georgia Monument* is a touching site. The stark stone memorial commemorates the five companies of volunteers who made the journey from Georgia to fight with the Texans in their revolution. The majority were killed with Col. James Fannin in the famous massacre at Goliad; nearly 20 years later the Georgia legislature invoiced Texas for $3,000 for guns but waived payment if the Lone Star State would erect a monument to the victims. Thanks to the citizens of Albany, that was finally accomplished in 1976.

JUNE'S FAVORITE ANNUAL EVENTS

Rattlesnake Roundup
Sweetwater, second weekend in March

Buffalo Gap Wine and Food Summit
Buffalo Gap, mid-April

Bob Wills Day
Turkey, last weekend in April

Fort Griffin Fandangle
Albany, last two weekends in June

Texas Cowboy Reunion
Stamford, first weekend in July

Texas!
Palo Duro Canyon, June through August

XIT Rodeo and Reunion
Dalhart, first weekend in August

Cowboy Symposium
Lubbock, mid- to late September

Panhandle South Plains Fair
Lubbock, late September

Punkin Days
Floydada, weekend closest to
Halloween

Also downtown at City Park, the ***Ledbetter Picket House*** occupies the corner of S. Main and S. 1st Streets. The restored 1870s frontier ranch has been relocated from near Fort Griffin so people can better inspect the interior, with items from the Ledbetter Salt Works, built in 1860. *Picket* is the term used for the construction style in which walls are built with vertical rather than horizontal boards. To tour this place, make an appointment with the chamber of commerce; (325) 762-2525.

When it's time for a meal ***Beehive Restaurant and Saloon,*** just west of the Albany square on US 180 (325-762-3034; www.fortgriffinandbeehive.com), is not only a good place to dine but also a self-contained point of interest. Chef and co-owner Ali Esfandiary is a petite, jovial man who is retired from Dyess Air Force Base, but he originally comes from Iran. Ali is all smiles and jokes, and as he talks with patrons, it's obvious that he's quite a local favorite. The restaurant is all roadhouse upon first impression, but its interior surprises with homey touches such as curtains and antiques. The menu is fashioned after an old-time newspaper, full of noteworthy items and lore from the 19th century. Atmosphere and details aside, the rib-eyes are fork-tender and simply the best in memory, the beautiful prime rib is the size of most placemats, and red snapper and fresh zucchini strips are other delights from the mesquite grill.

From town head 15 miles north on US 283 to ***Fort Griffin State Historical Park*** (325-762-3592; www.tpwd.state.tx.us), occupying 500 acres along the Clear Fork of the Brazos River. The fort was established in 1867 during the federal reoccupation of Texas after the Civil War, and the cavalry stationed here fought Kiowas and Comanches and helped end their domination of north

Texas. Some people know the park chiefly as the home of the state longhorn herd, whose story is as impressive as any in the state. Fort Griffin was along one of the routes through which some 10 million head of Texas longhorns were driven north to the beef markets a century ago. The longhorn was nearing extinction around 1920, and western author J. Frank Dobie was among a handful of men who helped preserve the stock. Descendants of the Dobie herd live at Fort Griffin, while other animals in the state herd live at state parks including Possum Kingdom, Palo Duro Canyon, and LBJ. By loan agreement, University of Texas mascots bearing the name Bevo are obtained from the Fort Griffin herd.

The park grounds also hold a restored bakery, replicas of other fort buildings, and some ruins, with a model of the fort and an exhibit on fort history inside the visitor center. In addition, there are nature and walking trails, restrooms, showers, a picnic area, a playground, and campsites, some with water and electricity.

The Chisholm Trail's Western Trail split off and came through Fort Griffin, and, like Fort Worth, this town was one of the West's wildest for gunslingers, gamblers, and outlaws—and that's where the ***Fort Griffin Fandangle*** comes in. The grand outdoor musical has been staged by locals for more than 50 years and is one of the more endearing annual events in Texas. Lawlessness and the fortitude it took to endure that, as well as isolation and Native American scares, are celebrated in song, dance, and pageantry, with longhorns and horses helping to create the mood. Close to a quarter of the townspeople—about 300—are involved in the spectacle, which takes place the third and fourth weekends in June. The show begins at 8:30 p.m. on pageant nights, with a barbecue dinner taking place earlier. For reservations and information call (325) 762-3838 or visit the website at www.fortgriffinfandangle.org.

If you go back through Albany, then west 8 miles on Highway 6 and south 27 miles on Highway 351, you will arrive in ***Abilene,*** the Taylor County seat and home to 116,000 residents. A sizable stop on I-20, Abilene is best known as the location of ***Dyess Air Force Base,*** I-20 at US 277 (325-793-2199; www .dyess.af.mil), which is a closed base requiring you to obtain a pass at the main gate to enter. Having done that, head for Dyess's ***Linear Air Park,*** where 25 World War II, Korean, and Vietnam War aircraft displayed outdoors include the C-47 Skytrain and B-17 Flying Fortress, plus B-1 bombers for training and combat. The date changes from year to year, but you may be lucky enough to catch an air show featuring the USAF Thunderbirds. Admission is free, and the air park is open during daylight hours.

For another collection head for the ***Grace Museum*** (102 Cypress St., Abilene; 325-673-4587; www.thegracemuseum.org), a cluster of three museums.

In the Children's Museum, kids learn, in a participatory way, scientific principles and technology's uses and applications in daily life; at the Fine Arts Museum, exhibits generally include classical to abstract art, using various media; and the Historical Museum profiles Abilene's history, with emphasis on the recent past. Numerous traveling exhibits make stops at this museum center annually. A small admission fee is charged; the museums are open Tues through Sat from 10 a.m. to 5 p.m., and for Thursday Family Night from 5:30 to 8:30 p.m.

Be sure the kids get to see the *Abilene Zoo and Discovery Center* (3 miles east of the center of town on Highway 36, in Nelson Park; 325-676-6085; www.abilenezoo.org.). The plains of Texas and Africa are represented by 500 species of animals, including coyotes, javelinas, zebras, ostriches, and bison. The herpetarium houses more than 70 different species of reptiles and amphibians. At the Discovery Center, visitors can learn more about various biomes. Open daily 9 a.m. to 5 p.m., with extended hours between Memorial Day and Labor Day. A small admission fee is charged.

Don't miss the chance to explore rough-and-tumble Texas history at *Frontier Texas!* (625 N. 1st St., Abilene; 325-437-2800; www.frontiertexas.com). A state-of-the-art center spreading over several acres, this ultra-interactive destination's high-tech capabilities let you connect with the people who carved a life out of the wilds across the state, putting you inside a herd of stampeding buffalo, a card game gunfight, Indian battles, and scary prairie weather. This is the perfect jumping-off point for wandering the 700-mile-long Texas Forts Trail, and the museum also has a gift shop stocking a wealth of books, toys, clothes, and home decor, all in a western theme.

It won't take too long to claim a pair of custom-made boots at *James Leddy Boots* (1602 N. Treadway, Abilene; 325-677-7811), one of the renowned names in Texas cowboy boots. Order now and you should have your eel, snakeskin, calfskin, lizard, or other exotic leather boots within 2 or 3 months.

Sweet Old Baird

The town of *Baird,* just east of Abilene via I-20, was settled in 1880 and was named the *Antiques Capital of West Texas* by the state legislature in 1993. In town you'll find the *Old Rock Jail* at 100 W. 5th St., which was moved from the former county seat of Belle Plain; each block was numbered and the jail was rebuilt exactly as it had been. It's now used as a *Boy Grumpe's,* a candy factory at 206 Market St., which is one of only four candy factories in the US that produces lollipops for business advertising, and one of only two that puts messages on both the stick and the candy.

Prices start at around $500 and top out at about $3,500. Don't forget to order a belt or wallet to match. Open Mon through Fri 8 a.m. to 5 p.m.

The longtime favorite dining destination in Abilene is *Joe Allen's Pit Barbecue* (301 S. 11th St., Abilene; 325-672-6082; www.joeallens.com), a legendary stop for old-fashioned, no-frills Texas 'cue. If your palate demands the very best beef with sides of pampering, you'll put *Perini Ranch Steakhouse* (2003 FR 89, Buffalo Gap; 325-572-3339; www.periniranch.com) situated in *Buffalo Gap Historic Village,* about 6 miles south of the Abilene city limits, on your must-go list. Owner-chef Tom Perini has served his famous beef at the White House in Washington, D.C., and at the James Beard House in New York, so you're assured of something pretty special. In a rustic setting, diners enjoy 16-ounce roast ribeyes with cowboy potatoes and ranch beans, or baby-back ribs cooked over mesquite. You can get margaritas and good wines to go with your steaks, too, but be warned that weekend crowds may mean a sizable wait for a table. Open Wed and Thurs for dinner and Fri through Sun for lunch and dinner. Call (325) 572-3339 for reservations. If you're looking for a big weekend of Texas cuisine, check out the *Buffalo Gap Wine and Food Summit,* held in mid-April at Perini Ranch, where new and exceedingly comfortable guest quarters are now an option for overnight stays.

Spend time before dining to explore *Buffalo Gap,* a restored frontier complex that was once a stopping place along the famous Dodge Cattle Trail, containing relocated historic buildings such as the Taylor County Courthouse and Jail, circa 1879; a railroad depot dating to 1881; Abilene's first blacksmith shop; and Buffalo Gap's own Nazarene Church, built in 1902. A charming trip back in time, Buffalo Gap is open mid-Mar through mid-Nov Mon through Sat from 10 a.m. to 6 p.m. and Sun from noon to 6 p.m.; and mid-Nov through mid-Mar Fri through Sun 10 a.m. to 5 p.m. A small admission fee is charged. Call the village at (325) 572-3365 or visit www.buffalogap.com.

Another look at history is found north from Abilene 14 miles on FR 600, where the *Fort Phantom Hill Ruins* consist of monolithic, cactus-crowded, crumbled masses of stones. These ruins have a particular poignancy about them, especially in the day's first or last light—it's easy to imagine that desertion was a problem here because of monotony and loneliness. Fort Phantom Hill was established in 1851 for protection against the Comanches as the westward settlement activity spread. The fort was abandoned in 1854, as the water supply was insufficient; although it mysteriously burned shortly afterward, the fort was later used as a Texas Rangers outpost and as a US Army outpost during the Indian Wars of the 1870s. The ruins lie on private property today, but the owner keeps the site open to the public daily from dawn to dusk. Admission is free.

Abilene serves as a good pivot point to reach two more marvelous pockets of the Old West. First is **Anson,** 24 miles northwest of Abilene via US 83/277, the seat of Jones County. The town was long known and widely criticized until a few years ago for banning dancing—except at the Christmas Ball—for religious reasons. Times have changed slightly, but most citizens still choose to go dancin' in Anson only for the three days every December when Anson hosts its historic **Cowboys' Christmas Ball,** usually held the weekend prior to Christmas. Anson has quite a time letting its citizens cut a rug, and western crooner Michael Martin Murphey has put into song and video the century-old poem honoring the ball, written by rancher Larry Chittenden. If you miss the dancin', check out the other element that drew the locals' ire: The Depression-era mural in Anson's post office offended folks at its 1941 unveiling, as some townspeople felt it was wrong to illustrate the fun people were having on the dance floor. (This is the Bible Belt, remember.) See the mural depicting the Christmas Ball in the post office on tiny Main Street (325-823-2241).

Now point your car to our next side trip, to **Stamford,** 17 miles north of Anson on US 277, still in Jones County and with a population of 3,800. You're in true cowboy country here, as Stamford is home to the **Texas Cowboy Reunion** held for three days over the weekend closest to July 4. Begun more than 60 years ago, it hosts unquestionably the world's greatest amateur rodeo, drawing more than 500 competitors and thousands of fans. The festival includes chuck wagon meals, a huge western art show, and lots of music. Call the chamber of commerce at (325) 773-2411 or visit the event site at www.tcrrodeo.com

For a better understanding of Stamford's cowboy history, head to the **Cowboy Country Museum,** 113 S. Wetherbee St., Stamford (325-773-2411; www.stamfordcoc.org/museum). Well-known cowboy artists have paintings and prints displayed here, and other exhibits include ranch and farm artifacts from a century ago, as well as a blacksmith shop. The museum is open Mon through Fri from 9 a.m. to noon and 1 to 4 p.m. Admission is free.

We'll Leave the Light on for You

Drive 46 miles east of Abilene via I-20 to the town of **Cisco** in order to visit the **Mobley Hotel,** 309 Conrad Hilton Ave. (also Highway 6). In 1919, Conrad Hilton, who needed a place to sleep, purchased the old hotel. It became the first in a chain of Hilton hotels when Hilton realized he could make a bundle by letting rooms to oil-field workers who would rent by the shift. Today the restored hotel serves as a chamber of commerce office and community center.

There may not be a better place to capture on film the heritage of this region than at the ***Mackenzie Trail Monument,*** at the intersection of US 277 and Highway 6. This immense, sand-colored stone marker was hand carved to depict the days of the famous Mackenzie Trail (1874–1900) and the buffalo, Native Americans, pioneers, and early ranchers who figured into this history. Open at all hours.

Now we're off to rattlesnake country: Head west from Abilene on I-20, following it 42 miles to ***Sweetwater,*** seat of Nolan County and home to 12,000 salty Texans. The community came about when buffalo hunters in the 1870s camped on Sweet Water Creek simply because they preferred the sweet, clear water there over the area's other, gypsum-flavored streams. The humble beginnings continued with the opening of a dugout trading post in 1877; then the town charter—first established in 1884—failed twice due to blizzard, drought, and resulting evacuation. After the 1902 incorporation held, the area grew during World War II, when the Women's Air Force Service Pilots training program was based at the local ***Avenger Field.*** The world's first and only all-women military flying school produced a little more than 1,000 pilots out of 25,000 applicants. The 39 who died in service are honored with a bronze statue and a walk of fame on the campus of Texas State Technical College–Sweetwater at Avenger Field, on I-20 West at Sweetwater Municipal Airport (325-235-7300). Open during daylight hours.

Plan your arrival in time for lunch, as you wouldn't want to miss a chance to use your boardinghouse reach at ***Allen Family Style Meals*** (1301 E. Broadway St., Sweetwater; 325-235-2060), not unlike Sunday dinner with a big family. For less than $10 you can eat family-style from a long table spread with a plastic tablecloth and set with unmatched plates. For lunch your table will be filled with plates and bowls weighted down with not only fried chicken but also cream gravy, beef brisket, buttered potatoes, candied sweet potatoes, potato salad, turnip greens, green beans, stewed summer squash, corn, English pea salad, pinto beans, fruit salad, rolls, peach cobbler, and iced tea. The restaurant has been a favorite for more than 40 years and will soon be one of yours. Open Tues through Sun for lunch and a buffet dinner, which is served in a newer building found next door.

If good fortune was in your planning, you'll have arrived in Sweetwater on the second weekend in March—that's when the town is jumping, thanks to some 20,000 or 30,000 folks who show up for the annual ***Rattlesnake Roundup.*** Some six or seven tons of rattlesnakes are gathered during this, the world's largest such event. Several other Texas towns have followed suit, but Sweetwater's is the oldest, having begun in 1958 when the Jaycees pitched in to help local ranchers and farmers deal with their tremendous rattlesnake problem. The roundup became a festival, and the rest—as is widely said in the western reaches of this state—is history. The weekend is filled with a parade, the Miss Snake Charmer Queen Contest, real hunts for western diamondback rattlers, professional snake-handling demonstrations, snake-milking for medical research, a 10K run, a dance, a tour of rattlesnakes' natural habitats, and a rattlesnake-eating contest. Fried rattlesnake is available, as are numerous other—and less exotic—snacks. And there's a weigh-in and prize ceremony for the most snakes captured and the largest. All the fun takes place at the Nolan County Coliseum at the north end of Elm Street. Call (325) 235-5488 or visit www.rattlesnakeroundup.net for schedules, details, and ticket information.

Now it's time to head into the Panhandle Plains: take I-20 west 8 more miles until you pick up US 84 and follow it 30 miles north to **Snyder,** found right at the US 180 West exit. This is the seat of Scurry County, with a population of 12,000 and—more important—a monument saluting a rare beast, the **White Buffalo Statue,** on the courthouse lawn at College and 25th Streets. One of the many, many buffalo hunters who killed off the valuable herds here claimed that among the 22,000 buffalo he killed was a rare albino, shot near Snyder. To honor the herds Snyder's townspeople put up this life-size replica of the albino buffalo. Some say the beast began as a bull buffalo, but respect for delicate sensitivities rendered it a cow instead.

You won't go hungry in Snyder at **The Shack** (right on US 180; 325-573-4921). Open for lunch and dinner, the restaurant offers everything from a rib-eye sandwich, taco salad, and fried chicken to a 16-ounce sirloin steak, grilled chicken breast, and fried shrimp. The restaurant also has a small gift shop selling crystal pieces and ceramic figurines.

Cap Rock & Canyons

Now we head into some of the most physically compelling country, if regarded with respect by those who spent lifetimes trying to tame it. Taking country roads at this point is the way to best drink in the often parched land, fascinating to anyone with an eye for prehistoric aesthetics. From Snyder, take Highway 208 north 57 miles to the town of Spur, passing through Clairemont. Now skirting the Cap Rock's eastern edge, head north 20 miles on FR 836 to US 82, then go west just another 6 miles, actually driving onto the famous escarpment. Watch for a roadside park on the left, and you'll have found **Silver Falls Park,** a stop said by many to be the finest of all roadside parks in the vast state. The White River courses through this part of the Cap Rock and its canyon land on its way south to join the Brazos River, and state engineers were wise enough to place picnic tables and carve riverside hiking paths here for journey makers like yourself. Perhaps you've picked up snacks or sandwiches on the way; this is a perfect place to stretch your legs and take some scenery photos.

It's just another 4 miles west to the town of **Crosbyton,** seat of Crosby County and home to 2,000. It's in the heart of an agricultural land, and the local Associated Cotton Growers is said to be the world's largest cotton-processing plant of stripped cotton, serving more than 500 cotton companies in a 50-mile area. Crosbyton is also home to the *Pioneer Memorial Museum* (101 Main St., Crosbyton; 806-675-2331; www.crosby countymuseum.com). Inside, the pioneer lifestyle is illustrated with home replicas and admirable collections of vintage housewares, arts, and farm equipment. Native American relics and artifacts relevant to the local ecology are exhibited, too. Open Tues through Sat from 9 a.m. to noon and 1 to 5 p.m. Admission is free.

texastrivia

The world's largest (and oldest) rattlesnake roundup is held every March in Sweetwater.

From here head north 23 miles on FR 651 to **Floydada,** seat of Floyd County, home to 3,700 Texans and the undisputed Pumpkin Capital of the US. If it's autumn, you've no doubt seen some awesome pumpkins—they call the hundred-pounders "Big Macs"—at markets and along roadsides in Texas, and you can bet they came from here. The town's annual *Punkin Days* is a festival held on the courthouse square the weekend closest to Halloween. Stop in for some pumpkin bowling, pie tastings, seed-spitting contests, and carving competitions. Most events are free. Find the fun at Main and Missouri Streets; for details call (806) 983-3434.

Now it's time to cross the Cap Rock again, heading east on US 62/70 from Floydada 24 miles to Matador, where you'll pick up Highway 70 north, following it 28 miles to *Turkey,* a Hall County town and site of the *Bob Wills Museum* (on 6th Street at Lyles Street, Turkey; 806-423-1253 or 806-423-1491; www.turkeytexas.net), intriguing to anyone with even a passing interest in the music called Western Swing. The museum's collection dedicated to the King of Western Swing—who was born just outside of town and whose daughter has moved back to Turkey to run the foundation—includes fiddles, boots, hats, recordings, sheet music, and photos belonging to or representing the Texas Playboys, Wills's band.

Open Mon through Fri from 8 a.m. to noon and 1 to 5 p.m. and weekends by appointment. Admission is free; however, donations are accepted. Inquire, too, about Bob Wills Day, usually held the last weekend in April, with a parade, fiddlers' contest, dances, and performances by members of the original Texas Playboys.

The town is home to, naturally, the *Hotel Turkey* (3rd and Alexander Streets, Turkey; 806-423-1151). Restored in the late 1980s, the cluttered but comfortable hotel draws plenty of Bob Wills fans, as he played here in the late 1920s, as well as people who simply enjoy old hotels. Guest rooms are filled with original furniture and wallpaper adorned with hand-sewn decorations, while the front parlor downstairs is furnished with century-old sofas, chairs, and tables. The 40-seat dining room is decked out with antique photos of Turkey's residents. A hot breakfast is served to guests, and a modest gift shop sells new and used knickknacks.

From Turkey, turn west on Highway 86 and travel 13 miles to RR 1065, following it north for just over 3 miles until you reach *Caprock Canyons State Park,* just inside Briscoe County and 3 miles beyond the tiny town (population 500) of Quitaque (KIT-a-KWAY). You may want to stock up on some groceries and camping goods in that town or back in Turkey, as this little-known park is an ideal place to kick back a while and savor this rugged country. The views here of mountains, canyons, streams, and indigenous flora and fauna are simply breathtaking, and a visitor center offers an interpretive area plus an archaeological site, with artifacts representing the canyon for some 250 million years. There's a 100-acre lake for swimming, fishing, and boating, but the real draw—besides the vistas, of course—is the hiking trails, 25 miles of paths coursing through the mountainous, 14,000 acres of parkland. Be on the lookout, especially on mountain trails, for buffalo and antelope, among several species

Horse Heritage

The *American Quarter Horse Heritage Center* at 2601 I-40 East, Amarillo (806-376-5181; www.aqha.com), explores the magnificence of the quarter horse from its days as the working ranch horse of the American West to the equine competitor of the modern world. Its life is examined from the 17th century, when the breed was developed in the Western Hemisphere, to the present day. The recently renovated, updated complex is also the international headquarters of the *American Quarter Horse Association,* the world's largest horse registry. Open Mon through Sat from 9 a.m. to 5 p.m. and Sun from noon to 5 p.m. Call ahead for a guided tour. A small admission fee is charged.

Where's the Beef?

"The Pride of Texas on a Bun" is what the *New York Times* called several Lone Star hamburgers in a 1998 cover story in its Dining Out section. The first of a handful cited in the story was that found at **Arnold Burgers** in Amarillo (1611 S. Washington St., Amarillo; 806-372-1741; www.arnoldburgers.com), where the house specialty is the Arnold Double Burger, a 5½-inch patty weighing three-quarters of a pound. Owner Gayla Arnold also makes a burger that can feed 12 to 18 people. See? Everything is bigger in Texas.

of wild animals. Joining you on the paths may be horseback riders, mountain bikers, or campers who brought their own mounts. Camping is in both primitive and improved campsites. The park is always open, and a small admission fee is charged. Call (806) 455-1492 or visit www.tpwd.state.tx.us for more information.

After the relaxation you can get to **Amarillo,** seat of Potter County and home to 173,000 people, by driving north from Caprock Canyons on Highway 86 not quite 9 miles and taking Highway 256 west another 9 miles until you reach Highway 207 North, which will put you on a scenic route across the majestic **Palo Duro Canyon,** which we'll explore in detail later. For now stay on Highway 207, 48 miles until you reach US 287 at the town of Claude, and follow that highway west 28 miles to the Amarillo city limits.

Amarillo's humble beginnings date to its 1887 establishment as Ragtown, a railroad workers' tent camp. Today it's a mammoth center of cattle trade, and there are wonderful places to buy western artwork and clothing. Some lovely historic homes are on view, as are an art museum and a well-known science and technology museum.

To get a taste of Amarillo's tremendous cattle heritage, make your first stop at the city's **Livestock Auction,** held in the stockyards at 100 S. Manhattan St., Amarillo, every Tues from 9 a.m. to 5 p.m. As you walk in, the auctioneer's rhythmic patter with odd inflections meets your ears as assorted cows and bulls are moved quickly for viewing through the main room's bottom, from which rise bleachers for spectators and bidders. Outside, the purchased cattle are herded into pens one at a time, usually by a few no-nonsense cowgirls, who are the only indication that anything has changed in the past 100 years. To understand the significance of this place, note that more than 300,000 cattle are sold here every year, making this the largest individually owned auction in the state. It's the world's largest weekly livestock auction, and annual sales are close to $75 million. Even if you miss auction day, you can look around the place; admission is always free.

At the adjacent **Stockyard Cafe,** also at 100 S. Manhattan St., Amarillo (806-374-6024), you can fill up on massive breakfasts (get the green chile omelet) and monster lunch portions of chicken-fried steak, sandwiches, and home-baked pies, sitting down with cowboys and ranchers. It's open Mon through Sat for breakfast and lunch and for dinner Fri and Sat only.

For a day of cowboy life, head for the **Bar H Dude Ranch,** an hour's drive east of the city via US 287 in Clarendon (806-874-2634 or 800-627-9871; www.barhduderanch.com). Ride horses or haywagons, do a little work with the cowboys and cowgirls, pitch horseshoes, fish, take square-dancing lessons, and even stay the night if you like. Call ahead for reservations and prices.

Explore Amarillo's high-tech side at **Don Harrington Discovery Center and Planetarium,** in the 50-acre Amarillo Garden Center at 1200 Streit Dr., Amarillo (806-355-9547 or 800-784-9548; www.dhdc.org). Named for a local oil mogul and philanthropist, the complex presents a number of special films that make science fascinating for kids and adults alike. The Discovery Center also presents Smithsonian traveling exhibits and several interactive displays for all ages.

And in tribute to Amarillo's standing as chief helium producer in the US, a leggy, four-pronged **Helium Monument** stands in front of the Discovery Center. The structure functions as a futuristic sundial, and its limbs are time capsules filled with newspapers, a Sears catalog, and a piece of apple pie sealed in helium. The Discovery Center is open Tues through Sat from 9:30 a.m. to 4:30 p.m. and Sun from noon to 4:30 p.m. Admission is charged. Planetarium shows are included with admission.

Antiques hounds will love the **Old San Jacinto** area, located on 6th Street along historic Route 66 (between Georgia and Western Streets). Those in the

The 72-ounce Steak Challenge

The quintessential, Texas-size experience is found in lunch or supper at the **Big Texan Steak Ranch,** 7701 I-40 East at Lakeside exit (806-372-6000 or 800-657-7177; www.bigtexan.com). Resembling a circus arena, the cavernous interior is fun and fascinating, with a giant wooden Indian, a stuffed grizzly greeting you at the entrance, and big-game trophies covering every wall. Chairs and benches are fashioned from horseshoes, of course. The menu is laden with buffalo, rattlesnake, rabbit, calf fries (the most private of calf parts), chicken-fried steak, and rib-eye steak. The fanfare, however, surrounds the presentation of a 72-ounce prime steak dinner that's free if the diner eats the whole thing—with the accompanying salad, shrimp cocktail, baked potato, bread, and butter—in 1 hour. Some do it, but it's a true challenge. The luckiest diners happen by when the Kawahadi Indian Dancers are scheduled for a performance. The restaurant is open daily for lunch and dinner.

know think this is becoming the premier antiques center of the Southwest, with dozens of delightful shops selling treasures dating from the turn of the 20th century. While away the morning or afternoon browsing, then stop at any of the several cafes along the strip. Most shops are open Mon through Sat from 10 a.m. to 5:30 p.m. and Sun from 1 to 5 p.m.

Right in the same neighborhood, there's the ***Golden Light Cafe*** (2908 W. 6th Ave., Amarillo; 806-374-9237), a hamburger joint dating from 1946. This creaky little place gets its atmosphere from neon beer signs and cooking that would never be deemed acceptable by the American Heart Association. Regulars mosey in and plan to sit a spell, waiting on handmade burgers and other bodacious platters of food, along with cold bottles of Shiner Bock beer. Grab a booth and get ready to travel back in time.

After shopping and lunch, treat yourself to the happiest surprise in this dry, flat city. At the recently renovated and updated Amarillo Botanical Gardens, you'll find the new ***Mary Bivins Tropical Conservatory*** (1400 Streit Dr., Amarillo; 806-352-6513; www.amarillobotanicalgardens.org). Within its glass pyramid, you'll roam through more than 6,000 square feet of lush flowers and trees meant to transport you to a South American rain forest. Sit by the rock waterfall and pond and feel stress slipping away. Depending on the calendar, you may stumble upon a horticulture workshop or lecture or perhaps catch an art exhibit on display.

For more visitor information call the ***Amarillo Convention and Visitor Council*** at (800) 692-1338 or (806) 374-1497, or visit the website at www.visit amarillotx.us.

Just outside of town, 12 miles to the west on I-40—also the epic Route 66—***Cadillac Ranch*** is the unique creation of Stanley Marsh 3 (as he is faithfully called), land and broadcasting baron and easily one of the more powerful of all the personalities of modern Texas. Known always for his noteworthy and eccentric ways, he made his contribution to pop culture in a cotton field with a lineup of 10 Cadillacs buried nose-down, exhibiting tail-fin designs from between 1949 and 1963 diagonally into the air. Worth noting is that the cars are buried at precisely the same angle to the ground as the great Cheops pyramids. Graffiti artists have made their own contributions, as the art display—called Amarillo's "bumper crop"—is always open. No admission is charged.

From the ranch take Highway 136 north to ***Alibates National Monument,*** a mostly undeveloped site popular with hikers and archaeology buffs. The area atop a high ridge overlooking Lake Meredith contains an ancient quarry of flint, unique for its amazing colors. Farmers and Native Americans distributed Alibates flint over the Southwest and Great Plains from 10,000 BC until the 19th century. The quarry itself is overgrown with grass and shrubs, so you won't know you've found it until you're in it. The stones are flat, somewhat smooth, and shaded with muted blues and grays, black, maroon, and orange. Nearby, great pits of buffalo bones have been found, along with pottery dating to AD 1250. A Native American village was excavated in a 1938–39 project, and pictographs were found in huge dolomite boulders. Ranger-led walks, extremely helpful for visitors, conclude with flint-chipping instruction. Free tours are offered during summer at 10 a.m. and 2 p.m. and by appointment for the balance of the year. Admission is always free, and the monument is open during daylight hours. Call (806) 857-3151 for information and reservations.

The monument lies on the south shore of Lake Meredith, site of *Lake Meredith National Park.* Fashioned from the Canadian River, the lake is 2 miles wide in places and 14 miles long, offering 100 miles of shoreline. The National Park Service has created eight recreation areas with swimming in a lake and swimming pool, fishing, sailboating, and waterskiing. There are places to play golf and tennis, too. If you've picked up provisions in Amarillo or in nearby Fritch, you can choose a place from several bluffs and canyons around the lake for picnicking and camping. Open at all times, admission is free, but there are fees for boating. Call (806) 857-3151 for information.

Plan a day of touring northeast of Amarillo to experience a wealth of Texas heritage. The first stop is in the town of *Panhandle,* 30 miles northeast of Amarillo on US 60. The *Carson County Square House Museum* (5th and Elsie Streets, Panhandle; 806-537-3524; www.squarehousemuseum.org) illustrates the history of the Panhandle, from its early Native American cultures to present-day industries and technology. The historic 24-foot-by-24-foot Square House was built during the 1880s with wood transported from Dodge City, Kansas. Other parts of the museum include a hall of natural history, two art galleries, railroad exhibits (housed in a caboose), and a barn. Open Mon through Sat from 9 a.m. to 5 p.m. and Sun from 1 to 5 p.m. Admission is free, but donations are accepted.

Continue your journey along US 60 another 27 miles to the town of *Pampa,* a ranching town with a strong oil and agricultural background. As you follow the ribbon of highway, you'll see skyscrapers appear on the otherwise bare horizon, but soon you'll realize they're grain elevators that characterize much of the landscape in the Panhandle.

The rewards in Pampa are of the gastronomical kind, starting with *Dyer's BBQ* (Highway 60 West, Pampa; 806-665-4401). A family restaurant whose walls are decorated with spatulas, old coffeepots, and potato mashers, Dyer's specializes in homemade smoked sausage and pork ribs, as well as simple but very good pinto beans. Also in Pampa make a point to visit *Coney Island Cafe* (114 W. Foster St., Pampa; 806-669-9137), a charming diner opened in

Adobe Walls

History buffs will want to seek out the site of the **Battle of Adobe Walls,** where two famous Native American battles were fought. In 1864 Col. Kit Carson fought his last fight when his US troops barely escaped defeat by Kiowas and Comanche who had been molesting wagon trains and settlers. Ten years later, in 1874, Quanah Parker and Lone Wolf led a tribe in an attack on a buffalo hunters' camp, but they were eventually scared away when the famous shot by William "Billy" Dixon took a brave from his horse at a distance of roughly 0.8 mile. The Adobe Walls site is roughly 18 miles northeast of Stinnett, which is northeast of Amarillo and near Lake Meredith. Inquire in Stinnett as to local tours.

1933 by Greek immigrants. The chili dogs and stew are very popular, but the homemade pies—buttermilk and apricot are among the 16 daily varieties—are outstanding and worth every calorie.

Continuing east along US 60, you'll cross the magnificent, scenic Canadian Breaks, eroded almost to canyons by the legendary Canadian River. Fifty miles beyond Pampa, you'll come upon the marvelous little town of **Canadian,** tucked into a wooded bend of the river, grown from a settlement once known only to cavalry soldiers, railroad builders, and cowpokes. Today you'll find a surprising collection of elegant, historic homes, lovingly restored buildings, good dining, bed-and-breakfast lodging, boutiques, an art center, and even a day spa.

If you can't stay overnight in Canadian, allow at least half a day to explore. Be sure your stops in the downtown district include the **W.C.T.U. Building** at 500 Main St., which is the only building in the nation built, owned, or maintained by a local Women's Christian Temperance Union chapter. Built in 1911, the ornate structure houses the county library today. Other worthwhile stops downtown include the **Palace Theatre** at 210 Main St., opened as a vaudeville house in 1909 and operating as a first-run movie house today; and the **City Drug Soda Fountain** at 224 Main St., a renovated 1910 structure that uses authentic soda fountain equipment and original furnishings today.

Make a quick detour immediately north of town via US 60/83 to see the **Canadian River Historic Wagon Bridge,** originally constructed in 1915, when it was the longest metal truss bridge in the state. Restored in 2000, its wood planking serves as a trail across the river for walkers, cyclists, birders, and other wildlife watchers.

You won't go hungry long in Canadian. Barbecued brisket and mesquite-grilled steaks are best at the **Cattle Exchange** (2nd at Main Streets, Canadian;

Panhandle's Little Tree

About 5 miles southwest of the town of Panhandle, which is the seat of Carson County, you can visit *Thomas Cree's Little Tree,* the site of the first tree planted throughout the entire Panhandle. On the plains that were once a sea of grass, pioneer settler Thomas Cree brought a sapling *bois d'arc* (pronounced "BOE dark") for planting behind his dugout home in 1888. The tree lived until 1969, when an agricultural chemical was accidentally used here; county residents planted a new tree, which sits behind a protective fence at the south edge of US 60. Be sure to note two State Historical Markers and a medallion from the National Men's Garden Clubs of America.

806-323-6755; www.cookya.com/). Greek salads, homemade chili, and exquisite desserts are among the good fare at *Our Fillin' Station* (217 S. 2nd St., Canadian; 806-323-6504; http://ourfillinstation.net).

Among several interesting accommodations choices in and around Canadian, one of particular note is the *Arrington Ranch House Lodge* (9765 County Road 5, Canadian; 877-325-6924; www.arringtonranch.com). Featured in the final scene in Tom Hanks's film *Cast Away,* the 5-bedroom home was a mail-order house built in 1918. The original owner was a Texas Ranger known as Capt. George Washington Arrington, and his great-grandson owns the home today. Perfect for family reunions, the home is roomy and extremely comfortable, with impressive views of the sunrises and sunsets. For more Canadian information, visit the *Canadian Visitor Center* at 216 S. 2nd St., or call (806) 323-5397.

Another good side trip from Amarillo is that to *Dalhart,* seat of Dallam County, home to almost 6,300 residents. To reach it from the north side of Lake Meredith, follow RR 1319 north about 11 miles to Highway 152, follow it west 20 miles to Dumas, and then go west on US 87, 39 miles to Dalhart. The route from Amarillo is north on US 287, 49 miles to Dumas and west on US 87, 39 miles to Dalhart.

The reason for this journey is to explore the heritage of the world-renowned *XIT Ranch* and today's *XIT Museum.* Here you'll discover the considerable history of the XIT, which in the 1880s was the largest ranch in the world under a single fence, which stretches 6,000 miles. It was created when investors from up north were contracted to erect the $3 million granite capitol building in Austin in exchange for this 3 million acres of land. The ranch spread across an area that today covers nine counties and was 27 miles in average width and 200 miles long between north and south fences.

The XIT Museum (108 E. 5th St., Dalhart; 806-244-5390; www.xitmuseum
.com) tells the whole story, which involved 150 cowboys and the running of
150,000 head of cattle. The investors lost interest, however, and sold off the
cattle and split the ranch into pieces. The museum lies inside a renovated art
deco building and contains photographs, documents, an antique gun collection, and reconstructed period rooms such as a parlor, bedroom, and kitchen.
Native American relics and Peter Hurd paintings are exhibited as well. The
Pioneer Chapel, created from pieces of Dalhart's first six churches, today is
frequently the site of weddings. The museum is open Tues through Sat from 9
a.m. to 5 p.m. Admission is free.

To see more of the XIT legacy, drive to a traffic island adjacent to the
underpass at US 87 North and US 385. There you'll find the *Empty Saddle
Monument,* honoring all XIT cowboys. The story behind it concerns an XIT
cowboy who died just before the annual reunion; his widow requested that his
horse be allowed to participate in the parade, and today's parade is always led
by a saddled horse without a rider.

Plan your arrival in Dalhart to coincide with the first Thursday, Friday,
and Saturday in August, and you'll enjoy the *XIT Rodeo and Reunion,* held
in Rita Blanca Park, US 87 South at FR 281 West. This is the world's largest
amateur rodeo and features a free barbecue of six tons of beef. The parade,
junior rodeo, nightly dance, antique car show, and 5K run add to the revelry.
For information and ticket prices, call (806) 244-5646.

The final side trip from Amarillo is a bit ambitious but may be worth it to
those who have Irish blood coursing through their veins. *Shamrock,* a town
of 2,200 residents, in Wheeler County, is located 86 miles east of Amarillo via
I-40. This is the site of Texas's own *Blarney Stone,* in Elmore Park, 400 E. 2nd
St. Someone in this town convinced the keepers of the original in County Cork,
Ireland, to donate a small piece of their famous rock; it sits on a pedestal and
is offered at all hours to anyone who cares to kiss it. Legend holds that those
who do are given the gift of eloquence. The Irish celebration of St. Patrick's
Day is held annually on the weekend closest to March 17 all over town. There's
a carnival, bazaar, old settlers' reunion, beard contest, fiddling contest, chili
cook-off, dances, cowboy roping contests, and a Miss Irish Rose pageant. Call
the chamber of commerce for information at (806) 256-2501.

Now it's time to make a trek back down the Panhandle, stopping first at
Canyon—just 16 miles south of Amarillo via I-27—seat of Randall County,
home to nearly 13,000 Texans, and site of the exceptional *Panhandle Plains
Historical Museum.* Found on the campus of Texas A&M West University,
1 block east of US 87 at 2503 4th Ave. (806-651-2244; www.panhandle plains
.org), the museum holds the honor of being the state's largest historical

center. Up front, the building's busy 1933 art deco exterior offers friezes depicting an array of Texana designs from spurs to brands. Inside, a time-line approach is used to relate the geological, social, cultural, industrial, and financial development of northwest Texas. Murals in the main hall overwhelm onlookers with an overview, and dinosaurs liven up the geological displays. Pioneer life, Native Americans, and Texas ranching have individual exhibit areas, and the three-floor annex is outfitted with a 1925 cable tool drilling rig. Other oil-patch relics piece together the story of oil and gas discovery and development in west Texas. Several excellent art galleries offer permanent and traveling exhibits, and a good gift shop sells books, games, jewelry, and art. Open Memorial Day through Labor Day Mon through Sat from 9 a.m. to 6 p.m. and Sun from 1 to 6 p.m. From Labor Day to Memorial Day it's open Mon through Sat from 9 a.m. to 5 p.m. and Sun from 1 to 6 p.m. Admission is charged.

Then you'll want to continue east of town 12 miles on Highway 217 to **Palo Duro Canyon State Park.** Here the Panhandle's arid climate, chilly mornings, cool evenings, and clean air are pleasingly exaggerated during spring, summer, and fall in the spectacular chasm, cut 120 miles long by a branch of the Red River. Rich in geological, Native American, and pioneer history, the canyon's rock formations rise and fall a little more than 1,000 feet, showing 90 million years of earth formation, baring brilliant walls colored ocher, red, and coral by the spirits of time. The Coronado expedition took shelter here in 1541 while looking for the fabled Quivira, and they decided *palo duro*—meaning "hard wood"—was appropriate for the tough juniper trees that still flourish here. What's so surprising and invigorating about the Palo Duro Canyon are its green trees and even greener meadows when the rain's been plentiful. Most of the canyon's beauty secrets are revealed in the state park, covering a 16,400-acre portion of the canyon.

An 8-mile paved road takes you rim to floor and affords unforgettable vistas. Hiking, camping, picnicking, and horseback riding are loads of fun. Open in summer daily from 6 a.m. to 10 p.m. and from 8 a.m. to 10 p.m. the rest of the year; admission is charged. Call (806) 488-2227 for reservations and information.

Inside Palo Duro's park, the **Chuck Wagon** (806-488-2152) sells snacks, drinks, and souvenirs and serves breakfast, lunch, and dinner daily. Visitors also can rent horses year-round for an off-road tour of the canyon. For infor-mation call (806) 488-2231.

The park's **Pioneer Amphitheater** on the canyon floor is the scene for an outdoor drama called *Texas,* which lights up the sky on summer nights. The story of the Panhandle, its gritty people, and the spirit that helped them conquer the land is told through such characters as Quanah Parker, the last great Comanche chief; Col. Ranald "Bad Hand" Mackenzie, Civil War hero and Parker's main nemesis; buffalo hunters Billy Dixon Jorge and Maria Hinojosa, who celebrate their Mexican heritage every day of their lives; Freedom Jackson, a cowboy from a slave family; and J. C. Travis and Sara Gray, a young couple whose love for each other just might overcome the obstacles between them. An updated dramatic musical score and spectacularly special effects continue a tradition begun in the 1960s on this very stage. For reservations and information call (806) 655-8121 or visit www.texas-show.com.

Among the more popular ways to enjoy Palo Duro Canyon between mid-April and mid-October is to join the Cowboy Morning Breakfast, now offered by the *Elkins Ranch.* Longtime purveyors of chuck wagon dinners and Jeep explorations, the family-owned Elkins Ranch has taken over the cowboy breakfast offering from the former operators. The ranch covers thousands of rangeland and canyon acres and can be found next to the entrance to Palo Duro Canyon State Park on Highway 217, about 25 miles from Amarillo. Visitors board giant

texastrivia

Talk about hot: It was 120 degrees in the shade in Seymour (the Baylor County seat, in north Texas) on August 12, 1936, says the Department of Meteorology at Texas A&M University.

Jeeps for 15-minute trips into the canyon, where a cowboy campsite awaits. A massive breakfast, cooked over the campfire, is served, including scrambled eggs, country ham steak, ranch-hand potatoes, sausage gravy, Dutch-oven biscuits, fresh fruit, orange juice, and cowboy coffee. After breakfast, local singer/songwriter Ed Montana entertains the crowd. The breakfast is offered by reservation only, April 15 through October 15, on weekends and holidays; adults are $20, children 4 to 12 $15, under 4 free. Book at (806) 488-2100 or (800) 658-2613 or visit www.theelkinsranch.com. Inquire also about evening chuck wagon steak dinners and Jeep tours.

If you'd prefer a bit more pampering, you can stay in a motel or book a room at the *Hudspeth House,* Canyon's bed-and-breakfast place at 1905 4th Ave., Canyon (806-655-9800 or 800-655-9809; www.hudspethinn.com). A famous former resident was the late artist Georgia O'Keeffe, who taught at the local university. There are 6 bedrooms, some with private baths and fireplaces, and decor includes beautiful antiques, tins, plates, dolls, grandfather clocks, and musical instruments. The breakfast table is set with linens, china, and crystal, so you'll enjoy a lavish breakfast or brunch in elegance. A spa, fitness room, sundeck, and gazebo are on the property as well. Call well in advance for reservations.

The Staked Plains

From Canyon follow US 60 southwest 30 miles and then take US 385 south 40 miles. At US 70, head west 24 miles to reach *Muleshoe,* seat of Bailey County and home to the peerless *National Mule Memorial*—what else? Found at the intersection of US 84 and Main Street, the memorial to the West's original draft animal is a fiberglass model measuring 15 hands (5 feet) in height. The mule's statue was built in 1965 thanks to donations from people all over the country—even a mule driver from the former Soviet Union sent a 20-cent contribution.

Another 20 miles south on Highway 214, you'll see *Muleshoe National Wildlife Refuge,* the oldest such refuge in Texas, founded in 1935. As it is situated on a central flyway between Mexico and Canada, hundreds of thousands of waterfowl stop by during migration between September and March. The park consists of about 5,800 acres of rolling, mostly treeless sandhills planted with sorghum and wheat (bird food) punctuated by lakes, which are occupied during the season by the country's largest concentration of sandhill cranes. Observation areas are available in the refuge, and picnicking and camping are allowed. Admission is free, and the refuge is open Mon through Fri from 8 a.m. to 4:30 p.m. for day visitors. Call (806) 946-3341 for information.

Just south of the refuge, pick up FR 37 and follow it almost 20 miles to US 84, which will lead 46 miles to *Lubbock,* nicknamed "Hub City," or hub of the Panhandle. Seat of Lubbock County, the city is home to 200,000 people and the expansive Texas Tech University. On its campus you'll find the remarkable *Ranching Heritage Center* at 4th and Indiana Streets (806-742-0498; www.depts .ttu.edu/ranchhc), a living, authentic center of ranching in the American West. Each year 100,000 people visit here to tour the 12-acre grounds filled with more than 30 restored structures, dating from 1838 to 1917. Among them you'll find one of seven division headquarters of the XIT Ranch, a century-old schoolhouse, milk and meat houses, a granary, a blacksmith shop, log cabins, a grand Victorian ranch home, a bunkhouse, a barn, and a train depot. There are horseshoeing, bread-making, sheepshearing, spinning, and weaving demonstrations, and changing exhibits include saddles, bronzes, and western art, plus wagons and branding irons. As was the case a century ago, windmills are more plentiful than trees, and the ranching center offers windmills of varying designs. A gallery has been created from a room at the enormous 6666 Ranch, complete with ornate mantle, saddle, brass bed, Oriental rug, grandfather clock, and family portraits. Open Mon through Sat from 10 a.m. to 5 p.m. and Sun from 1 to 5 p.m. Admission is free.

Among Lubbock's other interests is that of music, since the city gave the world rock 'n' roll pioneer Buddy Holly. You'll find the *Buddy Holly Statue and Walk of Fame* at 8th Street and Avenue Q, where an outdoor park honors

Holly and other west Texans—including Mac Davis, Waylon Jennings, and Jimmy Dean—who made significant contributions to musical entertainment. It's open 24 hours and is free. Holly's grave is found in the Lubbock Cemetery at E. 34th Street at Quirt Street. Marked by a small, plain stone, the site is visited by a steady procession of fans, many from the United Kingdom. There's also a fine collection of Holly memorabilia on display at a nice little museum, the **Buddy Holly Center** (1801 Crickets Ave., Lubbock; 806-775-3560; www.buddy hollycenter.org). A small admission is charged.

Head for **Lubbock Lake National Historic Landmark,** N. Indiana Street and Loop 289 (806-742-1116), one of the largest and most productive archaeological excavations in North America and thought to be the continent's only place where deposits relate to all cultures known to have lived on the Southern Plains. Covering the periods of the Clovis Man and the Folsom Man, Texas residents of 10,000 to 15,000 years ago, the site's digs have turned up remains of the mammoth, extinct horse, camel, and bison, plus a giant armadillo. A more recent addition to the park is a pair of sculptures, life-size replicas of a Columbian mammoth and her baby. The mother mammoth weighs 6,800 pounds and has a trunk reaching 15 feet into the air, as she "runs" through Yellowhouse Canyon with her 1,200-pound offspring. Follow a 0.75-mile trail through the 20-acre excavation area and look for interpretive signs along the way. A new interpretive center offers exhibits, a children's center, a gift shop, and an auditorium. Open Tues through Sat from 9 a.m. to 5 p.m. and Sun from 1 to 5 p.m. A small admission fee is charged.

Children also get a kick out of **Prairie Dog Town,** within Mackenzie State Park at 4th Street and Avenue A (contact the **Lubbock Convention and Tourism Bureau,** 800-692-4035 or 806-747-5232). One of the last remaining colonies of its kind in the whole country, it's home to cute little critters who are playful and endlessly amusing and who share their habitat with burrowing owls and a few rabbits.

In the same neighborhood at Mackenzie Park you'll find the impressive **American Wind Power Center** (1701 Canyon Lake Dr., Lubbock; 806-747-8734; www.windmill.com). Run by a nonprofit organization, the museum land is scattered with dozens of windmills from the 19th and early 20th centuries. Manufactured by more than 700 companies, these windmills—some of which are very unusual—were used throughout the Great Plains. Inside the exhibit hall, you'll see more than 60 windmills, many of which have wheels more than 25 feet in diameter. The museum store has fascinating gifts.

Texas's most award-winning winery is here in Lubbock. Find **Llano Estacado Winery** just over 3 miles east of US 87 at 3426 E. FR 1585 (806-745-2258; www.llanowine.com). Winery founders discovered ideal conditions in the loose, sandy soil, hot days, and cool nights of the Panhandle Plains. Some 15 or more varieties are grown at a time, and 11 or 12 different wines—plus one sparkling wine—are bottled each year. Plan to spend an hour here touring the winery and tasting four wines. Open Mon through Sat from 10 a.m. to 5 p.m. and Sun from noon to 5 p.m.; tours are free and offered every half hour daily, with the last tour at 4 p.m.

Make like the locals and hang out at *Spanky's Sandwich Shop* (811 University Dr., Lubbock; 806-744-5677), where the Texas Tech faithful line up for great burgers, fried cheese, and ice-cold beer.

For more information on Lubbock and the area, contact the *Lubbock Convention and Tourism Bureau* at (800) 692-4035 or (806) 747-5232 or visit the website at www.visitlubbock.org.

South Plains wanderers in search of a ranch experience should consider a trip to the *Guitar Ranch,* about 45 miles east of Lubbock at the town of Spur. Established in the late 1890s by John Guitar, the cattle ranch invites guests to explore the land by hiking and mountain biking, while fishing, wildlife-watching, photography, and hunting are popular, too. Guests stay in attractive little cabins that offer beautiful views of the sunset, and meals are cowhand hardy. Book by calling the ranch at (915) 673-8329, or visit www.guitar-ranches.com.

Southeast of Lubbock 42 miles on US 84, the town of *Post*—seat of Garza County and one of Texas's more famous speed traps—is located, thanks to cereal magnate C. W. Post, who bought nearly a quarter of a million acres here and founded Post City in 1907 with the intent of developing his own utopia. He built a sanitarium, hotel, business district, cotton gin and textile plant, and farm homes, but his project never saw true success because he couldn't make it rain, and the lack of water during the 1911 drought was devastating. He died

Buddy Holly's Legacy Lives On

Buddy Holly died before I knew any tunes other than "Jesus Loves Me" and "The Eyes of Texas Are Upon You" (the first songs my mother taught me, in that order). But since I saw the 1979 film *The Buddy Holly Story,* it has remained one of my very favorite films. I find it extraordinary that the son of a very ordinary Lubbock family achieved so much in a career and laid groundwork for landmark artists such as the Beatles before being killed at the tender age of 23. When I visited the 8½-foot bronze statue of Holly in Lubbock, I felt a great thrill. I was even more moved upon visiting his grave site, as others were before me: There, on top of the headstone engraved with a guitar and musical notes, are flowers and guitar picks left by his fans.

in 1914, but his statue on the courthouse lawn keeps something of his memory alive.

Post is home to the *Garza Theater* (226 E. Main St., Post; 806-495-4005), which was one of the first movie houses in west Texas when it opened in 1920 with silent films. It was adapted to sound in 1929 but closed in 1957. In 1986 it was renovated and reopened for use by a local theater production group. Musicals and plays are presented some weekends, and a barbecue dinner is usually offered as well. Call for schedules and ticket information.

About 6 miles southeast of town on US 84, find the *Llano Estacado Marker,* one that helps travelers more easily understand the geography of this remarkable area. It details the flat-topped mountains of the Cap Rock Escarpment and the Staked Plains, or *llano estacado.*

From Post you can trace the lowest reaches of the Cap Rock as it unwinds to the Panhandle's reach into deep west Texas. Follow FR 669 as it meanders along mesas and buttes, about 70 miles south to *Big Spring.* This is the Howard County seat and home to 23,000, and where a nice resting spot is *Comanche Trail Park.* Find this beauty at Whipkey Drive off US 87, immediately south of FR 700 (432-264-2376). A large spring indeed is the focus of this 480-acre park, which offers a swimming pool, lighted tennis courts, an 18-hole golf course, small fishing lake, playground, hiking and biking trails, nature trails, a flower garden, and improved campsites. In summer you'll especially enjoy the huge amphitheater—cut from native limestone during the Depression—which hosts summer concerts. Admission is free, and the park is open daily from dawn to 10 p.m.

Other Places to Stay in the Texas Panhandle

ABILENE

Courtyard by Marriott
4350 Ridgemont Dr.
(325) 695-9600
www.marriott.com

ALBANY

Foreman's Cottage at the Musselman Ranch
FR 601
(325) 762-3576
Situated on lonely, rugged ranchland about 10 minutes from the historic Shackelford County square, the 1950s cottage is simple but comfortable, with 3 guest rooms and 1 private bath, kitchen, living room, and dining area.

AMARILLO

The Big Texan Motel
I-40 at
Lakeside Drive
(806) 372-5000
www.bigtexan.com
Next to the Big Texan Steak Ranch, this 2-story complex has a funny Old West facade, 54 guest rooms, and a swimming pool.

Parkview House
1311 S. Jefferson St.
(806) 373-9464
www.parkviewhousebb
.com
This inn offers 4 guest
rooms, 1 suite, and 1 cottage. Guests are offered a
hot tub and sauna, plus a
full breakfast.

CANADIAN

Canadian Courts Motel
220 N. 2nd St.
(806) 323-8058
www.canadiancourts.com
A nicely restored motor
court with great landscaping, this 2-story complex
has 48 rooms with sleeper-
car themes.

LUBBOCK

Residence Inn by Marriott
2551 S. Loop 289
(806) 745-1963
www.marriott.com
This 2-story complex
features 80 rooms with
fireplaces and some
2-bedroom suites, heated
pool, and complimentary
drinks in the evening.

POST

Hotel Garza
302 E. Main St.
(806) 495-3962
www.hotelgarza.com
This 1915 inn, straight out
of the Old West, has a
good selection of comfortable rooms and suites, as
well as cottages nearby.
Breakfast is included in
your stay, and Wi-Fi is
available.

Other Places to Eat in the Texas Panhandle

AMARILLO

**Beans N Things
Bar-B-Que**
1700 Amarillo Blvd. East
(806) 373-7383
This friendly, no-frills cafe
serves up a fine plate of
barbecue, along with chili,
stew, great homemade
corn bread, and desserts.

BL Bistro
2203 S. Austin St.
(806) 355-7838
Romantic in the evening,
special at lunch, and delicious all the time, this hip
spot does a nice job with
dishes like sesame-crusted
tuna, salmon tortellini, and
seared beef tenderloin with
crab beurre blanc.

LUBBOCK

Cagle Steaks
W. 4th Street and FR 179
(806) 795-3879

Whistlin Dixie BBQ & Grill
3502 Slide Rd.
(806) 445-0000
The best barbecue in town,
this restaurant offers great
ribs, smoked chicken,
and spicy Louisiana-style
riblets.

WILDEST WEST TEXAS

Early life in west Texas wasn't easy, and seeing the land even today is proof. The land is lonely, honest, tough—like the pioneers who conquered it, the cowboys who worked it, and the people who call it home. Everywhere you look, the long histories of Native Americans, cavalry units posted at forts to protect pioneers and settlers, and oil-field discoveries bringing startling fortunes are unfolded.

The country wasn't always harsh. Sixteenth-century explorer Cabeza de Vaca wrote in his diary that he walked around completely unclothed in the soothing surroundings, and the earliest ranchers wrote that grasses here grew as high as cows' bellies. But herds of several thousand head of cattle were allowed to graze uncontrolled, and the ground was left bare. Apaches didn't mind the desolation, and outlaws were grateful for it. The open skies and spaces of west Texas invited pioneers to forge a new existence. Those hardy settlers who didn't find this part of the Rio Grande utterly impassable assigned names to spots like Camp Misery and Murder's Cove. They were preceded, of course, by the Comanches, whose war trails can still be seen. In 1882 the Southern Pacific Railroad connected the Trans-Pecos towns of Alpine and Marfa to

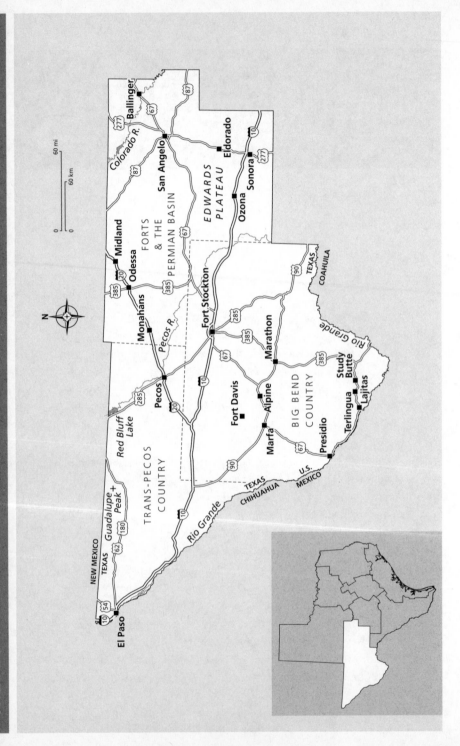

its line, and Terlingua, a bit south, became the quicksilver (mercury) mining center of Texas. Faint remains of those and other long-past ventures can be found in the area.

West Texas's great wealth of natural history is defined, revealed, and studied in the sensational form of Big Bend, a name for a region, a national park, and—for many—a state of mind. Within the elbow of the Rio Grande, where it pushes deeper into Mexico, 800,000 acres were set aside by the National Park Service in 1944 for preservation of a complex array of huge canyons, numerous clusters and stretches of mountains, and exotic plant and animal life. Many who live here say it claims a place in the soul, and even geology textbooks found in area shops contain descriptions with mystical undertones; one Native American legend holds that after the Great Creator made Earth with its stars, fish, sea, and birds, he threw all his leftover stony, dusty materials into one heap—the Big Bend. Because it's such a long way from anywhere, the Big Bend is one of the 10 least-visited parks in the nation, and that's what makes it all the more desirable.

So it's time to embrace the Chihuahuan Desert—roll down the windows and smell the cool scent of sagebrush. Walk around, but watch your step and keep quiet so deer will appear. Wear sturdy boots for protection and train an eye to the roadsides, as rattlers may dart out and recoil just as rapidly; that other brownish streak of movement into the brush is the regional mascot, the roadrunner. Low-slung mountain ranges, bearing names from Christmas to Chisos to Chinati, first appear like little more than bluish shadows nudging the horizon. Broom-weed lies low in oversized patches of vivid yellow in fall, and robust

JUNE'S FAVORITE ATTRACTIONS

Chinati Hot Springs
Ruidosa

Cowboy and His Horse Statue
Ballinger

Davis Mountains State Park
Fort Davis

El Cosmico
Marfa

Fort Concho National Historic Landmark
San Angelo

Front Street Books
Alpine

Gage Hotel
Marathon

Hot Springs
Big Bend National Park

McKittrick Canyon
Guadalupe Mountains National Park

Presidio County Courthouse
Marfa

bluebonnet blooms spring forth with zeal in February. Rafters floating along the Rio Grande marvel at the changing purples, tangerines, and corals in massive canyon walls, and formations of tuff, a hardened ash from volcanic activity millions of years ago, rise like deformed sand castles, followed by layered pink and gray rock cliffs, interrupted with soft carpets of grassy hills. Travelers from as far away as Japan and Germany, as well as those from far-flung corners of Texas, express awe at towering hills of rock, mountain lion warning signs, tough gray-green scrubland, and lush riverside grasses and palms.

Names of places and life-forms often ring of the Spanish-Mexican culture or are pioneer impressions of the land itself: Rosillos Mountains, Mesa de Aguila, Dagger Flat, Dugout Wells, Mule Ear Peaks. And there is such diverse vegetation; most eye-catching are the sotol, century plant, Spanish dagger, and ocotillo, the latter featuring tall spines sprouting bright green, tiny leaves just after the late summer rainy season and brilliant scarlet blooms in spring. The lechuguilla blooms pinkish orange in spring, too, progressing from top to bottom. The Davis Mountains north of the Big Bend wrap comforting arms about you, and the Limpia River is still the crystal, gentle vision it was when settlers arrived 130 years ago. Frontier life is present in a hotel and a distinguished cavalry post. Just don't try to rush through this generous corner of the state, because it takes time to feel and see. West Texas is by turns dusty and sensual, sweltering and refreshing—but always gratifying in a deeply spiritual way.

Forts & the Permian Basin

You'll likely pick up this reach into the Texas "badlands" where you left off at the end of the Panhandle, striking southeast from Big Spring on US 87—better stock the cooler with cold drinks and snacks, as this is the first of several somewhat long but always satisfying hauls. Drive 86 miles on this one highway, leaving Howard County, crossing Sterling and a corner of Coke Counties, to ease into Tom Green County and its seat, *San Angelo.* Home to about 90,000 Texans, the town grew from the exceptional *Fort Concho,* founded in 1867 where the north and middle branches of the lovely Concho River meet. Local lore holds that one of the town's first personalities was the Fighting Parson, who held church in the town's gaming halls; the only time anyone ever objected, the parson gave the protester a knock in the head with the butt of his six-shooter. An early cattle- and sheep-ranching center, San Angelo today is the country's largest primary wool and mohair market and a significant livestock auction site.

Old Fort Concho is one of the state's best-preserved frontier military forts, a 40-acre National Historic Landmark with 23 original and restored buildings

JUNE'S FAVORITE ANNUAL EVENTS

Texas Cowboy Poetry Gathering
Alpine, first weekend in March

Fiesta del Concho
San Angelo, third weekend in June

West of the Pecos Rodeo
Pecos, late June

Viva El Paso!
El Paso, June through August

Marfa Lights Festival
Marfa, Labor Day weekend

TransPecos Festival of Music and Love
Marfa, late September

Christmas at Old Fort Concho
San Angelo, first weekend in December

quite close to downtown. It served for 22 years for the army, stationed here to keep peace on the frontier. Among the cavalry and infantry forces there were the heroic Buffalo Soldiers, black troops named as such out of admiration by their Native American enemies. The fort today contains three museums featuring frontier life exhibits, officers' quarters, enlisted men's barracks, and a chapel. Throughout the year, special events, demonstrations, and reenactments are held at the fort. Christmas at Old Fort Concho is a particularly colorful event, with artists, dancers, and musicians adding to the celebration. Open Tues through Sat from 10 a.m. to 5 p.m. and Sun from 1 to 5 p.m. A small admission fee is charged. Fort Concho is located at 630 S. Oakes St.; (325) 481-2646; www.fortconcho.com.

A somewhat unexpected find is the *San Angelo Museum of Art* (1 Love St., San Angelo; 325-653-3333; www.samfa.org), a $6 million masterpiece in its own right. The swooping roofline resembles a saddle, fittingly, and interior works range from classic paintings to contemporary ceramics.

Still in the frontier vein but more expressive in some ways is *Miss Hattie's Museum,* 18 E. Concho St., San Angelo (325-653-0112; www.misshatties .com). One of several bordellos that thrived along this street, it was opened in 1896 and was a successful "gentlemen's social center" until the Texas Rangers closed it in 1946. Still in its original location, Miss Hattie's has been restored to its former glory, complete with furnishings, plus clothing worn by the girls and the cowboys, soldiers, and businessmen who were patrons. Open Tues through Sat from 10 a.m. to 5 p.m. Admission is charged. There's a cafe and saloon next door, too.

While you're downtown, check out the *Cactus Hotel* (36 E. Twohig St.; www.cactushotel.net), Conrad Hilton's fourth hotel—reportedly his most ornate—built in 1929 for $900,000. Rising 14 stories high with lavish ornamentation, the hotel is home to a coffee shop and an old-fashioned barbershop.

The pretty Concho River is the setting downtown for the ***River Walk,*** a landscaped and lighted stretch of more than 4 miles of river winding beneath huge pecan trees through parks, gardens, gorgeous homes, fountains, and waterfalls.

You'll want to take along a camera to photograph the beautiful ***Pearl of the Concho,*** a magical sculpture of a mermaid created by the late Jane Charless Beck, found in the Concho River near Celebration Bridge. A bit larger than life size, the bronze mermaid holds in her outstretched hand a Concho pearl, the freshwater gem found only in these waters.

Note that from Celebration Bridge you can walk to historic Fort Concho along ***El Paseo de Santa Angela,*** a walkway with pecan-tree shade, fountains, historic ranch buildings, and a windmill. The short route follows a footpath used by soldiers at the fort all those years ago.

Inside the restored Historic Orient–Santa Fe Depot, the ***Railway Museum of San Angelo*** (703 S. Chadbourne St., San Angelo; 325-486-2140 or 325-651-4506 for tours; www.railwaymuseumsanangelo.homestead.com) offers a changing selection of railroad artifacts and memorabilia, including a permanent model-train layout depicting San Angelo in 1928 when multiple railroads came through town and shared the depot. Other permanent displays include a restored caboose and 4 running displays (1 caboose, 2 locomotives, and a boxcar). The museum is open Sat from 10 a.m. to 4 p.m. A small admission fee is charged.

For more San Angelo information, contact the convention and visitor bureau at (800) 375-1206 or visit www.sanangelo.org/tourism/.

texastrivia

The Concho River in West Texas produces freshwater pearls ranging in color from pink to purple.

Just outside of San Angelo, you'll get plenty of peace and quiet at a retreat called ***Dry Hollow Hideaway*** (RR 380, 7 miles west of Paint Rock; 325-732-4272; www.dryhollowhideaway.com). Guests have free run of the very nice ranch home, transformed from a historic army barracks, situated on a 700-acre ranch. There are 2 spacious bedrooms, a huge living room and kitchen, and a porch with rockers overlooking a pond that attracts all manner of wildlife. Ask the owners about resident ghosts.

In the tiny town of Paint Rock, you'll find ***Ingrid's Custom Hand-Woven Inc.*** (US 83, Paint Rock; 325-732-4370), a shop where crafters hand weave rugs and saddle blankets on old-fashioned looms. You can see how the artists finish the items with latch hooks or by hand knotting the fringes. Open Mon through Fri from 8 a.m. to 4:30 p.m. and Sat from 10 a.m. to 5 p.m.

An interesting side trip to make while you're in the neighborhood—relatively speaking, as the neighborhoods out here are pretty big—is one for a photo op at the town of *Ballinger,* 36 miles northeast of San Angelo via US 67 in Runnels County. The county seat and town of 4,000 is worth finding for the *Cowboy and His Horse Statue* on the courthouse lawn, at the intersection of US 83 and US 67. The handsome memorial was sculpted by the acclaimed Pompeo Coppini, who was commissioned by the family of Charles H. Noyes, a local cowboy killed in a range accident.

About 45 miles south of San Angelo is the town of *Eldorado,* jumping-off point for stays at the *X Bar Ranch Lodge & Nature Retreat,* a 7,100-acre spread at Eldorado (888-853-2688; www.xbarranch.com). Bring your mountain bike and hiking boots so you can wander the dozens of miles of handmade trails that course through the rocking, rolling terrain. Various seasons bring watchers of birds, butterflies, rabbits, and armadillos, and there are turkey- and dove-hunting packages in fall and winter. In summer you might want to just hang by the pool by day and, at any time of year, study the brilliant sky at night. Accommodations include a cool guesthouse, cabins, and a lodge, all with kitchens where you prepare your own meals.

If your wanderings from Eldorado take you eastward along the San Saba River toward Menard (see Hill Country chapter), you'll notice a lovely, lonely lot of scenery along US 190. Your company will be hundreds of goats, prickly pear cactus, and ancient, crooked live oak trees populating the rocky hills on this scenic drive.

Still another diversion in this neck of west Texas is found in *Sonora,* a 63-mile drive due south of San Angelo on US 277. Go 8 miles west of Sonora on I-10 and take exit 392 to the *Caverns of Sonora* (325-387-3105 or 325-387-6507; www.cavernsofsonora.com). The founder of the National Speleological Society said of this site, "This is the most indescribably beautiful cavern in the world. Its beauty cannot be exaggerated, even by Texans," which is saying something. Cave experts say some of the delicate crystal growths are "impossible." Ceilings, walls, and floors are covered by phenomenal formations, millions of years in the making, that are seen on guided tours. Do note that the tours can be strenuous for some visitors and that everyone should wear rubber-soled shoes. The park contains picnic grounds, camping areas, shower facilities, and a gift shop. A covered-wagon dinner theater is offered Friday and Saturday evenings from mid-June through mid-August. Open daily, hours vary according to season. For admission fees and tour times, call ahead.

From San Angelo, the next destination is **Midland,** on I-20, 112 miles northwest via US 87 and Highway 158. The seat of Midland County, with a population of about 95,000, Midland lies on the old Chihuahua Trail, the Emigrant Road to California, and the Comanche War Trail. Its name came from its position between Fort Worth and El Paso. Midland was founded in 1885 by Midwestern farm families and supported by agriculture until the 1923 discovery of oil in the region's lucrative Permian Basin. The skies over this incredibly flat land are pointed to by skyscrapers built on the oil booms and by those boom-producing oil derricks.

First stop is **Permian Basin Petroleum Museum, Library, and Hall of Fame** (1500 I-20 West, Midland; 432-683-4403; www.petroleummuseum.org), a complex devoted to fossil-fuel origins, discovery, and resulting industries. This is where you can understand the significance of the wealthy Permian Basin, told in paintings and exhibits. There's a marine diorama of the prehistoric Permian Sea, containing 200,000 replicas of sea creatures; a re-created 1920s boomtown; an assortment of antique rigs; and a display on oil and gas well fires. Open Mon through Sat from 9 a.m. to 5 p.m. and Sun from 2 to 5 p.m. Admission is charged.

Midland is also home to the **American Airpower Heritage Museum and Commemorative Air Force Headquarters,** at the Midland International Airport (9600 Wright Dr., Midland; 432-563-1000; www.airpowermuseum.org). Widely considered the nation's best and most complete collection of flyable World War II combat aircraft, this moving museum was founded by dedicated pilots who wanted to make sure future generations would understand the importance of such astounding American air power. The museum is committed to acquiring, restoring, and preserving at least one example of each type of World War II plane. The array today includes—among many—the P-40 Warhawk, P-38 Lightning, P-47 Thunderbolt, P-51 Mustang, P-36 King Cobra, F4F Wildcat, F6F Hellcat, F4U Corsair, plus the British Supermarine Spitfires, a German Messerschmitt, and several Japanese planes. Also find a B-17 Flying Fortress, B-29 Superfortress, and a D-47 Skytrain. The second weekend in October, you can see these craft in flight demonstrations at the CAF "Airsho," and don't miss the museum's 30-minute film on the Ghost Squadron, shown daily at the museum. Open Mon through Sat from 9 a.m. to 5 p.m. and Sun from noon to 5 p.m. A small admission fee is charged.

Another Midland museum to take in is the **Museum of the Southwest** (1705 W. Missouri Ave., Midland; 432-683-2882; www.museumsw.org). Art and archaeology exhibits make up the permanent collection, a children's museum and a planetarium are on-site, and visiting exhibits are of the caliber of Ansel Adams's photography in a 1934 mansion bearing a National Historic Site marker. Open Tues through Sat from 10 a.m. to 5 p.m. and Sun from 2 to 5 p.m. Admission is free.

For more information about Midland, call the **Midland Chamber/Convention and Visitor Bureau** at (800) 624-6435 or visit www.visitmidlandtx.com.

Hitting the road again, we go 20 miles west on I-20 to Midland's sister city, **Odessa,** seat of Ector County, with a population of 90,000. Established in 1881, Odessa was named by railroad workers from the Ukraine for their home city, which this prairie land resembled.

Lest you think oil country is without culture, Odessa offers its very own **Globe Theatre of the Southwest** (2308 Shakespeare Rd., Odessa; 432-332-1586; www .globesw.org), on the Odessa College Campus. A nearly perfect replica of William Shakespeare's Globe Theatre in London, this one also was built specifically to host plays by the Bard. His works are performed throughout the year, with much celebration made of the Spring Shakespeare Festival, held close to his birthday, April 23. Another replica, the Anne Hathaway Cottage, is home to a Shakespeare library and archives. Branching out, the Globe Theatre now has a live country-and-western program called the Brand New Opree. Open Tues through Fri from 10 a.m. to 6 p.m. and Sat from 2 p.m. to 6 p.m. Admission is charged.

Odessa has another distinction in its **Presidential Museum** (4919 E. University Blvd., Odessa; 432-363-PRES; www.presidentialmuseum.org), the only facility in existence dedicated solely to the office of the US presidency. The campaign and election processes are both studied, and collections of campaign memorabilia, presidential medals, and an array of first-lady inaugural gowns in miniature replicas are all quite interesting. Traveling exhibits are almost always on show, as well. Open Tues through Sat from 10 a.m. to 5 p.m. Admission is charged.

Fans of kitsch won't want to leave town without having pictures taken with what is (reportedly) the **World's Largest Jack Rabbit,** a 10-foot-tall statue at 802 N. Sam Houston St., Odessa. You'll see plenty of his ilk in the wild, but none are quite this big.

For more information about Odessa, call the **Odessa Convention and Visitor Bureau** at (432) 333-7871 or (800) 780-4678, or visit the website at www.odessacvb.com.

Before departing this area, take a side trip west via I-20 just 30 miles to **Monahans Sandhill State Park,** immediately north of the interstate (432-943-2092; www.tpwd.state.tx.us). As you're driving west, you'll cross over a tiny corner of Crane County and drive into Ward County. That's when the flat, barren land gives way to hundreds, maybe thousands, of sand dunes, just like those at the coast. You almost think that the beach must be nearby. Wind-sculpted sand dunes resembling those in the Sahara spread over a 4,000-acre park area but also extend into New Mexico. Most of the dunes are still active, growing and assuming various shapes, and are odd also for their proliferating Harvard oak forest, covering 40,000 acres in all. The trees aren't immediately seen, as they grow no more than 3 feet in height, yet their roots reach some 90 feet into the ground. The park's interpretive center offers illustrations of the dunes' history, as well as that of the ranchers, Native Americans, and oil prospectors who once called this area home. There's a 2-mile drive around the dunes leading to picnic and hiking areas and campgrounds, plus a 0.25-mile nature trail allowing you on the dramatic mountains of sand. Inside the interpretive center you can rent huge, flat plastic disks (think of an enormous Frisbee) for $1 for sliding down the dunes. The shop also sells books on area geology, plants, and animals, as well as souvenir T-shirts. The park is open daily from 8 a.m. to 10 p.m., and the center is open from 8 a.m. to 5 p.m. Admission is charged.

blastfrom thepast

The town of Monahans, famous for its miles of white-sand dunes, is home to the **Butterfield Overland Stagecoach & Wagon Festival,** usually held in late July. The celebration of long-bygone stagecoach days features everything from a parade, live music, and street dancing to bull riding and barbecue.

In the town of **Monahans,** founded in 1881 as a stop on the Texas and Pacific Railroad and situated today just a couple of miles west of the state park via Business I-20, you'll find a handful of places to grab a bite. Highway 18, a north-south thoroughfare, is the town's main street and home to Emma's Kitchen, Howard's Drive-In, and Hero's Pizza. While you're here, don't miss the **Million Barrel Museum** (US 80/Business I-20, 432-943-8401; www.mona hans.org), located in the town's 1928 oil storage facility, and an adjacent, relocated railroad hotel. Antique oil-field equipment and other period artifacts are displayed.

Now it's time to venture south a while, traveling down US 385 for 53 miles to the town of McCamey, where you'll pick up FR 305 for 19 miles, then make a 4-mile jaunt west on US 190 to I-10. Now head back southeast 33 miles via I-10, Highway 349, and a particularly scenic, cactus-lined Highway 290 to **Fort Lancaster State Historic Site.** The site is worth finding if you like ruins, as this briefly occupied fort has a poignancy lingering amid its rubble in a breathtaking little valley carved by the Pecos River. Founded in 1855 to protect the many settlers traveling the San Antonio–El Paso Road, it was abandoned during the Civil War and was only briefly used again after the war's end. It had an important role, however, on the frontier—a story told in the modern interpretive center on-site. Open Mon through Fri from 8 a.m. to 5 p.m. Admission is free. Call (432) 836-4391 or visit www.tpwd.state.tx.us for information.

If you're a real fort fan, continue east another 30 miles on I-10 to the lonely town of **Ozona,** the Crockett County seat, with a population of 3,500. Unique for being the only town in the county—a county that's larger than the state of Delaware, by the way—and the largest unincorporated town in the nation, Ozona also offers the **Crockett County Museum** (404 11th St., Ozona; 325-392-2837). Housed there are artifacts and relics pertaining to Native Americans, the Spanish, and pioneers that were found at Fort Lancaster. Open Mon through Fri from 9 a.m. to 5 p.m. and Sat from 10 a.m. to 3 p.m. A small admission fee is charged.

Make time also to explore the park facing the courthouse. A magnificent monument to Davy Crockett bears a dramatic likeness of the hero, with his quote, "Be sure you are right, then go ahead." A bronze honoring the brave pioneers who settled the area sits at the park's center; titled *The Tie That Binds,* it depicts a man, woman, and child in period dress, facing the horizon.

Big Bend Country

West of Fort Lancaster 67 miles via I-10 is **Fort Stockton,** seat of Pecos County. This town of 8,000 residents began with the establishment of Camp Stockton in 1858 by troops forming from the First and Eighth Infantries of the US Army. The town grew into its modern form after the Yates oil-field discovery in 1925 in the eastern part of the county. The massive drilling rigs are still part of the skyline, but historical sites are the reason for stopping.

The first thing to catch your attention in town, however, is the unforgettable **Paisano Pete,** pure Texas kitsch on Main Street immediately south of US 290 at FR 1053. *Paisano* means "companion" in Spanish, and this statue of a roadrunner is 11 feet tall and 22 feet long, making Pete the largest companion of his kind in the world. You'll see these creatures everywhere in west Texas, but you will never see another like Pete, so take this photo now—otherwise, no one back home will believe you.

To explore the admirable local history, have a look around the **Annie Riggs Memorial Museum** (301 S. Main St., Fort Stockton; 915-336-2167; www .annieriggsmuseum.com). Housed in an 1899 hotel and a popular stop on the Overland-Butterfield Stage line, the museum was named for a colorful local figure—a twice-divorced, hardworking woman who ran the hotel for more than 25 years. The building, called territorial in design, features adobe brick and wood with a wraparound veranda and heavy gingerbread trim. The local historical society assembled the collection here, but the salt cedar that Annie planted in the courtyard was already in place. The parlor boasts one of the first pianos brought west of the Pecos River, as well as a giant cranberry-glass chandelier made in Ohio before the Civil War. The hotel's 15 rooms are filled with relics, such as an 1880s baby christening gown, a man's collar box, furniture, lanterns, and a profusion of kitchen and outdoor cooking gadgets, as well as artifacts relating to the area's archaeology, geology, ranching, and religion. Open Mon through Sat 9 a.m. to 5 p.m.; closed Sun. A small admission fee is charged.

Immediately adjacent to the Annie Riggs is the **Courthouse Square,** surrounded by wonderfully restored old buildings important to the history of Pecos County. These include the 1883 courthouse, an 1875 Catholic church, the 1883 schoolhouse, and the Zero Stone, a marker placed by a survey party in 1859 that was used as a point of origin for all land surveys in this part of west Texas for many years. There's also the photogenic Grey Mule Saloon, now a private residence.

For more information about Fort Stockton, call the **Fort Stockton Visitor Center** at (432) 336-2264 or visit www.ci.fort-stockton.tx.us. You can request a 16-point driving-tour map and audiocassette.

Now delve deeper into the land of the Big Bend by following US 385 south 58 miles, cutting through the Glass Mountains and arriving in the Brewster County town of **Marathon,** with a population of 500. This is definitely a place to set a spell, as we sometimes say in west Texas. And there's no place better to do that than at the **Gage Hotel,** right in the middle of town on US 90 (432-386-4205 or 800-884-4243; www.gagehotel.com). This 1927 creation by west Texas architect Henry Trost exudes the Old West in mood and looks, with a contemporary, stylish addition of beautiful landscaping, a gorgeous swimming pool, and all sorts of decor for rooms and public areas, such as branding irons, chaps, saddles, horseshoes, and spurs. The popular adobe wing added rooms, all of which are more luxurious—some have fireplaces and parlors—than those in the original building. The dining room, now called the 12 Gage, offers southwestern dishes with sophisticated treatment, including the pork chops with chipotle sauce and garlic mashed potatoes, grilled quail, shrimp enchiladas, and rainbow trout. Watch the sun fall from the sky on a front-porch rocker or ask the management to help you arrange a raft, Jeep, or hunting trip.

Travelers not familiar with Marathon will be surprised at the development in such a tiny town. Since J. P. Bryan of Houston bought the Gage Hotel in 1978 and supervised its marvelous expansion, he has also bought up most all the other buildings in town for renovation as art studios and galleries, boutiques and gift stores, and cafes. Whereas Marathon had been simply a launching point for journeys deep into the Big Bend region, it's now a place where travelers can hang out for a couple of days before continuing.

Bryan's vision for the still-sleepy town—you'll see goats and chickens and windmills in residents' yards, and there are virtually no stop signs or street signs to be found—has resulted in the opening of Gage Gear, which sells hats, book bags, shirts, and such with Gage Hotel logos; Front Street Books, selling new and used books; the Evans Gallery; French Company Grocery, selling gourmet foods and cool hats; and the V6 Collection, Bryan's store, which sells watercolor prints, Mexican glassware, and home decor in the ranch/cowboy vein.

These are all within a few steps from the front door of the Gage. In the next block east along US 90, you'll also find beautiful regional art at the James Evans Gallery (www.jameshevans.com).

Chisos Gallery is where you'll inquire about lodging in the fabulous **Adobe Haciendas** (800-550-0503; www.chisosgallery.com), expertly restored adobe cottages with full kitchens, living areas, and tiled baths.

Less than a mile west of the Gage, the **Marathon Motel** (432-386-4241; www.marathonmotel.com) is a wonderfully restored 1940s tourist court on 10 acres with excellent views of sunsets. Motel rooms are basic but very comfortable and clean, with double beds, TV, and showers. At the center of the property, a courtyard offers a large fire pit and a thoughtfully furnished seating area. Also on-site, a guest kitchen lets you cook your own meals, and the breakfast cafe called Courtyard Kitchen serves stout burritos, plates of eggs and bacon, and lighter meals of fruit and yogurt daily.

Kicking back in Marathon at a place with an eye toward the future means a stay at **Eve's Garden** (Avenue C and N. 3rd St., Marathon; 432-386-4165; www.evesgarden.org). This bed-and-breakfast and ecology resource center might serve as a microcosm of what our world would be if it were to function in a purely green manner. Adding onto a pretty, old adobe home, owners Clyde T. Curry and Kate Thayer have expanded their holistic hostelry to include 5 guest suites, a lap pool, a wondrous greenhouse, and a coffee-break/Wi-Fi room—all from papercrete blocks, astonishingly lightweight bricks composed of recycled newsprint and Styrofoam, which they've finished with layers of stucco and paint. You'll feel as though you're wandering through a fairy-tale land with rooms of curved shapes and lines, all cozy, colorful, and rich with texture. The suites, decorated with fabrics from India and appointments like glass chess sets, surround the pond-filled greenhouse, where Thayer grows squash, tomatoes, chard, purple pea pods, sweet potatoes, bok choy, and calla lilies. Eve's Garden is complete with a cartoonish, papier-mâché snake, festooned with colorful pieces of broken glass.

For more information on Marathon lodging, shopping, and dining, call the chamber of commerce at (432) 386-4516 or visit the helpful website at www .marathontexas.com.

If you'd rather camp nearby and save your money for later Big Bend adventures, consider **Stillwell's Store** (432-376-2244; www.stillwellstore.com), the only camping option near the park's northern entrance. It's 40 miles south of Marathon via US 385, then 6 miles southeast via FR 2627. The drive itself helps you become even more acclimated to the spreading region; just about 15 miles south of Marathon on US 385, the scrubby, hunchbacked mountains come upon you, huge and enveloping. Here you'll find 25,000 acres for primitive camping, as well as RV hookups. Camping is anywhere from $3.50 to $15 per night, and the store has plenty of provisions. An on-site bonus is **Hallie Stillwell's Hall of Fame,** a great little collection of Big Bend antiques and artifacts from the turn of the 20th century, kept in a building next to the store. Admission is free—you just ask the storekeepers for a key. Stillwell's Store is generally open daily from 8 a.m. to 9 p.m., but you might want to call ahead just to be sure.

Now it's time to explore the incomparable **Big Bend National Park.** The northern entrance is where US 385 reaches its southern terminus, 40 miles south of Marathon. On your drive down, note the Woods Hollow Mountains encroaching on the highway from the east. This image of purplish blue mountains slumping low against the horizon will become very familiar to you as you explore this magnificent region.

Once inside the park boundaries, you'll immediately come upon **Persimmon Gap Visitor's Center,** where you'll pay a $15-per-vehicle entry fee, good for one week. The visitor center has bathrooms, water fountains, books, and park literature. Another 26 miles south, you'll come to Panther Junction, site of **Big Bend National Park Headquarters** (432-477-2251; www.nps.gov/bibe) and the point at which the park's three main paved roads meet. You'll stop here for a variety of reasons: An abundance of free and inexpensive but vital pamphlets and brochures regarding roads, sightseeing, flora and fauna, hiking, camping, lodging, and ranger-led activities is offered; necessary backcountry permits are issued; and a huge relief map of the park helps you better understand the undertaking ahead of you. This is also the place to inquire about weather, river, and road conditions. Less than a mile west, you'll find a gas station–convenience store where you can buy basic supplies and water. You'd be wise to bring lots of bottled water with you, however.

Having gathered the copious amounts of information that define the park, you are ready to dig in. From Panther Junction, your most immediate option for exploring is to head east on the paved road. It ends at **Rio Grande Village,** near Boquillas Canyon; here you'll find RV camping with full hookups and a shower house, and a store selling snacks, camping permits, and bottled water.

About 3 miles upriver, 2 miles off the main road, is an abandoned resort called *Hot Springs,* a place that was all the rage in the 1920s. The drive down here cuts through dry, white limestone and shale shelves, and the road finally turns to white, powdery sands. The rest can be seen on foot. Out of nowhere appears a long-abandoned, whitewashed stone structure that was the post office for many years and functioned as a concession until 1952. Past that, a vacant rock lodge shaded by a grove of palm trees looks down the sandy path to the river and the therapeutic hot springs on the river's edge. Several healthy cows will probably stare vacantly at you from across the river in Mexico, but pay them no mind and go on exploring the few remains of the bathhouse in the water. When the river is low, those 108 degree waters still soothe tired bones. Ease down onto a small sitting area and feel the gush of hot water—moving at a rate of 250,000 gallons daily—revive your body and spirit.

Boquillas Canyon points up the Sierra del Carmen, rising 8,500 feet into the Mexican sky, blanketed by pine and fir forests. A great 2-hour hike into the canyon delivers sensational views and a wonderful sand dune to play on. Other options to consider exploring in the park's eastern area are those off-road adventures, such as hiking or biking. It's a good idea to make sure your vehicle is ready for the dirt roads first, and rangers can supply you with that information. Some excursions include the trek into *Dagger Flat,* reached from the Old Ore Road that splits off from the main road into the park from the north. It's a little-sought delight on a graded dirt road and an excellent primer to the extraordinary desert vegetation so abundant here. The 7-mile road leads to a strange grove of massive dagger yucca, shooting nearly a dozen feet into the air; these are stunning, especially when topped with blossoms in spring. Hike around here if you're armed with a guidebook. Pick up a 50-cent guide at the road's entry and follow the numbered posts to learn more about the landscape and plants.

Another detour to make off the main road is into *Dugout Wells,* reached by leaving the road that took you to Rio Grande Village. Here is a microcosm of the diverse Big Bend, as hardwoods commingle with all sorts of desert plants, in the company of a windmill and desert critters that are most commonly spied at sunup or sundown. Watch for the marker for the Chihuahuan Desert Nature Trail, a simple 0.5-mile path bearing descriptive signs regarding the odd plants you see.

Heading west to the park's center by paved road, you will reach *Chisos Basin,* situated in a 1,500-foot depression—hence, the basin. It rests right in the middle of the mile-high Chisos Mountains and is the busiest part of Big Bend

National Park, since this is where the park's only lodging and dining facilities are. It's also the coolest part of the park, and in summer everyone comes here for relief from the heat. As you drive up the twisting road to the Basin, you'll see a marked change in scenery. Here, there are trees—rich, rare shade is provided by evergreen and deciduous trees. The Basin's **Chisos Mountain Lodge** (432-477-2291; www.chisosmountainslodge.com) is often booked months in advance, and the comfortable rooms with spectacular views are the reason. The restaurant here offers above-average food for breakfast, lunch, and dinner daily. The adjacent store sells candy and basic foods, some camping supplies, drinks, T-shirts and hats, and postage stamps.

The Basin also has lots of campsites up numerous hillsides, but those, too, are often booked far in advance; for spring break, the park's busiest period, reservations are made a year in advance. Unfortunately, there is no longer horseback riding inside the park. Excellent riding opportunities await, however, in Study Butte and Lajitas.

Hikers will enjoy the route from the Basin to the South Rim and to the popular Lost Mine Trail, which can be a 2- to 4-hour hike but the easiest in these mountains. This is an area where extensive wildlife is sighted, including the black bear. Rangers advise hikers to take along 1 gallon of water per person. Photographers will take a special interest in **The Window,** a narrow slit of a gorge through which all Basin drainage flows to a 75-foot fall below. When there is heavy rain in the mountains and rocks rush and bounce through The Window, it's easy to see how the Basin was formed. **Mule Ear Peaks,** southwest of the South Rim, draws both hikers and photo buffs to its twin angular rock fragments and remains of volcanic rock flow. This is a 4-mile hike that takes 3 or 4 hours to complete.

Southeast of the Basin is **Mariscal Canyon,** where the Rio Grande's southernmost dip cuts through 1,600-foot limestone walls of the Mariscal Mountains. You can explore this canyon, which is littered with abandoned quicksilver mining structures, if you're a very serious, experienced hiker. This, along with other canyons pushing against the park from Mexico, is discovered most often on rafting trips. Among the nearby rafting outfitters offering trips lasting from a half day to several days—with hiking, lunch, and camping options—are Far Flung Outdoor Center (432-371-2633 or 800-839-7238; www .ffoc.net); Rio Grande Adventures near Study Butte (800-343-1640); and Big Bend River Tours (800-545-4240; www.bigbendrivertours.com). Guides are not only adept at the rowing and navigation of whitewater but also are trained to give you all the information you want regarding history, geology, plant and animal life, photography, and folklore. Exquisite riverside meals and entertainment can be arranged through these rafting companies, too. Tours on land are also offered by Texas Jeep Expeditions in Terlingua (432-371-2634; www .texasriver.com).

In the park's southwestern section, the village of **Castolon** is reached on a 22-mile paved road branching off from the main park road. Old cavalry barracks sit deserted where a US Army garrison and trading post was active from 1914 until 1916. A little store sells a few basics, such as T-shirts, snacks, books, souvenir coffee cups, and paper products. Grab some sandwich meat, cheese, and a loaf of bread for a picnic at Cottonwood Campground, adjacent to Castolon. There's superb scenery, too, down the 14-mile Maverick Road, but you need to ask a ranger if it's passable.

Morning is ideal for exploring **Santa Elena Canyon,** when the sunlight exposes walls of rose and rust. On the Texas side, the wall of steep cement steps you can ascend is called Mesa de Áquila, and the sheer cliff on the Mexican side is called Sierra Ponce. Santa Elena Canyon is the one most often seen on the shorter raft trips.

This is but a scant overview of a tremendously complex park. If you're itching to explore the lesser-known places bearing names like Devil's Den, Telephone Trail, and Grapevine Hills, ask at the headquarters for appropriate maps and information. The rangers can also provide you with names and phone numbers of personable, knowledgeable guides for hire.

Barely 2 miles west of the western park boundary on RR 170 at Highway 118, **Study Butte** is a 24-mile drive from the park headquarters and has lodging and food. Pronounced STEW-dee B'yewt, this is where travelers relax at the **Big Bend Motor Inn and Mission Lodge** (432-371-2218 or 800-848-BEND; http://bigbendmotorinntx.com), offering clean but very plain rooms, gift shop, swimming pool, TV, gas, convenience store, and an above-average diner. At the Study Butte Store, you can buy gas, drinks, snacks, and lottery tickets; there's a liquor store adjacent, and the Maverick Rock Shop is facing this on the south side of the road. The Road Runner Deli in Study Butte will pack massive sandwiches into a picnic lunch sack for you (432-371-2364).

Just west of Study Butte is a fork in the highway, where RR 170 continues

texastrivia

West Texas was the first viticultural area in what's now the US: In 1662, a century before Junipero Serra planted the first vines in California, Franciscan padres from Mexico established vine-yards in the El Paso area to produce sacramental wines.

due west and Highway 118 reaches northward to Alpine. At the fork is the Terlingua Post Office and the Quicksilver Bank (432-371-2211), with the area's only ATM. Bankers' hours here are serious: Mon through Fri 8 to 11 a.m. and 2 to 4:30 p.m. and Thurs to 6 p.m. Near the fork also is *Big Bend Stables* (432-371-2212; www.lajitasstables.com), where you can book horseback rides to see pictographs and quicksilver mines for an hour to 3 hours or all day.

Just 4 miles west on RR 170 from Study Butte, *Terlingua* (pronounced Tur-LING-gwuh) is called a ghost town—although it isn't anymore. You'll see the turn off RR 170 at the sign announcing TERLINGUA GHOST TOWN; among more recent additions to the area's lodging scene is El Dorado Motel (432-371-2111; www.eldorado-hotel.net), a 20-room offering in Terlingua.

Formerly an abandoned quicksilver mining camp, Terlingua isn't really a ghost town anymore, but the name stuck and you can find photo ops in ruined houses, a jail, and a rocky cemetery bearing aged wooden crosses. This is where musicians like Butch Hancock (one of the Flatlanders trio, of Lubbock fame) and myriad other poets, authors, and artists have retreated for a life of peace and quiet. Sure, it's anything but quiet the first weekend in November, when thousands of beer-soaked revelers turn out for two world-championship chili competitions, but Terlingua Ghost Town is, nevertheless, the quintessential jumping-off place in Texas.

At the heart of Terlingua, beyond the cemetery, is an aging building that houses the *Starlight Theatre* (432-371-2326; www.historic-terlingua.com), a spruced-up old movie house dating from 1931. This is where you load up on suppers of tofu with lentils, soy-seared yellowfin tuna, and green chile enchiladas while listening to live music, or where you can get a Sunday brunch of filet mignon with eggs and hash browns. Bring your laptop, as there's Wi-Fi, too. Open Sun through Fri from 5 p.m. to midnight and Sat from 5 p.m. to 1 a.m.

Next door to the Starlight—past the ubiquitous guy sitting on the porch bench happily drinking his Budweiser, smoking a cigarette, and staring off toward the horizon—is a nice trove of shopping inside *Terlingua Trading Co.* Here you can buy every manner of T-shirt; lots of western, Mexican, and folk music on CD and cassette tape; Mexican glassware; trinkets crafted from rock and stone; and stuffed animals. Also, inside the store is a little museum tucked off in a corner. Here you see old photos and artifacts from the region's early settlement days, when wagon trains from Marathon brought supplies, soldiers, and merchants and huge newspaper ads proclaimed "Presidio—the Coming Metropolis of the Big Bend Country."

Best among new developments in the old ghost town, *La Posada Milagro* (432-371-3044 or 432-386-6496; www.laposadamilagro.net) is an artfully crafted, four-room guesthouse sitting in one of the restored dry-stack rock buildings on a scenic hillside. Rustic but lavished with luxurious appointments and well-chosen decor, the inn offers fire pits, sundecks, and outdoor kitchens and spectacular views of the Chisos Mountains. Sitting outside your room at sunset, you'll be tickled that you stocked up on beer or wine at the Rancho Fandango Liquors (432-371-2552) in nearby Study Butte.

Between Terlingua and Study Butte there's the dependable *La Kiva* (432-371-2250), a very cool and funky rock cave sort of establishment, entered underground and built into the side of Terlingua Creek. The bar is inside, and an amazing patio is outdoors—you have to see it to understand it. This little hangout will keep you from worrying that the Big Bend might be overtaken by upscale interests. A handwritten wine list posted behind the bar offers three choices: red, white, and pink. The staff works on its own relaxed clock, as does the whole town of Terlingua, so you'll be a lot happier if you aren't in a hurry. Live bands from the area play most nights. You'll probably like what you hear, and you're likely to enjoy the kitchen's renditions of steaks, barbecued brisket and chicken, grilled fish, quail, and sausage. Open daily for dinner.

Another 13 miles west on RR 170, you'll reach the old frontier post town of *Lajitas,* which underwent a multimillion-dollar renovation. Now called *Lajitas Resort and Spa,* the town has become a very exclusive destination. If you look hard enough, you can find traces of the original site, established by the US Army as a post in 1895 and frequented by Pancho Villa and friends. There's a lovely old chapel, visited on one of the resort's guided walking tours, as well as the old trading post, where you can buy a beer—and all sorts of groceries—and pay a visit to Clay Henry III, the friendly goat whose title is Mayor of Lajitas.

The developers of the contemporary Lajitas have expanded the golf course to include a hole that sits across the Rio Grande in Mexico, which is more than a novelty. There's also a private airport, where the resort's Lear jets are kept, and a very impressive equestrian center. Updating to the resort lodgings has rendered the rooms at the Cavalry Post and in the main hotel very luxurious

Beer-Guzzling Goat

Whether or not cows can fly, it's certain that goats can drink beer. Proof is found at the *Lajitas Trading Post,* (432) 424-5000, where the mayor—a goat named Clay Henry Jr.—once guzzled beer on a daily basis. His predecessor, Mayor Clay Henry, was a huge hit with tourists who would stop in for a beer and see the mayor's pen littered with beer cans and bottles. When the curious would ask, someone at the trading post would kindly put a beer up to the goat's mouth, whereupon the goat would get a grip on the bottle with his mouth, tip his head back, and down the whole thing. It's said that old age, rather than liver problems, finally took Clay Henry a few years ago, but C. H. Jr. and C. H. the third have filled his shoes. Or hooves, as it were. Today the goats are just for show and photo ops.

indeed, with elegant bedding and bath linens, as well as beautiful furnishings. You can have a massage or facial in the spa, or play a round of golf—as long as you don't mind the high price tags. Daily activities for guests include watercolor classes, yoga, wine tastings, birding, morning and sunset walks, and putting lessons. For information call (432) 424-5000 or (877) 525-4827 or check www .lajitas.com.

Just shy of *Presidio,* 50 miles west of Lajitas, *Fort Leaton State Historic Site* is on RR 170 (432-229-3613; www.tpwd.state.tx.us). The private fort and trading post was originally a Spanish mission founded in 1759 but was taken over in 1848 by frontiersman Ben Leaton, who monopolized profitable trade with the Native Americans in the area. The adobe fortress now holds a museum covering Leaton's controversial personal and business ethics, along with the area's Mexican, Native American, and pioneer heritage. Exhibits offer bilingual signage and include natural history, along with chronology of commerce, settlement, and cattle and silver industries. A slide show covers the desert ecology. Open daily from 8 a.m. to 5 p.m. Admission is charged.

Presidio, settled in 1683 by Franciscan missionaries, sits in some of the most rugged land Texas can offer, an isolated Rio Grande settlement that's often mentioned in the news as having the hottest temperature in the country. Besides that, it's the self-proclaimed Onion Capital of the World and a good jumping-off place for travelers wishing to journey southwest into Mexico to tour the magnificent Copper Canyon.

If you arrive in Presidio hungry, head right to *El Patio Restaurant* (513 O'Reilly St., Presidio; 432-229-4409), an inexpensive, family-run spot serving fajitas, enchiladas, tacos, and other Mexican specialties, as well as salads, soups, and ice cream. It's open daily for breakfast, lunch, and dinner.

For more Presidio information and help with planning trips into Mexico, contact the *Presidio Chamber of Commerce* at (432) 229-3199.

If you're in pursuit of something more remote than you ever dreamed possible, continue west from Presidio via RR 170 about 36 miles down a teeth-rattling road to the speck of a town called Ruidosa. From there you'll veer onto rough Hot Springs Road for another 7 miles until you reach *Chinati Hot Springs* (Pinto Canyon Road, 432-229-4165; www.chinatihotsprings.com), one of the most restorative places on Earth. Towering cottonwood trees line a running stream, and hot mineral baths will help work out your troubles. People don't come here to party, although you'll see plenty of guests who have brought a cooler of beer or several bottles of wine for their stay. Some folks will grill steaks outside the community kitchen, which is surrounded by cactus and bougainvillea, while others heat up stew inside. Try to book the adobe hut called Patron, a little charmer with a private toilet and sink, plus a minifridge and comfy queen-size bed and a tiny patio with a deep tub, fashioned from an old trough. Light candles and soak under the stars while listening to the desert's silence.

From Presidio, follow US 67 north 61 miles, looking first to the west along the drive at the slumping Chinati Mountains, followed by the Cuesta del Burro Mountains. Keep an eye out for the sign indicating Lincoln's profile in a mountain formation to the west; sure enough, there's a clear profile of a reclining Abe's face. Soon after that look to the east side of the highway for Shafter Ghost Town. A turn from the highway will take you into a small, nearly abandoned historic mining town with scenic stone building ruins. Be sure you have a camera on hand.

Another turn to watch for from US 67—about 25 miles north of Presidio—is that to Cibolo Creek Ranch, the most luxurious, remote resort in Texas (see Other Places to Stay, at end of chapter, for details). Watch carefully and you'll spot some pronghorn antelope hopping and bounding along in the tall grasses to the east. You'll wind up in the ultra-western town of *Marfa,* seat of Presidio County and home to 2,400. The town is becoming well-known for a mysterious phenomenon called the *Marfa Ghost Lights.*

If you're around for Labor Day, you'll get to help celebrate the *Marfa Lights Festival,* which includes a fun run, street dance, food and arts booths, parade, evening concert, Mexican folkloric dancers, and mariachi musicians. For details call the chamber of commerce at (432) 729-4942 or (800) 650-9696.

By daylight, Marfa shows off its beautifully restored *Presidio County Courthouse,* at the north end of Highland Street, a stone-and-brick creation in the Second Empire design, built in 1886. The view of the surrounding land is stunning from the dome up top, which is open Mon through Fri from 8:30 a.m. to 4:30 p.m. Admission is free.

A few yards away, the *Hotel Paisano* (207 N. Highland Ave., Marfa; 866-729-3669; www.hotelpaisano.com) is a beautiful example of Trost architecture dating from 1927; it has hosted Franklin D. Roosevelt, Harry S. Truman, and John F. Kennedy, among other dignitaries. Bearing state and national historical markers, the hotel is beloved by movie buffs for having been the home of Elizabeth Taylor, Rock Hudson, James Dean, and Dennis Hopper, plus all the other actors who appeared in the epic film *Giant,* shot close by. Past the fountained courtyard, inside the Spanish-detailed hotel lobby, there are glass-fronted cases of *Giant* memorabilia, including signed photos of the cast, clippings from *Life* magazine, and numerous news clippings regarding the shoot.

A much-needed and painstaking renovation has made the Paisano quite grand again. Rooms and suites are pretty and comfortable, and there's a TV in a little room off the lobby that plays *Giant* continuously. Perhaps best of all,

Ghost Lights of Marfa

Nobody seems to know why, but there have been some strange lights appearing off the horizon near Marfa since the late 1800s. Various stories and theories circulate about what the **Marfa Ghost Lights** are, but not even the scientists who have studied them have come up with a sure explanation. Most people who have observed them say the lights sometimes glow softly and then brighten to the intensity of a searchlight. You can see for yourself by driving (after dark, of course) east from Marfa on US 90/67 about 8 miles.

Pull over on the south shoulder of the road where a new visitor center and viewing station await. Look southwest toward the Chinati Mountains and just wait. You'll probably wait just a little while, then—poof! There's the first one, a little ball of light in the distance, bobbing just the tiniest bit. Then—poof! It splits into two slightly wavering, shimmering spheres. More will likely appear, but maybe not. Ask the folks around town about all the theories, and decide for yourself. The Marfa Chamber of Commerce has information at (432) 729-4942.

the restoration included the addition of an attractive restaurant called *Jett's Grill* (432-729-3838), named for the movie's James Dean character. Among good choices for dinner are the pistachio-crusted chicken-fried steak with chipotle gravy, penne with spinach and goat cheese, and creamy, rich shrimp bisque.

One of the gathering spots in town is the *Marfa Book Company* (105 S. Highland Ave., Marfa; 432-729-3906), a bookstore that would be at home in Manhattan, in San Francisco, or on Chicago's lakeshore. An emphasis on art books makes a lot of sense here, naturally.

In the next block, dine on the exquisite offerings at *Maiya's* (103 N. Highland Ave., Marfa; 432-729-4410; www.maiyasrestaurant.com), where specialties include cucumber soup and a salad of roasted beets with gorgonzola dressing. Open Wed through Sat for dinner only. The restaurant's owner, Maiya Keck, knows that foodies can't live on the meager offerings at the old-fashioned grocery store in town, so she opened a terrific little market called the *Get Go* (208 S. Dean St., Marfa; 432-729-3335; www.thegetgomarfa.com). This is where you can find imported cheeses, organic eggs and produce, lovely chocolates, Asian foods, a good wine selection, and more.

Marfa's blend of raw landscape and pure solace have long made it a magnet for creative forces. The late American sculptor Donald Judd moved to Marfa in 1972 and created the *Chinati Foundation* in 1986 as an art museum dedicated to permanent installations of very large works of art in 15 buildings and scattered around the grounds of the former army post called Fort D. A. Russell.

The museum is about a mile south of town and is open Wed through Sun from 9 a.m. to 5 p.m. For information call (432) 729-4362 or visit www.chinati.org.

Adjacent to the Chinati Foundation property is a new cultural center, **El Cosmico** (US 67, a few blocks south of US 90; 432-729-1950; www.elcosmico .com). A lodging site with numerous, magnificently restored travel trailers, this has become a magnet for artists, musicians, and people who embrace a lifestyle that blends sophistication with bohemian sensibilities. Your reservation includes all bedding, bath linens, cookware, and more. El Cosmico offers several special events throughout the year, including culinary classes and music gatherings, including the very popular **TransPecos Festival of Music and Love** in late September.

If you get high on golf, head 2 miles east from downtown on Gold Course Road and you'll find the **Marfa Municipal Golf Course** (432-729-4043), the highest golf course in Texas, sitting almost a mile in elevation above sea level. There are nine holes open to the public, and greens fees are $10.63 on weekdays and $15.94 on Fri, Sat, and Sun. Open Tues through Sun 8:30 a.m. to 7:30 p.m.

The most daring visitors may want to take to the skies on a ride with the **Marfa Gliders** at the Marfa Airport (4 miles north of town on Highway 17; 800-667-9464; www.flygliders.com). Owner Burt Compton, an FAA-certified flight instructor, will take you up in the wild blue yonder, and he can teach basic piloting and advanced soaring techniques. It's open year-round.

Just a few miles east of Marfa on US 90, find **Luz de Estrella Winery** (100 Starlight Way; Marfa; 432-729-3434; www.luzdeestrella.com), a new venture that replaced the defunct Blue Mountain Winery. Winemaker Patrick Johnson offers a tasting room you reach on a short drive past roaming Texas longhorns and antelope. Cabernet sauvignon, chenin blanc, and Paisano Rojo, a red table wine, are among the tastes to try. If you show up on a Friday, weather permitting, the winery offers a Marfa Mystery Lights viewing party. The wines have a pretty label that incorporates a star and bluebonnets, making the wine a great gift for people at home.

For a more in-depth look at the region, head west on US 90/67 for 26 miles to **Alpine**, seat of Brewster County and home to 6,000 west Texans and Sul Ross State University, right on US 90. On the campus you'll find the **Museum of the Big Bend** (432-837-8143; www.sulross.edu/museum), newly relocated in its original but renovated WPA rock building. Drink in the west Texas cowboy history and buy any number of books about Texas. Open Tues through Sat from 9 a.m. to 5 p.m. and Sun from 1 to 5 p.m. Admission is free, but donations are accepted.

Rock hounds will enjoy a trip to **Woodward Agate Ranch**, south of Alpine 16 miles on Highway 118 (432-364-2271; www.woodwardranch.net).

More than 70 varieties of cutting stones on this 4,000-acre ranch include gemstones such as red plume, pom-pom agates, amethysts, and opals. Ranch managers will tell you where to find the best stones, which cost $2 per head, $2 per pound. Open dawn till dusk; remember to bring a hat, sunscreen, and water.

Stick around a while and maybe rest up at *Holland Hotel* (209 W. Holland Ave., Alpine; 800-535-8040 or 432-837-3844; www.hollandhotel.net), a historic, 3-floor hotel with 12 restored rooms and 2 suites. The Holland, once a favorite railroad hotel, is smack in the middle of historic downtown. Even high in the hotel's tiny "penthouse"—a cute little hideout for those who don't mind a steep staircase—you can still hear the train whistling by every couple of hours. A tiny sign on the nightstand, accompanied by two little packages of earplugs, reads, WE THINK OUR TRAIN IS VERY QUAINT. BUT IF EARS IT PAINS, PLUG 'EM AND IT CAIN'T.

In this charming downtown neighborhood is a host of shops and galleries. Among these, find *Front Street Books* (121 E. Holland Ave., Alpine; 432-837-3360; www.fsbooks.com), an excellent bookstore selling plenty of Big Bend and west Texas titles, maps, natural history guides, rare and out-of-print books, as well as notecards, books on tape, the *New York Times,* and used books. It's open Mon through Sat until 7 p.m.

Have no doubt: Crowds still flock to the original *Reata* (203 N. 5th St., Alpine; 432-837-9232; www.reata.net), a mainstay in Alpine and the place to find filling goodies like beef tenderloin tamales, shrimp enchiladas, and grilled quail.

Baseball fans and lovers of historical architecture are sure to be fond of *Kokernot Field* (Loop Road; 432-837-5180), a scaled-down version of Yankee Stadium and a beloved memorial to the game of summer. Home to the Sul Ross Lobos, the stadium was built for the semipro Alpine Cowboys, who play on only in memory.

To celebrate Alpine's growing arts community, there's an annual *Gallery Night* held in November, during which more than 20 galleries keep special evening hours and invite you to stroll and peruse special exhibits. For details on this event, and to get a wonderful walking-tour map of Alpine, visit the chamber of commerce at 106 N. 3rd St. in Alpine, call (432) 837-2326, or check out the website www.alpinetexas.com.

If you're ready for more adventure, head out for Jeff Davis County and its county seat, *Fort Davis,* north 26 miles via Highway 118. A cavalry post was established in 1855, the town later became a haven for sufferers of respiratory problems, and commercially grown Delicious apples eventually became a primary industry. The highest town in Texas at just over 5,000 feet, Fort Davis is cool enough to warrant wearing at least a sweater 11 months out of the year.

A good home base in town is the **Hotel Limpia,** on the square in the middle of the tiny town (432-426-3237 or 800-662-5517; www.hotellimpia.com). The hotel was built in 1912 by the Union Trading Company, was remodeled, and is a member of the Historic Accommodations of Texas. There's an upstairs balcony and an enclosed veranda full of rocking chairs, potted flowers, and oak tables—plus a lovely view of the sunset. The front desk's stained-glass detail and an old ranch house door add to the period mood. High-ceilinged rooms and suites are filled with antique oak furnishings, and the big main lounge has a native-stone fireplace. The Limpia's lodgings have been expanded to include—in addition to the main hotel and the annex out back—the Mulhern House, a renovated adobe home built in 1905, now offering 3 suites; Limpia Cottage, with its back pressed to the mountains; and the Dr. Jones House, a 1903 home that has been restored.

The Limpia's dining room features home cooking, with steaks, chicken, sandwiches, and soups, plus good pies and breakfast. Also part of the Limpia are Sutler's Club, a friendly little place to wet your whistle; the Hotel Limpia Gifts, a pretty store specializing in glassware and home furnishings; and Javelinas to Hollyhocks, an artistic boutique selling books and maps, candles, pewter photo frames, and sweatshirts.

A few blocks north of the Limpia, find **Cueva de Leon** (100 W. 2nd St., Fort Davis; 432-426-3801), a friendly, no-frills cafe famous throughout the area for its handmade chiles rellenos and cheddar cheese enchiladas in red chile sauce.

The best orientation to the area's wonders is found by driving the **74-Mile Scenic Loop Road**, beginning and ending in Fort Davis. An array of mountain vistas, Madera Canyon, and roadside parks bounded by ancient boulders are the rewards for following Highway 17 south of town just 2 miles to Highway 166 west to Highway 118, then southeast back to Highway 17 and Fort Davis.

Then it's time to see the reason Fort Davis came into being: As Indian raids increased with the numbers of settlers arriving or traveling through this part of the state, usually en route from San Antonio to El Paso, a cavalry post was built in 1855. **Fort Davis National Historic Site** is the restored site, named for US Secretary of War Jefferson Davis, who ordered the army's posting here. Active from 1854 until 1891, with lapses during the Civil War, when fire destroyed the fort, it was home to 12 cavalry and infantry companies—numbering up to 800 men—stationed here in 50 buildings. The renovated stone-and-adobe remains sit in a scenic box canyon, sheltered on the west by towering cliffs, and are as complete and impressive as any in the Southwest. This indoor-outdoor museum was also the post for black troops from the Ninth, Tenth, Twentieth, and Twenty-fourth US Cavalries. As was the case at Fort Concho, the enemy

Comanche and Apache soldiers named these men the Buffalo Soldiers, which has been interpreted as a term of respect.

During the summer a living-history program demonstrates pioneer and fort life with costumed participants; the fort's Labor Day celebration draws as many as 2,000 spectators, and a special Black History event is a February highlight. Otherwise the place is easily seen on self-guided tours with a slide-show introduction. A bugle sounds twice daily, starting the audio of a formal ceremony on the parade yard. Images of hundreds of mounted and marching soldiers in full dress are easy to see in the mind's eye. The commander's house was occupied the longest by Col. Benjamin H. Grierson, and his original furnishings show luxury's spotty hand in a usually mundane frontier post life. Antiques, silver, and linens decorate the parlor and dining areas; giant beds and ornate wardrobes are characteristic in the oversize bedrooms. A museum in the main building contains a display illustrating Trans-Pecos frontier days, the overland gold rush, stagecoach and Indian raiding routes, plus artifacts such as an officer's scabbard, pistol, and musket. A gift shop sells books and more books, including Old West cookbooks, art books, and children's coloring books.

Fort Davis is open daily from 8 a.m. to 5 p.m. A small admission fee is charged. The fort is situated immediately north of town on Highway 118; call (432) 426-3224 for more information.

You can be enveloped in the area's solitude and natural beauty by a stay in **Davis Mountains State Park,** 4 miles north of town on Highway 118 (432-426-3337; www.tpwd.state.tx.us). Sandwiched ideally between the grassy desert plains and the fragrant, woodsy mountains, this 2,700-acre park offers numerous hikes, from easy to challenging, as well as a rewarding Skyline Drive. Camp if you like, or call ahead for a room at the nicely renovated **Indian Lodge,** a pueblo-style motel with plenty of amenities, plus the hand-carved cedar furniture fashioned by Civilian Conservation Corps workers, who also built the lodge in the 1930s. The park is open daily for day use from 8 a.m. to 5 p.m. and at all hours for campers. Admission is charged.

texastrivia

Nine of the giant *Texas Ruby Red grapefruit* (the state fruit) equal the volume and mass of 12 regular grapefruit.

Or hang your hat at the **Prude Ranch,** also just north of town on Highway 118 (432-426-3202 or 800-458-6232; www.prude-ranch.com). A working ranch run by the same friendly west Texas family and open to guests since 1921, it offers bunkhouse and motel-style lodging, horseback riding, tennis, a Jacuzzi, and plenty of ranch-hand chow. To honor the ranch's centennial (it was founded in 1897), the Texas State

Historical Commission bestowed a historical marker in 1997 that details the ranch's history.

Stargazing travelers will want to drive up to the ***McDonald Observatory,*** a University of Texas operation reached by driving from Fort Davis 17 miles northwest on Highway 118, then 2 miles southeast on Spur 78. Sitting atop 6,800-foot Mount Locke, the observatory features a 107-inch telescope, plus tours for visitors to see its 160 tons of moving parts. Programs at the spectacular new visitor center include solar viewings, and star parties are staged Tuesday, Friday, and Saturday evenings for looking at celestial objects through small telescopes. Even if you're not in time for a viewing, pay a visit anyway to see the fascinating 30-minute video on the universe, produced by NASA. A great gift shop with unusual goods and the Stardate Cafe are on-site. The visitor center is open daily from 9 a.m. to 5 p.m. Solar viewing programs are offered. Call (432) 426-3640 or (877) 984-7827, or visit www.mcdonaldobservatory.org, for information and times. Admission is charged.

If you're hungry, belly up to the soda fountain called ***The Drug Store*** (113 N. State St., Fort Davis; 432-426-3118). The burgers and root beer floats are the stuff of your childhood dreams.

Next door along the boardwalk, facing the Hotel Limpia, is the ***Harvard Hotel*** (109 State St., Fort Davis; 432-426-2500; www.harvardhotelandlodge .com). Every room is a suite with microwave, refrigerator, TV/DVD player, Wi-Fi, pillow-top mattresses, and western decor. Book well ahead and you'll get one of the suites with a great balcony overlooking the street. The hotel owners offer similar suites on their ranch, along with a rock cabin, outfitted with a full kitchen and washer-dryer. At the ranch you can sit in a hot tub, shoot skeet, take a Jeep tour in the beautiful and scrubby Davis Mountains, or arrange a guided hunt for elk, mountain lion, deer, antelope, javelina, and birds.

For more lodging and dining information, contact the ***Fort Davis Chamber of Commerce*** at (432) 426-3015 or (800) 524-3015 or log onto www .fortdavis.com.

Trans-Pecos Country

Driving north from Fort Davis along Highway 17, the gorgeous winding road courses through slumping rock formations as it follows Limpia Creek; if you take along some snacks, you can stop at one of several roadside picnic sites and enjoy the scenery in relative quiet, as there isn't a lot of traffic along the route. Watch on the east side of the road for a 1956 Texas Historical Marker, noting Wild Rose Pass.

From Fort Davis the next stop is **Balmorhea State Park,** north on Highway 17, 39 miles away. Truly unusual in this modern day is a pool like the one here: Said to be the world's largest spring-fed swimming pool, Balmorhea's measures nearly 2 acres, is 30 feet deep, and contains 3.5 million gallons of water. Talk about cool—the water is between 72 and 76 degrees year-round, so your only swimming opportunities fall between the end of May and Labor Day. In addition to a vintage bathhouse and concession stand, you'll find tent and RV campsites and a small hotel, called San Solomon Courts, on-site. The grounds are green and roomy, so even if you miss the pool season, this is a delightful place to kick back and plot your next move down the road. Call (432) 375-2370 for reservations. Open daily from dawn until dusk. Admission is charged for park entry and pool use.

If the San Solomon Courts in Balmorhea State Park are full, look for a room in the town of Balmorhea at a new lodging called the **Eleven Inn** (504 S. Main St., Balmorhea; 432-275-2263; www.eleveninn.com). There are—you guessed it—11 rooms in this renovated motor court, all spanking clean and updated with iron or wood beds, cool antique or retro furnishings, and flat-screen TVs. No two rooms are alike; two have microwave ovens and minifridges. The grounds have picnic tables, grills, a fire pit, and clotheslines where scuba divers hang their wetsuits after exploring the depths over at the park's spring-fed pool.

Keep your eyes peeled in this area for some of the purely Texan things that make this part of the world something you won't forget. On the section of Highway 17 that is the main street in Balmorhea, for example, there's a yellow road sign with just a turkey on it—as in, turkey crossing. And on Highway 17 between Balmorhea and Pecos, look at the tops of telephone poles. More than likely, you'll see a hawk perched on high, looking for lunch in the fields.

If you've come at the right time, this is the point at which to make a detour 33 miles north on Highway 17 to **Pecos,** home in late June to the world-famous **West of the Pecos Rodeo.** The massive affair has been held annually since June 1883, when cowhands from the Hashknife, W, Lazy Z, and NA ranches argued in Red Newell's saloon over which one had the best ropers and riders among its brethren. Ever since, the summer holiday has been set aside for competitors in saddle-bronc riding, steer roping, bulldogging, and plenty of other tough events. Things have progressed considerably since that first rodeo, when 1,000 spectators showed up to watch the cowhands compete for a $40 prize—the numbers have increased by the thousands. Pecos, known far and wide also for its cantaloupes, hosts its **Cantaloupe Festival** the first weekend in August, as well as a **World Championship Bar-B-Q Contest** the first weekend in October. For tickets and information call the tourism office at (432) 445-2406, or stop by at 111 S. Cedar St.

Sorry, No Muppets Here

The Winkler County seat of **Kermit** became a boomtown in 1926, when oil was discovered nearby in the Permian Basin. If you're passing through, stop to see the town's oldest structure, the **Medallion Home,** built in 1907 about 5 miles south of town. It was dismantled and moved into Kermit in 1910 and was occupied until deeded to the city in 1967. Find it in Pioneer Park. For details call (432) 586-2507.

Should you decide to stick around and explore Pecos for a spell, pay a visit to the **West of the Pecos Museum** (1st Street at US 285/Cedar Street, Pecos; 432-445-5076; www.westofthepecosmuseum.com), occupying the old Orient Hotel. You can see bullet holes from the last gunfight in town, which took place more than 120 years ago, and explore 50 rooms on 3 floors filled with area relics, as well as period exhibits pertaining to such folks as the local sheriff, doctor, rodeo queens, Rotarians, and so on. A popular exhibit is the replica of the Jersey Lilly Saloon, where Judge Roy Bean reigned as "the Law West of the Pecos" down in the town of Langtry. Another exhibit honors Clay Allison, the gentleman gunfighter who "never killed anybody who didn't need killing." The museum is open Tues through Sat from 9 a.m. to 5 p.m.

All this is bound to work up a hunger, so it's a good thing the **La Nortena Tortilla Factory** (211 E. 3rd St., Pecos; 432-445-3273) is right around the corner. It's nothing fancy, but the homemade tamales and tortillas are rewarding.

Whatever the season, your path from Balmorhea is northwest to **Guadalupe Mountains National Park.** You can reach it by driving west for 71 miles, through parts of Reeves, Jeff Davis, and Culberson Counties to the town of Van Horn. Here you'll turn north on Highway 54 and go 55 miles to the park. Note that once inside the park, you've entered Mountain Time. This former ranch land is blessed with 80 miles of hiking trails, assorted mountains (some up to 8,700 feet high), breathtaking overlooks, ancient canyons colored in ridges of brilliant oranges and reds, abandoned ranches, springs, and spectacular foliage in autumn—all of it a photographer's delight. Because of its remote position, this isn't ever a crowded park; those mountaintop pine-and-fir forests are usually just yours to relish. The only company you might have is that of mountain lions, elk, wild turkeys, and black bears. More tame in the way of wildlife are cacti blooming with purple, pink, and ruby flowers. Stop at the visitor center first and inquire about ranger-guided hikes, programs in the amphitheater, and the best places to view or photograph McKittrick Canyon, El Capitan, and Guadalupe Peak. Camping is available at Pine Springs and Upper Dog Canyon campgrounds in the park. The headquarters visitor center is open

Mon through Fri from 8 a.m. to 4:30 p.m. Call (915) 828-3251 or visit www.nps .gov/gumo for more information. The entrance fee (payable at any trailhead) is $5 per person (good for seven days).

If you head west on US 62/180, 70 miles to FR 2775, then make a turn north and follow it 8 miles to **Hueco Tanks State Park,** you'll find odd, blob-bish rock formations with caves and cliffs containing some 2,000 ancient Native American pictographs, some from the Apaches, as well as ruins of an old But-terfield stage station. The park's name comes from the vast, natural rainwater basins, or *huecos* (WHAY-coes) in Spanish, making this spread a giant oasis for dwellers and travelers for as long, some studies reveal, as 10,000 years. Camp-ing, picnicking, rock climbing, nature study, and rock art tours are offered. Open daily 8 a.m. to 6 p.m. (until 5 p.m. for campers). Admission is charged. Call (915) 857-1135 or visit www.tpwd.state.tx.us for information.

Your final area for west Texas exploration is **El Paso,** 30 miles west of the Hueco Tanks turnoff, via US 62/180. Jammed into a pass of the mile-high Franklin Mountains, the ancient city clings to and curves around the mountains' base. Inspirations all around are as Native American and pioneer as they are Mexican and Spanish. Combined with Juarez, El Paso's twin across the Rio Grande, the population pushes 1.5 million—and some days there's the smog to prove it. In spite of all those people, El Paso feels wide open and very much a part of the Wild West. The purple and orange–layered sunsets soften the craggy mountains, giving them a blue cast and the city a somber backdrop. Annual visitors number around 15 million, due in part to the sunshine, which brightens at least 300 days each year. The story goes that World War II servicemen sta-tioned at massive Fort Bliss discovered the margarita, but they were preceded in discoveries by the 16th-century Spanish conquistadors who found this pass to the north from Mexico, and so named the place for its use.

don'tyou walkonby . . .

In **Wink** there's the **Roy Orbison Museum,** named for the native son and rock 'n' roll legend who became famous for "Pretty Woman," "Only the Lonely," and many other popular songs. See memorabilia from his youth and his career, including albums and sin-gles and his trademark sunglasses. For tours call (432) 527-3545.

Older even than California's, **El Paso's historic missions** occupy a lower valley along El Camino Real, or the Royal Highway used by the mission-aries and conquistadors and the longest historic road in the US. The first to explore is the **Ysleta Mission,** situated at Zaragosa and Alameda, next to the Tigua Indian Reservation. Founded by Franciscan padres in 1680, this mission has been rebuilt several times and is thought to be the nation's oldest mission and possibly the oldest continuously used parish in the nation. Don't be confused, but the church's official name is Our Lady of Mount Carmel, yet there's a St. Anthony statue on the outside, as he is the patron saint of the Tigua Indians, who fled New Mexico during the Pueblo Revolt in the 17th century. All missions are open daily from 8 a.m. to 5 p.m. Admission is free.

Socorro Mission, 3 miles southeast of Ysleta Mission on FR 258, was also founded in 1680. This one is of the classic, stark adobe design, and its ornate, hand-hewn roof beams are the oldest in Texas. Travel 5 miles southeast to *San Elizario Presidio Church,* also on FR 258, to see the 1770s architecture in a lovely courtyard. This is still an active Catholic church. Note that drives to the missions are prettiest in autumn, when cotton fields are overrun with white bolls, pecan groves stretch without end, and row upon row of chiles and onions burst in reds and greens. Farmers are usually found on roadsides tending their stands, selling roasted chiles or big, fat ristras, those hanging bunches of chiles that are very fashionable in southwestern decor. For more history and information on the missions, visit www.co.el-paso.tx.us/history/missiontrail.htm.

For a deeper look into history surviving to the modern day, visit the *Tigua Indian Reservation* (119 S. Old Pueblo Rd., El Paso; 915-859-7913; www.ysletadelsurpueblo.org). Also called Ysleta del Sur Pueblo, this is the home of descendants of those Tiguas who fled during the Pueblo Revolt in New Mexico more than 300 years ago. There's a living-history pueblo, with demonstrations of pottery, jewelry, and weaving crafts, plus bread baking in dome-shaped ovens. Tribal dances are performed during special events, while the 21st century threatens to impose itself, as the Tiguas prepare to bring high-stakes gambling to the reservation to increase tourism income. In the Cultural Center,

A Slice of the Wild West

Take off for an Old West retreat by visiting *Indian Cliffs Ranch at Cattleman's Steakhouse,* 30 miles east of El Paso on I-10 and 5 miles north on FR 793 (915-544-3200). The multilevel complex is part sprawling ranch, part adobe, part movie set, and all romance. Longhorn cattle and buffalo graze here, but primarily it's a place of entertainment and social interest. There's a restaurant with huge steaks and Mexican dishes, a gift shop with plenty of jewelry, and a terrace from which to watch achingly beautiful sunsets over a spread of cacti and corrals. A ride aboard a wagon pulled by huge Belgian horses takes you to Fort Misery, an 1860s fort replica for overnight guests and campfire dinners. Call ahead or visit www.cattleamanssteak house.com for activities schedules and reservations.

you'll find handcrafts for sale. There's a wellness center on the reservation, too. Open daily from 8 a.m. to 5 p.m. Admission is free, but donations are accepted.

Of El Paso's two scenic drives, the **Scenic Road** is shorter and easier to access. Drive behind the Sun Bowl and wind between formidable walls of rock for 2 miles west to east, from Rim Road to Richmond Avenue. From Murchison Park at the road's apex 4,200 feet high, your vista includes two cities, three states, and two countries. You can see a stone peg that marks the end of the Rocky Mountains, a giant Christ statue on Sierra del Cristo Rey, and several war memorials. Sadly, you may also see a fair amount of graffiti and trash.

The other route is the more lengthy **Transmountain Drive,** a highway cutting through Smugglers Gap in the North Franklin Mountains. The summit is almost a mile above sea level, and the Wilderness Park is up there with great Chihuahuan Desert hiking trails. A nature trail passes replicas of a Pueblo ruin, kiva, and pithouse. The view of mountains reveals geologic history—gray shades indicate where ancient inland seawaters lapped, and reds are the leavings of volcanic lava flows.

The **Franklin Mountains State Park** is in this area, too. The 24,000-acre wilderness offers mountain bikers, hikers, rock climbers, and horseback riders more than 100 miles of trails. After $1.5 million in improvements, the park is now open to overnight campers, too. Guided tours led by park rangers are given the first and third weekends of each month, and there is an aerial tramway to ride. Call (915) 566-6441 for reservations, or visit www.tpwd.state.tx.us for information.

In town, El Paso's cultural offerings are as diverse as they are plentiful. Downtown find the **Bridge Center for Contemporary Arts** (127 Pioneer Plaza, El Paso; 915-532-6707), a nonprofit gallery featuring work in contemporary and experimental art by emerging and nationally recognized artists. It's open Tues through Sat from 11 a.m. to 5:30 p.m. Across the street have a look inside the **Camino Real Paso Del Norte Hotel** (101 S. El Paso St., El Paso; 915-534-3000; www.caminoreal.com), built in 1912 and listed on the National Register of Historic Places. The 80-year-old Tiffany glass dome is a commanding sight in the hotel's elegant Dome Bar. Guests here over the years have included Pancho Villa, President Taft, and "Black Jack" Pershing.

Three fine museums are **El Paso Museum of Art** (1 Arts Festival Plaza, El Paso; 915-532-1707; www.elpasoartmuseum.org), featuring the Kress Collection of European Art, with masterpieces from the 13th to the 18th centuries; **El Paso Museum of History** (510 N. Santa Fe, El Paso; 915-351-3588; www.elpaso texas.gov/history/) has a new, beautiful home in downtown El Paso, where colorful exhibits detail the history of Native Americans, conquistadors, vaqueros, cowboys, and cavalrymen who played a role in taming the Southwest; and the *Magoffin Homestead* (1120 Magoffin St., El Paso; 915-533-5147; www .tpwd.state.tx.us), a state historical park featuring the adobe hacienda built by settler Joseph Magoffin in 1875, with some original period furnishings.

Two more museums, the *Fort Bliss Replica Museum* (915-568-4518) and the *US Army Air Defense Museum* (915-568-5412), are found at Fort Bliss on Pleasanton Road, near the airport. The largest air defense center in the world, the base was founded as an army post in 1849 and named after Lt. Col. William Wallace Smith Bliss. Both museums are wonderful in detail. Call for hours. Admission is free, but donations are accepted.

At the *Border Patrol Museum* (4315 Transmountain Rd., El Paso; 915-759-6060; www.borderpatrolmuseum.com), visitors learn about the US Border Patrol's history since the days of the Old West. Exhibits include aircraft and vehicles used by the patrol, surveillance equipment, confiscated items, and more.

You can find a little bit more history at *Concordia Cemetery* (just northwest of the intersection of I-10 and US 54), a graveyard begun in 1856. Find the section that was El Paso's "Boot Hill," where illustrious gunfighter John Wesley Hardin is buried.

Duffers can revel in the dry, mountain air at two renowned courses. PGA champ Lee Trevino made famous the historic *Emerald Springs Golf Course* about 20 miles east of town (take I-10 East to Horizon City; 915-852-9110), built on an actual desert spring. Another top-ranked course in Texas is *Painted Dunes Desert Golf Course* (12000 McCombs Rd., El Paso; 915-821-2122), surrounded by desert plants and purple blue mountains.

People drive from all over west Texas and southern New Mexico to while away days just eating and shopping in El Paso. Among the favorite places to eat is the *H&H Car Wash and Coffee Shop* (701 E. Yandel Dr., El Paso; 915-533-1144), an old-fashioned institution where you can have your car hand washed while the kitchen staff inside makes you an unforgettable meal. Best bets are the carne picada, or sautéed beef tips with tomato, onion, and jalapeño, or the amazing huevos rancheros and other spicy breakfast treats.

Long considered the town's most romantic restaurant, *Cafe Central* (109 N. Oregon St., El Paso; 915-545-2233; www.cafecentral.com) is also thought to be the best, as well. A blend of contemporary and classic cuisines, the menu offers smoked salmon paired with crab and caviar, as well as tender osso buco in red wine.

It's possible to do nothing for days but shop for wonderful Texas and Mexican gifts and goods in El Paso. The first two of several stores of special note is *Justin Boot Factory Outlet* (7100 Gateway East at I-10, El Paso; 915-779-5465), a superstore selling a complete line of boots as well as belts, hats, and all kinds of western accessories; and *Lucchese Boots* (6601 Montana Ave., El Paso; 915-778-8060), the factory store for the famous bootmaker, established in 1883. You'll find boots at up to 50 percent off retail prices, as well as cool old photographs, boot casts, and memorabilia of famous people who have boasted a pair of Luccheses. *Tony Lama Factory Stores* (call for directions to three locations, 915-772-4327) sell leather western boots made right in El Paso. *El Paso Chile* (909 Texas Ave., El Paso; 915-544-3434; www.elpasochile.com) is a booming family business that sells salsas, barbecue sauces, margarita mix, gift baskets, and cookbooks.

Galeria San Ysidro (801 Texas Ave., El Paso; 915-544-4444; www.galeria sanysidro.com) is a 3-story treasure chest of antiques, lamps, handcrafted wrought-iron decorative pieces, and collectibles from Mexico, Spain, India, and North Africa.

For a look at the Texas-Mexico connection, visit the *Chamizal National Memorial* (800 S. San Marcial, El Paso; 915-534-6668; www.nps.gov/cham). Built on land that became part of the US when the Chamizal border dispute with Mexico was settled in 1963, the grounds cover 55 acres and feature a museum and amphitheatre. Open daily from 8 a.m. to 5:30 p.m. Admission is free.

Other Places to Stay in Wildest West Texas

ALPINE

Maverick Inn
1200 E. Holland Ave.
(432) 837-0628
www.themaverickinn.com
A contemporary ranch-style makeover of an old motel; sand-colored stucco walls, Saltillo tile floors, heavy Mexican furniture, Indian rugs, flat screen TVs, Wi-Fi, Egyptian cotton bed linens, and cushy down bedding make for a chic stay.

BALMORHEA

San Solomon Courts
inside the state park
(432) 375-2370
All 18 adobe units are within a few steps of the celebrated pool. Some have kitchenettes.

EL PASO

Camino Real Hotel
101 S. El Paso St.
(915) 534-3000
www.caminoreal.com
This beautiful hotel, built in 1912, has a luxury floor, where rooms have honor bars and refrigerators. In all there are 360 rooms. A coffee shop, an upscale restaurant and bar, and a small swimming pool are on the premises.

FORT DAVIS

The Veranda
1 block west of courthouse
(432) 426-2233
www.theveranda.com
Opened in 1883 as the Lempert Hotel, this adobe building with 2-foot-thick walls has wood floors, high ceilings, period furniture, porches, courtyards, and gardens. There are 7 rooms, all with private baths, ranging from the large bedroom with 2 double beds and a fireplace inlaid with quartz to the 2-room king suites with

mountain views. There's also a private carriage house in an orchard of apricot and peach trees. Breakfast is included with stay.

MARFA

Cibolo Creek Ranch
30 miles south off Highway 17
(432) 229-3737
www.cibolocreekranch
.com
This 25,000-acre working ranch with horseback riding offers tours of lands where bison, elk, and longhorn roam. The ranch consists of three lavishly restored, 19th-century forts named El Cibolo, La Cienega, and La Morita. El Cibolo, the largest, has 11 guest rooms, which start at $250 and top out at $500 or so (meals are included), and has a heated pool, Jacuzzi, stocked reser-voir, and an exceptional museum. Decor in all areas is a tasteful, stylish blend of western and Mexican designs.

Thunderbird Hotel
601 W. San Antonio St.
(432) 729-1984
www.thunderbirdmarfa
.com
Renovation of an old motel has delivered a desirable, contemporary oasis in west Texas. This hotel has 24 rooms, some with private patio or balcony. Features include flat-screen TV, DVD player, fabulous appoint-ments, nice pool, and

outdoor fireplace. Dogs allowed. Rates start at $125.

Other Places to Eat in Wildest West Texas

ALPINE

La Trattoria Coffee and Juice Bar
901 E. Holland Ave.
(432) 837-2200
www.latrattoriacafe.com
Have breakfast burritos and pastries in the morning, panini and salads at lunch, and pasta, shrimp, and stuffed chicken at dinner. Wi-Fi is available, too.

BALLINGER

Lowake Steak House
about 6 miles south via US 67 and FR 381
(325) 442-3201
This legendary steak joint has unbeatable T-bones, rib eyes, filets, and strips, plus the best onion rings and baked potatoes. Open Tues through Sun for lunch and dinner, meals average $10.

EL PASO

Doña Lupe Cafe
2919 Pershing Ave.
(915) 566-9833
www.donalupecafe.com
A former 1960s drugstore soda fountain in the historic Five Points district has

been a mainstay for home-made chiles rellenos and other Mexican specialties for nearly 50 years. Open daily for lunch and dinner.

MARFA

Cochineal
107 W. San Antonio St.
(432) 729-3300
Exceptional food that you might find in New York or San Francisco includes handcrafted pastas and salads made from locally produced ingredients. Very nice wine list, too.

Food Shark
By the train tracks at Highland Avenue
No phone
www.foodsharkmarfa.com
A lunch truck and gathering spot for locals, this eatery dispenses an always-changing menu of Middle Eastern–inspired dishes and some unforgettable baked goods.

Pizza Foundation
100 E. San Antonio St.
(432) 729-3377
Exceptional pizza topped with such goodies as feta, ricotta, spinach, fresh basil, local tomatoes, and chorizo. Don't miss the tomato-bread salad. BYOB.

MIDLAND

Manuel's Country Store and Deli
3905 TX 349 South
(432) 682-2258
Homemade tortilla chips, burritos, brisket tacos,

and chicken enchiladas are great reasons to come here. Open for breakfast and lunch.

Sedona Grill
2101 W. Wadley St.
(432) 570-9600
Shrimp tacos, green-chile empanadas (savory turn-overs), and tortilla soup have patrons panting at this southwestern cuisine hot spot. Lunch and dinner are served, and prices are moderate.

ODESSA

Manuel's Mexican Food
E. 2nd Street/Business I-20
(432) 333-2751
This might be the one, true must-go place in town.

You can't miss the sprawl-ing orange brick place with the vintage signs from the 1950s. Popular since before anyone can remember, this is the place for giant Mexican plates as well as steaks. Open Tues through Sun for lunch and dinner; open Mon for lunch only.

Permian Basin Hamburger Co.
520 N. Grant St.
(432) 333-4971
This quaint diner in the heart of old downtown serves breakfast and lunch Mon through Fri.

Rockin' Q Smokehouse
3812 Penbrook St.
(432) 552-7105
Delectable pork ribs and beef brisket are smoked over a hickory fire for tasty delights. Open for lunch and dinner daily; moderate.

PECOS

Abi's Kitchens
425 W. 3rd St.
(432) 445-3433
Serving American and Mexican food. Closed Sat.

Index